Coalitions for Justice

The Story of Canada's Interchurch Coalitions

Edited by Christopher Lind and Joe Mihevc

NOVALIS

In-house editors: Michael O'Hearn
                   Louise Pambrun
                   Christopher Humphrey
Cover and layout: Gilles Lépine
© 1994 Novalis, Saint Paul University,
    Ottawa, Ontario K1S 1C4 Canada
Business Office: Novalis, P.O. Box 990,
    Outremont, Quebec H2V 4S7 Canada
ISBN 2-89088-670-0
Printed in Canada

CANADIAN CATALOGUING IN PUBLICATION DATA

Main entry under title:
    Coalitions for justice: the story of Canada's interchurch
coalitions

ISBN: 2-89088-670-0

    1. Church and social problems—Canada. 2. Interdenomina-
tional co-operation—Canada. 3. Sociology, Christian. I. Lind,
Christopher, 1953-   . II. Mihevc, Joe, 1954-   .

BR570.C63 1994   261.8   C94-900301-8

NOVALIS

Contents

PART II

* * *

Introduction

This book is both a record of and a reflection on an extraordinary period in the life of the Canadian churches. In the late 1960s and early 70s, issues of social justice were rising on the public agenda. Poverty was thought to be a solvable problem and the federal government was soliciting help from the churches to secure a guaranteed annual income. The Auto Pact between Canada and the United States had become a model for fair trade and economic development, and the Canadian churches were responding to calls from overseas partners for assistance in economic development. Human rights became a language that crossed political, religious and geographical boundaries to describe a universal longing for protection and support.

In response to the spirit of renewal that followed from the Second Vatican Council, Roman Catholics in Canada were reaching out to experiment with new ecumenical relationships. While formal links through the Canadian Council of Churches seemed a long way off, Protestants were pushed by this surge of Catholic energy to build new models for peace and justice work. These became known as the interchurch coalitions, which the Protestant churches experienced as an opportunity to rediscover their own Social Gospel tradition.

These coalitions began in an ad hoc manner with little thought to their significance for the long term. What was important was the issue. It didn't matter whether it was refugees from Latin America or oil exploration in the Arctic: organizers went with what worked. The impact of these small organizations was so large, however, that governments, businesses and representatives of the World Council of Churches quickly noticed them.

Most Canadian church members will be surprised to hear this; they saw only one or other small aspect of the coalitions' work and were unaware of the movement which lay behind it. For some church members, their connection was attending an ecumenical meeting in a church basement on a cold February night. The topic of the meeting was probably food and hunger, sponsored by the local Ten Days for

World Development Committee. Others will have put stickers on their cheques which read 'No Loans to South Africa,' little realizing that this campaign was co-ordinated through the Task Force on the Churches and Corporate Responsibility. Still others will have watched on television as torture survivor Carmen Gloria Quintana testified before the United Nations about human rights abuses in Chile. Yet few will have known that the Inter-Church Committee on Human Rights in Latin America played a key role in getting this story before the world.

These small, ad hoc ecumenical organizations are now 20 years old and older. They have built astounding levels of expertise and well-deserved reputations for faithfulness in the mission of justice. This book serves as a record of their achievements – and more.

The late 60s and early 70s were a period of great ferment in the theological world. At that time, theologians and church leaders in the Third World began to realize that they had to combat the impact of colonialism and neocolonialism in their thinking about God. The life and career of the Latin American theologian Gustavo Gutiérrez serves as a good example of this development.

Gutiérrez was a Peruvian from the slums of Lima who showed great promise as a priest and teacher in the church. As a result, in the 1950s he was sent by the Roman Catholic Church to study at the best European universities. When he returned to Peru and began to teach what he had learned, he faced great difficulty. What he had to say seemed irrelevant to his students. After some reflection with colleagues he realized that he had gone to Europe to study 'Theology' and had learned 'European Theology' instead. That is, he had learned the answers to the questions European Christians were asking. When he returned to Peru he had begun to teach the answers to questions Peruvians had not asked. His response to this insight was to return to the theological drawing board and ask, "What are *our* questions?" His answer was published in English in 1972 as the now famous book, *Liberation Theology*.

This shift was repeated time and again around the world. The new movement became known as 'contextual theology.' It accepts as a basic assumption that all theology is contextual whether that is recognized or not. It does not say that the answers provided by others are wrong, simply that we need to pay attention to the context out of which our questions about God's action in the world arise. In

Canada we are also afflicted by a colonial attitude to theological work, namely that theological reflection can only be done by experts from away, from London or Tübingen, from Rome or New York. As a result, there is a paucity of sustained theological reflection on questions that have emerged from the struggles of Canadians to bring about a more just and peaceful world. This book is one attempt to address that deficiency. Here we have tried to listen to our own voices and, like Gutiérrez, we have tried to 'drink from our own wells.' It is more than a record of the work of the interchurch coalitions, it is also an example of contextual theology.

In this book we have asked the coalitions to tell their own story. Though the story may have a single person's name attached to it, it has been authorized by the coalition and circulated and revised by many people associated with the coalition's work. This was done to ensure the telling of a collective story rather than an individual one. These stories form Part One.

All too often, the lives of coalition staff and board members are so busy that little time is left for reflection on their experience of doing justice work. For this reason we chose a different group of people to work on the second half of the book. The work on Part Two did not begin until the coalition stories had been gathered. We did not want to give priority to one coalition story over another so we waited until we had at least a first draft of all the stories. At that point, the stories were circulated to a group of people with some knowledge of the work of the coalitions but who represented diverse disciplinary, geographical and denominational contexts. We asked the writers of Part Two to read all of the stories and identify themes that emerged from the stories themselves. We did not suggest themes but tried to be open to new ideas, voices and concerns. In our response to suggested themes, we attempted only to avoid unnecessary duplication and commissioned the essays. The task in writing these essays was to push the questions beyond where the coalitions had left them. By including the stories along with the reflections, we have also invited the reader into the process of theological reflection. In reading the stories yourself, themes and patterns may occur to you that have not been mentioned in this volume or you may disagree with the theme writers. You have the same material available to you that they did. The purpose of this exercise is not to close a process but to open one.

In this way we have attempted to embark upon an 'action-reflection' model of theological work. The church activists have told the story of their active involvement in the mission of the Church. This storytelling has made public what would otherwise have been private. Another group of people, committed to supporting this justice work of the churches, has reflected on the strengths and weaknesses, similarities and differences among the stories. They have found much to praise, but also much to challenge. If the process cannot be closed with the publication of this book, neither can it be completed this way. It would not do justice to the contextual model. A process that begins with action must also return to action. The process can only be completed as denominational officials, coalition board and staff members, church members, partners and you respond to these voices with critical dialogue and committed action.

The process exemplified in this book also has another more particular genesis. In October 1981, one of the coalitions described in this book, the Canada China Programme, convened a conference in Montreal entitled "God's Call to a New Beginning." An international conference, it included among the delegates Virginia Fabella and Sergio Torres of the Ecumenical Association of Third World Theologians. The Association had just held its 5th conference in August in New Delhi, at which time the members had decided to invite some First World theologians into a dialogue on what it means to do theology in a divided world. During the Montreal gathering Virginia and Sergio circulated a draft proposal for just such a dialogue to take place in Geneva in 1983. Four Canadian representatives were to attend (two francophone and two anglophone), each with his or her own case study on the churches' response to injustice.

The anglophones and francophones organized their contributions separately. A group based in Toronto took on the task of animating one contribution from the national coalitions and one from western Canada. Frances Arbour became the Toronto delegate. Executive director of the Inter-Church Committee on Human Rights in Latin America, Frances' case study focussed on this coalition. Bob Haverluck, a United Church minister and Director of the Prairie Christian Training Centre, became the Saskatchewan delegate. His case study focussed on Manitoba's Inter-Church Task Force on Northern Flooding of which he had been a member.

Even at that early point it was obvious that the Committee saw itself involved in a broader purpose. Committee members had already been influenced by the movement toward contextual theology in the Third World and wanted to use this occasion to "encourage theological reflection by Canadians on our own experience and heritage."[1] The case study on the work of the Inter-Church Committee on Human Rights in Latin America was included in the Geneva conference proceedings and published as *Doing Theology in a Divided World*.[2]

In the fall of 1982 a larger vision of nurturing theological reflection began to emerge. After experimenting with a variety of formats, a group began to meet monthly over a noon hour. On each occasion someone from one of the interchurch coalitions would be invited to 'tell the story' of the coalition and the people assembled would reflect on commonalities and differences between the stories. By the fall of 1983, this had become the Canadian Theological Reflection Project.

This group met on a consistent though irregular basis over the next seven years. A large number of people participated for at least part of the time in these reflections. What emerged from this experience was an identifiable pattern for the storytelling. Coalition members were asked to reflect on significant events and key moments of change in the life of the coalition. They were asked to focus on how their understanding of the church and of society had changed over time. They were also asked to identify how their strategy had changed over time. Alongside the time line of the coalition, these categories of church, society and strategy were found to contain all the basic material required for theological reflection. When the material from several coalitions was compared, significant parallels and equally significant disjunctions were revealed.

Like the coalitions themselves, this methodology emerged as a result of trial and error. We went with what worked. The project came to an end for both personal and institutional reasons. At a personal level, key people moved on and the priorities of others changed. At an institutional level, the project had done what it could do through informal means. It was widely agreed that the story should be recorded and the methodology employed in a more substantial manner. The editors were both members and animators of this project at different times. In the fall of 1991, conversations began in earnest about translating the work of the Canadian Theological Reflection Project into a book.

There is much that could not be included in this volume. These stories do not exhaust all that might be said about faithful Christian witness in this country. These stories do not even exhaust all that might be said about interchurch coalitions in Canada, since there are many that have been doing exemplary work on a regional basis like the Manitoba coalition mentioned above. The stories included in Part One are the stories of the 12 interchurch coalitions that are funded by the national bodies of the various denominations. The difference between the interchurch coalition in Manitoba and the coalitions in Part One is that the latter have an official mandate that comes from the national level of each of the supporting denominations, while the regional coalition does not.

Because of that national structure and the need to be close to denominational officials, all but one (PLURA) of the national coalitions are headquartered in Ontario (though not all in Toronto!). Though the coalitions deal with areas of the world as diverse as China and Latin America, they are sometimes thought to have a certain central-Canadian bias. The staff may be able to converse fluently in Mandarin or Spanish, yet the working language is typically English and not French. This means that neither this book nor these coalitions have been able to transcend the contradictions of our life as Canadians. As editors, we think of this volume as a contribution to Canadian theology, conscious that one of the essays in Part Two was translated from the French original.

We are also conscious of the particular time in which this is being written. At a local level, all the denominations are having to reduce their budgets. This is prompting some painful and sometimes acrimonious debate about priorities. How much money should be spent on Christian education, how much on human rights in Africa and how much on residential schools in Canada?

At provincial and national levels, governments are also debating priorities at a time of economic recession and rising budgetary deficits. How much should we spend on peacekeeping, how much on health care, how much on welfare? In this atmosphere, few people have the confidence that many had 20 years ago that governments could solve social problems if only they moved in the right direction.

At an international level, issues become somewhat clearer. Though we didn't realize it when the interchurch coalitions were being formed in the early 1970s, the world was also being reorganized. We now call that process 'globalization.' Starting as early as 1971, the international financial markets began to be integrated from many small national markets to one global capital market linked by computer 24 hours a day. This has changed the power balance away from national governments and toward transnational corporations.

This reality, which is already upon us, is not fully comprehended, yet we can already discern a number of important implications. One is that now is another time of transition for the churches' mission of justice. Strategies which relied on the willingness and ability of governments to lead in the struggle for justice need to be reassessed. Similarly, assumptions about the dominance of church voices in Canadian society also need to be rethought. On the other hand, this is a world where power has become transnational. In spite of our denominational identities, all our churches have strong, historical ties that also cross borders. This is a unique heritage that has served and can still serve as a powerful witness for discipleship.

The coalitions were created in a time of optimism as well as hope. In the spirit of ecumenism, church leaders saw that it was possible to do together things that it may have been impossible to do alone. Today, a new spirit is upon us. It is a spirit of pessimism born of scarcity. We fear that this spirit is more protective of the old growth of denominational loyalty and theological retrenchment than of the tender shoots of ecumenical co-operation for justice.

Still, today is also a time of hope. Our hope lies not in economic predictions but in our trust that God will always be present. Because we know that God will always be present to the suffering of the world, so we are called to stand with God as the 'church in the world.' In the spirit of a cherished ecumenical principle, we believe as churches that we should not do by ourselves anything that we might do together instead.

This book celebrates the generation of creative, faith-inspired, Spirit-led work that has gone on to date. It represents a call to the leadership and the membership of the churches to notice the wonderful work that its children, the coalitions, have been doing. It is also a call to reorganize this work in such a way that it has a firmer foundation for the mission of the Church in the 21st century.

Christopher Lind   Joe Mihevc
Saskatoon   Toronto

January 1994

Contributors

Michel Beaudin was a regional animator and researcher for CCODP from 1974 to 1985. Since that time he has been Professor of Socio-Economic and Political Ethics, Faculty of Theology, University of Montreal.

Mary Boyd is in her 22nd year as director of social action for the Roman Catholic Diocese of Charlottetown. During those years she served on many local, regional, and national organizations where she used her 6 1/2 years of experience in West Africa and her M.A. studies in conscientization to develop action and analysis of injustices on local, national, and international issues.

Terry Brown is regional mission co-ordinator of Asia/Pacific in the national office of the Anglican Church of Canada. He is currently a board member of CAWG, TCCR and CCP.

Nancy Cocks is a teaching pastor at the Vancouver School of Theology. A former staff person with the CCC, she has represented the Presbyterian Church in Canada on the TCCR and the WCC's Faith and Order Commission.

Lee Cormie teaches in the Faculty of Theology, University of St. Michael's College and the Toronto School of Theology. His interests centre on the emergence of the voices of the previously marginalized and silenced in history and on the questions they have raised concerning the presence of the Spirit in the struggles to transform the world and the mission of the church.

Bill Fairbairn has worked with ICCHRLA for 11 years, serving as executive director since 1988. From 1976 to 1978 Bill lived and worked with the ecumenical community of Taizé in France where he first met refugees from Argentina and Chile. Bill is a native of Guelph, Ontario, who prefers salsa to marengue.

John W. Foster is national secretary of Oxfam-Canada. For 17 years a social justice staff person with the national office of the United Church of Canada, he was a co-founder or godparent of a number of ecumenical coalitions and a long-term board member and chairman of several. Dr. Foster often finds himself at the meeting place of "domestic" and "international" concerns.

Robert Fugere taught at Seneca College, York University and at St. Michael's College, University of Toronto, prior to becoming executive director of ICFID. A graduate of Harvard College and the University of St. Michael's College (Toronto), Dr. Fugere has published articles on development issues in *Grail* and prepared briefs for presentation to parliamentary committees.

Peter Hamel is rector of St. Paul's Anglican Church in Masset on Haida Gwaii. From 1977 to 1993, he was the Anglican Church of Canada's consultant on national affairs. During that time he served as an Anglican representative on TCCR, GATT-Fly/ECEJ and Project North/ARC. The Nisga'a call him "the birdman."

Dennis Howlett worked with GATT-Fly/ECEJ Justice from 1973 to 1993. He is currently the national co-ordinator of the Interchurch Committee for World Development Education which sponsors the Ten Days program.

Roger Hutchinson is Professor of Church and Society at Emmanuel College, University of Toronto. His most recent publication is *Prophets, Pastors and Public Choices: Canadian Churches and the Mackenzie Valley Pipeline Debate*.

Gary Kenny has been working with ICCAF since 1987, serving as co-ordinator since 1991. His broad African experience includes serving on NGO delegations to Mozambique and Sudan. Through ICCAF's Images of Africa Working Group he is helping to develop a media code of conduct, as well as curricula for primary school children.

David Langille teaches Politics at York University. His research and writing deal with the influence of transnational corporations on the Canadian state and the role of social movements in maintaining democracy. He draws on extensive experience in the labour, peace, and environmental movements, in development education and the pursuit of aboriginal rights.

Rebecca Larson is secretary for research and development education with the Lutheran World Federation (LWF). Previously she worked for the WCC in issues of justice, peace, and the integrity of creation. Rebecca is a pastor of the Evangelical Lutheran Church in Canada and lives in Geneva, Switzerland, with her husband Stephen and their two daughters.

Christopher Lind has served as Professor of Church and Society, St. Andrew's College, Saskatoon, since 1985. From 1978 to 1981 he was a staff member of CCP and from 1981 to 1985 an active participant in the CTRP. Chris' special areas of interest include ethics and economics, contextual theology, and ecumenical social justice.

Robert McKeon is a sessional lecturer at St. Joseph's College, University of Alberta, and a doctoral student in Theology and Social Ethics at the University of St. Michael's College, Toronto. Previously, Bob worked for 12 years with the Social Justice Commission of the Roman Catholic Archdiocese of Edmonton.

Cynthia McLean is the director of CCP. A graduate of Harvard University and Union Theological Seminary, she has been involved with China since the 1960s when, as a senior in high school, she had a choice of calculus or Chinese.

Lorraine Michael is the co-ordinator of the Women and Economic Justice program of the ECEJ. From 1973 to 1990, except for a period of time when she studied at the Toronto School of Theology, Lorraine was a church/social activist in St. John's, Newfoundland. For the last 10 of those years she was director of the Roman Catholic Diocesan Office of Social Action in St. John's.

Joe Mihevc is a city councillor in the City of York (Toronto) and director of the Globalization of Theology program in the Faculty of Theology, University of St. Michael's College. He is a former staff person of CCODP and the Canadian Churches Forum for Global Ministries. Joe has been active on a number of social justice issues over the last 15 years.

Jeanne Moffat has been an activist in development and human rights issues at local, regional, national, and international levels for the past 25 years. She was a staff member of Ten Days for 11 years, and national co-ordinator from 1985 to 1992. She is currently executive director of Greenpeace Canada.

Renate Pratt is a former vice-president of the YWCA of Canada, co-ordinator of TCCR (1975-86), and trustee on the Council of the International Defence and Aid for Southern Africa Fund (U.K.) until its repatriation to South Africa in 1992. She is also the author of "International Financial Institutions," in R. O. Matthews and

C. Pratt (eds), *Human Rights in Canadian Foreign Policy* (1988) and "From the Goldmines to Bay Street" in Bonnie Greene (ed), *Canadian Churches and Foreign Policy* (1990). She is currently completing a book on the contribution of the Canadian churches to the struggle against apartheid.

Ernie Regehr is policy and research co-ordinator for Project Ploughshares and has published widely on peace and security issues. He has worked as a journalist, a researcher for members of Parliament, and with the Mennonite Central Committee in Africa.

Edith Shore worked with several coalitions while on the staff of the CCC and also helped start the CTRP. She has held a variety of church positions, both professionally and as a volunteer. She freelances as a consultant and is working on her M.Ed. at the Ontario Institute for Studies in Education.

Henriette Thompson is a founding member of the Halton Hills Interchurch Refugee Committee. She has also been actively involved in the Ten Days network for 13 years, in British Columbia and Ontario. She is currently employed as development education resource co-ordinator at World Vision Canada in Mississauga, Ontario.

The Aboriginal Rights Coalition

Peter Hamel

The context

On September 1 1975, the Anglican, Roman Catholic and United Churches launched one of the most daring, creative and controversial experiments in ecumenical history. For some time aboriginal leaders had been urging the churches to do more than pass resolutions and issue statements on the continuing pattern of paternalistic, colonial development in northern Canada that was destroying aboriginal life and culture. The churches' response was the Inter-Church Project on Northern Development, soon shortened to Project North.

The Lutheran Church in America–Canada Section, the Mennonite Central Committee (Canada) and the Presbyterian Church of Canada joined in 1976. The Evangelical Lutheran Church in Canada joined the next year. The Society of Jesus (Jesuits), the Council of Christian Reformed Churches in Canada, the Religious Society of Friends (Quakers) and the Oblate Conference of Canada became partners in subsequent years.

The founding churches realized by the late 1960s and early 1970s that the historical relationship with aboriginal peoples, many of whom were church members, had to change drastically. This new direction for the Anglican Church was set by Charles Hendry's report to General Synod of 1969, *Beyond Traplines*.[1] His sweeping recommendations led delegates to adopt a justice agenda focussing on the "recognition of treaty, aboriginal and other rights and a just settlement of their land claims."[2] This relationship, based on solidarity with aboriginal peoples, would include political action with governments and corporations on social, economic, environmental and cultural issues.

The onslaught of several energy resource megaprojects across northern Canada in the early 1970s added a sense of urgency to this new church focus. Canada's 'last frontier' and the aboriginal peoples were under siege. Transnational and crown corporations had joined forces with governments to develop massive projects to exploit the resources of the north. The aboriginal peoples were once again being left out of the decision-making process.

In 1971 Quebec Premier Robert Bourassa proclaimed the James Bay hydro-electric development the "Project of the Century," costing $6 billion. Further west, Manitoba Hydro was pursuing its plan to divert the Churchill River into the Nelson River at a cost of $4 billion. It would flood thousands of acres of Cree land. In 1974 the federal and provincial governments announced a $500 million agreement that would transform northern British Columbia from Kitimat to the Yukon border. An additional $10 billion would come from industry to build dams, mines, sawmills, highways, a super-port and towns.

In March 1974, Canadian Arctic Gas Pipelines Ltd., a consortium of 27 major petroleum, pipeline and transportation companies, launched its campaign to build a $10 billion, 4,000 km natural gas pipeline to carry Alaskan and Mackenzie Delta gas through the Mackenzie Valley to southern markets. That same day the federal government appointed Mr. Justice Thomas Berger to conduct a full-scale inquiry into the social, environmental and economic impacts from this project.

This major energy proposal came only three years after the federal Minister of Energy, Mines and Resources had declared that Canada had 923 years' supply of oil and 392 years' supply of gas. By 1974, the National Energy Board was saying that Canada would have to import oil by 1982 and the gas consortium was insisting that a natural gas shortage was imminent. The consortium threatened Canadians with "freezing to death in the dark" if the pipeline were not built. This was the context in which Project North began its work.

A proposal for such a project was discussed during a meeting at United Church House on June 10 1975. In attendance were Howard Brock, Elizabeth Loweth, Tony Clarke, Russ Hatton, Karmel Taylor McCullum and Hugh McCullum. Within three months the coalition was operating. The first meeting was held in the McCullums' home on September 11 1975. Those attending were Elizabeth Boyd, Tony

Clarke, Russ Hatton, Elizabeth Loweth, Walter Shultz, Don Shepherd, Ernie Willie and the two project co-ordinators, Karmel and Hugh McCullum.

The beginning

Originally designed as a two-year project, Project North had a total budget of $25,000 equally funded by the three churches. It had the twofold purpose of assisting the churches in a) supporting the creative activities of northern native peoples in their struggles for justice and the settlement of their land claims; and b) challenging and mobilizing peoples in southern Canada to become involved in creative action on the ethical issues of northern development. A program of research, communication and education was developed. The basic approach involved visiting with the northern groups, responding to their requests and helping to communicate their struggles for justice to people in the south.[3] The manifesto for the coalition was the book *This Land Is Not For Sale,* written by the McCullums and published at the end of 1975.[4]

The Project worked on a shoestring out of Karmel and Hugh's home. Four key areas of concern were identified: Indian, Metis and Inuit in northern Quebec, northern Manitoba, northern British Columbia and the Northwest Territories. Its first job was to conduct a referendum on behalf of the Northern Quebec Inuit Association on their segment of the James Bay Agreement. Bishops John Sperry and Bernard Hubert counted the vote while Karmel and Hugh flew in to all the Inuit communities on Ungava and Hudson's Bay to act as returning officers.

Hugh and Karmel had many communications skills and extensive experience in the north. Later Neil Unrau, a Mennonite volunteer, took on the challenging job of office co-ordinator. Tony Clarke, official representative from the Canadian Conference of Catholic Bishops, was the first chairman. The administrative team also included staff from the Anglican (Russ Hatton) and United Churches (Clarke MacDonald). The intense level of work from the beginning is reflected in the fact that a press release announcing this new Project was not issued for three months!

One year later the Project co-ordinators reported they were spending 50% of their time in the field with native organizations and had travelled some 335,000 km. In those early years the native organizations paid Karmel and Hugh's travel and accommodation costs as part of a contractual arrangement. In 1977 this amounted to $30,000.

The Project was working with the Northern Quebec Inuit Association, the Manitoba Inter-Church Task Force on Northern Flooding, the Nisga'a Tribal Council, the Council for Yukon Indians and the Dene Nation. Soon after relationships were established with the Haida Nation on Haida Gwaii and Treaty 9 in northern Ontario. Connections were made with the local churches and public meetings/workshops facilitated in the south were to generate southern support groups.

In 1976 Project North presented 'expert' evidence at the Berger Inquiry in Yellowknife on the impact of large-scale development on northern native communities. A large delegation of church leaders appeared before the National Energy Board in Ottawa. It is worth noting that 20% of the 450 briefs presented to the Berger Commission in the southern hearings were given by church-based groups. Indeed, Thomas Berger might not have come south had Project North not offered to provide a forum for him—not just to hear briefs but to get visibility and media attention. Thus he could form a political base and support in the south for his recommendations.

In the summer of 1975, the Anglican General Synod and the United Church, Division of Mission in Canada, adopted resolutions supporting the native people in their struggle for justice through a just settlement of their land claims. They also called on governments to stop industrial development until those claims were settled. In September the Canadian Conference of Catholic Bishops issued a major Labour Day pastoral statement, "Northern Development: At What Cost?" It focussed on two sets of ethical issues in northern development—social justice for the native peoples and responsible stewardship of energy resources in Canada. The bishops also called for the just settlement of aboriginal land claims prior to industrial projects. This statement generated public discussion far beyond church circles.

Project North's on-the-ground working relationship with a number of native organizations kept it in tune with their aspirations and strategies. There was an internal dynamism between staff and committee members that made for a lively team spirit. This existed, says Clifton Monk, "because members of the Administrative Committee worked with staffers as a unit of equals on a variety of tasks. The church representatives gave to Project North time and effort out of all proportion to their other duties."[5]

In those early years the communications and lobbying skills of the staff were used widely by the native organizations in providing media support, pamphlets and books to publicize their land claims. This important function was gradually assumed by the aboriginal organizations.

Neocolonialism

The land rights struggle in the territories between 1975 and 1981 revolved around four major pipeline issues: Mackenzie Valley, the Alaska Highway, Polar Gas and the Norman Wells Pipelines. The Project reflected church policy that there should be no construction until the aboriginal land claims were settled and implemented. Major submissions by Project North and individual churches were made to the public hearings.

The primary focus, however, was on the Mackenzie Valley Pipeline. Project North was a significant player in calling for "a moratorium on all Northern resource development projects, including the Mackenzie Valley Pipeline, to give Canadians an opportunity to work together to develop alternative lifestyles, based on conserver rather than consumer attitudes."[6] Project North supported the Dene position that the pipeline proposal perpetuated the 'colonial' philosophy of development. The Dene were presenting an alternative 'community' philosophy of development through their land claim proposal.

In September 1976, in the middle of the pipeline debate, the federal government cut off funding to the Dene. The money was desperately needed for the Assembly in October that would finalize the Dene land claims proposal. The federal deadline for submission was November 1. In response to an urgent request, the Canadian Catholic Organization for Development and Peace and the Anglican Church's Primate's Fund arranged for $100,000 in grants and credit to fund the Assembly. The Dene later repaid the churches.

This funding crisis also precipitated Project North's activities on the international scene. We raised funds in a number of European countries for the Dene. Contacts with the World Council of Churches led to a grant from its Special Fund to Combat Racism in August 1977. The Dene were the first group outside Africa to receive funds and the federal government was furious. Shortly afterward, Hugh profiled the Dene struggle in an article entitled "No Last Frontier"[7] in a World Council of Churches publication. In 1982, Karmel travelled to Geneva to work on the World Council of Churches policy publication "Land Rights for Indigenous Peoples,"[8] which included documentation of the Dene struggle.

These efforts over five years helped the World Council of Churches to familiarize itself with aboriginal land rights issues in Canada. This work set the stage for a high profile presentation on indigenous land rights at the Vancouver World Council of Churches Assembly in July 1983. Clifton Monk and staff member Lois Kunkel worked on that agenda at the Assembly. Clifton was the official representative of the Lutheran Church in America–Canada Section for over eight years and chairman from 1981-83. Aboriginal leaders commanded the world's attention as they explained their positions before television cameras. The next year Anwar Barkat, director of the Program to Combat Racism at the World Council of Churches, visited the Lubicon in northern Alberta.

Project North worked closely with the Dene and their consultants, the Committee for Justice and Liberty Foundation which co-ordinated the churches' presentations before the National Energy Board. Presenters included GATT-Fly, the Latin American Working Group, network groups across Canada and a number of environmental organizations. In the end, Judge Berger became convinced that Dene claims must be dealt with justly before any pipeline construction in the Mackenzie Valley. The National Energy Board opted for the Alaska Highway Pipeline proposal in the Yukon.

Gospel connection

In the end, our effectiveness is dependent upon relating concerns for justice to our spiritual understanding. Project North's submission to Justice Berger did just that:

"The Gospel proclaims that God's sovereignty includes all realms of life. Nothing that is human can be outside the Church's mission. It is the love of God in Christ for man that is the basis of the Churches' social and political concern. In particular, this means that we stand in solidarity with the Native Peoples of Canada who face the inseparable connection between themselves as a people and the stewardship of the earth's resources.

"Most of us live in and benefit from a socio-economic situation which is *sinful.* By social sin, we mean that we create and sustain social and economic patterns of behaviour that bind and oppress, give privilege to the powerful and maintain systems of dependence, paternalism, racism and colonialism.

"The Gospel is more than mere propositions... It brings with it a radically new vision of man. In view of this new vision of man, Christians are called to take a critical stance regarding the social reality of each time and space. The Gospel sheds critical light on the structures and procedures of our institutions, governments and corporations and calls into question many of the images and norms which prevail in the mainstream of our economic, political and social life...

"We are calling for a conversion within our social and economic structures whereby policy making and decision making will begin to reflect and make practical the values of justice, dignity and fulfilment of every human being. Our corporate sins must be acknowledged and we must turn around if we are to have a society that truly reflects the social consequences of the New Commandment. To bless the established order unconditionally is to remain unconverted!"[9]

Project North's Moratorium position, which Berger adopted, and the right of aboriginal people to self-determination in the North caused the churches all sorts of problems with the energy industry and the federal government. The federal government attacked the Dene claim to the land and control over development as racist, separatist and unrealistic.

This critical approach to the pipeline debate from the Gospel perspective created an instant backlash within the church community. Business and corporate executives, especially within the petroleum industry, protested to church leaders. We also discovered that Imperial Oil had an active file on Project North. A number of retired church business people, together with a few former moderators, bishops and clergy, formed the Confederation of Church and Business People.

This group felt that Project North had gone too far in attacking the business community. Corrective action had to be taken before further harm was done to the free enterprise economy and the 'real church.' One member, who worked for Imperial Oil, wrote an article in the August 1978 issue of the *United Church Observer.* He accused Project North of "using the church to promote a one-sided economic view." The church has a right, he said, to speak out on economic issues, but has been promoting the wrong policies and attacking the wrong institutions. Moreover, "the United Church, through its support of Project North, has contributed to strife in many northern villages, division among many northern people and unemployment for large numbers of people."[10]

This debate was part of a vigorous discussion going on within the churches on the spiritual dimension of economic development and its impact on peoples and the environment. The historical colonial pattern was being challenged by the Dene and their emphasis on community control. They emphasized the wisdom of the elders and the need to protect and respect the land. They were challenging accepted economic theories and current management policies. The business community responded with an intensive lobby campaign among church leaders to withdraw support from the Project. In the north, churches with predominantly white congregations appealed to their national offices to terminate the coalition.

During the summer of 1977 the member churches reaffirmed their support for Project North for another three years.

Project North: The team spirit

It is hard to imagine the level of intensity maintained by the staff and Administrative Committee members. It was left to Tony Clarke to use all of his personal and professional skills to keep the Project from spinning out of control. He was chairman until 1981. Between attendance at Native Assemblies, mobilizing work with network groups across the country, writing books, newsletters, reports and submissions for a variety of hearings, Hugh McCullum and Russ Hatton found time to appear before the President's Council on Environmental Quality in Washington on May 23-24 1977. They were there with Daniel Johnson, chairman of the Council for Yukon Indians, and Georges Erasmus, president of the Indian Brotherhood of the Northwest Territories, the Dene Nation. The staff had already clocked 150,000 kilometres for the year!

Two days later Karmel and Hugh were resource and media people for a conference at the University of British Columbia entitled "Northern Development—Time to Consider." It was sponsored by the British Columbia Working Group for Moratorium. Over 300 representatives attended from labour, teachers', environmental and native organizations, Oxfam and the churches. Mike Lewis, a United Church layman, and Wes Maultsaid, an Anglican priest, were the prime movers of this conference. Wes was the director of the British Columbia Inter-Church Committee for World Development in Vancouver. He was a great community organizer, facilitator and strategist. During his time with the Inter-Church Committee it seemed that nearly every urban centre in the province had an active church-related group working on justice issues. Project North depended on this network for its action in the province. It was a sad day when the member churches terminated the committee.

The day after the U.B.C. conference, Hugh was a theme speaker at the Mackenzie Valley Pipeline seminars in Victoria. Over 400 people attended the three sessions and 96 signed up to continue the work—a letter-writing campaign, meetings with MPs and phone calls to cabinet ministers.

The next day Hugh flew to Whitehorse for four days of meetings with the Yukon Indians regarding the Alaska Highway Pipeline Inquiry. A day later, Hugh returned to Langley, British Columbia, to speak at the four-day meeting of the British Columbia Conference of the United Church. In between, there were meetings with James Gosnell, president of the Nisga'a Tribal Council, and Donald Rosenbloom, their lawyer, regarding their land claim proposal.

Anglican staff, Ernie Willie and Russ Hatton, joined Karmel the next day for a three-day pro-moratorium conference in Summerside, Prince Edward Island, sponsored by church groups. On one day they had media events followed by six hours of public meetings and seminars. The Canadian Council of Churches' annual meeting in Glace Bay, Cape Breton, was also on the itinerary. While Hugh was off in one direction, Karmel was at events in Yellowknife, Inuvik, Whitehorse, Kelowna, Halifax, London and Waterloo, all within a 16-day span.[11]

Menno Wiebe, Project North representative from the Mennonite Central Committee (Canada), Clifton Monk, representative of the Lutheran Church in America–Canada section, Tony Clarke and Russ Hatton were also on the run, attending meetings of their own or with staff. They still found time to attend the monthly Project North meeting in Toronto on June 21 1977. Items on the agenda included a national coalition of pro-moratorium groups, the Inuit Circumpolar Conference, meetings with five cabinet ministers and the Lysyk, Hartt and Thompson Inquiries. Plans were made for a two-day retreat in September of the same year!

The year 1979 was the high-water mark for Project North's work building southern support and solidarity with the aboriginal peoples of the North. For some it was the zenith of the coalition's history. There were 62 network groups at work during the Northern Native Rights Campaign. Plans had been worked out at a historic meeting in Saskatoon the previous October. It was here that leaders from the northern native organizations laid out their plans for 'aboriginal nations' with leaders from the churches and public interest groups from across the country. A public campaign would bring their case to southern Canada.

It was a monumental task. There were 33 regional organizers from all 10 provinces. Launching the Campaign on March 14 1979, Indian leaders from the Yukon to Labrador fanned out across Canada in five teams to speak at public forums and media events in 65 centres. As Tony Clarke pointed out, this public awareness project "served to set the stage for the constitutional agenda a few years later."[12]

This process of bringing together aboriginal leaders, the sponsoring churches and regional groups in solidarity spawned the current native rights movement composed of native and non-native groups.

By 1980 Project North groups in places like Victoria, Vancouver and Edmonton already had an incredible track record of action, research and public education on aboriginal issues. The Project was also working with 12 native organizations.

There was a recognition during the formative years that Project North consisted of three integral partners, namely its sponsoring churches, aboriginal organizations and the regional support groups. By 1980, however, in a revisioning and remandating process that Project North undertook, the organization recognized the fact that the success of the regional groups had created problems.[13] What were national and what were regional responsibilities? What was the relationship between the regional groups and local churches? What was the organizational base for regional groups in the future? The shift of focus from land claims settlements to underlying issues of native self-determination had also created confusion. These issues received much attention, but decisive action was not taken until 1988, when restructuring of Project North was discussed.

Soon after the Northern Native Rights Campaign, Hugh McCullum resigned to become editor of the *United Church Observer*.

Karmel Taylor McCullum continued as the co-ordinator. On April 1 1981, Clifton Monk was elected chairman.

The Constitution

Repatriation of the Constitution came to the fore in the late 1970s. Native self-government was once again an issue. During the Mackenzie Valley Pipeline debate, the Dene maintained that self-government was necessary if they were to have control over the resources and economic development in their territory.

The federal government responded with the Drury Commission in 1978. Over the protests of the aboriginal peoples, Drury recommended self-government be left out of the aboriginal claims negotiations. The National Energy Program of 1981 raised serious doubts about the federal government's commitment to aboriginal rights and land claims. That same year, Berger's call for a 10-year moratorium on northern industrial activity was shattered with the National Energy Board's approval of the Norman Wells Pipeline. The Dene changed their moratorium position and entered into a joint production agreement with Esso Resources. Bill C-48 gave unprecedented powers to federal ministers over oil and gas resources. It also put greater control in the hands of transnational corporations. Northerners were further marginalized in the decision-making process affecting political development, land claims and resource exploitation.

On November 5 1981, the federal government removed the section on aboriginal and treaty rights from the Patriation Resolution on the Canadian Constitution. Four days later, six aboriginal leaders appealed to the churches for help. "Your involvement with native issues in recent years," they wrote, "has established a solid bond of trust between us. Now, at this critical moment in our history, we need your support more than ever."

Project North, its network groups and church leaders joined in a very effective cross-Canada campaign. The aboriginal leadership fought hard to get their issues back on the national political agenda. Our role was to raise the consciousness of Canadians around aboriginal rights issues. In this way, our partnership, based on a solid bond of trust, developed and matured. On November 26, the House of Commons unanimously restored Section 35 with the addition of the contentious word "existing" aboriginal and treaty rights.

The coalition's work has depended upon effective ownership by the member churches. This has been amply demonstrated in the constitutional process over many years. On December 21 1982, church leaders met with Project North to create the Churches' Aboriginal Rights Forum. This was the special task force, staffed by Project North, to work on the First Ministers' Conference on aboriginal issues scheduled for March 1983. This Conference was to be a five-year process to define aboriginal rights. There were three objectives: to stimulate public awareness, to mobilize public support for the recognition and entrenchment of basic aboriginal rights in the constitution, particularly the right to self-government, and to monitor the conferences themselves.

Menno Wiebe, the official representative of Mennonite Central Committee (Canada) since 1976, was Project North's chairman from September 1983 to May 1986. During this period, church representatives attended the First Ministers' Conferences as observers at the invitation of the national aboriginal organizations. Church representatives held consultations with national and provincial aboriginal leaders; they met with federal cabinet ministers and provincial premiers; they participated in joint press conferences with aboriginal leaders; they sponsored public forums on aboriginal rights; and they published popular educational materials. Over one million copies of Project North's pamphlet, "You Can Help with the Next Chapter of Canada's History," were distributed.[14]

The constitutional focus marked a major change in our working style. We had worked with regional aboriginal organizations facing impacts from industrial activity. Now the constitutional issues required close ties with the national organizations.

Changing strategies

There were many issues to be faced in dealing with aboriginal issues on a national level. Not all aboriginal groups were in the discussions. Not all agreed that self-government should be on the table. But there was agreement among many aboriginal leaders that the entrenchment of aboriginal rights within the Canadian Constitution was an important stage in land claims negotiations.

The high point for Project North in the constitutional process was the production of the pastoral statement, "A New Covenant," by nine church leaders.[15] They presented the document to a special Aboriginal Summit in Toronto on February 5 1987, shortly before the last First

Ministers' Conference. Grounded in the biblical experiences of covenant making, the statement describes the need to establish a new covenant with the First Nations in the Canadian Constitution. In order to rectify historical injustices, "a new covenant is required, one that recognizes and guarantees rights and responsibilities concerning the aboriginal peoples of Canada."

Aboriginal rights include the right to be distinct peoples, the right to an adequate land base and the right to self-determination. The church leaders further stated that such rights need to be realized through "the explicit entrenchment of aboriginal self-government in the Canadian Constitution." All governments need to be "constitutionally obliged" to negotiate and implement the terms of negotiated self-government. In order for this to happen, the church leaders recommended that aboriginal self-government should be an "enforceable right in the constitution." Five years later, during the Constitutional debate of 1992, the Charlottetown Accord incorporated native self-government ideas in the final proposal.

The Nisga'a connection

The cry for justice from the aboriginal peoples in the mid-60s challenged the churches on many fronts. Project North quickly took an interest in issues of political development, self-determination, land rights and social justice. But it was not until we were challenged by the Nisga'a regarding the AMAX issue that we more fully understood the scientific and technological complexities of the aboriginal land rights struggle. The Nisga'a took the offensive at their annual convention in April 1980. They were concerned about the reopening of the molybdenum mine at Kitsault in northern British Columbia by the AMAX corporation.

In February, the Nisga'a had discovered that AMAX had received special permits from the federal and provincial cabinets to dump their toxic mine tailings into the ocean. What alarmed the Nisga'a was that the tailings contained several potentially dangerous heavy metals and radium 226. They were worried about the impact of such toxic substances on the fish and other marine life upon which they depended for food.

The special government permits significantly exceeded federal regulations contained in the Fisheries Act. Over the projected 26-year life of the mine, the company would dump 100 million tonnes of waste into Alice Arm. At their convention the Nisga'a called on the governments to rescind the permits and initiate a full public inquiry to assess the environmental, social and health impacts.

This was the beginning of a national three-year campaign, unlike any since the Berger Inquiry. By the summer of 1980, the Anglican Church had taken a position. The Bishop of Caledonia, Douglas Hambidge, and the Primate, Ted Scott, were joined by the Roman Catholic Bishop of Victoria, Remi de Roo, in calling for a public inquiry. Both levels of government and AMAX tried to discredit the Nisga'a position by stating they were only using this issue to achieve a land claims settlement.

James Gosnell, president of the Nisga'a Nation, responded, "Even if our land claims had been settled years ago, we would still protest the dumping of mine wastes into the waters of Alice Arm. We eat the seafood from those waters, several times a week in fact; and we do not intend to let AMAX destroy them nor do we wish to eat contaminated fish and eventually destroy our own health."

Government and AMAX officials stonewalled growing support for a public inquiry. In March 1981, we learned through a leaked government memo that most of the government scientists were opposed to the approval of the special permits.

On January 23 1981, 19 Anglican bishops sent telegrams to the Prime Minister calling for a public inquiry. Two days later the Primate sent a petition to every Anglican parish in Canada. Jim Fulton, the Member of Parliament for Skeena, was an invaluable ally in Ottawa. He presented over 100,000 signatures from every province and territory on petition forms in the House of Commons. He also presented a list of 51 organizations supporting a public inquiry.

The campaign intensified. Project North in Vancouver and Victoria went into action. They organized public demonstrations in Robson Square in Vancouver and on the steps of the legislature in Victoria. Over 1,000 articles and editorials appeared in newspapers across the country calling for a public inquiry.

In the fall of 1980, the General Synod of the Anglican Church of Canada and the Diocese of Caledonia purchased four shares in AMAX. On December 16, they filed a resolution with the company urging the shareholders to vote for a moratorium on the marine disposal of tailings until a public inquiry had been held. It was sent to its 36,000 shareholders.

Armed with overwhelming support from the Anglican House of Bishops, Nisga'a leaders, Project North and the Taskforce on the Churches and Corporate Responsibility descended on New York on May 5 1981. Two days later, Nisga'a chiefs James Gosnell and Rod Robinson, Ian Mackenzie, an Anglican priest in the Nass valley, Mavis Gillie, the invincible chairperson of Project North in Victoria, Renate Pratt, co-ordinator of the Taskforce, Don Rosenbloom, the Nisga'a lawyer, and Tim Smith, the executive director of the Inter-Church Committee on Corporate Responsibility in New York spoke to the shareholders. They were joined by Alice Richards, the daughter of the founder and former president of the company that later became AMAX Inc. The shareholders rejected a moratorium, but the Nisga'a received 1.5 million votes of support.

The three-year campaign did not produce a public inquiry. The mine operated until November 1982, when it shut down because the price of molybdenum went below $5 per pound. It was, however, a splendid example of how the churches can work effectively with aboriginal peoples in a broad coalition of environmentalists, labour, scientists, medical associations and other sectors of society.

Benefits to the churches

Our work with aboriginal peoples in the struggle for justice has brought incredible dividends to the churches. Our understanding of creation has been greatly enhanced. The aboriginal peoples have taught us that social justice is inextricably linked to environmental justice. Justice in the social order cannot be achieved in isolation from a recovery of the integrity of creation.

In its early days, Project North also facilitated meetings that brought together, for the first time, aboriginal leaders from across Canada to discuss their struggles. At the North/South Consultation in Saskatoon in October 1978, these leaders were able to share and develop strategies with Project North actors from across Canada. It was here that our first contacts were made with the Innu in Labrador. The decision was also taken to organize the Northern Native Rights Campaign for the following March.

The coalition has also provided, at an early stage, support for aboriginal peoples whose land rights struggles were being ignored by government, industry and Canadian society. It was in the summer of 1983 that Fred Lennarson approached the churches about the tragic experience of the Lubicon Cree at Little Buffalo in northern Alberta. In November, Anwar Barkat of the World Council of Churches visited Chief Bernard Ominayak and his people. In a letter to the Prime Minister, Barkat said that "the Alberta Provincial Government and dozens of multinational oil companies have taken actions which could have genocidal consequences."[16]

In March 1984, Project North organized a church leaders' visit to Little Buffalo. At a press conference the leaders condemned the treatment of the Lubicon by the federal and provincial governments. They called on the federal government to begin immediate negotiations with the band "to ensure their traditional and aboriginal rights are respected" and to provide necessary funding for the band to continue the court battle for its rights.

Eight years later, the Lubicon Cree still do not have a land base. The pulp and paper transnational, Daishowa, has joined the oil industry in further devastating the lands of the Lubicon people.

Project North has helped to focus public attention in the national media through a number of campaigns. The Edmonton Inter-Church Committee has organized many events at the local level and has kept in close touch with the Cree. Church leaders have been involved several times. On October 15 1988, when all avenues for justice had been exhausted, the Lubicon Cree asserted their own jurisdiction through checkpoints and blockades on four roads into their territory. Project North and the Edmonton Inter-Church Committee were there. Our chairwoman, Elaine Bishop, and another Project North member, Betty Peterson, were among the 27 people arrested five days later by the RCMP.

Through its first 12 years Project North was blessed with very gifted and experienced chairpersons, including Tony Clarke, Clifton Monk and Menno Wiebe, and committed staff, including the McCullums, Milly Malavsky, Lois Kunkel, Bill Skidmore, Heather Ross and Neil Unrau, plus a number of church representatives. Network groups across the country kept up a furious pace of public education and advocacy. We have also developed relationships of deep trust with over 17 tribal organizations.

Organizational crisis

The national structure of Project North came crashing down in 1987. The problem was that the Project's structure did not allow for effective involvement by the network groups in decision making. They had no formal access.

Project North in the beginning saw itself as part of a social movement, but as time went on it became more institutionalized. The program became mired in church bureaucracy and lacked the spontaneity of the early years. Little did we realize that the church leaders' statement, "A New Covenant," presented to the Aboriginal Summit on February 5th 1987 was also speaking to us. It was time to rediscover our roots. It was time for the churches to establish a new covenant with the aboriginal peoples of Canada and with our fellow workers in the network groups.

We had lost sight of our common prophetic vision of solidarity with our aboriginal partners in the struggle for justice. We needed to review our history over the past 12 years and the consequences of the failed First Ministers' Constitutional Conference in March 1987. We also needed aboriginal representation on the staff and administrative committee.

Other factors contributed to the demise of Project North as such. We had lost the sense of participating in a social movement. Burnout was taking its toll. The spontaneous response to crises, so crucial in earlier successes, was replaced by personal rivalries around the Administrative Committee table. The level of trust was low. Church representatives and staff were split into divisive factions. We were unable to reach consensus on major administrative issues affecting the staff. Some committee members had little connection with aboriginal people at the community level and did not participate in program field work. Bureaucratic wrangling took over. What happened to our team spirit?

What made it painful personally was the fact that I was now the chairman. It was I who presided over the termination of Project North as a national organization. In March 1987, the Administrative Committee recommended to the sponsoring churches and church bodies that "1988 be a year of research, consultation and transformation."

On September 23 1987, our traditional partners—representatives from the churches, aboriginal organizations and the network groups—assembled at the Bond Place Hotel in Toronto to share in our agony and to begin a new covenant relationship. The tables had been turned. Now the aboriginal peoples and network groups were standing in solidarity with us.

The birth of the Aboriginal Rights Coalition

The year 1988 was one of intense evaluation and consultation leading to the development of a new interchurch coalition on aboriginal rights. In March a consultant was contracted to conduct an extensive evaluation/consultation of Project North's history and future directions. Seventy-five people representing the three traditional partners were sent a detailed questionnaire. The results and analysis were presented in the Benson Report in May. From June 20 to 23, 50 delegates from the churches, aboriginal organizations and network groups gathered for a historic four-day meeting at the Villa Marie Centre near Winnipeg. The participants worked on the basic ingredients of a new structure and a vision statement. On December 7 1988, the Aboriginal Rights Coalition was launched. The first meeting of the new steering committee was held January 11 1989. There are now 10 participating churches and church bodies.

Its structure recognized the new reality. It would be "a coalition of churches working in partnership and alliance with both aboriginal (political) organizations and regional network groups." The operative words would be 'partnership' and 'alliance.' Its common mission would be "to strive for a new covenant that will ensure aboriginal justice in this country."[17]

The new coalition would be based on a decentralized model, with the emphasis on consultation, participation and networking. A national assembly would be held every two years to set priorities. There would be strong delegations from the three partners. Integral to the process would be the presence of native and non-native spiritual leaders to deepen spiritual reflection on the aboriginal justice concerns.

A steering committee, meeting three times a year, would be responsible for administration and the ongoing program. In addition to church representatives, there would be four aboriginal participants from political organizations and four from the regional network groups. These would be chosen by their respective caucuses at the National Assemblies. An executive committee would work with the staff. It was further decided that $35,000 of the budget would be allocated to network groups for their work. This was further recognition of the major role they were playing within the Coalition.

The Aboriginal Rights Coalition has now been working for three years out of its new office in Ottawa. Its chairwoman, Elaine Bishop, official representative from the Quakers, has done a remarkable job in facilitating the work. Lorna Schwartzentruber has struggled valiantly to staff the Coalition under incredible difficulties.

The Coalition's first biennial National Assembly in 1989 identified two key themes: land rights and self-determination. It also supported an Innu campaign against low-level flight training in Quebec and Labrador. Two years later the assembly focussed on the Lubicon struggle.

Learnings and the future

As I reflect back over the history of this coalition, I see a number of factors that have made us more effective. One has been the real presence of the churches in the aboriginal communities. Ian Mackenzie with the Nisga'a, René Fumoleau with the Dene, Menno Wiebe with the Lubicon and with the Northern Flood Committee in Manitoba and the Innu in Labrador, come to mind.

This also applies to network groups. I can think of the Edmonton Inter-Church Committee on the North in its work with the Lubicon and the Dene, the Project North groups in Victoria and Vancouver working with a number of aboriginal organizations in British Columbia, the southern Ontario groups with a number of tribes in the province and the Project North Newfoundland/Labrador group in St. John's and their work with the Innu. These historical relationships have greatly enhanced the churches' work.

Aboriginal organizations have now assumed many of the roles we once performed. There are many more groups and networks working on the aboriginal agenda. It is important, however, that we continue our work with aboriginal organizations, especially within the Inuit communities, where we have had little contact in recent years.

The struggle for aboriginal justice is the oldest human rights issue in Canada. The churches have a long, historical relationship with the First Nations. If the Aboriginal Rights Coalition is to be an effective vehicle to assist the churches in developing a new covenant, it requires adequate funding.

We have worked hard at developing a new structure that will deepen the working relationship with the member churches. What is also required is a broadening of the base of solidarity beyond the small core of activists. The interim committee of Project North in 1988 commissioned Murray Angus to study, among other things, ways of addressing this concern. He suggested that "non-native Canadians need to discover their own reasons for reshaping Canadian society in ways that would also benefit native people."[18] This was similar to advice given by one Dene speaker to a non-native person at an aboriginal rights conference in Edmonton in 1976, "The first thing you can do to help us in the North is for you to begin examining what is happening to you in the South." This still holds true.

The Coalition is in a unique position to facilitate a solidarity process in the larger church community. The current economic restructuring, the focus of government and business today, is threatening and undermining aboriginal rights, culture and the struggle for self-determination and also victimizing many other sectors of Canadian society. The middle and working class is hurting, worried and losing jobs. Murray Angus points out that the Aboriginal Rights Coalition needs to identify the structural links between aboriginal peoples and many others in Canadian society. In this way "ARC could help non-native Canadians identify the basis for solidarity (and ongoing involvement) with aboriginal people." Conflict between aboriginals and non-aboriginals over resource use would be located within broader trends in society. Unless this happens, aboriginal peoples will remain disconnected and separate. We must demonstrate that the destiny of Canada is inextricably linked to the destiny of its First Nations.

There have also been significant changes within aboriginal communities and their leadership and styles. Some have developed complex regional organizational structures with administrative and political functions. They employ professional organizers, public relations firms and teams of skilled lawyers. In the 1970s, aboriginal leaders relied on the churches for expertise, organizational and financial support. In many cases, those demands have decreased. The result is a very different relationship with the churches.

Aboriginal justice is now big business. Universities and law societies recognize the fact and offer degrees and programs reflecting this new reality. This often means that the churches and the coalitions, involving many volunteers, are being left behind. When the issues were easier to grasp and the participants less sophisticated, Project North had many more network groups. It is much harder to mobilize people around the Constitution than a pipeline or a dam. The reality is that aboriginal peoples are doing much more of their own advocacy, usually with the help of professional advisors.[19]

We are also being challenged to address the internal reality within the institutional church. There needs to be a new covenant relationship between the churches and their aboriginal members. It is time to heal the wounds of the residential school legacy. National policies and actions ring hollow if the regional churches and congregations do not have ownership of this work. Despite the valiant efforts of a few across the country, those involved in work with aboriginal peoples remain a community on the fringe.

This is partly because we have not facilitated opportunities to deepen theological reflection and spiritual development related to the struggle for aboriginal justice. This is now a prime objective of the Aboriginal Rights Coalition. We have a major role in bringing the spiritual dimension to the issues. Our challenge is to talk in spiritual terms about the meaning of self-determination, aboriginal rights, economic development and resource exploitation. We are being challenged to deepen our own Christian spirituality, to relate aboriginal spirituality to our own Christian faith. If we are unable to do this, it will be impossible to create a new covenant with the aboriginal peoples of Canada.

Chief Rod Robinson was speaking not only for the Nisga'a and all aboriginal peoples, but also for us when he addressed delegates at the 1983 Council of Churches Assembly in Vancouver, "My fellow Christians, we the Nisga'a people, like our bishop, would hope that our struggle is indeed your struggle, that our dignity is indeed your dignity, that our truth is indeed your truth, that indeed we are one in Christ's truth and his love."[20]

The Inter-Church Coalition on Africa

Gary Kenny

London, Ontario, June 1984

A volunteer working group of the fledgling Inter-Church Coalition on Africa convenes an ecumenical conference on "Africa's Last Colony." For decades the southern African country of Namibia has been ruled, exploited and oppressed by South Africa's white minority regime. A member of Namibia's South West Africa People's Organization (SWAPO) addresses the largely grassroots audience. Not only is it the first time for most to hear about Namibia's struggle, it is also the first time to meet a real live 'guerrilla.' SWAPO is the major Namibian liberation movement fighting for Namibian independence and includes armed struggle—always a controversial subject for churches—as part of its liberation strategy. The SWAPO representative, a diminutive, soft-spoken woman, shatters people's preconceptions about what a guerrilla should look like and elicits compassionate support for the struggle of the Namibian people.

Robben Island, South Africa, December 1985

Archbishop Ted Scott, former Primate of the Anglican Church of Canada, visits the famed and legendary leader of the African National Congress, Nelson Mandela, in the notorious island prison near Cape Town. Archbishop Scott is in South Africa as a member of the high-profile Commonwealth Eminent Persons Group. The Group's task is to help find a peaceful solution to South Africa's problems. Scott's report back to the Canadian government and public on his experiences and findings will contribute significantly to the momentum of Canada's anti-apartheid movement and will help situate Canadian churches within that movement.

Toronto, Ontario, June 1986

Marg Bacon, then co-ordinator of the Inter-Church Coalition on Africa, and Wendy Hunt, member of a Coalition working group on Namibia, are denied visas to the South African colony by the white minority government in Pretoria. It seems that the Coalition's work against apartheid has brought the disfavour of the government of P. W. Botha. Annoyingly, the refusal comes just hours before Bacon and Hunt are to depart for Africa from Toronto. By chance, en route to other southern African countries, they encounter the general secretary of the Council of Churches in Namibia, the Rev. Abisai Shejavali. Not to be stymied by the visa refusal, the three begin planning for a visit of Namibian church leaders to Canada. The racist South African regime, they vow, will not have the last word.

Toronto, Ontario, May 1987

Using the Ontario capital as their starting point, members of a delegation of church leaders from Namibia fan out across Canada to tell Canadians about the struggles of their people. Although many Canadians know something of South Africa, given its high profile in news media, few have heard of Namibia. The Namibian clergypersons and the Inter-Church Coalition on Africa set out to correct this omission. They make news wherever they travel and increase awareness among the Canadian public about their country's plight. They also help the Coalition to strengthen its network of contact people and activists across Canada.

Toronto, Ontario, January 1988

An ecumenical delegation of three clergypersons from Mozambique meet with the Inter-Church Coalition on Africa Board of Directors. Passionately, they urge members to appeal to the Canadian government to provide military protection for shipments of aid into the Mozambican countryside. RENAMO, the South African-backed army of bandits fighting to topple the Mozambican government, they say, is continually attacking trains and convoys of trucks carrying desperately needed food and clothing to people in remote rural areas. Months later the Inter-Church Coalition on Africa would learn that the three church representatives were part of a larger Mozambican church delegation that had travelled to Washington on a secret mission to initiate peace talks between RENAMO and the Mozambican government.

Windhoek, Namibia, November 1989

Christine Ooshuizen, from Stephenville, Newfoundland, travels to Namibia as part of a program organized by the Council of Churches in Namibia to observe the process leading up to the country's first ever elections as a politically independent nation. The Inter-Church Coalition on Africa, in collaboration with the Namibian Council of Churches, sends Ooshuizen, an Anglican minister, and eight other people from across Canada to Namibia over a six-month period. A South African by birth, Ooshuizen applauds the Namibian people for the organized and peaceful way in which they guide their country away from South Africa's repressive colonial rule and into a new era of expected prosperity.

Harare, Zimbabwe, March 1990

Just one week after returning home from Canada on an Inter-Church Coalition on Africa-sponsored speaking tour, Father Michael Lapsley is nearly killed by a parcel bomb. Lapsley, an Anglican priest and outspoken foe of apartheid, tragically loses both hands and an eye. From his hospital bed in Harare, the irrepressible Lapsley vows to resume his struggle against institutionalized racism in South Africa. "The Boers have not won," he declares defiantly. Just one year later, Lapsley triumphantly returns to Canada for a follow-up speaking tour, also sponsored by the Inter-Church Coalition on Africa. Now with steel hooks for hands, he offers his disfigured body as proof to Canadians that apartheid, contrary to media reports, is a long way from over.

Nairobi, Kenya, April 1990

Nine Canadians from across Canada touch down at Jomo Kenyatta Airport and begin a two-week odyssey, sponsored by the Inter-Church Coalition on Africa, to "discover the human face of Africa's economic crisis." Branching out, they visit urban and rural development projects in Kenya, Uganda and Tanzania. Church partners in these countries organize programs that yield many important insights into the root causes of debt and poverty in Africa. Back in Canada, the group decides against writing a conventional report to be read by only a few national church staff and instead produce a popular resource to make the many stories and insights they gathered accessible to many more Canadians.

Tatamagouche, Nova Scotia, November 1990

Christians from every Canadian province and the Yukon Territories spend three days discussing and analysing political and economic trends in Africa. They recommend ways in which the Inter-Church Coalition on Africa might respond more effectively to the needs of African church partners and provide better resources to Canadian organizations and individuals committed to working in solidarity with African people. The conference binds together more tightly a cross-Canada ecumenical network of people and organizations committed to justice for Africa.

Maputo, Mozambique, October 1991

During a visit to a theological training school outside of Mozambique's capital city, Coalition co-ordinator Gary Kenny witnesses the wounds of one of Africa's most brutal and bloody civil conflicts. Canadian cleric Bob Faris, seconded to the seminary by the Presbyterian Church in Canada, relates how South African-backed bandits seeking to overthrow Mozambique's government have attacked and bombed the campus and terrorized its students and faculty. He displays what for him is a poignant symbol of the senseless war in Mozambique—a crucifix that students fashioned from an exploded mortar shell.

Saskatoon, Saskatchewan, June 1992

The Inter-Church Coalition on Africa program staff for Southern Africa, Elaine Bruer, accompanies Pule Tshangela of South Africa on a speaking tour of western Canada. Tshangela, representing South Africa's Transkei Council of Churches, establishes a sense of kinship with Canadian women by sharing stories about the plight of South African women who experience the double oppression of apartheid and sexism. Her visit to Canada is planned collaboratively with the National Committee for the World Council of Churches Ecumenical Decade of the Churches in Solidarity with Women.

Ottawa, Ontario, September 1992

John Mihevc, Inter-Church Coalition on Africa program staff for issues of economic justice, is invited to Ottawa to appear before the Parliamentary Standing Committee on Finance. The Committee has called Mihevc to give testimony based on the Inter-Church Coalition on Africa's work in the area of economic justice. He outlines for the Committee the devastating impact in human terms of World Bank- and International Monetary Fund-promoted structural adjustment programs. He strongly appeals to the Canadian government to stop supporting these dehumanizing programs and to help Africans develop viable alternative economic systems.

Ladysmith, South Africa, December 1992

Karen Baldwin and Lisa Cantwell, present and former co-ordinators respectively of the Alberta Youth Animation Project on South Africa, assume their duties as ecumenical monitors in South Africa. Their mission is sponsored in Canada by the Inter-Church Coalition on Africa, the United Church of Canada and the Canadian Council of Churches, and in South Africa by the Ecumenical Monitoring Program on South Africa. For one month they will work with regional councils of churches to monitor situations of civil conflict as the country struggles to end apartheid and erase its debilitating legacy. They offer much-needed solidarity and support to South Africans whose lives have been traumatized and turned upside down by apartheid's violence. Their reports home document not only the pain of transition, but also the hope and heartening determination which oppressed South Africans demonstrate in their tireless effort to build a non-racial democratic society.

Toronto, Ontario, February 1993

The Images of Africa Working Group, one of the Inter-Church Coalition on Africa's three volunteer committees, sponsors the Toronto premiere of "Africa: Art of the People," an exhibition of 35 contemporary African paintings. Some 30 classes of school children and youth, from grades 2 through 12, visit the exhibition and learn that there is much more to Africa than famine, war and apartheid. Through a combination of art interpretation, hands-on activities and short lectures, the students take away something of the joy and spirit of Africa and the continent's richness and diversity of cultures, religions and landscapes.

* * *

From Johannesburg to Tatamagouche, from Harare to Toronto, from Maputo to Saskatoon. Follow these roads linking Africa and Canada and you have travelled a few of the solidarity paths of Canada's Inter-Church Coalition on Africa. It was a commitment by Canada's major churches—to put Canadians in touch with the everyday realities of life for the African people—that first put Inter-Church Coalition on Africa on the solidarity trail in 1982. Since that time countless Canadians have, with Inter-Church Coalition on Africa and its member churches as their guides, walked with the people of Africa in their quest for social, political and economic justice. The story of the Coalition's evolution into the internationally known organization that it is today is rich and complex and intersects with many historical developments in Canada, Africa and the world. It is a story of tremendous rebirth across the African continent. It is a story of remarkable co-operation among Canadian churches known the world over for their capacity to work together ecumenically. It is a story of individual Canadians and Africans combining their energy and vision to build an organization capable of making a contribution to the struggle for justice and peace in Africa and the world. It is the story of Canadian and African churches working together to bring justice and peace, not only to their own lands, but to the entire global community.

Promise of a better future

The story begins, appropriately, with the 1960s, a significant decade—a turning point, even—for Africa this century. By the end of the decade, and after many long and costly liberation wars, most African countries had freed themselves from the debilitating nightmare of systematic colonial rule and exploitation. Political independence was charged with the promise of a brighter, more prosperous future. It was a time marked by celebration and euphoria throughout Africa. Africans were overcoming the indignities of colonialism and finding the confidence they needed to rebuild their societies according to their own dreams and visions. A buoyant world economy, favourable weather patterns and the remunerative prospects of expanded production and export of agricultural crops and minerals would provide the climate necessary for steady movement forward. Political independence—Africans were certain and the international community was hopeful—would be the ticket to long-awaited social and economic transformation and development in Africa.

Visionary African leaders added to the excitement of the times. Tanzania's President Julius Nyerere electrified his audiences when he said, in his familiar staccato Swahili, that while they might not be able to travel to the moon like the superpowers, Tanzanians could take their own giant leap forward in their fields and workplaces. In Ghana, President Kwame Nkrumah, appealing to his people's biblical and democratic traditions, proclaimed that it was time to seek the fulfilment of the 'political kingdom.' African churches, shifting the idiom a little, talked about a "biblical exodus from a colonial Egypt to an independent Canaan."

Dreams unfulfilled

But alas, with the dawn of the 1980s, Africa's famous copper sun did not, after all, shed light on the promised land. Instead, it illuminated a bleak landscape in which the optimism of the 1960s looked very misplaced indeed. Hard statistics tell the tragic tale. During the 1970s the majority of African countries had experienced static or declining production levels and per capita income. For Africa as a whole, though total income had risen, increases in population meant that by the early 1980s per capita income had declined in real terms to well below its 1970 level. In most countries, per capita food consumption had also fallen to below the levels of the previous decade. Far from 'trickling down' to the poor—an assurance offered to newly independent African nations by Western governments and their economic gurus—the meagre benefits of export-led growth had accrued only to a minority of Africans, to foreign business interests and to the industrial countries that depend upon Africa's tropical crops and minerals. The number of poor Africans, on the other hand, had increased dramatically and their poverty had worsened. The vast majority remained on the margins in rural areas, but ever increasing numbers swelled the shantytowns of such capital cities as Nairobi, Maputo, Lagos and Dakar. The World Bank estimated that, as the 80s progressed, 60% of Africa's population would be living a life of poverty beyond the imagination of most citizens of the affluent West.

To make matters worse, drought and other natural disasters brought the peoples of many areas of the continent to their knees. Internal political strife, too, took a major toll. In several countries ethnic, tribal and religious disruptions resulted in violent domestic conflicts. The widely publicized Biafran War of the late 1960s had been the first major signal that the glamour of political independence was giving way to the tragedy and devastation of civil war. Political independence, it was clear, was not the hoped-for panacea and many African analysts knew why: it had been constructed within the remains of an essentially colonial state framework.

Famine and war during this period generated an incredible five million refugees—the worst refugee crisis in the world. For many African countries, the emergence of refugees symbolized the stresses and strains of the new order unfolding in the 1960s. Africa suddenly found itself in the throes of a severe development crisis compounded by famine, war, massive human displacement and a crippling foreign debt. It would take more than political independence to turn the fortunes of the continent around.

In response to the crisis, African governments and foreign aid donors began debating its causes and planning an appropriate co-ordinated response. In Africa, churches were in the forefront of discussions. The All-Africa Conference of Churches was established in 1958 at the same time as its secular continental counterpart, the Organization for African Unity. Leading up to, and immediately following independence, the Churches played a central role in matters of public education and leadership formation. Now, with a substantial pool of talent and expertise to draw upon, they turned their attention, in tandem with the state, to the many problems that had arisen during the 1970s. Responding to Africa's many social, political and economic crises, as it turned out, would preoccupy the churches for the next decade.

African Churches appeal for support

The All-Africa Conference of Churches and many of its member national councils appealed vigorously to their counterparts abroad for support. Denominations in Canada, which for many years had supported their African church partners with missionary personnel, material and financial resources, and education and advocacy programs in Canada, were eager to help. As the appeals increased in number and frequency, however, denominational church staff began to recognize a need for a co-ordinated Canadian church response.

Denominational Africa Secretaries (or their equivalents) began meeting in the early 1980s to explore options. They included representatives of the United, Anglican, Presbyterian and Lutheran Churches, plus the Canadian Catholic Organization for Development and Peace, the Mennonite Central Committee (Canada) and the Missionaries of Africa. Inspired no doubt by the success of other ecumenical social justice coalitions, they quickly settled on the idea of an interchurch coalition to specialize in African concerns. The basic mandate would be heightening awareness among denominational constituencies. It was decided that advocacy for progressive policy on Africa—directed toward governmental and other policy-making bodies—would be considered over time and likely added as a second component of the mandate. A planning document summed up the general purpose of the Coalition as follows, "To provide for continuing ecumenical discussion and planning among Canadian churches so that their support to Africa may be as effective as possible for solidarity with the people [of Africa] and the educational impact on Canada may be as strong as possible through co-ordination."

The major goal of the Coalition, the same document records, was to enhance and expand the work of the denominations in Africa and to empower the Inter-Church Coalition on Africa to use its concentrated focus on Africa to help keep African issues on its member churches' agendas. The Inter-Church Coalition on Africa, it was stressed, was not to be a 'dumping ground' for solidarity work Canadian churches could not or did not want to undertake. Nor was it to be a means for them conveniently to conserve or cut back on funds and staff energies. The Inter-Church Coalition on Africa "will help us see Canada's role [vis-à-vis Africa] more clearly and give [Canadian churches] much more possibility of applying resources either together or separately in a more [effective] way."

Making decisions about the scope of the program was certainly challenging, especially considering the litany of pressing concerns emanating from Africa. Minutes of early planning meetings suggest lengthy debates about whether to make the program focus the civil war in the Horn of Africa, the continental refugee crisis, human rights in selected countries, long-term economic development, apartheid, or some of the many other concerns, all of seeming equal urgency. The question of whether the program focus should be thematic, country-specific, or a combination of both, also animated discussion.

One appealing option was to support the movement to end apartheid in South Africa, which had attracted considerable public support internationally. Charlotte Maxwell, on the Africa Desk at the Anglican Primate's World Relief and Development Fund and a member of the Inter-Church Coalition on Africa's Board of Directors, in recalling that debate, notes that the rising profile of the struggle against apartheid meant that Canadians were becoming increasingly familiar with South Africa and its issues. Competent support for the anti-apartheid campaign was being provided by several Ottawa- and Montreal-based non-governmental organizations and solidarity groups across Canada, such as the Toronto Committee for the Liberation of Southern Africa and the Calgary-based Canadians Against Racism. But the rest of Africa, particularly independent black Africa, Maxwell adds, was relatively unknown to Canadians. It made sense for the new Inter-Church Coalition on Africa to invest its energy and resources to support the political, economic and development efforts of some of these countries.

Modest beginnings

Two southern African countries were chosen, Namibia and Tanzania. Each was considered a microcosm of a range of issues common to independent black African states and countries still straining, politically or economically, under a colonial yoke. Each had potential for public education and offered strong educational and media appeal. Namibia was a client state of South Africa. As 'Africa's last colony,' it was often left in the shadows of the international anti-apartheid campaign focussed on its racist neighbour. Tanzania represented exciting new possibilities for alternative social and economic development which, if successful, could serve as models for other independent and developing black African states.

Also, in both countries there were indigenous churches with a history of close and collaborative relationships with their Canadian counterparts and which had recently appealed to international partners for increased solidarity support. Both also offered possibilities of collaboration with sister coalitions and the opportunity to build on their accumulated experience. The Taskforce on the Churches and

Corporate Responsibility, for example, had monitored Canadian banking and corporate activity in South Africa and Namibia for several years. The Interchurch Fund for International Development had channelled funds to promising new development projects in Tanzania.

With the mandate and program focus in place, the structure of the Coalition was laid out. It would function with a Board of Directors, volunteer working groups and staff. The Board would be composed of two representatives from each sponsoring church or church organization. Its function would be mandating the program, ensuring that denominational policy was integrated into the program, monitoring program implementation and generally overseeing budgetary and administrative matters. Major responsibility for the programs, however, would be borne by the volunteer working groups. Initially there would be two groups, one on Namibia and one on Tanzania. Each would design, plan and implement the programs for these two countries. Owing to modest start-up funds, the staff component would be limited, starting with a part-time co-ordinator only.

Starting principles

In the early stages of the formation of any organization, certain operating principles will emerge and become institutionalized, either formally or informally. For the Inter-Church Coalition on Africa there were two key principles. The first concerned the work of the Coalition in relation to the African church partners of its sponsoring denominations. The question of fidelity and faithfulness to African partners was considered to be of paramount importance. "How can we, as a coalition of churches, be faithful to our partners in Africa?" was a concern expressed in the earliest formational documents. That same question has been, perhaps, the most frequently posed question during the Coalition's lifetime. In 1981 the Rev. Garth Legge, then general secretary of the United Church's Division of World Outreach and currently a member of one of the Coalition's volunteer working groups, captured this sentiment with the phrase "Christians in Canada relating to Christians in Africa through their churches." The idea behind the church-to-church approach, it is important to stress, was not to limit the Coalition's work and relationships to exclusively church organizations and movements, but to prevent the possibility of Canadians imposing their own agendas, however well-intentioned, on the African people. Simply put, the Inter-Church Coalition on

Africa's founding denominations felt strongly that the issues taken up by the Coalition should be based on signals coming from churches in Africa. This did not imply the uncritical acceptance and blind pursuance of every partner appeal. It did mean being open to the signals as they came, interpreting them in the Canadian context and consulting with partners as often as possible about the progress of the work and changes in focus or direction that might need to be made.

Partnership, in fact, was something about which the Inter-Church Coalition on Africa's early planners were very circumspect. The Coalition, they insisted, would not be a 'funding' partner like the denominations; it would relate to African churches on a 'program-to-program' basis. This form of partnership, says Marg Bacon, the Coalition's co-ordinator from 1982 to 1990, meant that the Inter-Church Coalition on Africa was free of the constraints which often accompany conventional donor-recipient relationships. She recalls travelling to Africa and being met by partners who were used to conventional ways of relating to Canadian denominations and expected money. It took some time for the partners to get used to a relationship based on program and not funding, she says. Gradually, Bacon adds, African partners found something liberating about the new arrangement. "We could relate more freely to one another. We could share each other's stories and struggles and find a deeper sense of solidarity in that."

The second principle concerned the central function of the volunteer working groups within the Coalition's life and work. Early planning documents refer to them as "the main generators of the work," and they are that in many ways, notwithstanding the tremendous contributions of Board members and staff. In the words of Jim Kirkwood, United Church of Canada Area Secretary for southern Africa and a member of the Coalition's Board, they are "the heart and soul of ICCAF." Working groups consist of officially designated denominational representatives and individuals with a special interest in and commitment to Africa. The backgrounds of members have varied widely over the years and currently include teachers, journalists, graduate students, clerics, retired missionaries and professionals from many walks of life. Many Africans working or studying in Canada have also joined the working groups and provide a specialized knowledge and experience critical to the planning and implementation of a program that is sensitive to the social and cultural realities of African life. Several Board members, attracted to the working groups' capacity to combine task orientation with self-education and interpersonal fellowship, attend monthly meetings regularly and are an important communication link with the Board. Many volunteers have day jobs or attend school; all the monthly meetings are held in the evening to make it easier for them to attend. The Board invests a lot of confidence in the working groups to fulfill successfully the Inter-Church Coalition on Africa's program mandate.

Defining the activities

For its major inaugural task the Tanzanian Working Group organized an ambitious educational speaking tour of two Tanzanians, one from a Canadian church partner, the Council of Churches in Tanzania, and the other from the Department of Information in the Tanzanian government. An educational kit on Tanzania was produced and distributed widely by the Inter-Church Coalition on Africa member churches, who used it to raise the awareness of constituents about the root causes of underdevelopment and the possibilities for effective remedial action. The Namibia Working Group also chose to organize an educational tour of Canada by a delegation from the Council of Churches in Namibia and to produce complementary educational materials as well. The combination of educational tours and popular resources would become the hallmark of the Coalition's work over the next several years. Marg Bacon claims that the Inter-Church Coalition on Africa developed a reputation for bringing African voices directly to the Canadian people and for producing resources that could be easily distributed among and understood by the people in the pews.

Tours of Africans to Canada were especially effective, Bacon says. "Canadians could hear African people tell their own stories rather than hear those stories second hand from white, male missionaries." The direct contact, she adds, made a dramatic difference in terms of the impact the stories had on the Canadian public. She tells a story of a visit to Canada, in the early 1980s, of Abisai Shejavali, the former general secretary of the Council of Churches in Namibia. At the time, Namibia was a colony of South Africa and subject to its racist laws. Wherever he went in Canada, Shejavali always wore a red scarf around his neck, Bacon says. Whenever people asked him about the significance of the scarf, he would say, "I wear it as a constant reminder of the blood that my people are shedding for their freedom." It was a very dramatic and potentially shocking statement, Bacon admits. But made in the context of stories of the Namibian people's struggle against their South African colonizers, it made Canadians poignantly aware of the unique and powerful form of Christian witness before them.

Educational tours of African visitors, because they were organized across Canada, also enabled the Inter-Church Coalition on Africa to develop beyond the urban confines of Toronto, Bacon says. As a result of visitors like Shejavali, the Inter-Church Coalition on Africa became a more truly national and ecumenical organization, working through the national networks of the denominations and establishing key contact people in every region of Canada. By the latter half of the 1980s, the Inter-Church Coalition on Africa was working with individuals and groups in every province. In some provinces—Alberta, Ontario and Nova Scotia, for example—strong ecumenical committees formed that were dedicated to working with the Inter-Church Coalition on Africa as well as planning and implementing their own regionally based education and advocacy programs. The formation of the network greatly expanded the Coalition's capacity to make the problems, hopes and fears of the African people known to Canadians across Canada. It also added weight and authority to the Coalition's advocacy campaigns which were aimed at changing Canadian government policy on Africa.

After 18 months, the Board members evaluated the Coalition's work, were pleased with what they saw and decided to continue the focus on Namibia and Tanzania. The Tanzania Working Group was encouraged to broaden its geographic focus to take in the so-called Frontline States—the southern African countries falling under the hegemonic influence and control of South Africa.

Broadening the Inter-Church Coalition on Africa's horizons

Within the next three years, however, the configuration of working groups changed in response to developments in Africa, a process aided by formal remandating in March 1984. The Tanzania Working Group, with its focus on the challenges of long-term development, expanded its thematic focus to become the less geographically and more thematically defined Development Working Group. The Namibia Working Group was continued and a working group on Lesotho, a tiny country completely surrounded by South Africa and subject to its overbearing political and economic influence, was added. Also added was the Church Mission Working Group, the mandate of which was to help Canadian Christians appreciate and learn from the gifts and unique witness of African Christians. In 1985, under pressure of the intensifying struggle against apartheid and in response to requests from partner churches in South Africa, the South Africa Working Group was formed. While its principal focus would be South Africa, it would also monitor events throughout southern Africa. After two years the Namibia Working Group was folded into the Group.

When South Africa was officially added to the Inter-Church Coalition on Africa's mandate in 1985, church-supported anti-apartheid work in Canada had been largely denominational, with the exception of the Taskforce on the Churches and Corporate Responsibility and its work of pressuring Canadian banks and corporations to sever commercial ties with the racist regime. Two developments convinced the Coalition Board that a co-ordinated Canadian church program on South Africa was urgently needed. First, black organizations in South Africa, under the banner of a broad coalition of anti-apartheid groups known as the United Democratic Front, dramatically escalated resistance against the apartheid policies of the Pretoria regime. Second, South African churches and church organizations were becoming increasingly prominent in the struggle.

A particular incentive to the Board was the bold and courageous witness of the churches and the response which their actions drew from the international community. They dared to issue several prophetic statements, such as the internationally acclaimed "Kairos Document," which scathingly criticized South Africa's apartheid policies and envisioned a new South Africa that was transformed socially, politically and economically. They also demonstrated a deft capacity to act as mediators and reconcilers among conflicting groups within the anti-apartheid movement and between anti-apartheid groups and the government. High-profile church leaders were sent abroad to inspire the international community to redouble its efforts to fight racism and poverty in South Africa. The feisty, charismatic and highly quotable Desmond Tutu, Anglican Archbishop of Cape Town, after becoming the general secretary of the South Africa Council of Churches, received national coverage when he visited Canada. Tutu's stories of how the South African people were suffering under the brutality and indignity of the apartheid system and how they were laying down their lives for deliverance from that system, deeply moved thousands of Canadians including many church leaders and social justice activists. A year later, a similar visit to Canada by Archbishop Denis Hurley, general secretary of the Pretoria-based Southern Africa Catholic Bishops Conference, demonstrated how South Africa's churches were united ecumenically against apartheid. Solidarity with the churches in South Africa, in the form of an ecumenical Canadian church response, seemed the only fitting and logical course.

At roughly the same time, grassroots church activists as well as church property in South Africa were increasingly coming under attack by the apartheid government and its agents. Stories of local church leaders being persecuted, detained, tortured or killed were common. Security police raided and seized documents from the South Africa Council of Churches' headquarters in Johannesburg and, not long afterward, the building was completely destroyed by a massive bomb. Canadian newspapers published photographs of national church leaders, including Tutu, Chikane and Hurley, marching arm-in-arm to Parliament in Pretoria under bombardment of water canon and being harassed by police wielding clubs.

With its partners increasingly under attack for their activism, the Inter-Church Coalition on Africa Board gave the South Africa Working Group a mandate to expand its public education and advocacy work on South Africa in Canada. The Group also began participating in committees of the Canadian Council for International Cooperation, a forum in which churches, non-governmental organizations and South Africa solidarity groups were encouraged to pool their resources for effective and focussed education and advocacy campaigns. But a lack of financial resources continued to hamper the Inter-Church Coalition on Africa's capacity to produce needed educational print materials for the national churches and to contribute effectively to other anti-apartheid forums.

Partnership Africa Canada

The creation of Partnership Africa Canada by the Canadian International Development Agency (CIDA) in 1986, however, provided a needed boost. Partnership Africa Canada is a consortium of Canadian non-governmental organizations that supports long-term development in sub-Saharan Africa and development education in Canada. It was established as part of Canada's response to the general crisis of 1984-85 in Africa, which included severe famine in the Horn of Africa region and indications of continuing economic decline in many African countries. In its first five-year mandate, Partnership Africa Canada administered $75 million and recently began a second five-year mandate with another $75 million. Approximately 10% of each five-year budget is earmarked for development education in Canada, with the majority of funds going to development projects in Africa.

The Inter-Church Coalition on Africa applied for and received funding from Partnership Africa Canada to launch the four-year long Education Project on Southern Africa. The 'South' Africa Working Group became the 'Southern' Africa Working Group in response to the South African government's policy of regional destabilization and the increasingly devastating impact of that policy on neighbouring independent black states. The creation of Partnership Africa Canada, and the subsequent formation of the Education Project, was a major turning point in the Coalition's development. Part of Partnership Africa Canada's commitment to the organizations it funds is to improve their capacity institutionally to plan, implement and evaluate more effectively their work of development education and advocacy. The extra resources made it possible for the Inter-Church Coalition on Africa to expand its program and to add another full-time staff position, in addition to its then full-time co-ordinator and administrative support staffer.

While support for the Partnership Africa Canada-funded project among Board members was unanimous, not all were at ease with the prospect of accepting government money. The issue was not so much one of possible political strings attached; indeed, staff and working groups have not felt constrained to criticize Canadian government policy on Africa. Rather, the issue was the effect large infusions of money might have on the Inter-Church Coalition on Africa programs. When the Inter-Church Coalition on Africa Board first decided to apply for Partnership Africa Canada funds, Marg Bacon says, there were concerns that growing bigger might draw the Inter-Church Coalition on Africa away from its philosophical and theological commitment to mobilizing the Canadian public to bring about changes in Canadian government policy and send it in the direction of working more directly with government where the potential for co-option is greater. The concern was an important one that continues to be a source of reflection and debate in Board and working group meetings. However, the Inter-Church Coalition on Africa has been careful not to become too comfortable in its movements within government circles and chooses to relate to government on a strategic rather than an ongoing basis.

The struggle against apartheid

The anti-apartheid work of the Inter-Church Coalition on Africa and its member denominations has brought them considerable and favourable recognition among the Canadian public. Responses to the work by Canada's political officials, however, have not always been as positive. In 1988, for example, the Inter-Church Coalition on Africa and the Canadian Council of Churches wrote a letter to the Minister of State for External Affairs, the Hon. Joe Clark. The letter urged Clark to ensure that the Government of Canada honour a commitment made by Prime Minister Brian Mulroney, speaking to the United Nations General Assembly in New York in 1986, to impose comprehensive and mandatory sanctions against the apartheid regime if substantive action to end apartheid was not taken immediately. In the almost two years that had transpired since Mulroney's speech, the South African government had not demonstrated any political will to change its racist policies. Canada, disturbingly, still had not made good on its promise to impose tougher sanctions. The letter was faxed to Clark in Canberra, Australia, where he was chairing a meeting of the Commonwealth Foreign Ministers on Southern Africa. Although the Inter-Church Coalition on Africa recognized that Canada was exercising strong moral leadership within the Commonwealth and broader international community, its actions on the sanctions front were considered to fall far short of its rhetoric. The Inter-Church Coalition on Africa/Canadian Council letter pointed out this discrepancy in rather unceremonious terms, using provocative language like "betrayal of the people of South Africa" and "unkept promises."

Within 24 hours Clark shot back an angry and belligerent response. He berated the Inter-Church Coalition on Africa and the Council for their 'unsophisticated' understanding of the political situation in South Africa. He further criticized what he saw as a lack of appreciation for the political sensitivities required for Canada to have a positive influence with the apartheid regime. He avoided, however, the issue of the Prime Minister's promise of full sanctions. Recognizing that Clark's response could be used to gain additional public support for sanctions, Coalition staff released the exchange of letters to the media. The next day, *The Toronto Star* published a stinging editorial in which it questioned Canada's record on sanctions and berated Clark for his irate reaction to the churches. "Mr. Clark has seen the enemy," the editorialist wrote, "and it is [the Inter-Church Coalition on Africa and] the Canadian Council of Churches."

The South Africa Working Group also became known for giving priority to issues affecting women in southern Africa. In South Africa and Namibia, women were contributing significantly to the struggle against apartheid rule by organizing actions such as marches and boycotts. Not only did women in these countries suffer the oppression of institutionalized racism and poverty, but they also had to cope with the patriarchal and sexist traditions of their own racial communities. Women are also the principal food producers in southern Africa as they are throughout Africa, but South Africa's policy of economic destabilization and Africa's crippling foreign debt meant that women's capacity to provide for their families was seriously diminished. In recognition of the burden being borne by women in the region, the Working Group took special care to make women a focus of its development education program. Between 1987 and 1991, most southern Africans brought to Canada on speaking tours were women, from Zimbabwe, Zambia, Namibia, Tanzania and South Africa. Often their visits were carried out in collaboration with church-based women's groups in Canada linked to the Ecumenical Decade of the Churches in Solidarity with Women (1988-98). Popular resources produced always included sections on women. This commitment to women's issues and perspectives is reflected in the programs of all working groups and has today evolved into a special emphasis on women and development and, even more recently, the study of how relations between men and women determine or affect the social, political and economic conditions in which they live.

In February 1990, South African President F. W. de Klerk delivered a watershed speech in which he announced that liberation movements opposed to apartheid would no longer be banned and that Nelson Mandela would soon be released. De Klerk, who was immediately praised worldwide, declared that with his actions South Africa's transition to a non-racial democracy had begun. The change in political dynamics that de Klerk's speech set in motion had a definite impact on the Inter-Church Coalition on Africa member churches. Although still committed to seeing the anti-apartheid struggle through to the end, they recognized an opportunity to shift some of their resources and energies to address other pressing African concerns. Among those concerns was Africa's steadily worsening economic crisis. At the centre of the crisis was a massive foreign debt and severely restrictive economic structural adjustment programs imposed on African states by the World Bank and the International Monetary Fund. The bleak 1970s, sadly and tragically, had been followed by the even grimmer 1980s.

Recovery programs fail

Internationally funded efforts to put Africa back on the development path, foremost among them the five-year United Nations Program for African Economic Recovery (1986-90), were emerging as failures. Western governments and international financial institutions had promised to support African programs for self-sustaining growth and development. What Africa got instead, and most intensively during the mandate of the U.N. Program for Economic Recovery, were uniformly monetarist solutions in the form of structural adjustment programs. Under these programs, growth and development were defined largely in terms of an improved gross national product. Little regard was shown for human development or for the impact which the adjustment programs had on such vital social sectors as education and health.

The economic crisis, caused in large part by the failure of U.N. Program for African Economic Recovery and the destructive policies of the World Bank and International Monetary Fund, increasingly drew the attention of the All-Africa Conference of Churches and national councils of churches across the continent. They became alarmed at the plight of their constituents whom they watched sink deeper and deeper into poverty and despair. Effective countermeasures, they realized, would have to be organized on several fronts. Their own governments would have to be lobbied to better represent their citizens in regional, African and global economic policy-making forums. Their constituents would have to be empowered with a basic understanding of the complex web of local, national and international interests that were pitted against them. And appeals to partner churches around the world, for new and innovative forms of solidarity support, would have to be urgently registered.

Among Canadian churches and church organizations at this time, effective education on the debt was being carried out. Ten Days for World Development and the Ecumenical Coalition for Economic Justice had both implemented education programs and produced resources on the Third World debt and the impact of structural adjustment programs. But no program specific to the African debt existed.

Africa Economic Justice Project

To fill this gap, and in response to the urgent appeals of partners, the Coalition Board conceived the Africa Economic Justice Project. Also with funding from CIDA's Partnership Africa Canada, this Project sought to build on previous work on the effects of Africa's debt crisis carried out by the Development Working Group. A centrepiece of this work was a resource on the debt called "The Human Face of the Economic Crisis in Africa." It was based on an Inter-Church Coalition on Africa-organized visit by nine Canadians to Tanzania, Uganda and Kenya in 1990. The resource presented an aspect of Africa's economic crisis that the usual economic indicators fail to note, namely, the real life experience of African people. The emphasis on the human dimension of the economic crisis has remained fundamental to all of the Coalition's economic justice work.

Also central to the Coalition's work on economic justice is supporting the development of African alternative economic systems and models. The prolonged stress of the debt now compounded by World Bank-imposed structural adjustment programs has obstructed the emergence of indigenous alternatives. Increasingly Africans are working to explore such opportunities. A recent example is the African Alternative Framework to Structural Adjustment Programs, which has won recognition around the world, especially in developing nations, as an example of the kind of innovative, visionary and first-order thinking of which people of the so-called 'Third' World are capable.

To date the Africa Economic Justice Project has established an extensive file of research on and analysis of Canadian government and World Bank policies on debt, aid and trade relations with Africa. It has also undertaken several corresponding advocacy actions and has begun producing popular educational resources for Canadian churches. For its effort, it has won recognition from African partners, other international churches and non-governmental organizations.

New programs and activities

Recently, several other components have been added to the Inter-Church Coalition on Africa's overall program, to augment the geographically defined work on southern Africa and thematic work on economic justice. One is concerned with Africa's public image in Canada. Since its beginning, the Inter-Church Coalition on Africa has sought, through the various expressions of its work, to present a positive image of Africa and its people to counter the litany of negative and distorted images that are spread through the various channels of mass communication. Ask the person on the street what immediately comes to mind when he/she thinks of Africa and, more often than not, the answer will be 'famine,' 'war,' 'black-on-black violence,' or some other essentially negative and violent image. In 1989, meeting in Maseru, Lesotho, the All-Africa Conference of Churches recognized the public relations beating Africa was taking internationally at the hands of media that seemed uninterested in careful interpretation and analysis of events. An appeal was issued to international partners to work harder to counter the superficial and sensationalist orientation of their media and to tell the whole story of Africa—not only the problems, but also the many hopeful developments and possibilities.

In response to the All-Africa Conference of Churches' appeal, the Inter-Church Coalition on Africa moved to consolidate and intensify its 'images of Africa' work. A new group, the Images of Africa Working Group, was formed. Still early in its development, program plans include the creation of educational resources for elementary school-age children in secular and church schools, showcasing African art and culture as a celebration of Africa's cultural richness and diversity, and working with the media to encourage expanded, more balanced and positive coverage of African and African-related events.

Another new component of the Inter-Church Coalition on Africa's program is concerned broadly with human rights in Africa. It will not be the first time, however, that the Coalition has engaged in human rights work. South Africa, Zaire, Kenya and Sudan have been the subjects of ongoing focus from a human rights perspective. But human rights advocacy has always presented the Inter-Church Coalition on Africa with a troubling dilemma. As stated above, the Coalition takes its signals primarily from church partners in Africa. Because most of those partners have not been able or willing to speak out against the human rights records of their respective governments, the Coalition's hands have been tied in a sense. Although member churches might feel inclined to do so, publicizing human rights violations in various countries where such violations exist could easily place church partners there at great risk. Some churches or church organizations, the South African Council of Churches uppermost among them, have for some years accepted the risk entailed in challenging their government's human rights record. Many other partners have chosen to remain silent, no doubt waiting for the right conditions to develop before voicing their dissent.

Now, however, the wind of democratic change is blowing across the African continent. That wind has its source in the growing dissatisfaction of grassroots African people—dissatisfaction with the seemingly endless and worsening economic crisis and with corrupt, wasteful and repressive governing regimes. Africans in many countries and churches in these countries are finding their voices. The movement has already resulted in the ousting by peaceful and violent means of several autocratic rulers and their administrations. More changes will undoubtedly follow as the trend continues and gathers momentum. In many countries where the human rights records of governments are being challenged, African churches are front and centre. In Malawi, Kenya and Sudan, to name only three, churches are providing strong and prophetic leadership in the process of securing protection of peoples' basic human rights.

While the Inter-Church Coalition on Africa has refrained generally from raising human rights concerns in countries in which church partners have not also adopted such a stance, there have been exceptions, Zaire among them. In the late 1980s, the Inter-Church Coalition on Africa facilitated the formation of what was to become the *Table de concertation sur les droits humains au Zaïre* (Roundtable on Human Rights in Zaire). Based in Montreal, the Roundtable brought together Zairian exiles living in Canada and several Catholic mission and development organizations with historical links to Zaire. It sought to provide various forms of support to the growing movement for democracy in Zaire and for the removal of the repressive and corrupt regime of Mobutu Sese Seko. Significant in the formation of the Roundtable was the fact that it was based in Quebec. This brought the Inter-Church Coalition on Africa into regular contact with several Catholic organizations and introduced the Coalition to an active francophone social justice network. Instrumental in the building of these relationships were the bilingual capabilities of the then-co-ordinator, Marg Bacon. Today, the Roundtable has expanded its operations to include the skilful lobbying of the Canadian government for strategically effective support of the democratic movement in Zaire, the publication of a weekly update on the situation in Zaire, as well as periodic popular education resources. Although the Roundtable continues to collaborate with the Inter-Church Coalition on Africa, it is a fully autonomous organization. South Africa, Kenya and Sudan have also been subjects of the Coalition's human rights focus. In 1990 the Coalition submitted briefs on the human rights situations in these three countries to the 47th session of the United Nations Commission on Human Rights.

The Inter-Church Coalition on Africa's new program on human rights has regularized the practice of preparing annual human rights briefs on selective African countries, starting in 1993-94 and the 49th session of the U.N. Commission on Human Rights. It has also included research and advocacy in the area of economic rights and the right to development. Helping to make economic rights a focal point of future U.N. deliberations on human rights is an objective that the Inter-Church Coalition on Africa will vigorously pursue in the next few years. Africa is experiencing economic injustices which are systematically affecting the human rights of its people. In particular, structural adjustment programs are increasingly weakening the social infrastructure of many countries. The resulting discontent among people over inadequate health services and educational opportunities and lack of food and buying power to purchase food, often prompts governments to resort to strong-arm tactics to quell rising unrest. Structural adjustment programs, therefore, can be linked directly to violations of civil and political rights as people's demands for security and the basic necessities of life, all of which are eroded by structural adjustment programs, are met with ever increasing violence.

Yet another new program component is the thematic focus on democratization and gender relations. Activities under this theme focus on the efforts of African partners to help democratize their societies. African churches are becoming increasingly involved in the process of nation building. They are supporting initiatives by the African people to gain a greater voice in political and economic decision making. In 1990, they participated in a major continental conference on 'popular participation'—the name given to the process whereby the African people assert their right to full participation in the affairs of state. The conference, held in Arusha, Tanzania, produced a document entitled the "African Charter for Popular Participation in Development and Transformation," which has become a seminal treatise in the debate on nation-building processes. Local democratic initiatives by the churches have included national voter education programs like that mounted in 1992 by the National Council of Churches of Kenya.

All of the Inter-Church Coalition on Africa's major programs— on economic justice, human rights, democratization and gender relations, and Africa's public image in Canada—have been organized under the project banner of "Africa Millennium." The project receives financial assistance from Partnership Africa Canada.

Over its life span, the Inter-Church Coalition on Africa's basic organizational structure has remained essentially the same, with a few refinements. Currently, the Coalition consists of a Board of Directors, three working groups and a staff of five (a full-time co-ordinator, an administrative support staffer and three part-time program officers). The working groups, Board and staff intersect in the Co-ordinating Committee, composed of a Board designate, working group chairpersons and staff. All component parts of the Coalition form the Africa Forum, which meets twice a year and whose agenda can vary from self-education and review of denominational policy to recreation and celebration.

The future

Famine, war, corrupt and autocratic governments, poverty, debt, structural adjustment programs and the ever increasing marginalization of Africa by the developed world have virtually paralysed social and economic development across the continent. The African people, however, are demanding change. Their voices are getting louder and their mood less conciliatory as they stand face to face with the internal and external forces that oppress them ("the enemy within and the enemy without," in the words of one African development analyst). If Africa's future is to be marked by justice, peace and prosperity, then its people must confront these two enemies, says the Rev. Jose Chipenda, general secretary of the All-Africa Conference of Churches. Africans themselves must formulate and put into action counterstrategies to develop political and economic systems more indigenous to Africa. The African Alternative Framework to Structural Adjustment Programs is one such initiative. For Chipenda, such action is critical: Africa is at a "crossroads between promises and terrible problems, new hope and total hopelessness. It is time to make a choice."

What African churches must choose, Chipenda believes, is to take an active part in the process of nation building. Many churches and church councils are already doing so—by promoting economic alternatives rooted in a sense of biblical justice, by standing up to state authorities for people's fundamental democratic rights and by initiating programs to make people aware of their basic human rights. It needs to lead the continent with a vision of the future, like it did during and after the exuberant 1960s, Chipenda says.

What will Canadian churches choose in response to the challenges that face the African people? Coalition-sponsoring churches have answered that question with projects like "Africa Millennium": intensive education, mobilization and advocacy programs geared to what our African church partners say is critical for the continent in the 1990s and beyond. On the Canadian and international fronts, however, a number of obstacles have arisen that threaten the capacity of the churches to support their African partners both denominationally and ecumenically through the Inter-Church Coalition on Africa. Among those obstacles, shrinking denominational revenues, reductions in Canada's Official Development Assistance envelope, proposed structural changes to CIDA and what seems like the intensification and compounding of wars, civil conflicts and human rights violations around the world—all of which threaten to place debilitating constraints on the important work of social justice. It seems a foregone conclusion that church solidarity work, whether on behalf of partners in Africa, Latin America or Asia, will have to restructure itself to withstand and overcome these new challenges. New strategies must be developed and new alliances built. Perhaps, years into the future, those who believe and participate in Canada's social justice coalitions will regard these turbulent times as having reinvigorated the work we all hold dear. From that thought let us draw hope.

The Taskforce
on the Churches
and Corporate Responsibility

Renate Pratt

Introduction

Large church corporations are powerful members of Canadian society. Their policies and practices affect the well-being of millions of people in Canada and around the world and can have a substantial impact on the natural environment. Canadian churches have seen it in their mandate to challenge those corporate activities which contribute to social injustice, to violations of human rights, increased militarism or ecological abuse.

The Taskforce on the Churches and Corporate Responsibility was formally established on January 1 1975, after a two-year planning process. The participating churches and religious orders committed themselves to react to Canadian corporate decisions which would adversely affect groups of vulnerable people who have no power to change those decisions.

In developing the Taskforce, the member churches had been influenced by the example of their American sister churches who, as shareholders, had begun to protest American corporate involvement in the Vietnam War and in the apartheid system in South Africa. Canadian churches were asked by their American colleagues to respond to shareholder resolutions on issues of corporate social responsibility.

Although some Canadian churches had refrained from investing in alcohol and tobacco companies, the active involvement in corporate decisions of churches as shareholders presented new and complex challenges which the founding members of the Taskforce set out to meet.[1]

The Taskforce was thus given the mandate to assist participating churches in the implementation of their policies. Official representatives of the churches serve on the board of the Taskforce as links with their own decision-making structures. In this way, the member denominations and religious orders retain control over the choice of activities in which they wish to participate; Taskforce briefs, letters and policy statements reflect their considered views and policy positions. The Taskforce itself owns no shares. Shareholder or other interventions occur only when the share-owning denominations or religious orders decide to take action.

Throughout the life of the Taskforce, there were, of course, personalities who left larger footprints than others. Their contribution, however, would not have been possible without the many Board members, volunteers and staff who cared for each other, helped to nurture the organization, gave it credibility, shaped it and kept it financially afloat and in good order.

There were the pioneers of active shareholdership who braved the hostile atmosphere of early shareholder meetings; supporters on committees and in congregations who defended this new form of mission activity when a powerful attack was mounted and the existence of the Taskforce hung in the balance; ministers and priests who dealt with distressed business people in their congregations without compromising their commitment to the actions of the Taskforce.

Important as these actors were who gave leadership and support to the work of the Taskforce, they share its accomplishments with international partner churches and their progressive organizations working for justice under conditions of poverty and human rights violations. The example of their courageous struggles has been a constant source of inspiration and renewal to the Taskforce.

Early critics of the Taskforce

Although church participation in company shareholder meetings has been but a brief annual event in a continuum of Taskforce activity, it has also been very much a public contest and has elicited spirited public objections. In 1977 a sustained effort to neutralize the activities of the Taskforce was begun by a number of senior members of the business community and clergy of all denominations who established the Confederation of Church and Business People. The Confederation championed corporate decisions which were being challenged by the churches. Inevitably the Confederation became apologists for regimes such as apartheid South Africa or Pinochet's Chile, which were benefiting from corporate decisions. They charged the Taskforce with biased information and alleged manipulation of church policy in favour of an antibusiness ideology.

Individual member churches responded to this powerful attempt to silence the Taskforce by demonstrating to their critics that denominational policy was indeed being applied in their joint activities as an ecumenical coalition. In rejecting the charges of the Confederation of Church and Business People, the churches protected the Taskforce and its programs from time-consuming and energy-draining involvement in this controversy. By the mid-1980s, much of the early criticism had dissipated. Thanks to the resolute commitment of the member churches of the Taskforce, the rights of all shareholders to challenge corporate policy is more widely respected.

International bank loans: Then and now[2]

Human rights and racism

Opposition to the system of apartheid was an early unifying force in the policies of the member churches and led to ecumenical action even before the establishment of the Taskforce. Since 1974, apartheid in South Africa and Canadian responses to it have remained a major agenda item.

A print-out sent anonymously in 1974 from the Frankfurt office of the European American Banking Corporation revealed multimillion dollar loans to the South African government and its state agencies made by Western banking syndicates. The Interfaith Center on Corporate Responsibility in New York in turn published the "Frankfurt Documents," itemizing the involvement of Canadian and other banks in large, long-term loans to South African state agencies.[3]

The "Frankfurt Documents" occasioned a strategy of responses by the Taskforce which has proved useful and has been retained ever since. Typically, the Taskforce verifies as thoroughly as possible the information received and requests a meeting with senior management. Confirmation of the South African loans was requested from each bank, along with a commitment from senior management to cease lending to South African state agencies until apartheid was abandoned. Citing client/banker confidentiality, the banks refused to discuss the loans. Church shareholders then began to attend regularly the banks' annual meetings, where they explained their position and distributed to the other shareholders fact sheets about their banks' complicity in the apartheid system. Bank chairmen fiercely defended the legality of these loans and even claimed that they benefited black South Africans. One bank chairman maintained that to halt these loans "would not be morally defensible nor morally consistent." Altercations concerning such social justice issues between bank chairmen and dissident church shareholders—the latter vigorously supported by the late Senator Eugene Forsey on one occasion—were a completely new phenomenon in Canada and attracted increasing media attention.

Codes of practice

Efforts to influence bank policy had placed the issue on the public agenda, but had not moved the banks. Senior management and the majority of shareholders were united in their opposition to the churches' 'interference' in bank decisions. Members of the Taskforce were more successful when they began to seek agreement on fundamental social criteria which the banks were applying to loan decisions. This was the Taskforce's initial venture in the strategic value of advocating corporate 'codes of practice.' Progress was slow but fruitful, though discussion of actual—as opposed to hypothetical—South African loans continued to be a problem.

Since then, codes of practice have become effective building blocks in the work of the Taskforce. They articulate a corporation's social and environmental obligations. They are the standard by which corporate commitment can be measured. When the Ontario Business Corporations Act was revised in 1981, the Taskforce proposed legislation for a permanent social responsibility committee of companies to advise the board of directors on emerging social, political and environmental issues. This committee, the Taskforce argued, should also oversee and report annually on the effective implementation of the company's code of practice.

Public pressure

To help people understand the importance of bank support for the apartheid system, the Taskforce published and periodically updated "Banking on Apartheid," a brochure detailing South African loans by banks, amounts, recipients and dates. The Taskforce exchanged information with international networks and profited from research done by the Corporate Data Exchange of New York, the World Council of Churches' Program to Combat Racism and others.

Canadian bank loans to South Africa had provoked widespread public protest actions. Many important organizations and individuals publicized the transfer of their accounts from banks with loans to South Africa to alternative lending institutions. The Taskforce assisted the protest by printing small 'No Loans to South Africa' stickers (soon matched by a 'No Loans to Chile' series) which were very popular. They were affixed to bank cheques and reached a great number of businesses and institutions. The United Church used them on their pay cheques.

Turning point

Public protests and media attention put enormous pressure on the banks. In 1978, the Royal Bank pledged to halt loans to South Africa where it judged that they would support the policies of the apartheid system. After acquiring the Orion Bank in England, the Royal added that the Orion would be covered by the same policy.

In 1979, the Toronto Dominion Bank notified the Taskforce that it had made a new loan to the South African electricity company, which the bank assumed would benefit the black community. Member churches were able to convince senior management that this loan was far more likely to aid South Africa's nuclear program. As a result, in early 1980 the Toronto Dominion became the first Canadian bank to announce an unconditional halt to new loans and to any renewal of loans to the South African government and its agencies.

In time, other banks let it be known that they too were avoiding new South African loans. Slow as were Canada's banks to respond, the Canadian government was slower still. The Taskforce can take some credit for the fact that Canada's banks had ceased lending to South Africa long before Joe Clark, then Secretary of State for External Affairs, included in his 1985 sanction packet a 'voluntary' ban on private loans to South Africa. A voluntary ban of a different sort was also achieved in the same year when the Chase Manhattan abruptly ceased lending to South Africa, causing all but the hardiest of international banks to panic and do the same.

Watching the lawmakers

The story of international bank loans illustrates the incremental nature of the Taskforce's activities. Concerned about the secrecy of international loan decisions with important political consequences, the Taskforce raised the subject with Canada's legislators on several occasions. Two examples come to mind. The significant rise in petroleum prices in 1973 generated huge deposits of 'petro-dollars' in Western banks, including Canadian ones. Bankers in turn began to deposit billions of dollars into the treasuries of Third World countries. Many of the banks' clients at the time were Latin American regimes of threadbare creditworthiness, with a record of instability and abuse of human rights. The Canadian Export Development Corporation for its part indiscriminately extended credits to facilitate exports, including military exports, to some of these unsavoury regimes.

Thus when the Bank Act was revised between 1978 and 1980, the Taskforce called for greater transparency of such international lending. Under the watchful eyes of a delegate of the Canadian Bankers Association, the Taskforce argued before the House of Commons Finance Committee that, in the interest of public and shareholder accountability, a revised Bank Act should require uniform and equitable disclosure of Canadian bank loans over $1 million to foreign governments or their agencies. The churches contended that where private loans are extended to regimes repugnant to our government and to very many Canadians, bankers become the undeclared but actual practitioners of Canadian foreign policy. Although the proposal for new disclosure rules was not accommodated in the revised Bank Act, pressure not only from the churches, but also from the investment community and financial analysts soon led to greater transparency of the banks' international business through new reporting formats.

International financial institutions

Staying with causes which initially appear hopeless has proved to be worthwhile. Such pursuits prompt questions from other concerned organizations and, with time, gain public currency. The Taskforce followed its line of enquiry about international loans from private to public financial institutions. It began to monitor decisions taken by Canadian executive directors in international financial institutions such as the World Bank, the International Monetary Fund and regional development banks. Working closely with the Center for International Studies in Washington, the Taskforce found that, through the executive directors of the international financial institutions, the Canadian government approved credits to regimes which were violating human rights and also receiving commercial loans. Indeed, Canada turned out to have a two-track policy on the protection of international human rights. In foreign policy pronouncements it was condemning human rights abuses, while in the international financial institutions Canada was ignoring them. In 1982, for example, the Taskforce launched a cross-country campaign to protest Canada's support for $1.07 billion (U.S.) in International Monetary Fund credits to South Africa, notwithstanding rising repression there and Canadian diplomatic condemnation of it.

To argue their case in tangible terms, members of the Taskforce designed a set of minimum human rights criteria focussing only on security of the person which, they said, the Canadian government should apply as minimum standards of behaviour for governments applying for credit from the international financial institutions. This position was first presented to the Minister of Finance in 1983 when parliamentary approval was required for an increase of Canada's financial commitment to the International Monetary Fund. Since then, the Taskforce has appeared before a number of official enquiries, yet successive governments continue to reject the notion of human rights criteria on the grounds that it would politicize the international financial institutions. Our argument was included, however, in the recommendations of two parliamentary committees.[4]

Today, minimum standards of human rights are increasingly recognized even by the international financial institutions. In 1988, Ibrahim F. I. Shihata, vice-president and general counsel of the World Bank, noted that human rights violations may well adversely affect the "ability to carry out World Bank projects."[5] In 1990, the World Council of Churches' Commission on the Churches and International Affairs consulted the Taskforce about the wording of a human rights clause to be included in the charter of the new European Bank for Reconstruction and Development, an organization founded to serve the new democracies of the Eastern Europe. Canada is a member of the European Bank and, despite its opposition to human rights criteria in other international financial institutions, is now partner to this clause in the new bank's Charter. In 1991, the World Bank postponed development funding for Kenya pending the return of a modicum of human rights standards there.

Academics and activists alike have absorbed into their concepts and literature much of our research and experience in the pursuit of human rights standards in international lending and have acknowledged the Taskforce's pioneering work in Canada in this area.

International debt

A few brief years of immense international lending has left in its wake a decade of misery and devastation in much of the Third World. Mesmerized by the astronomical debt of countries such as Brazil or Mexico, debt capable of threatening the very survival of the international financial system, people in the lending countries have paid far less attention to debtor countries which were suffering more, but posing less of a financial threat. For the churches, the debt crisis, like human rights abuse, was quickly recognized as a development issue and partner churches in debtor countries called for joint North/South advocacy action.[6] In Latin America in particular, a cruel irony was visited on the poor in countries where multiparty elections had only just been held. Under previous military dictatorships, they had endured unemployment, reduction in wages, cutbacks in social services and a rise in the cost of basic food items. The poor had not benefited from private loans that had sustained their rulers. Now the International Monetary Fund was making identical demands as conditions for credits and new private loans, and the poor became poorer still. Other states, particularly those in sub-Saharan Africa, never had qualified for private loans but had accumulated enormous debt obligations to Western governments.

Beginning in 1985, the Taskforce made a sustained effort to develop policy for an ecumenical approach to the Canadian government, Canada's private banks and the Export Development Corporation to seek debt relief for those countries most adversely affected and for the poor within them. Member churches consulted with a number of African embassies, the North-South Institute and with the North-South Working Group of the United Church. They also held an Ecumenical Consultation on International Debt with church representatives and senior bankers.

Taskforce staff drafted a position paper for discussion and revision by the Debt Study Network, an intercoalition working group. The result was a major study published in 1989, "The International Debt Crisis: A Discussion Paper Prepared for the Canadian Churches."[7] "The Debt Paper" was used extensively in subsequent years to challenge government and parliamentary committees, the Export Development Corporation and private banks to reduce the debt.

The study begins with widely representative testimonials from partners by indebted countries, such as the statement by Archbishop Carter of Jamaica, "No reading of Scripture would oblige hungry people to starve themselves and their children simply to honour contractual obligations to repay rich people and institutions" (Pastoral Letter, 1987).

Recommendations to the Canadian government and banks refer to the harsh conditions attached to International Monetary Fund credits and call for new guidelines to ensure respect for basic human rights and for protection of those already poor from added hardships. The Discussion Paper counsels that, "the goal should be to end 'the debt crisis' by reducing each country's debt to the point where there is no longer a net outflow of capital and the country has sufficient resources left after servicing its reduced debt to maintain its responsibilities to its people and invest in its own development."[8]

The paper also requests the Canadian government to instruct the Export Development Corporation to write down or reschedule debts to sub-Saharan Africa for long terms and minimal interest.

Working with a number of interchurch coalitions including Ten Days and GATT-Fly, the Taskforce appeared before the Standing Committee on External Affairs and International Trade in February 1990. Many of its recommendations were subsequently included in the Standing Committee's report. The government largely ignored the substance of the report and, in March 1991, the Standing Committee renewed its request for urgent action in a new document entitled "Unanswered Questions/Uncertain Hope."

Private banks and public debt

Eighteen years ago, when international bank loans flooded the markets, members of the Taskforce had asked for the inclusion of social criteria in the banks' loan policies and for greater prudence in the choice of their clients. Undeterred, the banks had welcomed and supported with their loans the promotion of free-market policies. As the debt crisis deepened, however, the banks made full use of a Canadian government provision which permitted them to defer taxes on their increased reserve funds against default by debtors.

In meetings with the banks, members of the Taskforce argued that, while the banks have thus obtained protection for their interests, the arrangement does not at all help debtor countries. In 1990, therefore, church shareholders sought the banks' agreement to a proposal that the banks claim additional tax relief only when there is corresponding benefit to debtor countries through reduction in the debt burden. The churches and religious orders forcefully spoke to this proposal during the banks' annual meetings. The banks, however, were not prepared to circulate the shareholder proposal, much less to accept it.

As the net transfer of funds from impoverished nations to the developed world continues, the Canadian banks have long overcome the embarrassment caused by their recent international lending binge. In 1991 they earned \$3.7 billion in profits, the highest amount ever.[9]

North/South solidarity actions occupy much of the agenda of the Taskforce as it focusses increasingly on the right to sustainable development. That move had begun with the issue of international lending and debt.

Environment and development

Policies

During 1980-81, member churches and religious orders of the Taskforce were reviewing their priorities for corporate social action. Many of them found that, in addition to ongoing work related to southern Africa and Latin America, domestic concerns about methods of energy generation and their impact on the environment were high on their lists. Placing these new issues on the Taskforce agenda coincided with the appointment in the fall of 1981 of Moira Hutchinson as a part-time researcher. The enhanced research capability of the Taskforce made it possible to devote major attention to the new and complex issues of environmental concerns.

Over the years, the Taskforce has sustained its interest and widened its expertise and activities on environmental issues. Faithful to their standing procedure, member churches ascertained that there was sufficient consensus in their policy positions to move to ecumenical action. They agreed to respond flexibly to specific concerns across the spectrum of energy and environmental questions brought before them.

Pollution-related issues

In a number of pollution-related issues, the Taskforce either initiated or supported existing campaigns of other organizations.[10] A first example: prompted by its Jesuit members in 1984, the Taskforce joined with others in pressuring Environment Canada to enact regulations that would phase down or eliminate lead in gasoline. The Jesuit concern originated in their community health work in Toronto, where high lead levels were detected in children. Lead poisoning is particularly significant in the case of children as it causes development problems. The Taskforce discussed the matter with petroleum and lead-producing companies to seek compliance from companies which would be affected by the Environment Canada measures.

During the same year, under the leadership of the United Church of Canada, the Taskforce joined organizations concerned with acid rain in pressuring the government to set early and higher reduction targets for sulphur dioxide emissions. Member churches met with senior management of INCO and Noranda Mines (operating respectively in Sudbury, Ontario and Rouyn, Quebec) and attended their annual shareholder meetings. They urged the companies to accept federal and provincial reduction targets of 50% in sulphur dioxide emissions. Agreement with the companies was reached in 1986-87. The Taskforce feels that it has played a part in the successful attainment of these targets.

In 1983 a Nova Scotia court had found in favour of Nova Scotia Forest Industries, permitting them to continue aerial spraying of the herbicide 2,4,5-T, contaminated with dioxin. The Taskforce engaged in a lengthy argument with the company. Given that the concerned public had only the courts through which to challenge the alleged safety of the herbicide, the Taskforce began to question procedures that *a priori* excluded the public from decisions affecting the environment. Adequate opportunity for public involvement in environmental assessment of public or private development projects became a major preoccupation of the Taskforce.

Nuclear and uranium developments

A review of church policies showed common concern about the uses of nuclear power. While local concern about uranium mining and waste was already engaging the member churches, overseas partners were alerting them to the international dimensions of nuclear power.

Three projects helped launch a new Taskforce program. The first was the discovery of the importation of uranium from South Africa-occupied Namibia for processing and re-export by Eldorado Nuclear. Staff research related to this discovery provided insight into the structures and activities of a network of government departments, regulatory agencies and Crown corporations responsible for the Canadian nuclear industry.

The second project was a workshop in 1981 sponsored by several interchurch coalitions on "Global Perspectives for Canadian Church Policy on Development and Energy," which took advantage of the visit of Janos Pasztor, director of the Energy Program of the World Council of Churches. The workshop urged the churches to be wary of 'value-free' scientific data of those involved in formulating Canadian energy policy, such as government, industry and the scientific community.

The third project, a brief in 1982 to the Atomic Energy Control Board on the deep geological disposal of high-level nuclear waste in Canada, marked the beginning of a decade of critical exchanges with agencies and departments of the federal government and the nuclear industry.

In their brief to the Atomic Energy Control Board, members of the Taskforce questioned the propriety of appointing Atomic Energy of Canada Ltd. to develop proposals for assessing the concept of disposal of high-level radioactive waste. This company is a Crown corporation whose very business lies in developing, promoting and selling nuclear power. The churches also called for a national enquiry into the desirability of pursuing the nuclear energy option prior to any assessment of the concept of disposal of *future* waste. The government did not respond to this request.

Concerning methods of disposal of *existing* waste, the Taskforce called for the inclusion of social justice issues in the review process and asked that environmental review panels be representative not only of industry and the scientific community, but of the whole spectrum of public opinion. To ensure adequate, informed public participation, the Taskforce requested intervenor funding for the environmental assessment hearings yet to take place. The government has largely agreed to these requests. In 1990 the Taskforce was told that provisions for intervenor funding had been made.

The environment and the rights of aboriginal peoples

Some major environmental concerns in Canada intersect with threats to the rights of native peoples. In addressing these issues, the Taskforce has worked closely with the Aboriginal Rights Coalition and its predecessor, Project North.

The Nisga'a and AMAX

Member churches of the Taskforce initiated actions on numerous occasions when environmental hazards from energy and other resource companies posed a particular threat to aboriginal peoples' rights and livelihood. A few examples must suffice.

In 1981, at the request of the Anglican Church, members of the Taskforce attended the annual meeting in New York of AMAX Corporation, the American parent of AMAX of Canada. As shareholders they joined the Nisga'a Indians to protest the dumping of molybdenum mine tailings into Alice Arm, British Columbia, which threatened the physical and cultural survival of the Nisga'a. The operation was eventually halted. Two years later it was revealed that the dumping permit had been issued by the federal government after "an unusual and unexpected use of power." AMAX lawyers had helped draft the 1979 special dispensation with the help of cabinet ministers.[11]

The Lubicon Cree and resource industries

The Lubicon Lake Band in northern Alberta first appealed to the Canadian churches in 1983 for support in their struggle for recognition of their aboriginal rights. An isolated community, they had been overlooked in the signing of Treaty Number 8 which covers their territory. Although the Government of Canada had recognized the Band in 1939, it had neglected to establish a promised reserve and instead ceded jurisdiction to the provincial government which leased the land for oil and gas exploration.

Exploration and extraction activity soon began to destroy the Band's traditional economic base in hunting, trapping and fishing, with devastating social and health consequences. The Band's efforts to settle its claims through the courts and through negotiations with the federal government have remained unsuccessful. Starting in 1983, the Taskforce has supported the Lubicon Lake Band by keeping pressure on such resource companies as Numac, Norcen, Petro-Canada, Shell and Unocal to curb exploration. Members of the Taskforce corresponded and met with the management of these companies and participated in their shareholder meetings. Here they drew attention to the environmental, social and political impact of the companies' activities. The Taskforce worked in close co-operation with ecumenical support organizations in Alberta and with individual church initiatives at all levels.

When, in exasperation, the Lubicon Cree erected a blockade in 1988 to safeguard access to its traditional hunting and fishing areas, the Taskforce sought and received assurance from two of the energy companies involved, either that they would not force the blockade, or that the companies' operations were outside the blockaded area. Both companies supported an early settlement of the Band's claim.

In late 1989, Alberta granted the Japanese paper company, Daishowa, a 20-year forestry management tract that includes 11,000 square kilometres of land claimed by the Lubicon Band. The Taskforce has repeatedly called on Daishowa Canada not to log on land claimed by the Lubicon Band until its claims were settled. In September 1991 the Taskforce was able to facilitate a visit to Japan of Lubicon Chief Bernard Ominayak. Although the president of Daishowa refused to meet him, he received support for his cause from the Japanese Catholic Bishops' Conference and the Japanese Council of Churches. He also met with Japanese parliamentarians and with lawyers of the Japanese Federation of Bar Associations. Subsequently, the company agreed not to log in the disputed area during the winter of 1991-92.

James Bay II

Two interrelated issues in the vast Quebec Hydro Great Whale River Project have been identified for action by members of the Taskforce. These concern possible ecological damage and the need to protect the rights of the Cree and Inuit peoples. The Taskforce addressed both issues in a letter to managers of pension funds raising ethical questions concerning the purchase of Quebec Hydro bonds earmarked for the financing of James Bay II. The Taskforce has also requested a meeting with Quebec Hydro.

Greater co-operation is likely in the future between the Taskforce and aboriginal and environmental organizations over the implications of hydro-electric power in the whole of the Hudson Bay basin, including also areas of northern Manitoba. Members of the Taskforce expect contact with provincial power corporations over their concept of corporate social responsibility.[12]

Global warming

In 1984 the Taskforce organized a seminar on "Soft Energy Futures," which examined renewable energy sources and methods of conservation as effective alternatives to nuclear power and coal lique-faction. Global warming rekindles these interests, as the burning of fossil fuels has been identified as the major source of greenhouse gases. Taskforce members are challenging the government to commit Canada seriously to energy conservation and to the use of renewable forms of energy. They are also co-operating in encouraging churches in other industrialized countries to address global warming.

Environmental codes and forest land management[13]

Working with partners in Brazil, Africa and East Asia who are active in opposing deforestation, members of the Taskforce have been probing the ethical dimensions of the Canadian forest industry.

In 1986 the Taskforce wrote to about 50 Canadian forest compa-nies to ask whether they had any environmental codes or policies. The fact was that very few had and that those which existed were too general to be effective. This lack of policy was of great concern, particularly in light of the 1987 "Report of the National Task Force on Environment and Economy" which had been Canada's response to the Brundtland Report.[14] One of the key recommendations of the National Task Force was that "individual companies should adopt and implement environmental principles and policy guidelines." To initiate discussion, the Taskforce sponsored a consultation in 1989 on environmental codes of practice for forest land management which was attended by representatives from native organizations, the forest industry, universities, government, environmental organizations and trade unions.

Based largely on the results of this consultation, the Taskforce formulated its "Model Code of Environmental Practice for Forest Land Management." It is notably broader in scope than many company environmental policies. This is because the churches are convinced that questions of environmental impact are directly related to a wide range of questions about the allocation of land. Thus the Model Code contains clauses about the intrinsic value of the forest environment, processes for resolving land conflicts, responsibility to forest-dependent communities and respect for aboriginal and treaty rights. Today most forest companies have environmental codes of practice, albeit of varying quality.

But codes alone are not enough. The Taskforce holds that, for codes to have any impact on improving the quality of corporate forest land management, there have to be means of implementation, of monitoring compliance and of reporting the results to boards of directors, employees, shareholders and the public.

In 1990, church shareholders formally filed a proposal with Noranda for debate at the shareholders' meeting, asking that the company report annually on its compliance with its own forest land policies. They also proposed that Noranda initiate periodic independent audits on the implementation and the effectiveness of its policies. Although Noranda rejected the churches' proposals, it committed itself to improve its environmental reporting to its shareholders.

The Taskforce recognizes the predicament of companies like Noranda in their uncertainty about what to report. There are at present no auditing standards for environmental reporting comparable to financial reporting. The Taskforce is committed, in co-operation with others, to develop forest land management indicators to help standardize reporting across the industry.

In a paper commissioned for the 1992 United Nations Conference on Environment and Development in Brazil, the Taskforce cited its work on forest land management. It recommended establishing codes of practice for forest land management and standardizing environmental audit procedures for worldwide application. The Taskforce suggested that such measures could lead to fruitful North/South co-operation, "People in the South may experience the effects of corporations but have little opportunity for direct access to corporate decision makers. Northern groups, which often have much better access to information, may be able to assist Southern groups to analyse how decisions are made and how they can be influenced. Conversely, many Northern groups have less direct experience of the destructive impact of corporate activities. They can be aided in this by effective partnerships with Southern groups."[15]

Corporate governance

Choices in responsible investments

Just as the member churches of the Taskforce were the first investors in Canada to raise social justice questions at annual meetings of shareholders, they were also the first to submit a formal social justice shareholder proposal. They did so in 1981, taking advantage of new provisions in the Canada Business Corporations Act which eased the restrictions for minority shareholders to communicate with other shareholders through the management proxy circular.

Media attention sparked public interest and the Taskforce office was flooded with enquiries from individual and organizational investors about 'clean' companies or those to be avoided. The Taskforce was careful to limit information to its own actions: there was a danger of being taken for an investment counsellor, a role which the Taskforce did not seek. Instead the Taskforce gathered information on organizations in the United States and England which had begun to address responsible investment options and identified similar developments in Canada. In time the Taskforce established a Corporate Governance Committee, which co-operates with other interested institutions and individuals to provide leadership about choices for responsible investment.

The Committee distinguishes three models of responsible investment: ethical investment, which applies an ethical screen to investment decisions; alternative investment, which defines a social benefit as part of the return and may be content to accept lower financial returns and higher risks; and active shareholdership, in which investors use their rights and exercise their responsibilities to influence the policies and practices of a company.[16] A workshop in 1986 explored the concept of ethical or screened investment and a further workshop in 1987 focussed on alternative investment.

A conference on "Strategies for Responsible Share Ownership: Implications for Pension and Other Investment Funds," held in December 1990, was sponsored jointly by the Taskforce and the

Centre for Corporate Social Performance and Ethics of the Faculty of Management, University of Toronto. The conference brought together members of the Taskforce and academics, managers of church and secular pension funds, trade unionists, business people, corporate lawyers and researchers. In sponsoring this conference, the Taskforce sought to emphasize and draw attention to the importance of active shareholdership.

At the conference, Moira Hutchinson, then co-ordinator of the Taskforce, made this point, "I would argue that the truly responsible investor cannot avoid being an active shareholder. Once you have screened your investment portfolio, you will still have investments in companies that will not and cannot be expected to be forever perfect. You have a responsibility to monitor how these companies are using your investments and to try to persuade them to change practices which don't meet your criteria for responsible behaviour."[17]

Withdrawal from South Africa

In 1982 Taskforce denominations filed their first shareholder proposal with Alcan. They requested that a directors' committee investigate and report to all shareholders on Alcan's involvement in the military production of the apartheid state. Alcan recommended that its shareholders oppose the proposal because the directors were already informed about Alcan's South African investment. The church proposal nevertheless received 8% of the votes cast, a significant result given the novelty of the exercise and the overwhelming tendency of shareholders to vote with management.

A second proposal filed with Alcan in 1983 showed good results as well. The churches asked the directors for a report on the income earned from the sale of specialized products to the South African military. Alcan again recommended rejection of the proposal, advising shareholders that such sales were not significant. The churches nevertheless received 6.7% of the vote. Another 6.7% had registered abstentions, bringing the total to 13.4% of votes cast against the advice of management.

A third proposal in 1986 asked Alcan to withdraw from South Africa unless it could give assurances that its products were not used for military purposes. For the first time, the churches used the full range of permitted techniques to engage in concentrated proxy solicitation, canvassing Alcan's institutional investors throughout Canada and the United States.

This activity coincided with a Canadian Catholic mission to South Africa accompanied by Renate Pratt, then co-ordinator of the Taskforce. In Archbishop Tutu's garden in Durban she met with workers of Alcan's South African affiliate who confirmed what had long been suspected: that the company produced military components such as rocket shell casings, stabilizer fins for bombs and specialized sheet metal for armoured vehicles. Upon public release of this information in Canada and one week before the annual general meeting, Alcan announced its withdrawal from South Africa.

Secret ballots

In 1984 the churches submitted a shareholder proposal to the Canadian Imperial Bank of Commerce, asking it to adopt a secret voting policy for shareholder proxies and ballots. This followed logically from an incident in 1983, when Bank management contacted shareholders who had returned their proxy votes in favour of the churches' proposal for increased disclosure of foreign loans. According to *The Globe and Mail*, an official of the Canadian Imperial Bank of Commerce stated that "a significant number" had decided to change their ballot after being contacted,[18] fair evidence that proxy ballots were hardly secret. The Bank opposed the 1984 secret-ballot proposal and won overwhelming shareholder support for its position. Yet at the end of the shareholder meeting, Canadian Imperial Bank of Commerce management reversed itself and agreed to adopt the spirit of the churches' proposal, the proxy votes of the majority of the shareholders notwithstanding.

Since then, and for a variety of reasons, many companies have adopted secret-ballot policies and shareholder support for them has been rising. Recently, new impetus has been given for secret-ballot voting by the increase in corporate takeover bids and attempts by companies to ward off the raiders through share manipulations. One such issue sparked a 25% support vote from INCO shareholders for secret ballots to protect their right to express themselves freely. A 1989 tabulation in the United States of the voting on 39 secret-ballot proposals shows an average support vote of 27.4% in favour.

The trouble with Section 131 (5) (b)

In 1987, a precedent was set in a successful court action by Varity Corporation (formerly Massey-Ferguson), which allowed the company to exclude from the management proxy circular a church shareholder proposal for disinvestment from South Africa. The court agreed with Varity's interpretation that, according to Section 131 (5) (b) of the Canada Business Corporations Act, the "proposal was primarily submitted for the purpose of promoting general economic, political, racial, religious, social or similar causes" and could be excluded on those grounds.

As the Bank Act has a similar clause, this precedent has made it difficult for shareholders to submit any proposal relating to a company's social responsibility which does not immediately fall afoul of the very wide interpretation given to companies in Section 131 (5) (b).

As they have done with other issues, members of the Taskforce have turned to the lawmakers, in this case to the Department of Consumer and Corporate Affairs, to seek revisions to the Canada Business Corporations Act which would restore appropriate minority shareholder rights. In 1991 federal officials encouraged the Taskforce to submit their views on the present asymmetry in which corporations have unilateral power to interpret the motive of a shareholder filing a proposal, while shareholders have no recourse but the courts to seek redress.

The Taskforce is investigating a variety of means to pursue this complex area of shareholder responsibility.

Conclusion

North/South solidarity actions are bound to occupy the agenda of the Taskforce as it focusses increasingly on the right to sustainable development. That has already begun with the issue of international lending and debt and with concerns for the global environment. As the Taskforce approaches its 20th anniversary, the distinction between international and Canadian issues is becoming increasingly blurred.

The Taskforce has tended to adapt its organizational structure to the needs of shifting priorities in order to address them as effectively as possible. For example, when international bank loans to, and

Canadian investment in, South Africa and Latin America were priority concerns, the structure evolved from working subcommittees designated by geographical areas to subcommittees with generic titles such as 'banks' and 'corporations.' When a new subcommittee on Canada (Energy & Environment) was added in 1981, it was flexible enough to accommodate a number of issues under this heading. Later, issues related to international debt were addressed in a new structure conducive to intercoalition consultation and so on. Combining the domestic issues subcommittee with the international issues subcommittee to form a larger unit in 1992 provided greater flexibility for addressing agenda items thematically.

The nature of the 1992 agenda no longer suited identification as either domestic or international. Indeed, questions of Canadian corporate social responsibility become international through the transnational nature of corporate activity—by export, investment, foreign subsidiaries, patent rights and so on—generating concerns at different times and in different countries for human rights, social justice, development and environmental protection or any combination of these. So one might question certain Canadian military production in Canada and also in affiliated companies abroad. It was no longer helpful to cover the ill effects of large-scale hydro dams on aboriginal peoples in Brazil in one subcommittee and discuss the same problem affecting northern Quebec in another. Global warming, also on the 1992 agenda, would know no borders.

The 1992 structural changes could therefore be interpreted as giving recognition to the globalization of corporate activity and to the links between environmental protection and the right to development. They could also simply reflect a time-honoured pragmatism in finding the most effective structure to accomplish the work with limited resources.

The member churches of the Taskforce will continue to be involved in intense North/South solidarity work. They hope to be instrumental as well in creating effective international networks of church organizations concerned with corporate social responsibility. Such networks can serve as mutual resource and information centres for those best placed to raise issues with corporations or banks.

The Canada-Asia Working Group

Terry Brown

Beginnings

The Canada-Asia Working Group was formed in late 1977 after several years of discussion and a series of exploratory meetings involving church representatives and other interested individuals. Most of the initiative came from the Division of World Outreach of the United Church of Canada and its Asia Secretary, Frank Carey. Carey's initial proposal (dated March 23 1977) cited the importance of Asia in terms of population, diversity of religion and culture, economic influence and church partnership. He noted that Canadian churches already had much information on Asian human rights struggles in Korea, the Philippines and other Asian countries. However, he noted, "there is one area where the lack of information is glaring... the Canadian impact, often adverse, on the life of these countries." From its beginning, the Canada-Asia Working Group's mandate was to concentrate on the Canadian connection. A more developed proposal, circulated ecumenically in late 1977, presented a broader mandate, still concentrating on the Canadian connection. It noted Canadians' lack of information about events in Asia and Canadian economic and political involvement there. It observed the "need for more information on Canadian trade, aid and investment links with Asia" to enable a "broad public education strategy" around Asian human rights issues. It also cited requests from ecumenical church partners in Asia "to provide them with information and to communicate their concerns to people in Canada."

Out of these concerns, the 1977 proposal put forward five primary tasks for the Canada-Asia Working Group: human rights advocacy ("drawing public attention to human rights violations and bringing public pressure to bear on government"); research and documentation on Canadian aid, trade and investment links with Asia; education on "human rights and economic justice issues in Asia through the publication of a newsletter, pamphlets, public meetings, etc."; support to groups in Asia (for example, the Christian Conference of Asia Urban Rural Mission network, Asian Fund for Human Development network) "through documentation on Canadian links to Asia and through dissemination of information from them"; and co-ordination of churches' and other groups' efforts around Asian issues in Canada.

The proposal defined the Canada-Asia Working Group's geographical area of concentration as south, southeast and east Asia, excluding Australia, New Zealand, China and the Middle East. (The Canada China Programme was already in existence.) It suggested that the coalition initially concentrate on two or three countries, naming South Korea and the Philippines. The choice of these two countries reflected both the seriousness of the human rights situations there (South Korea under Park Chung Hee and the Philippines under Ferdinand Marcos) and the strong partnership relations between most of the founding member churches of the Canada-Asia Working Group and churches in the two countries.

Founding members of the Working Group were the United Church of Canada (Division of World Outreach), the Canadian Catholic Organization for Development and Peace, Scarboro Foreign Mission Society (Roman Catholic), the Anglican Church of Canada (World Mission), the Presbyterian Church in Canada, the Canadian Friends Service Committee (Quakers), representatives of the Korean and Filipino communities in Toronto and other individual volunteers. Besides Frank Carey, early members of its steering committee included Fred Bayliss, Katharine Hockin and Sang Chul Lee (United), Tom Johnston (Development and Peace), Fred Wakeman (Scarboro Foreign Mission Society), Rhea Whitehead (Anglican), Dennis Howlett (GATT-Fly) and Reuben Cusipag (the Group's first director). The Canada-Asia Working Group began with an annual budget of $12,000 (March 1978-February 1979), including support of one part-time staff. The Ecumenical Forum donated office space.

From its beginning, the Canada-Asia Working Group has functioned as a genuine 'working group,' with staff and steering committee members (some of whom officially represent member churches, while others are volunteers-at-large) sharing the work of research, writing, advocacy, solidarity, education, information sharing and co-ordination. Initially, there were two subcommittees in addition to the steering committee: economic links and human rights. These two subcommittees very much defined the work of the Canada-Asia Working Group until the mid-80s. Gradually, however, their work devolved onto staff and onto the whole steering committee and the two subcommittees ceased to function. Instead of permanent subcommittees, various ad hoc working groups have emerged from time to time around particular issues, such as developing relations with North Korea. The increase to two full-time staff in the mid-80s increased the work accomplished. Still, the steering committee of the Canada-Asia Working Group continues to function as a working group, with members taking on tasks in co-operation with the staff.

Canada Asia Currents began publication in late 1978. The Working Group's first director, Reuben Cusipag, put a great deal of effort into its development. Early issues of *Currents* reflect the work of the two subcommittees. In the area of Canadian economic links with Asia, concerns addressed in the late 70s and early 80s included Canadian uranium sales to the Philippines and South Korea, Canadian involvement in the electronics industry in southeast Asia, the sale of CANDU nuclear reactors to South Korea and Canada-Indonesia trade links. In February 1982, representatives of the Canada-Asia Working Group met with Mark MacGuigan, Minister of External Affairs, to urge him to block the export of a second CANDU reactor to South Korea, citing the South Korean government's abominable human rights record and the high level of military tension on the Korean peninsula. The group also urged the Canadian government to explore what creative steps it might take to defuse tension and contribute to the eventual reunification of North and South Korea. In a variety of ecumenical settings, the Canada-Asia Working Group put forward the case against strengthening trade relations between Canada and various oppressive Asian governments.

At the same time, the Canada-Asia Working Group strove to publicize situations of human rights abuse in Asia and sought to influence Canadian foreign policy in relation to these countries. Early issues of *Currents* contain extensive documentation of human right abuses in South Korea, the Philippines, Sri Lanka, Taiwan, Indonesia and other Asian countries. In January 1981, the Canada-Asia Working Group began annual meetings with, and the presentation of a brief to, the Canadian Ambassador to the United Nations Commission on Human Rights. The 1981 brief concentrated on South Korea. From 1981 onward, copies of the briefs and accounts of the meetings were included in *Currents*.

The U.N. Commission on Human Rights meetings in February and March each year in Geneva are an important international forum for demanding accountability from countries seriously abusing the rights of their citizens. The Canada-Asia Working Group has tried to influence the Canadian government's position at the hearings. Its briefs are also circulated to other governmental and non-governmental delegations there. Between 1983 and 1991, steering committee members and staff (Rhea Whitehead, Derek Evans and Robin Gibson) served as Canadian church representatives on the World Council of Churches' U.N. Commission on Human Rights team. The stature of the Canada-Asia Working Group at the U.N. Commission on Human Rights has steadily increased over the years.

From its earliest mandate, solidarity and partnership have been a part of the Canada-Asia Working Group's work. The focus on Canadian economic links with Asia and publicizing human rights abuses in Asia has meant giving strong support to Asian women and men struggling for justice in extremely difficult situations. In the early 1980s, the Canada-Asia Working Group began building solidarity links between the Filipino and Canadian labour movements by means of several visits of the Kilusang Mayo Uno trade union federation to Canada. The Canada-Asia Working Group has served as a resource to many solidarity groups travelling in both directions between Asia and Canada. In October 1984, it sponsored an ecumenical consultation on Vietnam, urging Canada to take a role in reducing that country's isolation.

Trends

If one charts the Canada-Asia Working Group's development from the mid-80s into the 90s, several trends emerge. First, the interest in Asian human rights issues has intensified. Despite some democratic openings, the overall human rights situation in Asia has worsened in the last five years: new oppressive regimes have emerged (for example in Myanmar, formerly Burma), longstanding difficult situations have worsened (Sri Lanka, Indonesia), and even countries which have gone through some process of democratization (the

Philippines, South Korea) have returned to a worse level of human rights abuse than before democratization. For our Asian partners, human rights have continued to have a very high priority. The Canada-Asia Working Group's increasing focus on the production of the annual brief for the U.N. Commission on Human Rights—and advocacy related to the brief both in Ottawa and Geneva—has been one response to this high priority.

In order to monitor human rights in Asia and to prepare the brief, the Canada-Asia Working Group's steering committee and staff made frequent visits to Asia. This has included listening to those whose lives have been so tragically affected by the injustices of Asia: internal refugees in the Philippines whose children have died of malnutrition, young men who have been tortured by the Sri Lankan military, tribal minority people in Myanmar whose whole existence is being destroyed by their own government. The Canada-Asia Working Group has tried to bring these situations to the attention of Canadians and the world.

A second trend which has emerged has been the success, especially in the Philippines, of the Canada-Asia Working Group in monitoring Canadian foreign aid offered through the Canadian International Development Agency and in helping to develop some alternatives to problematic patterns of aid. Following the defeat of the Marcos government in 1986, Canada offered massive foreign aid to the Philippines as a sign of support for the democratically elected government of President Corazon Aquino. Most of the aid was concentrated in two programs, the Philippine Development Assistance Program and the Negros Rural Development Fund. Partners in the Philippines soon faulted both of these programs (especially the latter) for favouring the middle class, including corrupt local politicians, while failing to address the needs of the most impoverished sectors of the Filipino population. Following discussions of the Canada-Asia Working Group staff and steering committee members with CIDA and a cross-section of non-governmental organizations in both the Philippines and Canada, a new CIDA-supported partnership organization was formed, the Philippines Canada Human Resources Development program. This program, bringing together a coalition of Canadian and Filipino organizations, has enabled the funding of human resource development for a broad range of people's organizations in the Philippines. Derek Evans, Robin Gibson and other Canada-Asia Working Group steering committee members were deeply involved in the formation of the partnership organization.

A third trend to emerge in the past five years has been Canada's role in tension reduction and peacemaking in the region. The Asian situation with the highest potential for global conflict remains the Korean peninsula. Since the 1984 international ecumenical consultation on tension reduction in northeast Asia, held in Tozanso, Japan, the international ecumenical community, co-ordinated by the World Council of Churches, has been encouraged to facilitate relationship building between the people and churches in North and South Korea and to help reduce North Korea's isolation from the rest of the world. In December 1985, the Canada-Asia Working Group issued its "Statement on North Korea," in which the Canadian churches declared their intention to support the Tozanso Process of tension reduction in northeast Asia.

In November 1988, five members of the Canada-Asia Working Group steering committee visited North Korea at the invitation of the Korean Christian Federation to the Canadian Council of Churches. Committee members were present at the opening service of the new Pongsoo church in Pyongyang. In October 1991, the Canada-Asia Working Group hosted a return visit of five members of the Korean Christian Federation to Canada. Mindful that the primary purpose of the Tozanso Process is to build positive relations between North and South Koreans, members of the 1988 Canada-Asia Working Group delegation to North Korea visited South Korea afterward and reported on the visit; likewise, the 1991 Korean Christian Federation visit to Canada included the participation of eight representatives of the (South Korean) National Council of Churches of Korea, thus providing opportunities for North and South Korean Christians to have direct conversation.

A report of the 1988 Canada-Asia Working Group visit to North Korea was published in a special edition of *Currents*, later translated into Korean for Korean congregations in Canada. Korean-Canadian congregations participated in the planning and hosting of the 1991 visit of Korean Christian Federation representatives to Canada. While not unaware of the problems of North Korea's present political system, the Canada-Asia Working Group has continued to urge the Canadian government to be more open to rapprochement with the Democratic People's Republic of Korea.

Difficulties

These three trends have taken up much of the attention of the Canada-Asia Working Group staff and steering committee members. As a result, other areas of interest have necessarily diminished. It has done less detailed research on Canadian economic relations with Asia. The Canada-Asia Working Group has continued to monitor this area broadly (for example, Massey-Ferguson and Placer Dome in the Philippines, Petro-Canada in Myanmar, INCO in Indonesia), but has not been able to produce detailed, comprehensive reports. After the important work of Dulce Hernando, a Frontier Intern in Mission appointee from the Philippines in the late 1980s, the Canada-Asia Working Group has been hampered by the lack of any full-time researchers. Likewise, overseas partners often do not have the time to do detailed monitoring of Canadian corporations in their countries. In some situations (for example, Indonesia), church links are weak. As Canadian foreign aid (and, indeed, human rights policy) is being tied increasingly to the country's potential for providing a profit for Canadian corporations, this is an area which needs more work, if additional funding for staffing or contract assignments were available.

Education has been a difficult matter for the Canada-Asia Working Group. Education of the Canadian public (and especially Canadian Christians) about Canadian complicity in injustice in Asia was part of the Canada-Asia Working Group's earliest mandate. *Canada-Asia Currents* was established as part of the strategy. Initially it was written in a popular, topical style, trying to arouse interest in Asian concerns among ordinary Canadians. But some found the strong stands it took 'excessively political.' With the increased Canada-Asia Working Group emphasis on human rights in the late 1980s, *Currents* took on a more objective and professional quality, a well-researched resource for those concerned with human rights in Asia and the Canadian connections. While every effort has been made to make *Currents* readable, the density of the material is forbidding for some. Attempts have also been made to use non-traditional educational means, such as popular theatre. In 1986, a Philippine Educational Theatre Association production toured across Canada.

The nature of the Canada-Asia Working Group's mandate is related to the question of its educational role. The Canada-Asia Working Group began as an ecumenical program of the national bodies of Canadian churches, church-related development agencies and religious communities. Various national synods, councils, conferences and boards officially approved the participation of Canadian churches in it. Churches and organizations who participate are usually represented by their Asia-related national staff. Input into the formation of the Canada-Asia Working Group policy comes from the Canadian churches through membership in the steering committee. Indeed, policy formation occurs in both directions. Canadian churches bring concerns to the steering committee (for example, the Presbyterian Church in Canada on Taiwan human rights, the Canadian Catholic Organization for Development and Peace on East Timor) and the Canada-Asia Working Group steering committee, through links with Asian people's movements and ecumenical human rights groups, commends issues to the Canadian churches (such as Korean reunification). For the most part, the Canada-Asia Working Group's policies on human rights, foreign aid, development, Korean reunification and so on have been backed up by resolutions of Canadian national church bodies. In this sense, the Canada-Asia Working Group is genuinely a Canadian church organization. Furthermore, there is not much risk of it breaking away from the Canadian churches and going its own way.

However, because the source of its mandate is in national church bodies, the Canada-Asia Working Group relates most often with national church bodies. It can be considered a broad-based grassroots or people's organization only insofar as Canadian national church bodies can be considered broad-based grassroots or people's organizations. Unlike some of the Canadian coalitions, therefore, the Canada-Asia Working Group has not sought to develop a national 'CAWG network.' Its resources are intended to be fed into the Canadian networks of the churches and organizations which are its members. Sometimes, however, these networks are not strong; sometimes a great variety of other resources are being fed into them; and sometimes the Canada-Asia Working Group resources have not been entirely suitable for them.

As the Canada-Asia Working Group is mandated as a national organization to do advocacy on Asian issues on behalf of the Canadian churches, it can speak with some authority. Canadian churches frequently have better grassroots links with the people of Asia through the Asian churches than the Canadian government does through its government and aid partnerships. For example, steering committee members visit a small village in the Philippines and hear how the people's small community organization, which they control, is being undermined by a corrupt local political official and his 'community organization' funded by the Canadian government. The official has managed to convince the local army detachment that the people's group is communist and the army is beginning to terrorize them. They are told they must disband their organization (funded by a Canadian church) and join the local politician's anticommunist organization, in which they will gain nothing. The villagers ask, "Why is the Canadian government supporting the corrupt politician and not us?" This is the kind of question the Canada-Asia Working Group tries to bring back to the Canadian government.

Linkages

All of the above is not to say that the Canada-Asia Working Group is unrelated to local congregations and Asia-related solidarity groups across Canada. Part of its initial mandate was also rooted in the Asian community in Canada. Representatives of Korean-Canadian congregations sit on the steering committee and shape the Canada-Asia Working Group policy and activities. The Canada-Asia Working Group supports and helps co-ordinate Philippines solidarity groups in Montreal, Ottawa, Toronto, Winnipeg and Vancouver. The Group has supported the formation of the Canadian Solidarity Forum on Sri Lanka, many of whose members are Sri Lankan refugees in Canada. The Canada-Asia Working Group relates with a variety of popular non-church groups in Canada working on specific human rights issues in Asia (for example, in East Timor and Taiwan). While the Canada-Asia Working Group is not well known to many middle-of-the-road Canadian Christians, it *is* well known to many Koreans, Filipinos, Sri Lankans and Taiwanese who have made Canada their home.

The Canada-Asia Working Group has also co-operated with other coalitions over the years, such as the Inter-Church Committee on Human Rights in Latin America and the Inter-Church Coalition on Africa, in the preparation and presentation of the annual U.N. Commission on Human Rights briefs. Over the years, the Canada-Asia Working Group has co-operated with the Taskforce on the Churches and Corporate Responsibility where Canadian transnationals have been identified as supporting unjust governments in Asia. Throughout 1991 and 1992, for example, the Canada-Asia Working Group and the Taskforce challenged Petro-Canada, through letters, telephone calls and personal interviews, on its decision to continue to drill for oil in Myanmar (Burma), one of the most repressive regimes in Asia. Finally, in November 1992, Petro-Canada announced its withdrawal from Myanmar—citing both financial reasons and the human rights situation. The Canada-Asia Working Group has also co-operated with GATT-Fly/the Ecumenical Coalition on Economic Justice in organizing exchange visits between the labour leaders (for example, in the garment industry) in Canada and Asia. The Canada-Asia Working Group has also worked with Ten Days for World Development on the debt issue.

Future prospects

As the Canada-Asia Working Group considers its future, the Canadian church context is one part of the picture. As noted above, that context sometimes includes inadequate communication between local and national church structures. Indeed, polarization between traditional pietistic Christians, whether Catholic or Protestant, and social justice-oriented Christians, whether Catholic or Protestant, occurs within every level of the church, from the parish to the national, and not just between local church supporters and national staff people. (This polarization is also a feature of the international church scene.) In this situation, the Canada-Asia Working Group relies on the local, congregational voices of justice-oriented Christians to help shape national churches' policies, so that, when the Canada-Asia Working Group in its advocacy claims to 'represent' the Canadian churches, it can do so with honesty.

As the Canada-Asia Working Group considers its future, the broader Canadian and international context must also be considered. Under the Conservative government of the 1980s and early 1990s, Canada has become a nastier place to live. The Free Trade Agreements with the United States and Mexico have brought about the undermining of the Canadian economy and Canadian sovereignty. The government's inability to take seriously the concerns of aboriginal Canadians and Québécois has brought the country near dissolution. On the international scene, the Canadian government has increasingly accepted former President Bush's 'New World Order,' which is the old world order of U.S. domination writ large. Canada is a full participant in World Bank and International Monetary Fund programs of structural adjustment, by which countries of the south are forced into free-market economies destructive to their people.

In this New World Order, the Canadian government sees Asia variously as economic rival, source of natural resources, of cheap labour and of capital, and market for Canadian exports. Asian Studies programs of most Canadian universities reflect this view. In such a perspective, human rights and structural adjustment become tools for furthering Canadian economic interests. Indeed, there is considerable danger that the New World Order will co-opt 'human rights' for its own political and economic ends. As evidenced in the history of the Canadian government's priorities over the last decade, it has become much more difficult to influence Canadian foreign policy in areas of human rights, development and foreign aid. Past prime ministers and other ministers have refused to meet with church leaders. National church pronouncements and advocacy by national coalitions such as the Canada-Asia Working Group may be dismissed as unrepresentative of Canadian church opinion. It has become much more difficult for the Canada-Asia Working Group to be given an interview with the Minister of External Affairs.

The Asian context is also in flux. Japan continues to dominate the region economically. The 'newly industrialized' dragons (South Korea, Taiwan, Singapore, Malaysia, Thailand) try to emulate Japan. The results have been low wages, suppression of labour unions, abridgment of human rights, pollution and environmental degradation. An Asian trade bloc is emerging to challenge the European Community and the North American free trade bloc. At the same time, Asian countries (Sri Lanka, India, Myanmar, Indonesia) are being torn apart by tribal, ethnic and religious conflicts. Situations of gross human rights abuse worsen. With the collapse of the Soviet Union and the introduction of a mixed economy in China and Vietnam, socialism and Marxism seem less viable options for Asian people's movements. These people's movements search for new patterns of political and economic organization that draw on the best of a variety of religious, tribal and ideological traditions. The New World Order and transnational capitalism (whether Western or Asian) remain a threat to these emerging new movements. These movements continue to be characterized by the New World Order as 'communist' and 'terrorist.'

In its history, the Canada-Asia Working Group has undergone extensive evaluation and remandating in consultation with the Canadian churches and overseas partners (1982, 1984 and 1989). From 1986 to the present, staff and steering committee members have spent at least one day per year in evaluation of the Canadian, Asian and international contexts and in priority setting for the year ahead. Out of the analysis made at the 1991 and 1992 meetings, a few general directions for the future have emerged.

First, it has become clear that it is becoming very difficult to do human rights advocacy (for example, at the U.N. Commission on Human Rights in Geneva) without a full analysis of the international economic situation and the role that international economic bodies play in it. Economic aid from the International Monetary Fund and the World Bank allows major human rights abusers such as Sri Lanka to flourish. Similarly, more concrete work needs to be done on the relation between international investment and human rights. The worst abuser of basic human rights in Asia—Myanmar—is able to function despite universal censure because of Japanese, Thai and Singapore investment and Chinese trade. Canada's erratic response to Indonesia's massacre of East Timorese civilians in November 1991 was similar: a proposed increase in aid was revoked; there were hints of a further cut, followed by a suggestion that the proposed increase might be implemented; Canada opposed a European Community-sponsored resolution at the U.N. Commission on Human Rights censuring Indonesia for the massacre and so forth. This suggests that the Indonesia trade relationship is still the prime determinant of Canadian foreign policy and that in-depth research needs to be done on it. It may well be that the Canada-Asia Working Group is being called back to its original mandate of extensively researching Canada's economic relations with Asia. However, staffing to do this remains a problem.

More also needs to be done on Japan's economic role in Asia. When Western human rights groups have been successful in reducing International Monetary Fund assistance or international investment in countries with poor human rights records, the Japanese government or Japanese investors have simply stepped in and made up the difference. Links ought to be strengthened with Japanese groups doing the relevant research and advocacy within Japan. Recently, more links have begun to be made with the National Christian Council of Japan. Similarly, more attention needs to be given to Korean and Taiwanese investment in Asia and, indeed, in Latin America and Africa.

It is also clear that the country focus of the Canada-Asia Working Group's U.N. Commission on Human Rights briefs in the past few years is not entirely appropriate to the Commission's framework for discussing human rights. While much lobbying takes place around the question of which countries will or will not be censured, the actual structure of the hearings has become increasingly thematic—issues such as the right to development, torture, impunity, minority rights, the rights of the child and so forth. Again, the abuse of many of these rights relates directly to the unjust international economic structures noted above. In fact, a broad human right, such as the right to development or the rights of minority peoples, provides a good framework for a critique of such economic structures. The Canada-Asia Working Group's 1992 brief to the U.N. Commission on Human Rights moved toward a more thematic approach to human rights, closer to the Commission's actual agenda.

New justice issues continue to emerge from Asia. For example, for the last two decades the Philippines has faced a situation of civil war. An armed people's movement, the New People's Army, has been in steady conflict with the Armed Forces of the Philippines. The Philippine government has actually declared total war on the New People's Army. The Philippine government has also sought to suppress the National Democratic Front, the political coalition of which the New People's Army is a part. The conflict between the New People's Army and the Armed Forces of the Philippines has resulted in enormous human suffering—deaths, torture, internal refugees, destruction of tribal cultures, environmental destruction, loss of income and economic instability. People are tired of the conflict and the destruction it has brought to the country. Partly encouraged by the Salvadorean peace process, in which the churches took an active part, Philippine Christians are asking if Canadian churches can join international ecumenical efforts to encourage peace talks between the National Democratic Front and the government of the Philippines. In early December 1992, the Canada-Asia Working Group organized an ecumenical visit of Canadian church leaders to the Philippines to provide support to the peace process.

It is also assumed that the Canada-Asia Working Group will continue to be a resource to the churches (both in Canada and internationally), the Canadian government and the general public. Over the years, the Canada-Asia Working Group has supplied Canadian media (newspapers, television, radio) with extensive material on Asian social justice issues. Similarly, the present Canadian Ambassador to the Philippines called on the Canada-Asia Working Group for a briefing before assuming his position in Manila. Relations of mutual respect have been built between the Canada-Asia Working Group and officials of the Canadian Department of External Affairs, despite disagreements over Canadian foreign policy. Because of the extensive experience, research and analysis of Asian issues by staff and steering committee members, the Canada-Asia Working Group is often first to be called by the media, and its representations command increasing respect.

Finally, the Canada-Asia Working Group must consider its relations with Canadian churches on the local level, especially in terms of its advocacy and educational roles. While some relations with local congregations that have Asian concerns are possible, the Canada-Asia Working Group lacks the resources and mandate to develop a national church network on Asian issues. Nor is it clear that such a nationally organized network would be appropriate. A more appropriate response might be, for example, a concentrated national campaign around a particular issue, using the existing networks of Canadian churches, church-related development organizations, religious communities and other ecumenical coalitions. However, this kind of advocacy has been limited in the past by the slim human and financial resources of the Canada-Asia Working Group.

The Canada-Asia Working Group has issued many 'appeals' through *Currents*. Such appeals are valuable in bringing issues to public attention. However, government often overlooks the letters which such appeals bring. If the Canada-Asia Working Group wants results in its advocacy, it will have to be more concentrated and strategic in using the networks. In its educational role, the Canada-Asia Working Group can develop more useful resources for use at the Canadian parish, diocese, presbytery and conference level. At the same time, Canadian churches should develop their justice-oriented mission and development networks, some of which are quite weak.

When local Asia-related groups emerge across Canada, the Canada-Asia Working Group can provide resources (people and research) and co-ordination; but the general feeling within the Canada-Asia Working Group is that such groups should grow and function independently, as appropriate to their local context, co-ordinating with the Canada-Asia Working Group and other organizations doing similar work. Such local groups can be easily mobilized for national campaigns and solidarity work.

The Canada-Asia Working Group presently has two staff, Daisy Francis and Bern Jagunos. In a departure from the former hierarchical staffing model, both share administrative and program functions. Country responsibility has been divided between them. Both have a high level of expertise, especially in the area of human rights in Asia. Both staff and steering committee members do the work of the coalition—the research and writing of briefs, advocacy, co-ordination of the Philippines Canada Human Resources Development program, organization of solidarity visits and so on. Staff and steering committee members work very much in partnership with one another in common commitment to justice in Asia.

The Canadian churches continue to affirm the Canada-Asia Working Group as their national ecumenical coalition responding to Asia-related justice concerns as they come to us from partners in Asia. And as we Canadians engage in our own struggle for a just and humane Canadian society, such links and solidarity with Asian sisters and brothers strengthen and encourage us.

The Ecumenical Coalition for Economic Justice

Dennis Howlett

Origins

The Ecumenical Coalition for Economic Justice began in 1973 under the name GATT-Fly. The name GATT-Fly comes from a pun on the word gadfly and the General Agreement on Tariffs and Trade (GATT). The idea was that GATT-Fly would be a gadfly, pestering the government on trade and economic justice issues.

The name GATT-Fly was coined by John Foster, a United Church of Canada staffer who was one of four Canadian church observers at the Third United Nations Conference on Trade and Development which took place in Santiago, Chile, in 1972. At a seminar back in Toronto they reported that Canadians could not be proud of the role which their government played at that conference. The Canadian government ignored the demands of the Third World and kept looking back to see how the U.S. delegation was voting and then followed its lead. It was at this seminar, held at St. Michael's College in Toronto, that the need for an ongoing church project to monitor Canada's trade policy with respect to the Third World was perceived and that the upcoming GATT multilateral trade negotiations were identified as a possible focus.

GATT-Fly was formally launched in January 1973 with one full-time staffer, John Dillon, and the support of the Anglican, Lutheran, Presbyterian, Roman Catholic and United Churches. John was joined a few months later by Dennis Howlett and Reg McQuaid. Russ Hatton of the Anglican Church was the first chairman of the Administrative Committee. Its original mandate was to do research, education and action on trade and economic issues affecting the Third World.

From the beginning, the GATT-Fly team was committed to an action-reflection or praxis model of work. Research on a particular issue would be followed by action to try to do something about the problems identified by the research. The action in turn would be followed by reflection upon the research and the action.

Lobbying government on sugar

Early GATT-Fly actions were based on the assumption that lobbying the federal government to change Canadian trade policy affecting the Third World was the way to help the poor of the Third World. This assumption was challenged and rejected through a process of action and reflection, what Latin American activist-theorists such as Paulo Freire call 'praxis.' A good example of how this worked is the sugar issue.

One of the first actions GATT-Fly undertook was to present a brief to the Canadian government delegation to the International Sugar Conference. The GATT-Fly brief basically called for a more sympathetic hearing by the Canadian government of petitions from the Third World sugar-producing countries for a price agreement that would guarantee them a fair price for their sugar. The negotiations for an International Sugar Agreement eventually broke down and we heard from a number of trustworthy sources that Canada was largely responsible for this because of the hard line it had taken.

GATT-Fly responded with a public protest and delivered a very strongly worded letter to the Minister of Trade and Commerce denouncing the role that Canada had played in the breakdown of these negotiations. This got some media attention as well as some sharp reaction from the Canadian government.

Through this experience we learned that the Canadian Sugar Institute, which represented the sugar industry in Canada and which opposed price controls, had a lot more influence with the Canadian government than a polite lobby by the Canadian churches. In fact, the Sugar Institute even had one of their representatives at the negotiations in Geneva as part of the government delegation. The power of moral persuasion was no match for economic power. One of our conclusions was that changing government policy required organizing political pressure through the media and broad-based public participation and not just through well-researched briefs, moral arguments or polite meetings between government ministers and church leaders.

The irony of this story is that, in the absence of an international sugar agreement, free-market forces took over and sugar prices zoomed up to 64 cents per pound in 1974. Canada ended up looking very foolish for having scuttled the agreement.

Who benefits—Who loses?

When we examined the effect of high sugar prices we found that those who benefited the most were the transnational sugar companies. The 1975 annual report of Tate & Lyle (the parent company of Canada's Redpath Sugar) reported record profits. But the impact on sugar workers, among the poorest of the poor in Brazil or the Philippines, for example, was in many cases disastrous. A Brazilian sugar worker when asked by a journalist, "What do these higher prices mean for you?" was quoted as replying, "Now the sugar comes right up to their doors." What she meant by that was that the landowners, who had previously allowed their tenants to have at least a small plot of land to grow food for themselves, had taken that away and were planting sugar cane right up to the door. In the absence of strong unions able to defend the sugar workers, this meant more hunger, not a better life for the people of northeastern Brazil. Where unions were strong and able to operate, as in some of the Caribbean countries, workers had been able to win gains for their members, but on the whole it was naive to think that higher prices would automatically benefit the poor.

Dependence and self-reliance

This critical inquiry led us to re-examine the assumptions under which we had been operating. Very early in our history, within the first year of the project, GATT-Fly had produced a discussion paper entitled "Limitations of the Trade Issue," which questioned the assumption that more trade would lead to greater development.[1] From very early on, GATT-Fly's thinking was influenced by Third World theorists such as Andre Gunder Frank, Samir Amin, Clive Thomas and Walter Rodney, who saw poverty in the Third World not as a result of their being technologically 'backward' or 'less' developed than the Western industrialized countries.[2] Instead these theorists saw Third World poverty as a result of their having been 'under' developed by the colonial powers and of having their economies tied into the global capitalist economic system in a way which created dependence. Third World peoples were consigned to producing raw materials for export while having to import many basic manufactured goods, with the prices of their exports always lagging behind the increase in the prices of their imports. The way toward 'authentic' or people-oriented development lay not in promoting increased trade, but in 'de-linking' from the global economy and establishing more self-reliant national economies geared to serving the basic needs of citizens first and relegating international trade to a secondary role. GATT-Fly went on to break new ground in applying dependence and self-reliance theory to an analysis of Canada's economic problems.

Organizing public pressure on the food issue

We did not abandon attempts to influence government policy. When we organized around the World Food Conference in Rome in 1974, we did not just have a polite meeting with the government (though we did that too); rather, we organized a massive letter-writing campaign and an educational strategy to support such an action. We developed a network of local groups across the country, from Kamloops, British Columbia, to Charlottetown, Prince Edward Island, ready to act at a moment's notice. We dispatched a team of observers to the World Food Conference in Rome who reported back daily via phone and telex on what the Canadian government delegation was doing. A team in Canada got the information out to opposition MPs, the Canadian media and to the local action groups. These groups then sprang into action, flooding the government in Ottawa and the delegation in Rome with telegrams and phone calls. We were able to embarrass the government which was surprised to learn that opposition MPs were better informed about what was going on in Rome through our communication network than its ministers were.

We received front page news coverage and even an Opposition Day special debate in the House of Commons. We were able to shape the public debate and forestalled Canada supporting the U.S. in Henry Kissinger's plan to use food as a weapon. But our evaluation was that despite the profile we gained and impressions to the contrary, our influence on the government policy issues that mattered was almost negligible. We had not called for increased food aid. We argued rather that policies such as land reform, income redistribution and stabilization of commodity prices through commodity agreements were what was needed as long-term solutions to the food crisis. Yet the Canadian government's main response to the largest number of letters ever received by the Prime Minister's office on a single issue up until that time was to increase its food aid commitments.

Our own analysis of the food system also led us to question whether a U.N. Conference involving governments was the place where the real problems of land distribution and poverty, which were at the root of the hunger issue, could be effectively addressed. The leadership for change on these issues was coming more from people's organizations such as labour, peasant and women's groups, or what we called 'popular movements,' than from governments which often were undemocratic and oppressive and allied with the rich and powerful.

Three new emphases emerged from this experience: developing a popular method of education called the 'Ah-hah Seminar,' initiating research and action on Canadian as well as Third World issues, and working directly with groups which are marginalized or dispossessed on issues that affect them.

The Ah-hah Seminar

The development of the Ah-hah Seminar method of popular education[3] was inspired by the challenge of trying to explain the complexities of the food issue, the structures of land ownership, international commodity prices, trade and so forth, without over-whelming and demobilizing people. The more comprehensive a presentation we gave on the issue, the more it made people say, "Wow, he's a real expert; he knows what he's talking about, but this issue is too complicated for me to fully understand, so I can't do anything about it."

Inspired by Paulo Freire[4] and Latin American approaches to popular education, we developed the method of engaging people in sketching a huge picture on a wall. It was a picture of the global food system, which they could draw from their own knowledge and experience. Putting their collective knowledge together, supplemented by information from resource people like ourselves, groups were able to see that they could do their own analysis and develop strategies for action. We learned that often a barrier to people getting involved in action is not lack of knowledge, but a lack of confidence in their own ability to make an analysis and develop action strategies.

Cliff Monk, the Lutheran representative on the GATT-Fly Administrative Committee, coined the name 'Ah-hah' to describe the process, because people say "Ah-hah!" not necessarily when they learn something new but when what they know already, which is all jumbled up inside their heads, begins to fit together and make sense.

The Ah-hah Seminar was seen as a tool which could help people make sense of their own knowledge and experience and take action.

While the Ah-hah Seminar method began as a way to unpack the food issue, we soon learned that we needed to start where people were, getting them to put themselves into the picture first, before making connections to issues 'out there' such as the global food issue.

A major turning point in the development of the Ah-hah Seminar method came at a two-day workshop with the Mummers Theatre group, Oxfam, Ten Days for World Development local committees and the Newfoundland Fishermen's Union in St. John's in 1975. On the first day, we did the Seminar as we had always done until then, starting with the land in the Third World. But in the course of the discussion an interesting confusion set in as to whether we were talking about the Third World or Newfoundland. Finally one of the participants suggested that we start over again, drawing a picture of Newfoundland. A new sheet of paper was put up and when GATT-Fly staffer Dennis Howlett asked where we should start, the group responded, "Start with the fishermen!"

Participants became much more animated and involved when they were talking about themselves and their communities. The picture of the global economic system made a lot more sense when they could see themselves in the centre of the picture. But, most importantly, the discussion of action strategies became much more concrete when global issues were linked with local realities.

The Ah-hah Seminar became not only the primary educational method for GATT-Fly, it was also an important research tool. Through conducting Ah-hah Seminars with fishermen, farmers, workers, aboriginal peoples, church-based social action groups, immigrant and unemployed groups, in Canada as well as in many countries around the world, we were able to learn from people, from their experience and insights. We were also able to clarify what questions people were asking and what information people needed to take action. This helped to shape and give focus to GATT-Fly's research work.

The Ah-hah Seminar led to important theological insights as well. Doing Ah-hah Seminars with the marginalized and oppressed affirmed our faith in people. We saw that groups of people were able to do their own analysis of their situations and develop strategies to bring about their own liberation by working together. We were led to reflect on the difference between the Old Testament prophets' appeal to powerful kings or an all-powerful God for deliverance and Jesus' ministry of empowering the poor to realize their own liberation and bring about the Reign of God. In assisting groups struggling for justice to develop social change strategies, we also came to understand the importance of employing approaches that were consistent with our goals and vision for society. So if we are working for a society that is democratic and supports the participation of all in making decisions that affect them, then it is important to employ participatory educational approaches and develop action strategies that will allow for participation by many, rather than lobbying by a few leaders. The theological parallel is that the Reign of God can be manifested in the process of people taking action, working together to create a new reality, thereby realizing their creative and social nature. So rather than the Reign of God being only the Second Coming or some other apocalyptic event, we came to understand it as a process in which we can experience its partial fulfilment even before its final realization.

GATT-Fly published a book describing the Ah-hah Seminar method in 1983 and conducted training workshops for educators in Asia, Africa, the Caribbean, Latin America, New Zealand, the United States and Canada. Since then it has come to be widely used in educational programs of popular movements around the world.

Starting with Canadian issues

The lessons we learned about educational methodology also affected our political strategy. If we were to engage Canadians in political action in sufficient numbers to have an impact, we had to start with issues that were of immediate concern to them. While we continued to be concerned with Third World issues, we began consciously to take up Canadian issues and to try to link Canadian issues with Third World issues.[5]

Our analysis of the food issue had shown that there were many structural similarities between the crisis of agriculture in Canada and that in the Third World. The loss of family farms, unstable prices for agricultural products, high interest rates, high economic and environmental costs associated with dependence on chemical inputs and dependence on exports, for example, were issues common to both Canadian and Third World farmers.

Self-reliance emerges as key theme

Bill Luttrell, who came to work with GATT-Fly in 1975, played a key role in developing the theme of self-reliance as an alternative to the food and agriculture crisis in Canada and the Third World. GATT-Fly pointed out that the ability of people to feed themselves is lost when there is an excessive dependence on a few export crops. The alternative which GATT-Fly advocated was greater food self-reliance, defined as each country growing and processing the food which its people needs, ensuring that all people have either the land or income necessary to grow or buy the food they need and continuing trade in food and agricultural products only as a planned extension of production at home. While a number of Third World economists such as Clive Thomas and Samir Amin had developed and advocated self-reliance for Third World economies, GATT-Fly, in its publications "Canada's Food Trade—By Bread Alone?" (1978) and "Canada's Food—The Road to Self-Reliance" (1979), was one of the first to apply this analysis to industrialized economies like Canada's.

Applying lessons from the Third World to Canada's energy issue

GATT-Fly's work on energy applied experience and analysis from the Third World to Canadian issues. It was initiated in 1975 at the request of the Dene First Nation in the Northwest Territories and their allies in the churches who were opposed to the construction of a natural gas pipeline down the Mackenzie River valley. In order to support their struggle, the economic, social and environmental costs of energy megaprojects had to be demonstrated and a strong case had to be made that Arctic oil and gas reserves were not needed for Canada's energy needs in the immediate future.

Mary Bird, who joined the GATT-Fly staff team in 1975, co-ordinated a research group which did case studies of megaproject development in the Amazon and its implications for the Northwest Territories. This was presented as evidence before the Mackenzie Valley Pipeline Inquiry chaired by Justice Berger in 1976. GATT-Fly's research was also able to show that the pursuit of energy conservation and the development of alternative energy sources would not only make Arctic energy development unnecessary, but that such an alternative energy strategy would be less costly for governments and far more beneficial to the Canadian economy in terms of job creation and protection of the environment than the megaproject development of frontier energy which the energy corporations and the federal government were advocating.

GATT-Fly's work on energy led to close collaboration with another interchurch coalition, Project North, and with aboriginal, environmental, farm and labour groups. It marked the beginning of coalition-building strategies for change. In 1981 GATT-Fly published its first book, *Power to Choose,* on Canada's energy options.[6]

Empowering the powerless

GATT-Fly's frustrations with lobbying government on both the sugar and food issues led us to conclude that the fundamental social changes we sought were not likely to be supported by the powerful who benefited from the present unjust system. Rather than trying to convert the powerful, we began to focus on empowering the powerless.

In organizing for the World Food Conference we had already established links with Canadian farm organizations. Follow-up activity on the food issue involved further work with these farm organizations and rural church groups, including delving into Canadian issues of particular concern to them. This led to the publication of a number of popular resources on food self-reliance and on farm-product marketing boards. Research and education were pursued in collaboration with textile and garment unions (the Confédération des syndicats nationaux and the Canadian Textile and Chemical Union) on the issue of trade policy for the textile and garment industry and more self-reliant alternatives. Joan O'Laney, on the staff of GATT-Fly since 1976, took the lead in this area. In 1982 an organizer with the KMU union in the Philippines joined GATT-Fly for a four-month educational project with Canadian textile and garment workers and to provide a Third World perspective on the self-reliance proposals being developed for the Canadian unions. Work also was done in the early 80s with the Kayahna Tribal Council on development alternatives for the seven native communities in northwestern Ontario.

GATT-Fly's action on the sugar issue moved away from trying to influence government to working directly with sugar workers, both in developed as well as Third World countries. This led to the first International Sugar Workers Conference in Trinidad in 1977, which GATT-Fly co-sponsored with the Caribbean Conference of Churches. Sugar workers from 10 countries participated and were able to share analysis and develop solidarity networks. In the years following this conference, GATT-Fly helped to organize international solidarity responses to arrests and killings of sugar workers and provided resources for educational events organized by sugar workers in a number of countries. By the time of the Second International Sugar Workers Conference in 1983, the sugar worker unions were prepared to launch the International Commission for the Co-ordination of Solidarity Among Sugar Workers, which continued GATT-Fly's sugar work under the direction of sugar workers. Reg McQuaid, who had led GATT-Fly's activities on sugar, left GATT-Fly to help staff this new independent project.

Coalition building and Free Trade

In the early 1980s Canada experienced a major recession which led to high levels of unemployment and growing poverty. Government responses to the economic crisis at both federal and provincial levels were cutbacks, privatization, an attack on labour rights and an undermining of the social welfare system.

GATT-Fly called for coalition building among the social groups affected to press for alternative economic and social policies which would promote full employment, improved social programs and greater economic self-reliance.

Many of GATT-Fly's themes were picked up in the Canadian Catholic Bishops' Social Affairs Commission 1983 New Year's statement, "Ethical Reflections on the Economic Crisis." The statement's call for a re-ordering of economic priorities had a profound impact on public debate. Labour, antipoverty, women's and farm groups responded positively to the call to create a new social movement or coalition.

Solidarity coalitions sprang up in a number of provinces in response to neoconservative government policies. GATT-Fly actively supported these coalitions through research and publication of educational resources, by conducting Ah-hah Seminars with a number of local coalition groups and by encouraging churches to take a stand in support of these struggles.

In 1985 the GATT-Fly Administrative Committee identified the free trade issue as a new priority which could assist coalition-building strategies. GATT-Fly organized a Consultation on Free Trade early in 1986, which brought together representatives from labour, women, farm, cultural, antipoverty and church sectors. A year later, in February 1987, GATT-Fly organized a larger national Ecumenical Conference on Free Trade, Self-Reliance and Economic Justice. This Conference was able to lay the groundwork for the creation of the Pro-Canada Network two months later at the Maple Leaf Summit organized by the Council of Canadians. The Pro-Canada Network grew to include over 40 participating national organizations representing labour, women, peace, environment, artists, seniors, aboriginals, antipoverty, farm, nurses, students, teachers, development and church sectors.

GATT-Fly was an active participant in the Pro-Canada Network and played a key role in expanding the coalition beyond representatives from national organizations to include participation from provincial and regional coalitions. Catholic Social Affairs Commission director and member of GATT-Fly, Tony Clarke, was elected co-chairman of the Network in the fall of 1987 and GATT-Fly staffer Dennis Howlett became co-chairman of the Communication Committee.

In 1987 GATT-Fly initiated publication of the *Free Trade Action Dossier* which served a vital communication role for the Network. (The publication, renamed the *Action Canada Dossier*, continues to be published by the Action Canada Network.) GATT-Fly also made important contributions to the research and analysis team of the Pro-Canada Network and produced a number of publications and popular resources on the free trade issue. Just before the 1988 federal election campaign, GATT-Fly helped to co-ordinate the production and distribution of a series of church bulletin inserts on election issues.

John Dillon of GATT-Fly was part of a fact-finding mission to Mexico's *maquiladora* free trade zones in the fall of 1988, which reported on Canadian businesses moving to Mexico to take advantage of cheap labour and lax environmental controls. The mission pointed out how the Canada-U.S. Free Trade Agreement would allow duty-free access for many products with Mexican components and warned of U.S. intentions to expand the Free Trade Agreement beyond Canada to include Mexico and the rest of Latin America. Unfortunately the media and opposition party leaders did not pick up on this prophetic warning.

On the eve of the 1988 federal election, GATT-Fly held a press conference charging the Prime Minister with misleading Canadians during the televised debate when he denied that the Free Trade

Agreement would affect Canada's regional development programs. GATT-Fly released documents which showed that Canada's negotiators had offered to restrict regional programs severely. The news conference got a lot of media attention, particularly in the Atlantic region, and probably was a factor in the Conservatives' poor electoral results in that region.

Although the Mulroney government was re-elected in 1988, the efforts of GATT-Fly and others in the Pro-Canada Network did result in a shift of public opinion to a point where more people opposed than favoured free trade. Despite the disappointment of having the Free Trade Agreement go ahead, all those who participated in the Pro-Canada Network felt that the coalition should continue to fight against the imposition of a neoconservative corporate agenda.

In 1989, the Pro-Canada Network co-ordinated the fight against the first Free Trade budget, a budget which introduced 'claw-backs' of Old Age Security payments for those earning over $50,000 a year—marking an end to the principle of universality—and which cut transfer payments to provinces for health and post-secondary education as well as regional development. The Pro-Canada Network also opposed the changes to the Unemployment Insurance program which 'harmonized' Canadian benefit levels and qualification requirements down to American levels.

In 1990, the Network launched the Campaign for Fair Taxes which opposed the regressive Goods and Services Tax (GST) and advocated fair tax alternatives. The highlight of this campaign was the sign-up days which succeeded in getting over 2.4 million Canadians in three days to sign ballots opposing the GST and supporting fair tax alternatives. GATT-Fly was very influential in shaping the national campaign and in formulating the alternative fair tax program which was endorsed by a large number of groups. GATT-Fly drafted a cartoon booklet on the tax issue which was published by the Pro-Canada Network with over 750,000 copies distributed. GATT-Fly also produced a church bulletin insert on the tax issue and encouraged local parishes to participate in the sign-up days by distributing the inserts and by making the sign-up cards and ballot boxes available at Sunday services. Again as in the free trade battle, while the Pro-Canada Network was not able to stop the government from introducing the GST, it played a part in influencing public opinion, to the point where over 80% of the population was opposed to the government's actions.

Largely as a result of the leadership provided by the Pro-Canada Network, opposition to the GST did not fall into a right-wing tax revolt but came to be articulated in terms of 'fairness.' The moral and ethical issues were made central to the campaign: instead of just opposing a government policy, we put forward clear and detailed alternatives.

Continuing the international dimension: Debt and structural adjustment

While in recent years GATT-Fly's research and action program focussed largely on Canada, GATT-Fly continued to work on international issues. Its work on Canadian issues such as agriculture, energy, or free trade was informed by lessons from Third World struggles. Direct links between Canadian and Third World struggles were fostered, for example, in the project with Filipino trade unions on the textile and garment issue. A second example is the work on the global debt crisis and structural adjustment programs. Two books were published, *Debt Bondage or Self-Reliance* and *Recolonization or Liberation*, along with numerous articles on the subject.[7] GATT-Fly's work on debt has received wide international acclaim and GATT-Fly's books and articles have been translated and reprinted in a number of countries. GATT-Fly representatives have also been invited to participate and give presentations on the debt issue at a number of international events in Peru, Jamaica, Zimbabwe and elsewhere. GATT-Fly's work on debt and structural adjustment has also been foundational to the education and action campaigns of the Ten Days for World Development program.

A new name and a new mandate

In 1990 GATT-Fly changed its name to the Ecumenical Coalition for Economic Justice. The name change resulted from a remandating process GATT-Fly undertook with its participating churches. The name GATT-Fly, while catchy and easy to remember, was also problematic in that its meaning was not self-evident. The media and general public also were not sure whether a group with a name like that should be taken seriously. The new name, while not as flashy, was more self-explanatory.

Leading up to this remandating process there was much debate within the GATT-Fly Administrative Committee about how closely GATT-Fly should be linked to the churches.[8] Some felt that the

primary agents of change were the popular groups or people's movements and that the churches would always be constrained by the class
makeup of their membership to play a more conservative role in
society. A few even argued that GATT-Fly should become independent of the churches. Others felt that the church was not a simple
monolithic institution and that, while it often plays a conservative
role in society, there were progressive groups and tendencies within
the churches that could play an important role in supporting broader
struggles for justice.

While the debate within GATT-Fly centred on questions of
ecclesiology and the social role of the churches, within the churches
there was also much controversy about GATT-Fly. There was a
perception within some quarters that GATT-Fly was 'doing its own
thing,' with little accountability to the churches. GATT-Fly had come
under fire from some in the churches for the large amount of time and
energy that it put into working with 'non-church' groups, such as
labour unions, antipoverty groups and women's groups, and for not
spending enough time providing services to the church constituency.
Others felt that GATT-Fly had abandoned its original mandate of
helping Third World countries develop by improving the rules of
trade and promoting greater access for their exports to First World
markets. These critics coming from a liberal, developmentalist point
of view were unhappy with GATT-Fly's more radical analysis of
dependence and self-reliance which envisioned major structural
transformation, rather than *reform*, of existing institutions. Another
criticism was that GATT-Fly was not doing enough to influence
government policy making by presenting briefs, lobbying politicians
and so on.

While not all these issues were finally resolved, what emerged
from the dialogue of the remandating process was agreement both
within the Ecumenical Coalition for Economic Justice committee and
with its sponsoring churches: while the Ecumenical Coalition for
Economic Justice would continue to have the independence to do
analysis and develop policy recommendations for the churches, the
connections to the churches would be strengthened. In this way, the
Ecumenical Coalition for Economic Justice would not be doing its
work 'on behalf' of the churches, but rather would enable the
churches to better carry out their mission for justice.

The new mandate committed the Ecumenical Coalition for

Economic Justice to strengthen the churches' ability: 1) to maintain an active Christian presence among the poor and marginalized groups involved in struggles for economic justice; 2) to develop positions that both criticize and advocate alternatives to major issues of economic and social policy in Canada and their relations to the Third World; 3) to participate in building coalitions with a variety of popular groups struggling for economic justice; 4) to provide opportunities for Christians to become actively involved in ministries for economic justice; and 5) to develop a grassroots educational strategy to promote economic justice.

Research and action priorities identified by this mandate included: the global debt crisis, women and economic justice, free trade, tax and social policy reform and the development of just and ecologically sustainable alternatives.

Theology of mission

In its mandating document, the Ecumenical Coalition for Economic Justice articulates its theology of mission in terms of the prophetic tradition which understands that people come to know God by participating in the struggles for justice for the poor, the marginalized and the oppressed. Jesus' identification with this prophetic tradition (for example, Luke 4:18) and his teachings which encourage us to take the perspective of those who have become the victims of injustice in society (for example, Matthew 25:31-46) show that acting for justice is integral to our faith as Christians. The Ecumenical Coalition for Economic Justice mandate calls for the churches to carry out this prophetic mission today by denouncing economic and social injustices and by working with others to build a more just, participatory and sustainable society.

While GATT-Fly and the Ecumenical Coalition for Economic Justice have not often explicitly articulated this theology in their publications, underlying their whole approach has been a theology strongly influenced by Latin American liberation theologians such as Gustavo Gutiérrez.[9] It is a theology which not only understands the struggle for justice and liberation to be central to the Christian faith, but also sees the poor and oppressed and their struggle for justice and liberation as the place where we encounter God in history. The Coalition's work with poor and oppressed groups and its emphasis on coalition building as a strategy for social change flows from this theological conviction.

Social movement coalitions—Strategy for change

In recent years the Ecumenical Coalition for Economic Justice has given a high priority to coalition work. In addition to continuing participation in the Pro-Canada Network (which was renamed the Action Canada Network in 1991), the Ecumenical Coalition for Economic Justice initiated the Coalition Exchange Project, which has organized a series of seminars in South Africa, Canada, Mexico and the Philippines to share what has been learned from social movement coalitions in these countries and to build solidarity links among them. Coalition activists from each of these countries are also working together to produce a book describing their experiences with coalition politics. The Coalition has also used the Ah-hah Seminar as a tool for coalition building at provincial and community levels.

Our experience has confirmed that coalitions are one of the most hopeful means for social transformation. Not only do coalitions enable social groups to have more power and effectiveness by acting together rather than individually—what we have called the "arithmetic" of coalition politics—coalitions also create a "chemistry" through the interaction of different social sectors which educate and change the thinking of participating groups.[10] The Canadian labour movement, for example, has been greatly influenced by their association with environmental activists and those in the women's movement and have come to support strongly many of the demands of these groups. The Action Canada Network also played a key role in helping the Canadian Union of Postal Workers develop a job action strategy, which included the offer to deliver government pension and welfare cheques during the strike by postal workers in 1991. The Action Canada Network also worked to build understanding and support for the union's positions and got its member groups from the seniors and antipoverty sectors to sign a solidarity pact with the union. This display of solidarity was repeated in the strike by the Public Service Alliance of Canada and there was unprecedented public support for the unions during a public sector strike.

The Ecumenical Coalition for Economic Justice and its sponsoring churches have also been changed by the experience of working in coalition. We have been challenged by feminist and environmental perspectives and have attempted to incorporate them into our analysis. The interaction with farmers, workers and the unemployed has sensitized us to the problems these groups face and encouraged greater efforts at solidarity.

The challenge for coalition work in Canada now is the "art" of coalition politics, that is the visioning and creation of alternatives. Progress has been made in this regard through several statements: the declaration "A Time to Stand Together, A Time for Social Solidarity" by the Working Committee for Social Solidarity in 1987; the "People's Budget," produced by the Action Canada Network and the Canadian Centre for Policy Alternatives in 1991; the "Zacatecas Declaration" issued in 1991 by Mexican, American and Canadian coalition groups, a document which spelled out an alternative people's development and trade agenda to the proposed North American Free Trade Agreement; and the "Discussing Our Future" discussion paper published by the Canadian Centre for Policy Alternatives in 1992. But there is still much to be done in terms of articulating a clear alternative vision for our society and building public support for it. The Ecumenical Coalition for Economic Justice has played a key role in working on alternative social and economic policies and is currently giving this a high priority.

Mutual international solidarity

New forms of international solidarity have been pioneered in the work the Ecumenical Coalition for Economic Justice is now doing with Mexican and American social movements on the North American Free Trade Agreement. The Coalition played a key role in developing the Common Frontiers project which has given leadership in forming strong trinational co-operation. Coalition research on the energy and intellectual property rights aspects of a North American Free Trade Agreement has been particularly useful to Mexican activists. These solidarity links with Mexico are different from previous work in that we are not just supporting them in their struggle, but are supporting each other in a common struggle which affects all of us.

Women and economic justice—A new priority

In the past few years the Ecumenical Coalition for Economic Justice has developed a new focus in its work on Women and

Economic Justice. This new engagement recognizes the fact that women are usually the hardest hit by poverty and economic restructuring. It also signals a more conscious attempt to incorporate a feminist analysis into the Coalition's work.

Lorraine Michael, who joined the Ecumenical Coalition for Economic Justice staff in 1992, is helping to co-ordinate a research and action project on the Future of Women's Work in co-operation with the National Action Committee on the Status of Women. The Coalition is also participating in the Taskforce on the Feminine Face of Poverty, which is seeking to build solidarity between church women and poor women in Canada and the *Mujer a Mujer* project which links women in Canada, Mexico and the United States on issues of common concern. As a supporter of the Homeworkers Campaign, the Coalition is also fighting for better protection and working conditions for people who do piecework in their homes.

Conclusion

Almost 20 years after its inception, the Ecumenical Coalition for Economic Justice has in some ways come full circle in its focus on the trade agenda. In addition to its work on the North American Free Trade Agreement, the Coalition has been concerned in recent years with the way in which the same U.S. and transnational corporate agenda is being advanced in the current round of multilateral negotiations under GATT. The Coalition's commitment to a praxis model has resulted in analysis and strategies which have grown and changed so that it is a very different organization from when it was launched.

GATT-Fly began as an altruistic concern for the effects of trade on the poor and marginalized in the Third World. It has changed, however, to a concern arising more from a sense of common interest with Third World struggles. We have increasingly seen how a majority of Canadians are also adversely affected by free trade and economic structural adjustment policies. A more authentic, mutual solidarity with people's movements all over the world struggling for justice and real democracy is growing from this ground.

The Canada China Programme

Cynthia McLean

Introduction

The Canada China Programme/Projet Canada Chine is an ecumenical social justice coalition of the Canadian Churches, albeit a somewhat anomalous one. A concern for the welfare of all 1.15 billion Chinese people and solidarity with the Chinese people's struggles for independence, justice and peace are the *raison d'être* of the Canada China Programme. The organizing principles of the Programme, however, are partnership and mission. The theological question, including the critical justice dimension, has always been: What is God doing in China today?

In the course of tracing the history of the Canada China Programme rooted in relationships established a century ago, we will naturally be touching on social justice concerns pertinent to the context in which Chinese Christians live and witness. We continue to wrestle with 5,000 years of Chinese history and the socialist revolution of 1949, which challenge our deeply held Western assumptions about self, church and society. China, from whom we were estranged for several decades, brings different questions to debates about people's organizations, social development, environmental concerns, church/state relationships and human rights.

This chapter is divided into six parts: *Missionary background: 1888-1949* looks at the roots of the Canadian-Chinese Christian relationship; *Estrangement: 1949-70* covers the period during which there was minimal contact between the Chinese and Canadian peoples; *Organizational beginnings: 1971-81* traces the early years of the Canada China Programme prior to direct relationships with Chinese Christians; *God's call to a new beginning: 1981-89* describes the re-establishment of church-to-church relationships; *Tiananmen crisis: 1989* examines the crisis that rocked China in June of that year; and *Into the future: The 1990s* suggests some of the directions and tasks of the Programme in the coming decade.

Missionary background: 1888-1949

Canadian church involvement in China spans a century. The Presbyterians began work in Guangdong and Henan provinces in the 1880s; the Methodists arrived in West China in 1891; several French-Canadian orders of sisters and priests sailed for China after 1909; the Anglicans under Bishop White established themselves in Kaifeng, Henan, in 1910; the Scarboro Foreign Mission Society entered Fujian Province after World War I; many evangelical Canadians joined the work of the ecumenical China Inland Mission; young people went to China with the Student Volunteer Movement; Canadian Lutherans, Disciples of Christ, Baptists, Mennonites and Friends worked with American colleagues throughout China. The China missionaries represented the largest number of workers sent to a single mission field by the Canadian churches prior to the 1949 Revolution and the Korean War, after which all foreign personnel returned home from China.

The end of the 'Missionary Movement' in China was a trauma for all the churches involved. The missionaries were accused by the Chinese of being 'cultural imperialists': their schools, hospitals and evangelization work were implicated in a series of Unequal Treaties, which from 1842 on had reduced China to semi-colonial status at the hands of the Western powers. The Chinese revolution forcibly confronted both missionaries and mission boards with the need to account for this apparent disaster. Some saw no need for self-examination and, blaming the situation on the godless Communists, continued their work in other countries. Others, however, attended closely to the harsh critiques even Chinese Christians were making of the foreign missions and began the slow and painful process of rethinking their understanding of Christian partnership and God's mission in the world. Grounded in the Social Gospel—believing that Jesus Christ came to save not only individuals but the society in which people lived—they also wrestled with the economic analysis made by Chinese Marxists and further questioned whether capitalism indeed was the extension of Christian principles into the economic realm.

Estrangement: 1949-70

Canada, with outspoken diplomats like Chester Ronning (born in China of Lutheran missionary parents), was inclined to recognize the new People's Republic of China. The United States, however, with nuclear weapons and doggedly anticommunist diplomats like John Foster Dulles prevailing, fashioned a Cold-War world which imposed economic sanctions on the People's Republic and enabled Chiang Kai Shek's government in Taiwan to hold the China seat at the United Nations.

Except as a Cold-War 'bogeyman,' China largely faded from the Canadian world-view during the 1950s and early 1960s. Little was heard except for the occasional passionate voices of former China missionaries who recalled for Canadians the dire poverty endured by most Chinese people prior to 1949, which now was being addressed and ameliorated by socialism. Church assemblies as early as 1952, however, included calls for Canadian recognition of China; a major World Student Christian Federation consultation focussed on China was held in Montreal in the mid-1960s; and the United Church in 1968 prepared a remarkably in-depth and sensitive course for teenagers called "Now China."

Organizational beginnings and advocacy: 1971-81

Canada finally recognized the government of the People's Republic of China in 1970 (prior to ping-pong diplomacy and Richard Nixon's celebrated 1972 visit). Prodded by such people as E. H. (Ted) Johnson of the Presbyterian Church and Clair Yaeck of the Scarboro Foreign Mission Society, the World Concerns Secretary of the Canadian Council of Churches convened a Special Committee on Canada/China Relations in November 1971 to explore missiological questions in light of the 1949 Revolution. Early in 1972 a handful of Protestant and Roman Catholic churches contributed $1500 to the budget of a new China Working Group. Ted Johnson, while a secretary of the Overseas Missions Department of the Presbyterian Church in Canada, became the volunteer program director.

The mandate of the China Working Group was 1) to maintain and encourage a continuous study of contemporary China so as to understand as well as possible what was happening there; 2) to interpret events in China to the church and wider Canadian community; 3) to promote study of the theological implications of what was happening in China; 4) to explore lessons from China for Christian faith and practice in dealing with Canadian and world problems; 5) to develop a concern for, and a sharing with, Chinese people in Canada; and 6) to initiate and support the gathering of materials on China missions for placement in archives and to study the lessons of the China missionary experience.

In 1973 Ted Johnson and his wife Kitty visited China where they were able to talk with K. H. Ting and his wife Siu May Kuo, prominent Christians who had worked in Canada with the Student Christian Movement in the 1940s. Although deinstitutionalized and largely invisible, the Christian faith had by no means been extinguished by even the most severe ravages of the Cultural Revolution (1966-76), during which all religious institutions were closed.

The claiming of the United Nations' China seat by the People's Republic, in 1972, sparked new interest internationally in both the utopian goals of the Chinese revolution and the situation of Chinese Christians. Inspired by the Latin American bishops' call for "a preferential option for the poor" and impressed by Chinese accomplishments in sustaining 22% of the world's population on only 7% of the world's arable land, Western theologians began to take note of China. In 1974, under the auspices of the Lutheran World Federation and Pro Mundi Vita (Roman Catholic), conferences in Bastad, Sweden, and Louvain, Belgium, brought Roman Catholics and Protestants together to reflect on the "Theological Implications of New China" and "Christian Faith and the Chinese Experience."

In the spring of 1975, the Canadian churches committed themselves to finding the budget for full-time staff. In 1976 they called on Dr. Raymond Whitehead, who had been engaged in research and teaching in Hong Kong since 1961, to be the China Working Group's first director.

By 1978 the China Working Group had become the Canada China Programme/Projet Canada Chine, with a revised mandate which read, "The Canada China Programme was established in response to China's growing participation in the world community and to develop friendship and openness between our two peoples." From that time on, it has functioned in relation to the Canadian Council of Churches and it continues to receive support from Catholic and Protestant organizations and individuals.

The purpose of the Canada China Programme is to develop denominational and other networks which will interpret China to Canadian churches and to the community at large, to promote study and critical reflection on the meaning of China's experience for the self-understanding of the Church, and to deal creatively with the Chinese contribution to our common struggle for justice, liberation and development.

The late 1970s was an exciting time to be 'China watching.' We witnessed the passing of both Chou Enlai and Mao Tsetung, the official end of the Cultural Revolution and the fall of the Gang of Four, and the economic reforms initiated by Deng Xiaoping to open China to international markets. Increasing numbers of Canadians were able to visit China and see first-hand the changes brought by the socialist revolution. Although still poor, the Chinese people were not plagued by disease, famine and destitution; drug addiction, prostitution and exploitation of child labour were almost non-existent; the gap between the rich and the poor was very slim; the country was not crippled by foreign debt. In addition to interpreting these events, the Canada China Programme laid the groundwork for a conference that would explore the socialist threads of Canadian history alongside the China experience. In June 1979, a broad spectrum of Canadian Christians met at the Prairie Christian Training Centre, Fort Qu'Appelle, Saskatchewan, to discuss "The Churches and Social Change: Lessons from China and the Social Gospel."

The year 1979 marked a turning point for the Canada China Programme: by the end of the year the transition had begun from being an 'advocate for' China to being a 'partner with' the Chinese people, especially Chinese Christians. In September, K. H. Ting and three Protestant colleagues were members of a nine-person delegation from China to the Third World Assembly of the World Conference on Religion and Peace, convened in Princeton, New Jersey. Following the conference, Ting came to Canada where, in addition to catching up with colleagues he had not seen in 30 years, he preached and lectured at several churches and seminaries across the country. "Facing the Future or Restoring the Past?" and "Religious Policy and Theological Reorientation in China" made it clear that Chinese Christians themselves not only could, but would, define the needs and parameters of church life in China. Self-governing, self-supporting and self-propagating, never again would Chinese churches be a "dot on someone else's missionary map."[1]

In 1980 Ray Whitehead submitted his resignation, moving on to a teaching ministry at the Toronto School of Theology. Katharine Hockin served as interim director until the arrival of Dr. Theresa Chu in January 1981. Born in Shanghai and a Religious of the Sacred Heart, Theresa had extensive teaching experience in Korea and Japan.

The year of laying the foundations for the reinstitutionalization of the Protestant and Catholic Churches in China was 1980. Simultaneously, national church offices were being set up; churches were being repaired and reopened in many cities; Nanjing Theological Seminary was preparing for its first class since the mid-1960s; and discussions were under way for international people-to-people exchanges.

Due in good part to historic Canadian openness to the People's Republic of China, the Canadian Council of Churches was the first overseas church delegation to be the official guests of the China Christian Council. Heather Johnston, then Council president, headed a 16-person delegation from seven churches, including a Roman Catholic observer, which visited Christians in Canton, Shanghai, Nanjing, Kaifeng and Beijing from June 17 to July 5 1981. They reported back that there was one Protestant Church in China with various manifestations; denominations were a feature of the past. They also found that bibles were in short supply, but that no absolute scarcity existed; the smuggling of bibles by outsiders was regarded as a hostile act. Finally they observed that the Chinese Church opted for socialism in economic and social structures.

God's call to a new beginning: 1981-89

In early October 1981, the Canada China Programme hosted an international conference—"God's Call to a New Beginning"—in Montreal, where 150 Christians from around the world met for a week with seven Protestants and three Catholics from the People's Republic of China. Designed to be a sharing among equals, the Chinese presentations were some of the many made concerning the Gospel in diverse contexts—Canada, Haiti, the Philippines, South Africa, feminist North America, etc. The Chinese had come to learn more about theological developments in which they had not participated—such as Vatican II—as well as to share their experience of being Christian in a socialist society.

It was a historic and emotional event as colleagues separated by suspicion and silence for 30 years embraced and sat down to rebuild friendships. It was an event which gave the Chinese the opportunity to outline the principles upon which they felt future relationships between churches in China and elsewhere must be based: mutual respect, non-interference, independence. Frequent reference was made to the cultural, economic and theological domination of the Chinese churches by missionary agencies prior to 1949, a domination which had so coloured their church life that many Chinese had considered Christians to be denationalized, if not traitors to their own people. Never again would this be allowed, the Chinese delegates stressed; self-governing, self-propagating and self-supporting, their task was to be *fully Christian* and *fully Chinese*. Missionaries would not be invited to return, although goodwill visits would be welcomed.

The Chinese were clear about their co-operation with a socialist government, which they felt fundamentally did fulfill the aspirations and needs of most of the Chinese people. Yes, mistakes had been made and excesses had occurred, but Mao Tsetung's peasant revolution had been both necessary and in the long run positive. Several speakers spoke of being inspired by some of the atheist revolutionaries they had encountered, who had given their lives to improve those of others. This conversation was of special interest to some of the delegates from struggling Third World countries, whose governments often raised the spectre of the 'great Red dragon of communism' to thwart and suppress people's movements for justice and equality.

"God's Call to a New Beginning" was just that: a new beginning, not only for bilateral conversations and relationships, but for the entire Christian *oikoumene*. China had been the biggest mission field in the world during the 19th and early 20th centuries; community work there greatly contributed to the development of the modern ecumenical movement resulting in the World Council of Churches. With dialogue once again established, the hopes and experiences of nearly a billion people could now be factored into a Christian understanding of the world. Indeed, it was a *kairos* moment; the integrity of the church universal was strengthened at Montreal that fall of 1981.

The conference also furthered Catholic and Protestant co-operation and mutual understanding, both in China and Canada. For the first time in history, Chinese Catholics and Protestants worshipped together in Montreal. Sister Fleurette Lagacé, a Religious of the Immaculate Conception of Mary, was largely responsible for handling conference logistics. She was later joined by the Rev. Michel Marcil, S.J., and this work, done primarily by French-speaking Catholics with China connections, was the seed from which the Montreal-based *Amitié Chine* would grow. In 1983, the Canada China Programme published the conference proceedings as *A New Beginning: An International Dialogue with the Chinese Church,* edited by Theresa Chu and Christopher Lind.

Remandating by the churches came for the Canada China Programme in 1982. The Board left the 1978 mandate intact, adding only a fourth purpose to the list: To relate to the Chinese Church on the basis of the principles of mutual respect and genuine friendship. Now in regular contact with Chinese Catholics and Protestants, the major shift for the Canada China Programme was moving away from its own questions about China to working on questions posed by Chinese Christians.

Partnership requires sensitive and careful listening, and some-times means painful revision of what we think we know of a situation. After 30 years of near-silence, suddenly there was a veritable flood of information about China, much from the Chinese themselves. The who's, what's, how's, when's, where's and why's of events in China since the early 1950s began to emerge, some of it contradicting our previous interpretations. Stories about the Great Leap Forward and the Cultural Revolution were particularly disturbing.

'Serve the People' was a glorious ideal, but in retrospect most Chinese view the Cultural Revolution of 1966-76 as a vicious, polit-ical power-struggle which caused enormous suffering. Religion was condemned as the "opiate of the people," scriptures were burned, temples and churches destroyed and many religious leaders experi-enced beatings, constant interrogations, prison sentences and public shame at certain points during this period. Public church life ceased.

We also learned more about the famines and deaths following the utopian policies of the Great Leap Forward (1959-61); the infla-tion of production statistics by some rural cadres trying to curry favour with Beijing; the harassment of artists and writers who were forced to create-to-order; the fanaticism of some young people who took sledge hammers to ancient Buddhist monuments and dug up graves to 'struggle against' the dead; the personal vendettas carried out supposedly in the name of 'the People.'

Many of us were quite unprepared for these revelations. We were forced to realize that we had, to some extent, projected our own hopes and ideals on the Chinese people. Disillusioned during the 1960s and 1970s with the exercise of U.S. power and Canada's participation in a world order that exploited so many peoples in Africa, Latin America and Asia, we thought we saw in China the tumbling of the mighty from their thrones, the lifting up of the humble and meek. We were not entirely mistaken in our understanding—the status of women improved, barefoot doctors raised the standard of medical care in the countryside, agricultural collectivization and public works projects benefited the peasants, the 'iron ricebowl' (guaranteed job, housing, medical care, education) took care of the workers in the vast state enterprises—but certainly the Kingdom had not dawned in China.

Balancing reports of turmoil and suffering, Chinese Christians also told stories of integrity, courage, generosity and tremendous faithfulness under severe duress. More importantly, while deploring the excesses and horrendous mistakes of certain leaders, they staunchly defended the historical necessity of Chinese socialism and continued to view the 1949 revolution as a liberation from chaos and misery for the majority of the Chinese people.

A favourite Protestant hymn, written in the early 1980s by Wang Weifan of the newly reopened Nanjing Theological Seminary, was "Winter has passed, the rain is o'er; Earth is a-bloom, songs fill the air/Linger no more, why must you wait; Rise up my love and follow me." Rather than dwell bitterly on the past, Chinese Christians chose to celebrate the restoration of the policy of freedom of religious belief. Rebuilding the Church and beginning the slow and painful process of reconciliation within the Christian community were more important to them than assigning blame. Everyone had suffered; there had been no innocent bystanders during the Cultural Revolution.

Developing a balanced interpretation of China, which experienced dizzying changes socially, economically and politically during the 1980s, would continue to be a delicate task for the Canada China Programme. Partnership and solidarity demand that we strive to see events through Chinese eyes, not passing premature judgment rooted in Western assumptions. Faithfulness to our own Canadian context and understanding of the Gospel, however, requires that we sometimes raise difficult questions with our partners, while being open to theirs.

In the fall of 1983, the Canada China Programme arranged for Mr. Zhang Jinlong to study at the Toronto School of Theology—the first Chinese theological student to come abroad since 1949. Jinlong completed his Master of Divinity degree in 1986 at Emmanuel College, after which he returned to teach theology at Nanjing Theological Seminary. During the summer of 1985, six Protestant seminarians and a faculty member visited Canada for two months. One— Mr. Wang Zhenren—would return in 1988 for two years of study at the Vancouver School of Theology. The reception and nurture of seminarians would become a major part of the Canada China Programme's work during the second half of the decade. The Chinese Church needed to raise up a new generation of leaders fluent in Western languages and conversant with the theological trends of the worldwide *oikoumene*. Preoccupied with opening churches and training a new generation of church leadership, the China Christian Council could not give very much attention to its international relations. Yet it understood clearly that there could be no significant Chinese Christian selfhood apart from the church universal.

Following liberation in 1949, the government had relieved the churches of their schools, hospitals and social welfare organizations, thereby largely limiting church life to Sunday worship and the pastoral care of believers. In 1981, at the Montreal conference, Chinese Christians told the assembled that missionaries would not be invited back to China and that they had no need for developmental assistance. As the economic reforms deepened, however, the government began to invite the participation of Chinese voluntary groups in the area of social welfare. In 1985, Protestant leaders joined with secular educators and workers to open the Amity Foundation, an indigenous non-governmental organization designed to contribute to China's ongoing modernization.

One of Amity's first requests to Christian partners overseas was for language teachers. In 1986 three Canadians joined American, British, German, Japanese and Dutch Christians in Nanjing as Amity teachers. They were followed each year by Canadians who, abiding by a 'theology of presence,' contributed not only to the Chinese acquisition of technical skills, but to a growing awareness among Chinese of the presence of the Church, both local and international.

Although supported by individual churches, Amity teachers are not denominational 'missionaries,' but ecumenical workers belonging to all the churches committed to the Canada China Programme.

Due to the independent consecration of bishops in 1958 and the Vatican's diplomatic decision to recognize the Republic of China in Taiwan, relationships between Canadian and Chinese Catholics were more problematic than in the Protestant case. But in the spring of 1985, a delegation led by Fleurette Lagacé spent three weeks studying Catholic Church life in China with a focus on the newly opened seminaries. They returned exultant. The great warmth, collegiality and friendliness they had experienced led to hope that reconciliation was possible between the autonomous Chinese Catholic Church and Rome. Chinese Catholics remained spiritually devoted to the Holy Father and longed for worldwide Catholic fellowship.

The Canada China Programme continued to concentrate its energies on exchanges in 1986 and 1987. In 1986 Theresa Chu led delegates from the Ecumenical Association of Third World Theologians to China, a visit that overlapped with Nanjing '86, an international conference organized by the American National Council of Churches. The Canada China Programme helped to facilitate a China visit by representatives of the Christian Councils of Angola, Mozambique and Tanzania. In May 1987, eight Chinese Catholics spent three weeks in Canada as guests of Amitié Chine of Montreal and the Canada China Programme. Lois Wilson, of the Ecumenical Forum, and Ray Whitehead, of the Toronto School of Theology, led 27 theological students from across Canada to visit Chinese seminarians in Beijing, Shanghai and Nanjing in 1987. In September, Mr. Wang Zhenren, Mr. Kan Baoping and Mr. Zhu Xuandong arrived from China to begin graduate studies.

China appeared to be flourishing in 1988. The economy was booming, harvests were bountiful, tourists flocked to China filling the state's coffers with hard currency. Catholic and Protestant Churches continued to open with services which attracted thousands of inquirers; seminaries could accept only one in ten applicants; the Amity Foundation had expanded into medical and rural development projects; the Amity printing press was furiously producing bibles, in Chinese and in several minority languages. Government cadres increasingly seemed willing to co-operate with, rather than to obstruct, the Christians in their districts.

The same year, the Canada China Programme was busy with ongoing interpretive work, supporting the three seminarians at McGill, the Vancouver School of Theology and Waterloo, recruiting Amity teachers, and providing resources for the many Canadian Christians making China trips. Ms. Shi Lili and Ms. Jin Yan arrived during the summer to pursue graduate studies.

Feelings of optimism and ever-widening opportunities predominated, despite mutterings in the Chinese press about inflation, nepotism and corruption of officials, restrictions on intellectuals, youth unemployment, greed and materialism. But the dissatisfactions seemed normal for an economy which had expanded so rapidly and a huge population adjusting to major social changes. The Canada China Programme began to prepare for a visit in May 1989 by Bishop K. H. Ting and his wife, Siu May Kuo, who were to receive honorary doctorates from Victoria University at the Convocation of Emmanuel College.

At the end of 1988, the Canadian churches gave the following mandate to the Canada China Programme: 1) to be a national, ecumenical program of Canadian churches helping them to work in partnership with the churches in China, and 2) to promote the study, critical reflection upon and interpretation of the experience of the churches in China within their changing social context and of the involvement of the Canadian churches.

At the same time, the Catholics decided they needed to think through their participation in the Canada China Programme at a step removed from the Protestants. History, theology and the worldwide institutional structure of the Roman Catholic Church raised different questions for them in regard to their relationship with Chinese Catholics. They began to meet regularly at the Canadian Catholic Conference of Bishops office in Ottawa, forming themselves into the Canadian Catholic Roundtable on China. This decision brought appropriate Faith and Order questions into the work of the Canada China Programme; ecumenical engagement—although sometimes uncomfortable—deepened as Catholics and Protestants began to explore together their varying understandings of mission, of Church, of partnership.

Tiananmen crisis: 1989

The year 1989 opened brightly; no one was prepared for the tragedy which unfolded in June. On April 15, Hu Yaobang, an official dismissed for openness to student demands in 1987, died. Taking his death as an opportunity to voice their grievances, 6,000 students gathered in Beijing's Tiananmen Square. Within days, similar demonstrations sprang up in Shanghai, Tianjin, Wuhan and Nanjing. The numbers grew and included workers and ordinary citizens. Negative response to their petitions from the authorities stiffened student resolve and some went on hunger strikes.

In late May, after his visit to Canada, Bishop Ting publicly praised the students' patriotism but advised them to return to classes. On May 30 a ten-metre Chinese 'Goddess of Democracy' appeared in Tiananmen Square. Confrontation deepened, although many students began to go home. In the early morning hours of June 4 1989, the army moved in; hundreds of people were killed as the world watched the televised debacle in horror.

That summer and fall were grim months of anxiety and confusion for friends of the Chinese people everywhere. Would China return to the ideological fervour of the Cultural Revolution and curtail contact with the West? Would the authorities restrict religious freedoms again?

Word from our Chinese Christian partners eased our worst fears. The church was not experiencing extraordinary pressure, although the passports expected for three new seminarians were never issued and an international conference scheduled for Edinburgh, Scotland, in September was postponed. Most of the 86 Amity teachers had stayed and more were invited for 1989-90. Many Chinese Christians, the majority of whom live in the countryside, mourned the bloodshed but felt that the demonstrations had indeed turned to turmoil. Remembering the horror wreaked by idealistic students during the Cultural Revolution and fearing the disruption of economic reforms which had improved their lives, they felt the government had to intervene and restore order. Chinese Christians asked us for compassionate patience and not to mount a human rights campaign when the issues were so murky, opinions so divided.

Into the future: The 1990s

In April 1990, the Canada China Programme participated in a conference on Chinese theological education held in the U.S.A. with Bishop Ting. Students now had to work in China for several years before studying abroad, but the China Christian Council saw this as an opportunity to send mature leaders overseas to study 'church and society' issues. Michel Marcil, S.J., taught theology at Sheshan Seminary outside Shanghai and, in the fall, a five-member Canadian delegation spent three weeks in China visiting Catholic churches, seminaries and social services. Tension was evident in certain places, but the ongoing institutionalization of the churches—especially in training a younger generation of leaders—was evident. Vatican II was being studied and the faithful regularly prayed for the Pope.

Rhea Whitehead represented the Canada China Programme at an Amity Foundation Rural Development Seminar in November. Two Chinese Catholic sisters from the diocese of Nanjing visited Canada from November 1990 to January 1991, exploring the many social ministries of the Canadian Catholic Church. After three years in Canada, Mr. Wang Zhenren and Mr. Kan Baoping returned to teaching positions in Wuhan and Nanjing. In January 1991, after a decade of devoted work, Theresa Chu retired as director with plans to return home to Shanghai. Cynthia K. McLean, with a strong background in China mission history, was appointed her successor.

With a new director, the Canada China Programme spent 1991 taking stock and reflecting on future directions. It celebrated with the China Christian Council its reception as a 'member church' into the World Council of Churches in Canberra, Australia. Plans began to be formulated for a six-person delegation from the China Christian Council to spend five or six weeks exploring the role of the churches in Canadian society. The Canada China Programme participated in the planning of an international conference which included Chinese Protestants and Catholics and was held in Manila in November 1993. Xu Rulei, archivist of Nanjing Theological Seminary, worked in Canadian church archives in October 1991, collecting mission materials necessary for the writing of Chinese church history.

Interpretation has always been an important task for the Canada China Programme. Since 1976, the Canada China Programme has published *China and Ourselves* quarterly, carrying not only reports of Catholic and Protestant church activities and theological thinking, but also analyses of Chinese social, political and economic currents. The Chinese churches are incomprehensible apart from an appreciation of the challenges of livelihood and development for one billion Chinese people. In the aftermath of June 4 1989, interpretation has become an even more important—and somewhat problematic—Canada China Programme task.

Undue focus on human rights obscures China's enviable record of providing nearly a quarter of the world's population with the basic necessities of food, shelter, education, employment and health care. China pointedly asks whether social, cultural and economic rights are not as important as individual human rights. While the wealthy governments of the North rail about civil and political liberties, they are noticeably silent when pressed about a New Economic World Order that would assist the faltering economies of so many debt-ridden nations of the South.

On the other hand, it is impossible to overlook brutal assaults on the dignity of individuals. As Canadians we raise questions about China's sales of arms to repressive governments in Myanmar and the Sudan, just as we question such sales by our own government. The proposed damming of the Yangtze River gorges and the status of Tibet also require sensitive reflection and interpretation. It is at such times that partnership requires great trust from both parties. We have been told that a human rights agenda would be an inappropriate imposition of a Western agenda and set of assumptions. Avoiding a confrontational posture, Chinese Christian leaders themselves are increasingly protesting the interference by rigid leftist cadres in church affairs, the arbitrary closing of meeting points and the arrest of pastors, events that do occur in some areas.

Interpretation of the social, economic and political context of the churches in China will continue to be an important challenge for the Canada China Programme in the 1990s. 'Socialism with Chinese characteristics,' which means the introduction of capitalist market mechanisms, is irrevocably changing the lives and aspirations of the Chinese people. Of great concern is the privatization of industry, housing, medical care and education. Who will provide for those unable to pay for basic social services when the 'iron ricebowl' is removed? Mutual understanding will be especially important between now and 1997, when the sovereignty of Hong Kong reverts to China. Canada is the destination of choice of emigrating Hong Kong Chinese, currently the largest immigrant group in Canada. The Canada China Programme, therefore, will further engage Chinese Christians in Canada in dialogue, recognizing the many theological, cultural and political complexities and sensitivities involved. China no longer is 'out there,' but a dynamic reality in today's multicultural Canadian society.

Conclusion

The Canada China Programme's primary purpose is to build relationships of understanding, trust and solidarity between the Catholic and Protestant churches in Canada and the Peoples' Republic of China. This involves facilitating exchanges, providing English teachers and assistance for rural development work through the Amity Foundation, working with seminarians, and interpreting to Canadian Christians the efforts of our Chinese brothers and sisters to rebuild their churches and witness to their people in the context of exceedingly rapid social, economic and political changes. For the Protestant churches, the Canada China Programme is the primary ecumenical vehicle for church-to-church relationships in the absence of denominations in China.

Concern for social justice issues in China and in the world remains an ongoing Canada China Programme commitment. China—with close to a quarter of the world's population, one of the five permanent members of the United Nations' Security Council, a magnet for international investment capital, and a nuclear power—is playing an increasingly important role in world affairs. It is critical that the Chinese experience be factored into all discussions about the environment, human rights, development, population, the arms trade, poverty and so forth. As Canadian Christians, we need an understanding of China in order to develop a realistic world-view. The Canada China Programme believes that supplying the relevant information to make China's point of view clear, is one of its responsibilities.

Social justice issues, however, are only as central to the work of the Canada China Programme as they are to our partners—the Catholic and Protestant churches in China. And for the moment, they seek our support primarily as Christians, as fellow believers in Jesus Christ. A tiny minority, the major task facing them is the training of biblically grounded men and women to lead burgeoning congregations, most of which are in the countryside. Starting almost from scratch 10 years ago, they require the rebuilding and outfitting of seminaries, the development of libraries, the writing of theological curricula at different levels of sophistication and the recruitment of teachers, most of whom are older ministers and priests with heavy pastoral responsibilities. The Catholics are grappling with the enormous changes of Vatican II, such as a vernacular liturgy and the enhanced role of the laity; the Protestants are struggling to fashion a workable church order for a single church that inherited dozens of denominational models from their missionary mentors. Once restricted to Sunday worship, Chinese Christians now are gently exploring new roles for the church in Chinese society. Set apart for nearly three decades, they are just beginning to find a balance between their Chinese particularity and a Christian universalism in the worldwide *oikoumene*. And we must not forget that the reinstitutionalization of the Protestant and Catholic churches in China is occurring in a context which is still essentially socialist, a fact which raises for them very different theological and church-state questions.

Chinese Christians are in something of a 'brick and mortar' stage of development, erecting and opening new churches, while we in Canada are selling and closing many of our buildings. Our immediate concerns are very different and the nature of our church membership is very different; if we weren't Christians we would probably have little to do with each other. But we are, and Christian partnership does not require that we respond to the Gospel and act in the world in exactly the same ways. Quite the contrary: an important aspect of partnership is mutual learning—appreciating profoundly that there are many ways to be Christian and that God is more multifaceted than we can see with our limited Canadian lens.

Chinese Christians ask from us patience, understanding, a willingness simply to walk with them—and, above all, prayer—as they discern what God is calling the church to do and to be in China today. When Canadian missionaries set sail for China over a century ago, they aimed to plant self-governing, self-supporting and self-propagating Chinese churches. They succeeded, and today the churches in Canada and the churches in the Peoples' Republic of China work together as friends and colleagues, sharing the common task of witnessing to the love of God in Jesus Christ to the world.

PLURA

Mary Boyd

Antecedents

Some people connect the beginning of PLURA, a national agency devoted to the poor of Canada, with a 1968 church-sponsored workshop in Montreal entitled *Christian Conscience and Poverty*. The idea for the workshop came primarily from the Roman Catholic Church, but the workshop itself involved the four other founding churches (Presbyterian, Lutheran, United and Anglican). The result of that conference was not PLURA but the Coalition for Development, whose goal it was to involve church, labour and business in the struggle against poverty in Canada. Through this proposed national coalition, the churches came together and even inspired some community-based Coalitions for Development in places like Halifax and Windsor. Its success depended on the availability of church staff, however, and perhaps for that reason it never took off. Although the national coalition fizzled out, concern about poverty in Canada remained alive in the churches.

The Canadian Conference of Catholic Bishops, fresh from the Second Vatican Council, established the Canadian Catholic Organization for Development and Peace to fund socio-economic projects in Third World countries and thereby set the stage for PLURA. In addition to collecting money, Development and Peace had an educational component which brought Canadian Catholics together to reflect on the situation of poverty in the Third World. Questions were raised in its 1968 Lenten collection about what the Church was doing for Canadians caught in poverty. Roméo Maione, the organization's first executive director, believed that governments have ample resources to take care of the needs of Canadians. He said, however, "That doesn't mean that we shouldn't have contact with the poor."[1] Maione became one of the main voices for the establishment of PLURA.

Maione credits the media with inspiring more ecumenical agreement on the issue of poverty. All the churches wanted publicity, but they were told that the media couldn't cover 10 churches. "They told the churches to get together, and that challenge helped to foster a whole rash of interchurch organizations such as Ten Days for World Development, PLURA, the Interchurch Fund for International Development and others," he notes.

Maione recalls that PLURA was to be a vehicle for the poor in Canada to speak to Canadians. "If we preoccupied ourselves with the needs of the poor on an international level and didn't do something here, we would be perceived as hypocrites. I wanted to call the organization 'CULPA,' but some people didn't understand that, so we came up with PLURA."[2] (The name PLURA is an acronym made up of the first initial of each of the founding churches—Presbyterian, Lutheran, United, Roman Catholic and Anglican.)

The National Council of Welfare shared responsibility for the new awareness of poverty that gave birth to PLURA. This Council presented the first position paper to the Inter-Church Consultative Committee for Development and Relief. Roméo Maione was a member of that Board in 1970 and served as its chairman from 1971 to 1973.

The churches came together on June 11 1970 to present a joint brief from the Canadian Council of Churches and the Canadian Conference of Catholic Bishops to the Special Senate Committee on Poverty headed by Senator Croll. When Croll's report reached the public in 1971, it revealed that 30% of Canadians lived on incomes below the poverty line. The figures did not go unnoticed by certain church departments.

In 1971 the Rev. R. D. (Bob) MacRae of the Anglican Church of Canada played a key role in systematizing church involvement when he wrote a memo to titular heads, general secretaries and department heads of social action ministries in the various churches. He wanted to consult about more efficient ways of working together. "In order to get a policy on almost anything you had to go around in circles. I felt that it was time to do things in common."[3] The group met at the Anglican Church House on October 28 1971. Tom Johnston of the Canadian Catholic Organization for Development and Peace recalls that most of the agenda was about Third World issues, interchurch relations with CIDA, Emergency Aid Facility and Domestic Education on International Development. There was, however, a paper on domestic poverty prepared by the National Council of Welfare with "collaboration from the Anglican, United and Roman Catholic Churches."[4]

The working paper, "To Establish a Funding Body to Assist Low-Income Self-help Groups," figured prominently on the agenda of the group's second meeting in December 1971. Chairman Bob MacRae prepared a memorandum based on the paper entitled, "To Facilitate the Funding of Community Organizations and Development in Canada." MacRae urged the churches to move on the issue of domestic poverty. The Ad Hoc Committee agreed tentatively that "the revised document should be distributed to the churches for initial reactions"[5] and, further, that several representatives should sound out federal officials, including the Hon. John Monroe, Federal Minister of Health and Welfare. The Committee nominated Roméo Maione (Development and Peace), Bob MacRae (Anglican Church) and W. I. McElwain (Presbyterian Church) to represent them. Later, they added the names of Canon Maurice Wilkinson (Canadian Council of Churches), the Rev. Clarke MacDonald (United Church) and the Rev. Patrick Kerans (Canadian Conference of Catholic Bishops). Roméo Maione agreed to make a survey of what the churches were then doing regarding domestic poverty.

The Committee, calling itself the Inter-Church Consultative Committee for Development and Relief, met for a third time on February 22 1972. Members agreed to strike a special committee representative of the churches to establish common criteria for disbursement of funds, to take the necessary steps to co-ordinate the response of the churches to domestic poverty, to prepare an audit of the work that was then going on, to review the data from the National Council of Churches (U.S.) and report back to the parent body.

The beginnings of PLURA

The Committee was convened by the Rev. D. G. Ray (United Church). Its members were the Rev. R. D. MacRae, R. Maione, G. Maxwell (Canadian Conference of Catholic Bishops), the Rev. E. Reusch (Lutheran Church), Mrs. Elizabeth Loweth (United Church), the Rev. Wayne Smith and the Rev. M. Wilkinson. For the first time the Committee expressed the need to get representation from low-income groups.

On March 14 1972, Grant Maxwell, Roméo Maione, the Rev.

Don Ray, Bill Dyson from the Vanier Institute and Len Shefrin of the National Council on Welfare met with the Hon. John Monroe. They informed Monroe that the Churches were committed to expenditures of up to $500,000 for domestic poverty. They wondered if Monroe would match the money at a suggested ratio of at least four to one, since the five major denominations were in the process of co-ordinating efforts to enable self-help groups to take on the struggle of domestic poverty. The Minister indicated openness to the suggestion, especially if there was a co-ordinated effort on the part of the churches. The Committee left the meeting with a feeling that specific proposals would be welcome by the end of April.

By October 1972, Ray, deputy secretary of the Inter-Church Consultative Committee for Development and Relief, was able to write to heads of churches that the group had made some progress in developing a proposal for joint church action about domestic poverty. Ray went on to state that a "subcommittee has been meeting to develop a proposal to establish a funding body to assist low-income, self-help groups."[6] Ray illustrated church capacity to respond by pointing out that the churches involved contributed at least $250,000 in 1971 to fund requests from various groups. Ray considered the sum to be a conservative estimate because substantial amounts had been committed by the Roman Catholic Church at the diocesan level. The Anglican Church had also committed funds for domestic poverty and the United Church, another early motivator of PLURA, had earmarked $85,000 for its taskforce on poverty.

The Board of the Canadian Catholic Organization for Development and Peace made some suggestions about the fund for domestic poverty at its November 1972 meeting. They wanted the fund to be very decentralized, with funding decisions made as close as possible to the level where the work would be done. Funds should be made available without regard for race and cost of administration should remain below 10%. The name should be more positive than "a fund to help domestic poverty."[7]

Both the English and French staff at the Social Affairs Office of the Canadian Conference of Catholic Bishops raised questions about whether Toronto should serve as the constitutional headquarters and whether the Board should consist of individual members as well as representatives of organizations. They called for equitable distribution of funds among anglophones and francophones and among geographical regions. Harold Arnup of the United Church shared similar views. He pointed out "the need for direct participation by church people in local citizens' groups to avoid the churches being insulated by a second-hand approach from the real problems."[8]

By March 1973 preparation of bylaws had become a major agenda item. The United Church had a taskforce on poverty called "The Mustard Seed." It was suggested as a suitable name for the new organization. The Ad Hoc Committee had in mind that the Fund for Domestic Poverty would be structured with the usual centralized head office and staff. However, Development and Peace pointed out that "if we are serious about meeting the needs of marginalized people, we need to be where they are." It was agreed that this type of social action could not be done from a national office.

The Subcommittee on Domestic Poverty met with the Hon. Marc Lalonde, the new Federal Minister of Health and Welfare, in Ottawa in July 1973. Lalonde turned down the proposal to match funds. He indicated, however, that there might be a willingness to consider specific projects from the churches.

At the September 1973 meeting of the Subcommittee on Domestic Poverty, chairman Donald Ray listed a number of organizational matters that needed to be addressed: 1) concern for a decentralized model as exemplified by the Canadian Catholic Organization for Development and Peace—adopting this model would mean the formation of a national board with comparable regional boards in western Canada, Ontario, Quebec and the Atlantic region; 2) the name of the funding body; 3) the place of the national office; 4) who could serve as board members; and 5) how to ensure equitable representation among the sponsoring groups, noting that two representatives from each denomination would leave the Roman Catholic constituency with fewer representatives in proportion to total numbers.

The minutes of the Inter-Church Consultative Committee for Development and Relief meeting held September 24-25 1973 indicate that the Subcommittee on Domestic Poverty decided to continue without the block general grant from the Ministry of Health and Welfare. A meeting was called for October 31-November 1 to begin to accept requests for funding and to make grants. The interim Board was asked to proceed with work on the organization's constitution and its criteria for projects, to develop a workable method of receiving and considering grants and to select a representative group to report to the Inter-Church Consultative Committee for Development and Relief. Members also discussed the concern of Development and Peace for decentralization.

The only grant made by PLURA in 1973 was a $15,000 grant to the Canadian Civil Liberties Education Trust which was working on the legal needs of native peoples in northern Ontario.

In the fall of 1973, members of the interim Board travelled across the country to discuss the new organization with church councils and groups at the grassroots. PLURA would be a fund for social justice. Its projects would attack the root causes of poverty in Canada. The intention was not to give hand-outs or to fund service-type projects. The poor would be empowered to struggle for basic changes.

Quebec would also play a key role in shaping the direction of PLURA. In an April 1992 interview, Grant Maxwell stated that the founders of PLURA felt the need for projects in Canada like those of the Canadian Catholic Organization for Development and Peace elsewhere, with an educational program like that of Ten Days for World Development. These two elements, it was hoped, would empower the poor in Canada.

The PLURA constitution was approved by its interim Board in December 1973. This is probably when the name PLURA was chosen. The story told by Bob Lindsey is that Father Pat O'Byrne and a small group went to a pub after the first night of the board meeting. The next morning they offered 'PLURA' as the name for the new organization. In a 1982 article in *L'Église canadienne*, Father François Thibodeau points out that there is more to the name than initials—PLURA's Latin root means 'more abundant resources.' This, says Father Thibodeau, "indicates the intention of the churches to supply the necessary means for groups to fight against poverty and injustice."

The constitution of the new organization called for proportional representation from the churches, representatives of disadvantaged groups and persons of special competence. Regional and provincial PLURAs would decide which local self-help groups would be funded. Grants to national organizations and groups in the territories would be handled by a committee of the national PLURA Board.

The four Atlantic provinces formed a regional bloc, called Atlantic PLURA, which disbursed funds to groups in that region. Each province also had a PLURA committee to screen applications and reach out to self-help groups. Quebec constituted a region on its own, as did Ontario. The western provinces rejected the notion of regions and opted for four provincial committees. All regional and provincial committees operated under bylaws approved by the national PLURA Board.

The PLURA constitution has been revised several times. It was amended both in April and September of 1974. It underwent major revisions again in 1979 and 1984.

How PLURA works

In essence PLURA is a partnership of church and low-income groups working together in provincial committees on a volunteer basis to empower low-income self-help groups to struggle against the root causes of poverty. It is more realistic to refer to PLURA committees as made up largely of committed Christians prepared to build communication and partnerships. Some of the low-income members are not affiliated with churches. These PLURA committees are very aware that low-income people in Canada are becoming more and more impoverished as the political powers of the day press forward with their corporate agenda of free trade, privatization and deregulation. This partnership of church and low-income groups shares common goals and operates under democratic structures. Local groups decide what is the most realistic way to struggle for social justice in their area.

The criteria used to assess requests for funds was worked out in light of PLURA's purpose. A majority of membership in the group soliciting funds must be disadvantaged/low-income persons who make the decisions and take leadership in the group. Group members participate in planning and implementation of the project, agree to evaluate projects in terms of goals and objectives, and report according to a mutually agreeable schedule. Preference is given to projects which are oriented toward social change, the promotion of justice, respect for human rights, and the dignity and self-development of individuals and communities. The projects must combat the causes of poverty and injustice and promote collaboration with other groups where feasible. Community participation as well as community and individual commitment of resources (time, work, energy, equipment and so forth) are important. In addition, PLURA promotes research and education into the underlying causes of poverty, informs the public of the issues and problems arising from poverty, and promotes and encourages the collaboration of local churches with low-income, self-help groups.

In many ways PLURA is unique among interchurch coalitions. This truly decentralized coalition, with no head office and no paid staff, works well from the point of view of grassroots involvement. PLURA is present in all provinces of Canada and is further decentralized within the provinces. The specific purpose of PLURA is to make financial and other resources available to self-help groups made up of low-income persons in Canada who promote transformation and/or changes in social, economic and political realities which create poverty, attack the root causes of poverty, and enable the poor and the general public to become more aware of the causes of and the problems arising from poverty.

A second specific purpose is to promote and encourage the participation of churches with self-help groups of low-income persons at the local and regional levels.

PLURA since 1974

PLURA took off quickly, especially in Quebec. A former national chairman, Bernard Dufresne, explains that clergy responsible for PLURA were pastors of poorer parishes and involved with popular groups. They brought to PLURA their personal history, the experience of the popular movement and the social analysis capacity they had acquired from their involvement. Their experience of accompanying the organized self-help groups enabled them to break with the liberal understanding of the time.

Father François Thibodeau's article in *L'Église canadienne,* "PLURA: A Prophetic Work," noted that in 1981 the Catholic Church provided $145,000, the United Church $64,000, the Anglican Church $42,000, the Presbyterian Church $5,000 and the Lutheran Church $4,000. To Father Thibodeau, this represented considerable funding when one considers the financial situation of the churches. He called PLURA a remarkable ecumenical achievement in which the churches have truly passed "from words to actions."

The originality of PLURA doesn't stop there. Beyond being a coalition of churches and low-income groups, PLURA is an association in which churches and popular groups, as partners, have autonomy in making decisions in their work on the root causes of poverty and injustice. Thibodeau also made the point that priorities, politics and procedures differ from one region to another.

In eastern Canada, social analysis and commitment to Brazilian educator Paulo Freire's method of 'conscienticization' influenced Prince Edward Island PLURA from the beginning. A grant from Atlantic PLURA in 1981 financed a study on the quality of work on Prince Edward Island and pinpointed unjust wages and working conditions for women and youth in fast food outlets, non-unionized fish plants and other minimum-wage work places. The study also took a critical look at regional disparity and the priority of profit over people which motivates many businesses.

Other PLURAs used similar models, but groups lacking the background of Third World experience or popular movements in Canada tended to lean toward the charity model. As the various regional and provincial PLURAs came together for annual meetings, they exchanged ideas and increased their understanding of the criteria. Each region and province had to submit an annual report which was open to questions and discussion. Most PLURA annual meetings had a formation session which usually focussed on social analysis. An evaluation of PLURA carried out in 1982 by the *Coopérative d'animation et de consultation* contained a recommendation that PLURA annual meetings should de-emphasize business and emphasize formation and small group discussion.

The results of PLURA's work are significant and the examples are numerous. A group in Rouyn-Noranda writes that PLURA is unique in its way of helping people. Ontario's PLURA allowed their group to continue to exist by supporting people who wanted to do the work but had no other resources. A group in New Brunswick sees PLURA as a way for the churches to be involved in helping the poor get out of their poverty and constructing a more just society. A Montreal group wrote to Quebec PLURA that "the churches must be involved through PLURA in working with and for the most disadvantaged, so that church people can learn how to work together on socio-economic issues, and that such actions on the part of Christians give hope to the poor."

Father Thibodeau ended his article by stating, "Together we must stand up to the daily challenge of respect for and promotion of human rights. Justice is an integral part of the church's ministry of evangelization. The prophetic boldness that created PLURA must be implanted in all our communities and must continue to grow. So many times we have restated that the glory of God is woman and man fully alive... This is the challenge, that to glorify God in our midst, all our fellow citizens may have abundant life as men and women."

The report of the 1982 evaluation concluded that, although "education is a must to achieve valid social change, PLURA is not equipped to deal with that kind of goal for two main reasons." These reasons were that "PLURA's members are volunteers, and do not have the time nor the money to become involved at that level," and "PLURA members did not feel supported by the churches." The evaluators felt that the churches didn't really want this type of education, preferring to do their 'churchy things' rather than look at the causes of poverty.

PLURA members perceive a big gap between the social messages of the churches and their application. The same members believe, however, that the projects funded by PLURA help to achieve the goal of public education. Similarly, the evaluators noted that a similar study of the Canadian Council for International Cooperation revealed that the Council, which had $12 million in cash and kind in 1980, was not able to reach the non-organized public except through their fund-raising campaign.

PLURA members were negative about their second specific purpose, "to promote and encourage participation of local churches and church association with self-help groups." Some members were unaware of that particular goal. Others felt that it was too idealistic and that the churches lacked knowledge even of the existence of self-help groups. This opinion ran counter to a study carried out in Saskatchewan, however, where 83 out of 121 churches responding to a questionnaire were interested in working with self-help groups and one-third were interested in giving financial help.

PLURA's main emphasis, according to the 1982 evaluation, was funding self-help groups to empower them to do their work. Between 1974 and 1981, the churches committed $1.35 million to 609 projects sponsored by 455 groups. The size of the projects varied from province to province, as did the number of groups reached. This can be explained by the types of groups applying and the way that provincial PLURAs applied the selection criteria.

Understanding PLURA's criteria for project selection is key to

appreciating PLURA's effectiveness as an instrument for social transformation. There are differences between provinces arising from the
uniqueness of each situation. Differences sometimes lean in the direction of social service projects versus social action projects. Others
use the theological distinction between charity and justice to distin-
guish the types of projects that provincial PLURAs fund. The 1982
evaluation viewed social service projects and social action as being
on a continuum. According to the evaluation, in some provinces
social service projects could be the spark to bring social action later.
This appears to be the exception rather than the rule when one
considers that the social justice mandate is to transform society.
Social transformation does require certain conditions, including the
conscious practice of strategy and tactics.

Social service or charity projects tend to address the needs of
individuals. They deal with the effects of problems rather than the
causes. If people are hungry, ways must be found to feed them. This
is good work in that it helps to alleviate the current crisis, but it is
not enough. It does not change the reason why people are hungry.
All too often it creates dependence and makes clients out of the
recipients.

Social action or social justice work deals with the causes of
problems by analysing, mobilizing and speaking out for changes in
the policies and practices of social institutions (governments, corporations, international trading bodies and so on). When people are
hungry, questions are asked: Why are they hungry? Where are the
injustices and loopholes in the policies? What policies need to be
changed? How can they be changed? Social action promotes the
transformation of these unjust structures and also promotes the
empowerment of people. It works *with* people, rather than *for* them.
It requires analysis and action against the causes. It requires alternatives. It also requires commitment, dedication and patience.

A panel of popular educators in the Point St. Charles community
of Montreal made the point at the 1992 PLURA assembly: a project
to teach sewing to low-income people that does not address root
causes would not meet PLURA funding criteria. If the sewing project,
however, aimed at raising the critical awareness of the participants
to understand how assembly lines work, how the textile industry is
organized and so forth, it would indeed meet PLURA criteria. It
would help participants understand who holds power and how that

power is exercised in our society. It would help people at the bottom of the socio-economic ladder to understand, analyse and share their analysis with others. They would understand the importance of working together to bring about change. It is in sharing our practice in dialogue and in agreeing on criteria to address the causes of poverty that PLURA becomes a national force to overcome poverty.

In Quebec, where PLURA has few funds for many groups, priorities have been set with a clear option for justice. There is an option for groups oriented to social action and able to manage funds. In Quebec, PLURA is administered by people from the urban centres (Montreal and Quebec City) and from the peripheral regions. Quebec PLURA helps groups with an option for transformation through social action, with the exception of 10% of the budget which is set aside for projects with a symbolic meaning. These latter projects are important for their psychological impact. Preference is also given to groups which are likely to have a 'snowball' or multiplying effect.

In the 1982 evaluation report, self-help groups were highly complimentary about PLURA's impact and way of operating. They saw PLURA as gutsy, involving itself in the root causes of problems, and were impressed that five denominations could pull together to work with self-help groups. They stated that PLURA, unlike government agencies, deals with human beings and listens to the groups. PLURA avoids creating a dependence on the part of the groups they support. It is unique in that it funds social change groups before groups have proved themselves. Aboriginal groups are impressed that PLURA respects their traditional spiritual needs. Many self-help groups expressed their appreciation for the churches' commitment to social justice through PLURA. Some asked why the churches could not be more strategic and fund big projects which could be used as examples for the politicians to see.

PLURA members were also positive about their organization but considered the money to be insufficient. They were uneasy and impatient at the slow pace of social change. The evaluators recommended patience as a key to success and underlined the point that social change is difficult to measure.

The lack of funds can be illustrated by Quebec, which had 86 requests in 1990 and was able to fund 45 of them with its $75,910. In 1991 it paid for 51 projects with $69,999. Quebec PLURA funds projects which address the causes of poverty. Lack of funds seriously impedes them in their goal of social transformation.

The concept of regions gave way early to the realistic recognition of the problem of inter-regional communication, especially travel. The West rejected the concept of region from the beginning and the Atlantic, which began as a region, divided into provincial PLURAs in 1983. Newfoundland and Nova Scotia PLURAs preferred to work provincially, while Prince Edward Island preferred to keep the concept of regional PLURAs. New Brunswick at the time was also sympathetic to a regional PLURA, but was going through a restructuring of its own. It did not send a representative to vote at the spring 1983 meeting of PLURA.

The Atlantic region has many serious common problems which call for a common analysis. Uneven development under capitalism is apparent in all four provinces, which traditionally have had the highest unemployment rates, the lowest wages, the fewest services for the people and the lowest percentage of manufacturing and processing of primary resources. Emigration has been heavy in all provinces and government 'solutions' have failed to solve the economic problems.

Common root causes call for common actions aimed at transformation. Unlike Quebec, however, interprovincial boundaries created four sets of backgrounds. While Prince Edward Island favoured a model of 'conscienticization' to social justice issues, some of the other Atlantic provinces often leaned toward a social services model. The same variety of approaches exists among western provinces and within Ontario.

PLURA has a fine track record when it comes to closeness to the people. It is still working on improving the partnership between churches and low-income groups. The present objective is to have a 50-50 ratio of representatives of self-help groups and church members on each regional/provincial Board. This has been achieved by most PLURAs, including the national Board.

How does one measure the impact of PLURA? The August 1982 report stated that, in the Atlantic provinces, Alberta and Manitoba, "the poor are poorly organized." Perhaps the comment challenges PLURA in most provinces to be stricter in applying social justice criteria. In regions where the justice criteria are consistently adhered to, PLURA's projects have had a far-reaching impact. Grants to

struggling primary producers in the Maritimes are a good example
of how PLURA money has been well spent.

PLURA is a truly national organization operating from coast to
coast and respecting Quebec's uniqueness. Provincial Board membership is for the most part spread geographically throughout each province. Roy Shepherd, a 12-year PLURA veteran, former national
PLURA secretary and representative of the four Protestant churches
from 1984-92, believes that one of the most significant improvements
in PLURA came in 1984 with the constitutional requirement that
membership in provincial boards and the national PLURA Board be
50% from low-income groups and 50% from the churches. Provincial
PLURAs must never exceed a 40/60 ratio. This change added
momentum to the building of a large network of low-income, popular
groups across the country. Each year PLURA funds somewhere
between 140 and 175 self-help projects, with most of the money
going directly to low-income groups for projects which address the
socio-economic and political systems which create poverty.

In British Columbia, a self-help group used PLURA to establish
a school lunch program, with the aim of making the provincial
government take responsibility for providing a universal program.
By its action, this group got the ball rolling. The government now
funds the program under the watchful eye of the community. If British
Columbia PLURA had not set an example by funding a group which
set up a school program and by providing seed money to low-income
earners to travel to school meetings, the government might not have
moved on the issue.

Another British Columbia PLURA grant went to a social housing
group composed of people with mental disabilities. The group organized a community kitchen and training in other skills, which will help
them achieve their long-term goal of self-reliance. Joan Morelli, the
national PLURA Board member from British Columbia, reports that
"groups requesting funds from B.C. PLURA must be very grassroots." She also says that the committee wants to "build bridges rather
than walls."

In Nova Scotia, PLURA gave a grant to groups in Cape Breton
and Windsor to organize research/action projects which would raise
critical awareness about the problem of poverty and to work toward
empowerment of low-income groups to confront these problems.
Another PLURA grant went toward the organization of a small store

to empower women in the black community to have greater control over the nutritional quality of their food.

Alberta PLURA funded the Calgary Poverty Protest group to launch a public picket against widespread poverty in that province. The Alberta government refused to acknowledge the problem and turned a deaf ear to the protest.

In Prince Edward Island, PLURA funds helped a women's group of Irish moss harvesters to stand up to two transnational companies which were exploiting them by paying low prices for their product. The women were able to mobilize the whole region for a 25-day strike and almost doubled the price they received. They are now working on a pilot project which, if successful, will provide other markets and a co-operative which will sell seaweed as health food. The long-term aim is to replace the transnational buyers.

PLURA has funded innovative projects such as the Poverty Game, which helps players to experience for a few hours what it is like to be trapped in the prison of a welfare system which does not adequately supply the basic needs of food, shelter and clothing. It has inspired the Manitoba PLURA to build solidarity by organizing a yearly potluck supper for all recipients of PLURA grants.

Several provinces reported to the 1992 biannual assembly that they funded projects to combat racism (a creative example being a comic book in Manitoba). Alberta, Nova Scotia, Ontario and Quebec reported that their provincial government's hardline stance toward low-income groups and welfare recipients creates huge problems and victimizes many people.

The 1984 constitutional revision also ended the practice of having people with 'special competence' on PLURA boards. These 'experts' seemed to signal that PLURA lacked confidence in its own ability. In doing away with the 'special competence' category, PLURAs sent out the signal that the partnership of low-income groups and churches could stand on its own feet.

PLURA funds come from the development and relief agencies of the five sponsoring churches, with the exception of the United Church which funds PLURA through its Division of Mission in Canada. These churches are continually updating their criteria to meet the changing social and economic reality of poor Canadians. The concept of solidarity has come alive with new meaning and importance. These changes challenge PLURA to evaluate repeatedly the quality of its partnership, as well as the quality of its action for transformation.

This remarkable outreach helps attain PLURA's goal of a partnership between the churches and low-income groups. Church resources distributed through PLURA have made a major contribution toward empowerment of the poor.

Over the years PLURA members have had to learn the art of good stewardship of resources and financial accountability. When funds from churches did not increase to keep up with inflation, PLURA cut costs. The annual national meeting became a biennial affair and the number of representatives on the national board was reduced. National Executive meetings were cut from four one-day meetings per year to two meetings, each lasting one and a half days. This reduced executive costs by 50%.

PLURA today and tomorrow

There are new trends in Canadian society which concern PLURA. Coalition building in this country as well as in the Third World has become the new means of strengthening 'people power' in the face of global domination by transnational corporations. The right-wing policies of 'structural adjustment' and trading blocks are restructuring Canadian society profoundly and chipping away at the meagre progress we have made in creating a just society. Many social groups recognize the need to work together on the difficult and challenging task of defining the economic and political forces that cause poverty. Globalization and items on the political agenda such as free trade and structural adjustment require a response of shared research, analysis, dialogue and action.

PLURA recognizes the importance of working more closely with other interchurch coalitions, especially the Ecumenical Coalition for Economic Justice. Closer co-operation with the Ecumenical Coalition would increase the ability of PLURA members to do social analysis. PLURA members could benefit, too, from greater attention to the educational programs of the Ten Days for World Development as well as the development education programs of the various denominations. These programs make links between the needs and interests of the poor in the Third World and the poor in Canada. They point to global solidarity as an important way to confront poverty. Third

World visitors to Canada are especially interested in meeting self-help groups funded by PLURA.

The solidarity of PLURA with the social justice movement in Canada in fighting the program of free trade, privatization and deregulation can only enrich both movements. Some PLURA members have been discussing the quality of their relationship with labour unions, which are a major part of the Canadian social justice movement. In some provinces self-help groups have felt betrayed and intimidated by certain labour unions which seem interested solely in their own affairs. Other labour unions, however, are learning through their participation in organizations such as the Action Canada Network to extend their practice of solidarity to the larger community. Self-help groups and unions need each other at this moment in our history.

The pioneers of the modern ecumenical justice movement knew from the start that no one church could transform an unjust society on its own. They realized that transformation is a task which is greater than the force of all the churches together, but that the Christian community is called upon to do its part. They also understood that they would encounter resistance to their work for justice and that togetherness would strengthen them in the face of that opposition.

Small prophetic organizations and coalitions are important because they provide essential contexts for growth, contemplation and analysis. They also offer a dream: that one day the status quo will be transformed into a society which reflects the spirit of the Gospel. PLURA is important because it attempts to be that kind of coalition. It asks, "Who are the poor in Canadian society?... How can we get our hands dirty in the attempt to alleviate poverty?" In order to continue to be empowered, it needs allies and it needs to give itself space to experience the hand of God in its work.

Ten Days
for World Development

Jeanne Moffat

Ten Days for World Development is the story of thousands of
people across Canada. It has its beginning in the vision of ecumenically minded national church staff. Its life and growth have been
nourished by people in hundreds of communities in every province
and territory and by countless resource people from Third World
countries. Through Ten Days, these people have made connections
with partners in other countries, with people in many sectors and
occupations here in Canada and with policy makers in church,
government and business. Because each connection is a unique story,
there is no *one* story of Ten Days for World Development. I can only
attempt to capture some of the significance of these stories.

We begin with a very recent story. The theme of the 1992 Ten
Days program was "Freedom from Debt: People's Movements
Against the Debt." The purpose of the program was to urge Canadians
to see things from the perspective of the people of Third World
countries who are suffering under burdensome debt loads and to
consider seriously the alternatives and proposals that they have developed to address the resulting problems. All the resources of the Ten
Days program—print and human—were directed to this goal.

Two visitors from the Philippines were among our resource
people. Enrico Esguerra travelled to the Ontario/Quebec regional Ten
Days meeting and to the Atlantic provinces, and Filomeno Sta. Ana
went to Manitoba and northwest Ontario, sharing not only the story
of the Philippine debt crisis, but of the large organized people's
movement in the Philippines—the Freedom from Debt Coalition.

Among the platforms of the Coalition was a call to their government to disengage from loans that did not benefit the people, particularly those tainted with fraud. The Coalition was especially concerned
in early 1992 about the renegotiation of a package of commercial bank

debt which included several questionable loans. One particular loan to build the Bataan Nuclear Power Plant had a long and stormy history. Originally planned in the early 1970s, Bataan had been the subject of much controversy. For one thing, it had been built near a volcanic area and on an earthquake fault and thus it was a potential threat to human safety. Furthermore, questionable financing arranged between Westinghouse Corporation and the Marcos administration eventually came to light. The plant was partially built, but not one kilowatt of power had been generated by the time the project was mothballed in 1986 by President Aquino because of safety concerns. Charges of fraud and bribery were laid in 1988 by the Philippine government against Westinghouse Corporation in the New Jersey courts. In spite of this, the government of the Philippines continued to honour the debt for this plant and were paying $300,000 (U.S.) in interest daily on the Bataan Nuclear Power Plant.

During his stay in Canada, Sta. Ana, the secretary general of the Freedom from Debt Coalition, met with a Canadian banker who was a member of the Bank Advisory Committee responsible for renegotiating the commercial bank debt with the government of the Philippines. The banker felt that the deal was an excellent one for the Philippines and its people. Sta. Ana provided statistics, however, which demonstrated the negative impact of the debt burden on the poorest in his country. The 'economic growth' model, which the financial institutions and commercial banks championed, was not providing any growth for these people. In fact, it was quite the opposite.

Sta. Ana returned to the Philippines to face not only the imminent signing of the commercial bank package, but to hear the unexpected announcement that the government had agreed to work on an out-of-court settlement with Westinghouse Corporation. The settlement would lay the ground for Westinghouse to complete and operate the Bataan Nuclear Power Plant, selling the energy wholesale to the government of the Philippines, who would then sell it at a higher retail rate to the people.

The settlement outraged the Filipino people. Environmentalists, doctors, academics and scientists joined the protest. The Freedom from Debt Coalition, which already had 268 organizations among its membership, was encouraged by the formation of an even broader coalition. But they needed expressions of concern from outside, as well as research to help them argue their case. Sta. Ana phoned Ten

Days, assuming that the support was here. He knew that Canadians had already been writing letters to Canadian bankers and government officials, urging them to listen to the Coalition. He also felt deep appreciation for their letters of encouragement to the Coalition.

Sta. Ana asked for more letters of concern and more information concerning the safety of nuclear power plants. He also asked for details about the banking agreement that had that day "hit a snag," according to the Governor of the Central Bank of the Philippines. And he excitedly shared the news that a letter from school children from Pinawa, Manitoba, expressing their concern about the debt burden on the children in the Philippines, had appeared that day in the *Daily Globe* in Manila, a newspaper read by policy makers.

Within an hour of his call from the Philippines, our Manitoba/northwest Ontario co-ordinator was alerted. She was planning a Ten Days workshop the next day and could follow up on his requests for letters of concern and for information on the safety of nuclear power plants. From our national office, we contacted the banker who provided more information on the debt package.

Our five years of work on the debt—highlighting the impact of the burden on the poor of the South, demystifying financial jargon, pushing for church policy on the debt and on structural adjustment programs of the international financial institutions, meeting with MPs and writing briefs to Parliamentary committees, talking with local and national bankers—took flight in that hour. Connections were made, information was shared and people were mobilized in the task of working for justice. That hour was a microcosm of what Ten Days is all about.

How did all this begin?

The story begins on May 28 1970, when Roman Catholic and Protestant general secretaries and titular heads came together with social action and world development staff in the Inter-Church Consultative Committee for Development and Relief "to foster further co-operation of our churches in the whole field of development." The model of co-operation had been established in 1968 when a conference on poverty had been held in Montreal.[1] If this could be done on domestic issues, why couldn't it work on international ones? The nascent elements of Ten Days for World Development are reflected in a motion from that meeting that "we adopt the principle of a joint ten-day interchurch education program... in the pre-Easter period of 1971 using all of the resources available in the churches through the departments and programs of social action and justice, education, overseas mission development funds, communications, etc., to focus our development concerns and resources in that period."

The idea of a 10-day period evidently came from Roméo Maione, head of Development and Peace. According to Tom Johnston, who worked with him, Roméo was a 'seedbed of ideas' and a strong force behind the formation of a number of ecumenical coalitions.

In spite of the motion, it was not as easy to 'focus the development concerns' as it was to focus on the development of joint resources for fund raising and publicity. It was not until February 1972 that Johnston was officially asked by the Inter-Church Consultative Committee to convene a meeting of the representatives from the churches on development education. There was an indication at that meeting that the churches should earmark funds for development education in Canada, recognizing that "to change attitudes in Canada is a very major task."

On April 7 1972, the Inter-Church Committee on Development Education met for the first time, with the task of coming up with a plan for the period from September 1972 through August 1973. They developed a proposal that "during a concentrated period next March 1973, we raise before public opinion in Canada various development issues. To do this, we invite not only the churches but also the different sectors of Canadian society to participate in this venture." Key strategies were identified for the political, educational, economic, media and church sectors.

This group of ten people seemed undaunted by the work implicit in such a vision and by the co-ordination required to get it going. If this program were to change public attitudes, it would require maximum coverage in the press. For that, the committee agreed that there would need to be involvement of top church leaders, as well a 'Declaration of Concern' which would spell out the churches' concern about the inequities in the world. Archbishop Ted Scott received positive reaction to his suggestion to the heads of churches that they set aside a block of time in the spring of 1973 so that they might travel together, giving "visibility to joint action by the five Church leaders." The national effort could not happen, however, without the significant involvement of local people.

The plans for the first 'Ten Days' began to take shape and the churches committed themselves to a budget in the fall of 1972, which included a full-year staff contract with Robert Gardner. The Canadian International Development Agency approved a contribution. Gardner began the task of resource production for small group study and of firming up plans for the Church leaders' tour. It was a dizzying whirlwind of activity.

Gardner reported to the committee in late November 1972, after visiting local church people in Ottawa and Toronto. He observed that "the two groups, while being concerned and eager, were somewhat nonplussed by how much they needed to absorb at the first meeting and by the possible implications of the project." Just a few short months later, his report of that first year's program pays tribute to the "prodigious quantity of work done by the local interchurch committee and members of the national staff of the Canadian Conference of Catholic Bishops in preparation for the events in Ottawa." The tour depended greatly on the efforts of the people in each locality—from the London committee's considerable skills in reaching large numbers of people, to the "most impressive, high quality 'Teach-In' sponsored by the Halifax committee," to the "very well-planned and exceptionally helpful meeting" at the University of British Columbia planned by the Vancouver committee. The report also notes the imaginative work of the Edmonton committee in preparing an additional brief for presentation to the Alberta Government. It was this brief which lay the groundwork for the later establishment of Alberta's own program to match funds raised by individuals and groups for international development.

Even before the first year's 'Ten Days' occurred, the committee approved a long-term development education program. The historic motion of February 26 1973 was worded thus, "Because it is already evident that we can do together what we cannot do separately, the Inter-Church Committee on Development Education recommends to the Inter-Church Consultative Committee for Development and Relief that the various co-operating denominations which we represent continue to fund and plan a long-term development education programme; i.e., there should be an annual, interchurch educational thrust during a specific period comparable to the 1973 Ten Days for World Development." Two weeks later, the first 'Ten Days for World Development' was launched.

The Church leaders' tour took place between March 8-19 1973. They visited Ottawa, Quebec City, Vancouver, Calgary, Edmonton, Toronto, London and Halifax. Those participating were: Archbishop Edward W. Scott, Primate of the Anglican Church of Canada; Bishop William E. Power, president of the Canadian Conference of Catholic Bishops; Dr. John Zimmerman, president of the Lutheran Council in Canada; Dr. Max V. Putnam, Moderator of the Presbyterian Church in Canada (Dr. Donald MacDonald substituted for him in Ottawa, Quebec City, Vancouver, Calgary and Edmonton); and Dr. N. Bruce McLeod, Moderator of the United Church of Canada (Dr. George Morrison substituted for him in Ottawa and Quebec City and Dr. W. C. Picketts, president of the Maritime Conference of the United Church, represented him in Halifax). John Dillon, who had recently been hired to work on the GATT-Fly project, was a key figure in briefing these leaders.

The tour included public receptions and forums, workshops, meetings with federal and provincial government officials, labour officials, press interviews and conferences. The Church leaders delivered the Declaration of Concern, "Development Demands Justice," to the government and to the people of Canada. It contained two sections: "Alternate Policies for Development, Trade and Population," and "Citizen Participation in Policy Making." The latter section called on the government to develop an educational program around these issues, to provide possibilities for consultation with the Canadian public about these and to ensure Third World participation in these deliberations. It called for the composition of Canadian representation to GATT (the General Agreement on Tariffs and Trade organization) and to the U.N. Conference on Population to come from a broader range of backgrounds.

The fact that the leaders of the five major Christian churches in Canada had chosen to take such public positions relating to justice for the Third World was a major press story for radio, television, and the print media across Canada. An even more significant story for the future was the stimulation of a number of groups across Canada to study these issues.

The program takes root

The plans for the second year focussed on trade inequities as the central development problem. While the program aimed at church people, it was seen as absolutely necessary to work with social institutions in order to mobilize public opinion. In spite of the focus for action of Year I (the brief to government leaders), there is no mention of a similar focus in the plans for the second year. There *were* concerns that Ten Days should bring people from the Third World to help with the educational program, rather than rely on Canadian church leaders. This led to the invitation to Bishop Peter Sarpong of Ghana, who became the first of many Ten Days visitors to assist the program over the following years.

The 1975 program presented its audience with an analysis of dependence, citing examples of Third World countries and pointing to the anomaly of Canada as a rich but dependent nation. The Group of 77, the caucus of the Third World countries within the U.N. Conference on Trade and Development, developed a list of conditions considered necessary for the fair and just functioning of the world economy, under the title "The New International Economic Order." By 1976 the New International Economic Order became the focus for the work.

By 1976, approximately 35 committees were established and a national field worker hired. Tensions began to emerge as the program grew and developed. These concerned the dynamic between education and action, between local and national responsibilities and decision making, between church and public as the recipients and/or vehicle of our work, and between denominational and ecumenical interests. The story of Ten Days in the years since then has seen the resolution of some of these tensions and the emergence of others.

The three years from 1977 to 1979 highlighted food as a way of understanding the New International Economic Order. There was an explosion of activity across the country and many new committees formed, bringing the total to 80. The "Food First" analysis of Frances Moore Lappé and Joseph Collins, followed by the reflections of Gonzalo Arroyo, the Chilean agronomist, and of Susan George (author of *How the Other Half Dies*), all four of whom were Ten Days visitors, generated many questions about lifestyle, agribusiness and corporate power, Canadian aid and trade policy. Across Canada, spin-offs included the People's Food Commission, an attempt to define a Canadian food policy to benefit broader groups of people.

At the end of the second year on 'Food' (1978), Susan George offered her impressions of Ten Days and made several recommendations to a church leaders' seminar. First, those particularly concerned in social justice issues, she said, should avoid personal guilt trips: preoccupation with the contradictions of one's personal life can be paralyzing. The fight for social justice arises from turning outward and joining others. Second, it is possible to understand and predict the future effects of the global economic system in the Third World through understanding and analysing a local issue, thus making possible the prevention, or alleviation, of the dire effects of that system in the Third World. Third, Christian beliefs (for example, the incarnation, the resurrection) enable us to move radically with regard to the food issue. But we should be aware that in the future we will be accused of *politicization,* that is, some fellow Christians will complain that those concerned with social justice have become involved in politics at the expense of the Gospel. Nonetheless, we must not evade political involvement because we are already immersed daily in politics. Social justice cannot be done outside politics and there are real political enemies of social justice. Organization at the grassroots level, she added, is the key to success. Failure to achieve this organization means losing the battle; it means the deterioration and decay of the Third World, of our lives and so on. Sides must be taken in this conflict.

Shortly after that report, MP David MacDonald, in his keynote address to the 1978 annual meeting of Ten Days, asserted that the three-year commitment to the food issue had been particularly fortuitous. Not only had Ten Days committed itself to "an issue which is absolutely vital to our whole ethos as Christians trying to live responsibly at this point of time in history," but it had given birth to a focus much larger than the program itself. His question was, "Now, what we're faced with as parents is: How do we let the child go? How do we make sure that the child is going to grow and flourish and not simply disappear off into the bush after the third year?"

In fact, many committees did not want to 'let the child go.' When the National Committee determined after the third year on 'Food' that the work for 1980-82 would focus on 'Making a Living,' there was very little excitement. There were however a few outstanding exceptions of enthusiasm for the work issue. In St. John's, Newfoundland, the local committee co-published a book on the struggles of the Longshoremen's Union. In Montreal, teachers in a CEGEP (a community and pre-university college) used the Ten Days materials as major resources for their classes. In Winnipeg, local groups made connections with immigrant textile workers. In Kitchener-Waterloo, where racism in the immigration office was a major barrier to newcomers securing work permits, the committee worked with their MP to demand a federal hearing into that workplace.

Growing pains

Throughout the years on the food and work themes, two issues were emerging with particular clarity: the question of regional participation in the decision-making bodies and processes of the program and the implementation of a stronger focus on action. Both of these issues required a basic rethinking of the program's mandate and processes and led to major changes that have had profound effects on the work of Ten Days.

There had been a burst of new Ten Days committees during the work on 'Food.' But the decision to change the theme in the midst of an enormous burst of activity led to resentment about how decisions were being made and who was making them. Beginning in late 1980 and culminating in mid-1981, there was considerable debate in which the concerns of some of the national church bodies came up against the needs of the local committees. The churches nationally had been working toward a focussed, action-oriented program which required local support, as reflected in the working document on a basic policy statement developed by the Program Committee on December 15 1980, "It [the program] is therefore dependent upon effective work at the local level and needs a strong network of committed groups to take on the responsibility for local programs." The local committees asked Who? and How? Their concern was the lack of a strong support system for a network of committed groups.

Furthermore, they had no membership on the decision-making National Committee to help shape the program. In spite of the fact that regional delegates had been involved in annual consultations since 1973 and had participated on a program committee, the policy-making National Committee was still firmly in the hands of national church appointees. These appointees clearly were not of one mind about the advisability of bringing regional people onto the Committee. Regional people made their points well—through their spokespersons on the Program Committee, letters, submissions and reports of the staffer, and David Pollock, who was the national field

worker. They pressed for staff and financial back-up and full participation in the decision-making processes. Finally, in late May 1981,
the delegates to the Annual Evaluation and Planning Conference
resolved that "people serve on the national bodies as the elected
voting representatives of Ten Days regional committees." This was
passed on to the National Committee which a week later accepted
the principle.

That same conference in 1981 also reached consensus on a new
policy statement which declared that "Ten Days is a focussed development education program building to specific actions." The meeting
agreed that there is a "possibility for a particular single action if the
right process is followed." It should "never be imposed from above"
and "can be generated at the local level and shared through ongoing
newsletters." It must "be on the Ten Days theme and within the limits
of criteria agreed upon by consultation."

I began work as the program facilitator in October 1981. I developed and employed my listening skills in those first six months, as
we worked through two draft proposals for the next step. By the time
of the April 1982 annual consultation there was agreement to work
together on changing government policy in regard to Central
America. The exact policies and strategies for action were left to the
National Committee in consultation with other interchurch coalitions.
And so the 'focussed action component' of the program was born.

Building a network

The decision to allow regions to elect their representatives to the
National Committee was a manifestation of a principle that has since
guided our struggle to become a social change network stretching
across the country. This principle is that "a network for constructive
social change must function out of principles of justice." In June of
1989, I spoke on the new orientation to the National Development
Education Conference in Calgary, Alberta, "In practice, the first
principle meant that we had to understand and celebrate the regional
differences in our country. When we talked about a national program,
we could not see it as a program planned nationally in one office.
Instead, it had to be a program planned nationally by every community and every region. National structures had to guarantee representation from all the regions and regional input had to be honoured as
much as the national church input. The focus was not national staff,

but national volunteers right across this country. It meant that our most important resources were not finances, not structures, not print materials, but people—and that the people needed to articulate their needs, their fears, their strengths and their weaknesses. People needed to indicate what kind of support they required for the hard, front-line justice work in which they would be engaging. Support, in fact, might be in the form of finances, structures, print resources, ongoing communication, staff assistance and policy development."

By the mid-80s we had 150 local committees. In 1985, following Bob Gardner's retirement and David Pollock's resignation, Ten Days reassessed the needs of local committees. More support was given to the regions, including increased financial support for regional representatives and regional meetings. This enabled much more frequent networking and communication. Field work was added to the tasks of the three program staff and a new position of co-ordinator for regional communication and leadership development was created. David Reid, the former British Columbia regional representative on the National Committee, was hired to fill that position in early 1987.

Regional/provincial representatives began to take on much more responsibility for relating directly to the 150 local committees. Reid initiated an annual get-together of all the regional and provincial co-ordinators, enabling them to reflect on the needs of the regions and plan for ways in which the regions could strengthen the committees and the program. A consultative process begun in 1982 soliciting program ideas from all local committees, national churches, inter-church coalitions and Third World visitors helped established a high level of trust among all parts of the program.

As the committees felt more supported, a growing understanding of the potential of joint action developed among the people in the Ten Days network. Yet as they took on more action, they also experienced stronger reactions to the tough questions they were raising, not only in the broader public, but within their own church communities. A number of these reactions challenged the appropriateness of Christians getting involved in political discussions and strategies to influence public policy. Susan George's prediction in 1978, "be aware that in the future, we will be accused of politicization," was coming true. In 1986, Charles Elliott, a theologian-economist specializing in international development, toured Canada with Mosi Kisare, development research consultant with the All-Africa Conference of

Churches, helping Ten Days address the theme "Why Are People Hungry?" Reflecting on his time with people across the Ten Days network, Elliott identified a "total lack of training in seeing political power as a theological category." Related to this point, as well, was his observation that the "notion of a spirituality that relates to politics seems foreign to both clergy and laity."

These two realities—local committee experiences and Charles Elliott's analysis—pushed the issue of a 'spirituality for justice-making' to the top of Ten Days' agenda. Even the national church representatives who had argued that this was the responsibility of the denominations reconsidered and agreed that Ten Days might have a role to play. The staff suggested that this was such a priority that it might be important to have a moratorium on the Third World visitor program for one year (in order to focus, but also in order to find funding for this) while the participants in the program addressed the need for education in justice. The National Committee responded with a compromise. Half of the visitor program budget would be used to support a national leadership event in the next year for Ten Days people on the theme "Spirituality for Justice-Making." The other half would be used to bring resource people from the South for the ongoing visitor program.

Regionally appointed delegates spent several days together in early 1987 in Manitoba, examining the foundations of their faith and exploring strategies for putting across their concomitant under-standing of justice. It was not clear how well 'trained' they were to offer such workshops in their regions. The ripple effects were felt, however: the following autumn, all regional representatives reported that there had already been workshops or that more work on the question of 'spirituality' had been done as part of the regional meetings. One regional representative (a clergyperson) reported that "some fairly healthy struggling is going on; we're trying to do some-thing that is foreign to our psyche." The struggling continues.

Taking action

When we began our focussed action in the fall of 1982, there was already a history of work within the churches on Central Amer-ican issues. In particular, the churches had been challenging Canadian government policy in the Central American region through the Inter-Church Committee on Human Rights in Latin America. The analysis of the churches was that the conflicts in the region were based on years of poverty and inequality, supported and exacerbated by the presence of transnational corporate power and the military forces of the United States. Further, these conflicts were viewed through the lens of the Cold War. The Canadian government, while agreeing that poverty and inequality were the fundamental cause of the region's unrest, was reluctant to develop its policy wholly according to that analysis. The government was being pressured by the United States government to adopt Cold-War rhetoric.

Ten Days and the Inter-Church Committee on Human Rights in Latin America developed a clear agreement about how to work together. A newly established Policy Integration Committee brought coalitions and denominations engaging in Central America work together with Ten Days national and local committee representatives to advise Ten Days on the action component of the program. We have continued to have a Policy Integration Committee for whatever action thrust we have had. Its membership changes to include those who have expertise in the particular theme of the program. This committee is now often referred to in the churches themselves as a model of collaboration and co-ordination on an issue.

Over the three years of work on Central America, people across the country spoke to their members of Parliament and wrote to various government officials. Their reports and correspondence formed a major part of the action work of the Policy Integration Committee. A broad picture of MPs' positions on the region emerged and the Policy Integration Committee could often provide local committees with information to deal with those positions. The Minister for External Affairs, Allan MacEachen, decided to travel to Central America as a result of the push from people across Canada and asked for a briefing and debriefing with the churches and other non-governmental organizations. Our work had its effect: Canada's vote on one of the resolutions on El Salvador at the United Nations Human Rights Commission meetings changed and the Canadian representative ascribed the shift to growing public pressure in Canada.

Stories abound of people whose level of self-confidence grew in the course of a brief encounter with an MP. They learned that their MPs were not all-knowing, and they discovered that their sources of information (partners who represented the poor in each of the Central American countries) often offered a totally different perspective from that of their MPs. The determination of these people to stay in the dialogue was almost always strengthened.

Many politicians of all parties found the encounters helpful, although a few found them 'one-sided' and 'communist-inspired'! The impact in Ottawa was quite significant. The Prime Minister's office received more mail on Central America than on any other issue. We must note here that, while Ten Days was one major actor, there were a number of other networks involved in this issue at the same time, adding to the numbers of letter writers. Parliamentary librarians were overloaded with requests from MPs for information on Central America; some CIDA offices considered hiring additional staff to help deal with the mail relating to Canadian aid to the region.

In 1984 there was an unprecedented outpouring of human compassion in response to the Ethiopian famine. A call came from local committees for a deeper analysis of the root causes of hunger. Our next three-year focus, "Why Are People Hungry?" took us into analyses of land issues (control and use), wealth concentration and the feminization of poverty. It led also to action focussed on the Canadian response to hunger in the world. The questions were, "How is Canadian aid addressing these root causes of hunger? What should be the principles of an Overseas Development Assistance program that attempts to deal with causes and not just symptoms of hunger in the world?"

In 1987 the Standing Committee on External Affairs and International Trade launched an exhaustive study of Canada's Overseas Development Assistance. Our committees were ready and they forced the Standing Committee to hold hearings in seven, rather than four, provinces, as they had previously announced. Three Ten Days committees—Halifax-Dartmouth, Kitchener-Waterloo and British Columbia region—were called to testify and submitted in-depth briefs highlighting different concerns about Canada's Official Development Assistance program. Those were supplemented by written briefs from 35 other committees, as well as many letters. In the Standing Committee's final report, "For Whose Benefit?" (1987), one can see the influence of the churches and of Ten Days.

Our Third World partners clearly identified one of the causes of hunger: the impact of the international debt crisis on the poor. In the second year of "Why Are People Hungry?" Ten Days introduced the debt issue. We also met with an interchurch, intercoalition network on debt, called together by GATT-Fly, to co-ordinate our work.

This introduction led Ten Days committees to ask for a particular action focus on the involvement of commercial banks in the debt crisis. We decided that local committees should attempt to enter into dialogue with local bank managers about the impact of the debt on the poor and on the environment in the Third World. The committees would also inquire about bank policy in relation to the debt.

For some committees in farming communities on the Prairies, the painful issue of farm debt and their vulnerability to the banks led to their decision not to take this on. Others found creative ways to involve not only bank managers, but MPs as well, in roundtable discussions of the issue. Much to their surprise, Ten Days committees discovered that most local bank officials either did not know their banks' policies, felt too vulnerable to discuss the issues, or had been directed by their head offices not to talk with these church people! A few welcomed the opportunity to share perspectives. National bank offices, however, had to deal with many requests coming up through their systems from local bank managers and thus the dialogue did take place, although by correspondence.

While bank policies did not change dramatically, Ten Days people learned that this issue did not belong exclusively to the bankers and that their role was to make sure that the bankers heard the Third World voices. The issue was not only a financial question for experts, but an issue with profound moral and ethical implications as well.

In 1989, within months of the bank action, the Standing Committee announced that it would study the international debt crisis and Canada's role in it. Our committees immediately pressed the Committee to hear witnesses from the South. We even agreed to pay the expenses of a witness. The push was successful and the Committee agreed to spend one of its sessions with Ten Days and our special witness, Jaime Wright from Brazil. It was a victory for Ten Days to get the particular perspective of the South into this arena.

Jaime Wright and Ten Days committees across Canada, along with many other church people, had a significant impact on the parliamentarians conducting the study. When they made their final report in June 1990, "Securing Our Global Future: Canada's Stake in the Unfinished Business of Third World Debt," many of our concerns had been heard.

The government issued its response in November 1990. It did

not take up the clear challenge of the Standing Committee on External Affairs and International Trade to chart bold new directions in Canada's approach to the debt problem. The government agreed only to hold a seminar on international debt. That occurred in June 1992 and Ten Days again made sure that representatives of Third World non-governmental organizations were included.

While the government by and large did not adopt the Standing Committee's recommendations, the public debate had been broadened because of our program, a fact noted by the Committee in that report, "We believe that an informed citizenry that is moved to act is worth any number of reports which merely gather dust, no matter how heavy with good intentions or laden with statistics. That is the ultimate test and we hope to have made a small contribution toward meeting it. As a Committee, we have been impressed by the efforts of the churches and NGOs, notably through the Ten Days for World Development campaign, to dialogue with Canadian banks and to bring Third World debt issues to the attention of the public. And we were impressed by the sincerity of those who wrote to tell us of their deep personal concern."

The challenge for the future

We in Ten Days for World Development have reason for hope. The struggles of the past have given us strength, from which new undertakings and new visions can emerge. Not only must we trust our consultative processes, but we must build on the trust among ourselves and our partners and bring these strengths to broader networks of people of goodwill. Our vision of things will not be realized if we focus inward, on internal processes and structures.

Increasingly we see a trend in Canada and the world to protect the well-off from those who struggle to survive. The result is a destructive type of development, a kind of development which must be challenged by people who have a commitment to a different kind of world. How can we bring our unique strength into coalitions to define alternatives to the current destructive system? If we think of Ten Days as part of a movement for social change, what does this mean for our traditional way of working, that is, education/action designed for a particular time of year? Networking requires ongoing and in-depth work with occasional urgent responses; there is no single high-profile time for the work. We began to get some sense of what that might entail as we connected with the Freedom from Debt Coalition in the Philippines.

We are also challenged by the disappearance of boundaries between North and South, East and West and the emergence of a worldwide split between rich and poor in all countries, the 'North in the South' and the 'South in the North.' The participants in this program, at national and local levels, understand that a response to Canadian issues of injustice enables us to stand credibly in solidarity with others in distant places. While many Ten Days individuals are engaged in Canadian concerns already, should Ten Days attempt this on a national level, that is, beyond individual, local, or regional actions? Since our network is one of the few ecumenical cross-country social justice networks, we are frequently seen as the only place where important local/national work can be done. Can we do this and still remain faithful to our mandate to focus on international development? Maintaining a focus has been a major and key strength of our work. The push to try to be all things to all people will present a major challenge, both to our understanding and our way of working.

Working ecumenically will also present its challenges in the 1990s. Increasingly, there are pressures on the denominations. Church membership and finances are decreasing, necessitating cuts in program, committees and staff. The churches' prophetic witness and actions are coming under stiff questioning from some of our own constituents. The effect of these things on ecumenical social justice work could be quite profound. Within Ten Days it already means that denominational committees and staff have less time to research the international development issues and discuss the future of Ten Days as an ecumenical venture. It means that educational programs in the denominations are suffering and Ten Days is being asked to do more of the basic denominational work. If Ten Days does this, it may stand to lose its public witness and its broader impact on structures and policies in this country. That would be a serious loss.

I began with two stories—one about our links with the Freedom from Debt Coalition in the Philippines and the other about the first year of Ten Days. These stories not only inform us about the Ten Days program and people, but also challenge our understanding of church leadership in Canada. In the 1990s, when the media pay little attention to the appearances of church leaders and when ecumenical co-operation is no longer a 'new' story, Ten Days people are finding new ways of getting the attention of those in positions of economic and political power. The strategies of 1973 can no longer serve us in this moment. The people all across our network of local committees have assumed a mantle of leadership, having been empowered by this program—through contacts with southern visitors, discussion with their local groups about the issues, recognition of the common forces of oppression in Canada and the world beyond, struggle with their faith and how to express it in the world, engagement and challenge to their churches, dialogue with their bankers and MPs and interviews with the media. The women and men at the grassroots are taking increased responsibility for challenging the systems and structures of the world. *They* are the church leaders of the 1990s, declaring the same concern of the church leaders of 1973, "Development Demands Justice!"

The Inter-Church Committee on Human Rights in Latin America

Bill Fairbairn

Early beginnings: The Inter-Church Committee on Chile

On September 11 1973, the people of Chile awoke to the sound of martial music crackling over the radio, interrupted only by machine-gun fire. A state of siege was invoked, curfew imposed and a series of edicts pronounced which would signal 17 years of tyranny.[1] Announcers read long lists of names of persons being ordered to turn themselves over to the military authorities. At approximately 11 a.m., a Hawker Hunter aircraft of the Chilean Air Force passed over the Presidential Palace, scoring a direct hit with its bomb. Chile's proud democratic tradition was brought to an abrupt end.

In Canada reaction to the coup was swift among church leaders, missionaries, labour, student and various public groups. During the three years of the Allende government, a number of exchanges had taken place between Canadians and Chileans. At the time of the coup, the Toronto-based Latin American Working Group and the Student Christian Movement were planning one such exchange. Co-ordinating the visit in Chile were Florrie Snow and Arturo Chacon of the Chilean Methodist Church. Immediate phone contact with these friends and other contacts revealed the ferocity of the repression which had been unleashed.

These first-hand reports from Chilean friends and the coincident visit of two Canadian church leaders to Chile prodded Canadian churches to react quickly. The day after the coup, an emergency meeting was convened in the offices of the Ecumenical Forum of Canada. Among those present were John Foster, Tim Draimin, Fred Franklin and Frances Arbour, all of whom would become future committee and/or staff members of the Inter-Church Committee on

Human Rights in Latin America. Information was shared and analysed and an initial response developed.

On September 15 1973, the United, Anglican and Roman Catholic Churches issued a statement. It protested the coup d'état and appealed to the Canadian government not to give legitimacy to the military junta by granting recognition.[2] It urged the government to offer safe conduct and assistance to any refugees from Latin American countries living in Chile[3] as well as any Chileans wishing to come to Canada. Three days later, the Canadian Council of Churches issued a second ecumenical statement.

On October 3 1973, a delegation of Canadian church leaders met with the External Affairs Minister, Mitchell Sharp.[4] They presented him with a brief calling on the government to take immediate steps to open Canada's doors to Chileans whose lives were in immediate danger. The brief urged the Minister to use the diplomatic channels which the Canadian government had opened with the military leaders in Chile "to register the strongest protest against those violations of human rights perpetuated by the regime since its bloody seizure of power." The church representatives were met with questions, scepticism and even attack. The Minister and his senior officials insisted that this was just another Latin American coup of no great importance and assured them that the situation in Chile was already returning to 'normal.'

The events surrounding the coup in Chile deeply moved many in the Canadian church community. Ecumenical concern and co-operation continued and deepened in the following weeks and months with the establishment of an ad hoc body, the Inter-Church Committee on Chile. In the early days, the ad hoc committee would meet on a Friday in the offices of the Canadian Council of Churches. There was always an emergency that required immediate attention: some called it the 'Friday afternoon crisis club.' Later, one committee member noted, "We have experienced a phenomenal period of trust and co-operation within an ad hoc framework, which makes ecumenical concern truly possible. Much of this originates in a certain style of leadership at the top of the church denominations and councils, a willingness to be pragmatic, to work together rather than just talk in committees. Actual experience in the issue concerned or with the people concerned is important in the motivation of these actors."[5]

Florrie Snow who, together with her family, was forced to flee

Chile became the first co-ordinator of the Inter-Church Committee on Chile in early 1974. Clearly, the crisis was worsening and the response could not continue on an ad hoc basis. Between 1973 and 1976, the Inter-Church Committee on Chile[6] sponsored several visits to Chile by Canadian observers, among them Father Bill Smith, Father Buddy Smith and Frances Arbour. The Committee helped host visits to Canada by witnesses from Chile, including Hortensia Allende, Bishop Helmut Frenz and Swedish Ambassador Edelstam. Alone or with the Canadian Coalition on Chile—a grouping of labour, humanitarian and civil rights organizations—the Committee made frequent representations to the Canadian government.[7] It pressed the government to bring greater numbers of refugees to Canada, to take a more active stand in international forums for the restoration of human rights in Chile and to suspend official aid and all investment funds to the military government.

The initial representations did not meet with great success: clearly the government was reluctant to offer asylum to Chilean refugees. An important breakthrough occurred in the fall of 1973, when classified cables from Canada's Ambassador to Chile were leaked to the media. The cables from Ambassador Andrew Ross stated that the killings taking place after the coup were "abhorrent but understandable." Ross went on to claim that the prisoners being held in the National Stadium were nothing but "the riff-raff of the Latin American left." The leaked cable created a scandal in Canada, galvanizing many in the church and solidarity networks. The continued pressure of the churches and other non-governmental organizations led to the eventual decision of the Canadian government to accept some 10,000 Chilean refugees.

Faced with increasing international pressure, General Pinochet announced in December 1974 that the junta was willing to give condemned political prisoners the option of exile as commutation for prison sentences if other countries would receive them.[8] Shortly after this announcement, the Inter-Church Committee sent a delegation to Chile comprised of committee member George Cram and François LaPierre of the *Société des missions étrangères*. Working with Chilean church agencies (in particular the Vicariate of Solidarity) and the Canadian government, the delegation conducted direct interviews with relatives of the prisoners and was instrumental in the design and implementation of a program to facilitate the release and transfer to Canada of approximately 200 Chilean political prisoners.

In Toronto, Edmonton, Calgary and many other Canadian cities, people formed welcome committees and local 'interchurch' committees to receive refugees and press the Canadian government on human rights in Chile. The Inter-Church Committee on Chile, in co-operation with the local committees, assisted in the resettlement of several thousand refugees in Canada, providing assistance in cases of family reunification, legal complication and refugee appeals.

The need for a broader response

The work of the Canadian churches immediately following the coup revealed that the doctrine of 'national security' and the economic model being pursued in Chile were being replicated in a number of countries throughout the Americas. These twin policies laid the foundation for massive human rights violations in Argentina, Uruguay, Brazil and other countries and, consequently, streams of refugees, as was the case in Chile. The rapidly deteriorating situation in Argentina and Peru, together with the continuing reports of torture and imprisonment in Uruguay and Brazil, resulted in many appeals from prisoners and their families, trade unionists and asylum-seekers.

In October 1976, a group of Central American theologians addressed an open letter to North American Christians, "Friends and fellow Christians, it is time that you realize that our continent is becoming one gigantic prison and, in some regions, one vast cemetery... that human rights, fundamental to the Gospel, are becoming a dead letter, without force. And all this is happening in order to maintain a system, a structure of dependence that benefits those who have always held might and privilege, in your land and in our land, at the expense of the poor millions who are increasing throughout the width and breadth of the continent."[9]

Messages such as this and urgent appeals by the Argentine and Uruguayan communities in Canada led to the decision in the spring of 1976 to revise the mandate of the committee, enlarging its geographical frame of reference.

The last major initiative of the Inter-Church Committee on Chile, and one which served as a bridge to the formation of the Inter-Church Committee on Human Rights in Latin America, was a fact-finding mission sent in September-October 1976 to the 'Southern Cone.' The delegation included three Canadian members of parliament: Andrew Brewin (NDP), David MacDonald (PC) and Louis Duclos (Liberal).

The delegation visited Argentina and Uruguay, but at the last moment was denied permission by the military junta to enter Chile. The testimonies gathered during the visit—like that concerning a young woman, Monica Mignone, abducted in the presence of her parents from their home in Buenos Aires by a group of five heavily armed men, never to be seen again, and that concerning Laura Raggo, a 20-year-old student who died after being savagely tortured by the Uruguayan military—made an indelible impression on the members of the delegation. These and many similar human tragedies convinced the Canadian churches that they needed to stand in solidarity with victims of such abuses throughout Latin America.

Inter-Church Committee on Human Rights in Latin America

The Inter-Church Committee on Human Rights in Latin America was formally established on January 1 1977. Initially, the main geographical focus of the committee was the Southern Cone of South America. The Committee continued to respond to the situation in Chile, Uruguay and Argentina through a variety of means, including the sending of missions, the publication of special reports and ongoing advocacy work with the Canadian government and international bodies.

In 1978, the Canadian churches sent a five-person delegation to attend a human rights symposium in Chile. Bishop Adolphe Proulx, the vice-chairman of the Inter-Church Committee on Human Rights in Latin America, headed the delegation and was one of the speakers at the event. The visit provided a key opportunity to meet with Chilean colleagues, trade unionists, lawyers, educators and social workers as well as with the Association of Relatives of the Disappeared. Together with the Canadian Taskforce on the Churches and Corporate Responsibility, the Inter-Church Committee on Human Rights in Latin America produced a report on the event, entitled "Bread, Peace and Liberty," which provided the framework for the continued work of solidarity with Chile.

In November 1979, the Inter-Church Committee on Human Rights in Latin America sent another fact-finding mission to Chile to investigate the impact of Decree Law 2568 which was promulgated by the military government as a means of splitting up the indigenous communities. The report of this mission, entitled "Mapuches: People of the Land," was presented to the Canadian Ambassador to the United Nations Commission on Human Rights in January 1980. In early 1978, the Inter-Church Committee on Human Rights in Latin America also published a major report in conjunction with the World Council of Churches, entitled "Violations of Human Rights in Uruguay (1972-1976)."

Understanding of human rights

Because of the responsive nature of their work and the limited resources available, the Inter-Church Committee on Human Rights in Latin America and its predecessor, the Inter-Church Committee on Chile, have often focussed their attention on Latin American countries in which the most fundamental violations of civil and political rights have occurred. At the same time, the nature of the work undertaken and reflection with Latin American partners led Canadian churches to an understanding of human rights much broader than that traditionally applied by Canadian and other Western societies.

In 1981 the Committee submitted a brief to the parliamentary committee studying Canada's relations with Latin America and the Caribbean. It stated, "When we speak of the struggle for human rights, we are not only talking of torture, repression of freedom of speech, or arbitrary arrest—significant as all these things are—but also of the broader struggle for social, economic and political partic- ipation by all the people... A given nation may have a democratic constitution and may promise periodic elections but, nevertheless, if the Minister of Finance agrees to the implementation of International Monetary Fund requirements regarding food and cooking oil prices which may result in the deaths of half a million children, can we say that human rights are being observed or defended? If a given economic model, like that characteristic of Brazil after 1964, or the current economic model in Chile, requires the repression of trade union and civic political organizations... must not our defence of human rights entail a profound critique of the economic model and its military managers and defenders?"[10]

Focus on Central America

Within a short time, alarming reports attesting to a sharp dete- rioration in the human rights situation in El Salvador, Guatemala and

Nicaragua led the Committee to direct increasing attention to Central America. The fall 1977 issue of the Inter-Church Committee on Human Rights in Latin America's *Newsletter* reported, "This week... a list of 66 political assassinations in Guatemala during August and September, mostly of peasants and farm workers, their bodies found shot and often cruelly tortured, arrived as the latest harsh example of repression in Latin America."

The Canadian churches were shocked and moved to action as the Inter-Church Committee on Human Rights in Latin America began to help unearth news of the terror of the Somoza dictatorship in Nicaragua, the genocide occurring in Guatemala and the assassinations of priests, sisters, delegates of the Word and thousands of civilians in El Salvador.[11] In the midst of the horror, the deep faith and witness of many Central American Christians, among them Julia Esquivel, Ernesto Cardenal and Archbishop Oscar Romero, remained a constant source of strength and inspiration.

In November 1978, the Committee participated in an international ecumenical delegation to Nicaragua. Father Michael Czerny, the Committee's representative on the mission, became a fervent spokesman in future representations to the Canadian government. Together with other Christian and community groups in Canada, the Committee pressed the Canadian government to sever ties with Somoza and open contact with the popular sectors. Through its publications and urgent actions, the Inter-Church Committee on Human Rights in Latin America attempted to increase awareness of the situation in Nicaragua. The June 1979 issue of the *Newsletter* reported, "On June 15, the Red Cross reported 10,000 dead in Managua alone. General Somoza is heavily bombing civilian populations in many centres in order to kill as many Sandinista supporters as possible."

After July 1979, a new revolutionary government in Nicaragua began to usher in programs of sweeping social change, including a literacy crusade of remarkable proportions. Soon it was faced not only with internal and regional opposition but with a counter-revolutionary army created by the government of the United States.

With the arrival of the Reagan-Bush administration in Washington, it became apparent that fundamental battle lines were being drawn in Central America which would affect the future of the Latin American region. In its efforts to prevent the consolidation of an alternative social model in the region, the U.S. government sought to crush the Sandinistas through economic pressure, the covert mining of Nicaragua's harbours and the establishment of bases within Honduras for its *contra* army. Likewise fearful of a victory by the insurgent Farabundo Marti Front for National Liberation in El Salvador, the Reagan administration sent massive amounts of military assistance to prop up the repressive Salvadorean government.

Throughout this time, the Inter-Church Committee on Human Rights in Latin America sent mission after mission to Central America. Strong partnerships with church and human rights groups as well as with committees of mothers of the disappeared and political prisoners developed and deepened in Guatemala, El Salvador and Honduras. The Committee's executive director from 1977 to 1985, Frances Arbour, was instrumental in the establishment and nurturing of these relationships of trust.

To Archbishop Romero's assassination was added the killing of four American churchwomen, European reporters and thousands of Salvadorean citizens. As the military warred in the highlands of Guatemala, thousands of Guatemalan refugees joined the thousands of Salvadorean displaced people and refugees seeking safety from the helicopters, death squads and marauding armies. The *contra* forces escalated their attacks against Nicaragua from their bases in Honduras, resulting in the murder of thousands of *campesinos*.

The Inter-Church Committee on Human Rights in Latin America's member churches became convinced that the establishment of a just peace in the region was an absolute prerequisite to any improvement in the overall human rights picture. Consequently, in virtually all of its representations to the Canadian government, it urged that Canada adopt a stronger position in opposing the Reagan administration's militarization of the region. Further, the Committee pressed the Canadian government to support negotiated political settlements to the internal conflicts in Central America and to denounce the human rights abuses that were occurring in the region.

The Inter-Church Committee on Human Rights in Latin America's critique of the role of the United States in the region occasionally raised the ire of some,[12] among them journalist Barbara Amiel. In a January 1984 article in *The Toronto Sun*, Amiel claimed with regard to the Committee's 1983 annual country reports on the human rights situation in Latin America that "the language in which this document is written is not the language of the Western world" and that it "would be more at home in the pages of *Pravda*—where it could with no difficulty be reprinted word for word."[13]

While representations to the Canadian government frequently ended in frustration, there were occasional successes. Though it avoided any overt criticism of American policy, the Canadian government eventually began to provide greater support and backing to the Central American peace process. It also assumed an important role within the United Nations Commission on Human Rights in sponsoring resolutions on Guatemala.

Fundamental to the gradual shift in Canadian government policy toward Central America was the work the Inter-Church Committee on Human Rights in Latin America carried out in conjunction with another ecumenical coalition, Ten Days for World Development. During the years in which Ten Days maintained a focus on Central America, the Inter-Church Committee on Human Rights in Latin America worked closely with the Policy Integration Committee, providing ongoing analysis and policy recommendations. The Policy Integration Committee, which brought together various coalitions and churches engaged in work around Central America, was developed as a focal point for the consolidation of policy on the region. The country-wide network of Ten Days for World Development local groups was instrumental in deepening the knowledge and understanding of a significant number of Canadians concerning Central America. This grassroots support brought to the attention of the Canadian government the broad extent of support for new initiatives in Canadian policies regarding international economic development, diplomacy and human rights.

The Southern Cone and Andean region

Concurrent with the increasing demands of energy and resources which were needed to respond to the Central American crisis, the Inter-Church Committee on Human Rights in Latin America began to receive new requests from South America: from Peru, the committee received reports of the disappearance of hundreds of men, women and children from the highland Department of Ayacucho; in Chile, a series of mass protests launched in the spring of 1983 was met with renewed repression by the Pinochet government; in Uruguay, the military regime introduced a series of decrees suspending all political and trade union activity, enforcing censorship

on the media and outlawing *Servicio Paz y Justicia* (SERPAJ), the
only independent human rights organization in the country.

In 1983 the member churches of the Inter-Church Committee on
Human Rights in Latin America resolved to enhance the Committee's
capacity to keep its commitment to the Southern Cone and respond
more adequately to the deteriorating situation in the Andean region.
Two additional staff were hired, bringing the total number to five
persons.

From 1983 to the present, Committee staff and members have
participated in numerous missions to South America. Among the
most noteworthy were the 1990 and 1991 missions to Peru which the
Committee co-ordinated together with the Latin American Council
of Churches and the World Council of Churches.

In recent years the Inter-Church Committee on Human Rights in
Latin America has also developed and maintained relationships with
church and human rights organizations in Colombia and has sought
ways to respond to the human rights situation in Brazil. In April
1991, the Committee played a key role in an important fact-finding
mission to Colombia organized by the International Council of
Voluntary Agencies.

How does the Inter-Church Committee
on Human Rights in Latin America carry out its mandate?

From its inception, the Inter-Church Committee on Human
Rights in Latin America was envisioned both to have an active role
in defending victims of human rights abuses and to be a vehicle
through which the Canadian churches could assist Latin Americans
in their struggles against the root causes of such abuses.[14] The original
proposal stated its purpose, "The Latin American churches recognize
that they live a process of liberation which manifests the presence of
God in human history. By participating with Latin American struggles for freedom and justice, Canadian Christians experience the work
of the Gospel. The Committee should continue its active role in the
defence of human rights and refugees from political oppression. It
will assist Canadian churches in their relations with Latin America,
particularly making present the moral and physical support of Canadian Christians in situations of oppression. It will seek the co-operation of other church and non-church groups who share the concern

with promoting human justice and who will stimulate widespread solidarity action when crucial issues arise."[15]

Fundamental to the life and mandate of the Inter-Church Committee on Human Rights in Latin America is the formation of relationships of respect and trust with partners from church, human rights defence and legal aid groups, and from organizations of relatives of the detained-disappeared and of political prisoners in a number of Latin American countries. Close relationships were established with a variety of bodies, including the Archdiocesan Commission of Pastoral Work for Human Rights and for the Marginalized of Sao Paulo, Brazil; the Vicariate of Solidarity and the Foundation of Social Assistance of the Christian Churches in Chile; the Ecumenical Committee for Human Rights and the Permanent Assembly for Human Rights in Argentina; the Episcopal Commission on Social Action of the Roman Catholic Church in Lima, Peru; the Permanent Assembly for Human Rights in Bolivia; the Legal Aid Department of the Archdiocese of San Salvador in El Salvador; the Ecumenical Justice and Peace Committee of Guatemala; and a variety of national secular commissions on human rights. Thanks to the broad nature of its membership, the Inter-Church Committee on Human Rights in Latin America has been able to work closely with a variety of ecumenical partners, gathering first-hand information through on-site visits and regular contact with these colleagues.

Information and action initiatives are shared and developed with other international church partners, including the Human Rights Resource Office on Latin America of the World Council of Churches, directed by the Rev. Charles Harper, the National Council of Churches of Christ in the United States, and the United States Catholic Conference. Close working relationships have also been developed with a variety of other partners, including the Washington Office on Latin America.

In 1987, during an event marking the Inter-Church Committee on Human Rights in Latin America's tenth anniversary, founding committee member Fred Franklin remarked, "Over time, many visits to religious communities in Latin America, as well as return visits by some wonderful human beings, brought us face to face with the tremendous religious faith, buoyancy and steadfastness of the Latin American people. Knowing of the daily terror and persecution in their homelands, this affected us profoundly. It was our constant inspiration as we tried to tell their story to the Canadian public and to influence our government's policies."[16]

These links with partners in the South made the Committee acutely aware not only of the daily struggle for fundamental human rights in Latin America, but also of the daily threats against those who defend human rights.

Refugee/immigration policy and advocacy

The Inter-Church Committee on Human Rights in Latin America's original mandate contemplated "emergency action in response to urgent needs, including projects of concrete assistance to refugees." During its first years, the Committee continued to monitor closely Canadian government policy as it pertained to asylum-seekers from Latin America. It also received appeals for referral and assistance and took on a number of urgent cases.

The reality of refugee work in Canada changed dramatically during the mid-70s, dating principally from the passing of a new Immigration Act in July 1977. In the first six months of 1977, the Inter-Church Committee on Human Rights in Latin America struggled to have changes made to the new immigration bill, C-240. Together with the Inter-Church Project on Population, the Committee presented several proposals to the government. It was particularly concerned with inadequacies in the procedures by which persons who apply for refugee status upon arrival at a Canadian port of entry are assessed.

The Inter-Church Committee on Human Rights in Latin America continued to spearhead the churches' review and critique of the Immigration Act and, in March 1979, it submitted a major brief to the Minister of Immigration on "Recommended Changes in Canada's Refugee Status Determination Procedure." The brief was based on several months of investigation and the co-ordination of refugee cases under deportation order across the country. Following his review, the Minister of Immigration agreed to introduce 8 of the 12 recommended changes. At the same time, the Committee engaged in a series of meetings with the office of the United Nations High Commissioner for Refugees.

With the wave of Canadian interest in refugees from Southeast Asia in 1979 and the recognition of the need to engage in a more thorough and systematic review of Canadian refugee procedures, the churches decided to establish a refugee advocacy and support office.

In January 1980, Kathleen Ptolemy was hired as director of the Refugee Concerns Committee of the Canadian Council of Churches, eventually renamed the Inter-Church Committee for Refugees.

From 1980 on, the Inter-Church Committee for Refugees became the main vehicle through which the churches co-ordinated their joint efforts in the refugee field. The Inter-Church Committee on Human Rights in Latin America has co-operated with the Inter-Church Committee for Refugees in a variety of initiatives during the years, including a number of urgent refugee cases and fact-finding missions to Guatemala and Mexico in August-September 1983 and to Colombia in January 1993.

Other representations to the Canadian government

The Inter-Church Committee on Human Rights in Latin America has engaged in innumerable exchanges with representatives of the government of Canada. In all of its meetings, the Committee has pressed for greater coherence and transparency in policy decision making. The Committee has often raised concerns that Canadian statements on the global stage have not been matched by effective economic measures. Church organizations have asked business and government leaders why Canada is doing business in countries where there are gross violations of human rights and why Canadian dollars and Canadian expertise are being used in any way that reinforces repressive regimes.

Similarly, the Inter-Church Committee on Human Rights in Latin America and other church bodies, particularly Project Ploughshares, have questioned the Canadian government's failure to link human rights questions with a strategy for disarmament or a campaign to stop arms sales to repressive governments. In a 1979 brief prepared for the Canadian Ambassador to the United Nations Commission on Human Rights, the Committee asserted, "our Committee is concerned that Canadian international policy regarding human rights will amount to little more than a colourful balloon if it is not matched and connected with Canadian economic and defence policies."[17]

United Nations representations

In late 1977, the Inter-Church Committee on Human Rights in Latin America received an invitation to make representations to the Canadian delegation preparing for the 1978 session of the United

Nations Commission on Human Rights. The notice was very short and the Committee was unable to participate. However, one year later, in the fall of 1978, it participated in what was to be the first of many more annual consultations.

In the first meeting, the Inter-Church Committee on Human Rights in Latin America submitted a 12-page brief dealing with six countries, along with several hundred pages of supporting dossiers to Ambassador Yvon Beaulne and senior officials from the Department of External Affairs. Such efforts were to become a major focus of the Committee's yearly work plan. Since 1979, the Committee has prepared annual reports on the Latin American countries prioritized by its member churches. These reports are submitted to the Canadian government as well as to other member countries of the U.N. Commission on Human Rights and relevant U.N. bodies.

The decision to dedicate considerable time and energy to the United Nations system is the result of a number of factors. The most important of these was the call from several Latin American counterparts for the assistance of the Inter-Church Committee on Human Rights in Latin America and other church bodies in gaining access to the United Nations system. With its broad ecumenical makeup and the extensive network it had developed overseas, the Committee was able to relate well in government and United Nations circles. A landmark of this work was the witness of Carmen Gloria Quintana, a young Chilean woman who, together with a friend, Rodrigo Rojas, was set on fire in July 1986 by a military patrol. Rojas subsequently died; Carmen Gloria, however, survived despite burns to 62% of her body. With the Inter-Church Committee on Human Rights in Latin America's assistance, Carmen Gloria Quintana was able to testify before the 43rd session of the U.N. Commission on Human Rights in Geneva in March 1987.

Another important element in the decision to be involved in U.N. work was the fact that, since Canada was a member of the U.N. Commission on Human Rights, this forum provided an important occasion for action, an occasion where the Canadian government position was on the line. As the Inter-Church Committee on Human Rights in Latin America's work became better known internationally and its material cited in United Nation's documents or quoted in the speeches of foreign diplomats, the Canadian government began to pay closer attention.

The annual consultations with senior officials from the Department of External Affairs and the Canadian Ambassador to the U.N. Commission on Human Rights, while not without their frustrations, provided opportunities to press for a number of policy initiatives.

The expertise gained has made the Inter-Church Committee on Human Rights in Latin America an important partner to ecumenical and human rights partners participating in the U.N. process. On several occasions, the Committee staff and/or members have participated in World Council of Churches' delegations to the U.N. Commission on Human Rights or the U.N. General Assembly, allowing the Committee to follow more closely Canada's international posture with respect to human rights concerns.

The future?

The Inter-Church Committee on Human Rights in Latin America continues its work in the 1990s faced with new challenges. The brutal military regimes of Latin America in the 1970s have been replaced with civilian governments. While this has theoretically allowed for more 'space' for civil society to organize, real power remains largely with the military and the traditional oligarchies.

Latin American governments have responded with increasing sophistication to international pressure over continued reports of human rights violations. In many countries, governmental human rights commissions have been established, often serving more as public relations instruments than effective mechanisms to eradicate abuses. Impunity for the perpetrators of past and current abuses is widespread.

While the Cold War has ended, many Latin American partners speak of another more ruthless one: that of the growing social and economic inequalities between the North and South. The rigid application of structural adjustment programs and continental economic initiatives such as the "Enterprise for the Americas" and the North American Free Trade Agreement are resulting in a dramatic erosion of the most fundamental rights of millions of Latin Americans.

In 1983, then executive director of the Inter-Church Committee on Human Rights in Latin America Frances Arbour wrote that the issues of human rights and social justice in both Latin America and Canada confronted Canadian Christians with new challenges, "ones that touch on the confluence of church-state relationships and the very purpose of church institutions."[18]

Ten years later, economic realities and political pressures in Canada *continue* to test the commitment of Canadian churches to issues of justice and ecumenical co-operation. Ten years later, Canadian churches *continue* to face the temptation to retreat into narrow denominationalism in their international partnerships as well as in their witness in Canada. Forces opposed to the church taking up its calling to be prophetic and pastoral *continue* to be real in Canada as elsewhere.

For 20 years, the Inter-Church Committee on Human Rights in Latin America and its predecessor have been a sign and symbol of the belief of Canadian churches in the Gospel promise that "all may have life, and have it abundantly."

In 1987, long-time Committee member Fred Franklin reflected that, "We will never know just how much we lightened the burden of our Latin American brothers and sisters. We do know that we gained faith, insight and perspective, tools of analysis and a much clearer understanding of our own situation and part in it."[19]

Today, Latin American sisters and brothers continue to challenge us to live out the Gospel vision by standing with the marginalized and oppressed in Latin America and our own country.

Project Ploughshares

Ernie Regehr

Introduction

Admittedly, Tinseltown is an unusual source of inspiration for Canada's interchurch peace and justice coalitions. Nonetheless, a few years ago, Hollywood served up what seemed to be a routine police thriller that turned out to offer a surprisingly compelling insight into the role of church and other non-governmental groups in pursuing positive social change. The movie *Witness* pits a 'good guy' cop against corrupt colleagues, but its central gimmick is its setting in a rural Amish community. The role of the passive, isolationist Amish in advancing the plot highlights the social and moral power of the 'witness'—or, put another way, the social and moral power of the marginal or powerless. The Amish role as witness in this good guys/bad guys caper takes three distinct forms, all analogous to the social/political roles of the interchurch coalitions in general and certainly to the work of Project Ploughshares.

First there is the Amish child who, on a rare and frightening visit to the city with his mother, becomes eyewitness to a brutal murder in a train station washroom. Having witnessed the bloody killing, he is involved, like it or not. Inevitably his quiet, marginal, sectarian community is drawn into the plot. As the city cops (the bad ones in pursuit of the good cop hero) are drawn into Amish country, this marginal, out-of-it Amish community moves from being a passive eyewitness to actively bearing witness—demonstrating to the sophisticated city-types a way of life outside the conventions of violence that characterize more and more of mainstream society. Then in a powerful closing scene, as the crooked cops, loaded with all manner of weaponry, are about to finish off the hero in what they assume is the anonymity of an isolated backwater Amish farm, neighbouring Amish farmers, warned by a bell someone has managed to ring, descend in buggies and on foot to the scene of the unfolding crime. Unarmed, having left even their pitchforks behind, they circle the bad guys and their powerful arsenals and, simply by observing the scene (witnessing), they deny evil its anonymity and prevent the murder—leaving all, except the bad guys of course, to live happily ever after.

There are several obligatory Hollywood flourishes in the movie, but the theme of the witness works very well. How do churches and others who, though concerned about peace and justice, do not hold the levers of power, become effective agents of change? We become witnesses. First, we are witnesses to evil and therefore involved. Indeed, the point of organizing coalitions and of equipping them with research and travel budgets is to ensure that we become more than the accidental eyewitnesses that our young Amish boy was. Instead, we systematically identify injustice. And not only do we witness the bloody event, but an eyewitness has the authenticity to finger the one who 'dunit.' The eyewitness has knowledge to corroborate an allegation, to identify the culpable and to rob us of our collective non-involvement. Second, the churches, through the coalitions, bear witness to 'another way.' In the case of Project Ploughshares, this means the articulation of approaches to the security question which reject the notion of 'armed fortress security' in favour of principles of 'common security' (more on that later). And finally, the churches keep a standing watch, monitor social, political and military events and by such witnessing rob evil of its anonymity—a reminder to politicians at home and around the world that they are being watched, that there are witnesses out there who will not let the crime go unnoticed. This is the essence of Amnesty International's letter writing on behalf of prisoners of conscience; it is what Project Ploughshares means when it calls for 'transparency' in arms dealing.

Theological issues

Witnessing for peace and justice, of course, produces a theologically loaded agenda. Issues are informed, or sometimes clouded, by rich but diverse Christian traditions—traditions which an ecumenical coalition of one and a half decades' duration is not likely to bring into pristine harmony. But we deal with some problems by ignoring them—which in effect was the Ploughshares' strategy regarding theology. Besides the fact that some of the sponsors of Project

Ploughshares are secular organizations, the churches themselves quickly found that the information and analysis concerning current issues of militarism, arms control and disarmament, and conflict and war would be most useful if they were not first put through a theological screen. All information comes with a set of assumptions and Ploughshares information is no exception—it comes with the assumption that war is to be avoided, the use of force is to be minimized and conflict is to be resolved as much as possible in the interests of justice and without resort to violence. All the sponsors, in their varying Christian traditions or in their secular ethical orientations, share these basic values. So information is gathered and disseminated on that basis, with the church denominations putting it through their own theological screens within their own structures.

But in the process, something remarkable has happened on this theological agenda. In the last two decades the Christian traditions have evolved significantly. It is not that traditions have been abandoned. Rather, the churches found, when they turned to the fundamental war/peace teachings of each tradition, that the differences are much smaller than one might expect. This came through in Canada with exhilarating clarity during the 1990-91 Persian Gulf crisis and war. In the course of responding to that crisis, Christian groups as varied as the Anglicans, the Roman Catholics, the Evangelical Fellowship of Canada and the Mennonites, looking deep within their own teachings and understandings, all came to the urgent conclusion that the war could not be morally justified. It is not so surprising that pacifists concluded that resort to war was wrong and that states had a moral obligation to find non-military solutions. But in this instance, churches, and others in the churches who relied on the insights of the 'just war' tradition, concluded that in these circumstances states had a moral obligation to find non-military solutions.

One key to this evolution was the antinuclear movement of the 1980s. Then the just war tradition turned out to be a guide, not to the justification of war, as in perception and practice it frequently had become, but to understanding the limits of acceptable force. And in the nuclear debate, many mainstream Christian denominations concluded that nuclear weapons clearly violated the requirements for proportion and avoidance of non-combatants. Catholics, Anglicans and some evangelicals became in effect nuclear pacifists. That is, they held that under no circumstances could justice be served by the use of nuclear weapons and that in turn it is wrong as a matter of policy to threaten to do that which, if it were done, would clearly be immoral and unjustified.

Out of that debate, the same traditions took another look at conventional war. It was acknowledged that the general experience of modern war is that many more civilians are killed than combatants and that such war destroys entire societies and social orders. Given this, the same conclusion must be reached as in the case of nuclear war—that is, under no circumstances is the resort to war within the bounds of 'the justified use of force.' This was not an argument for pacifism, but the pacifists and the 'just war' folk have obviously come a lot closer together. There remain many circumstances in which justice requires the use of military force, but largely in the manner of policing and patrolling as part of the task of preventing war. So the 'just war' ethic is in the process of being restated in terms of the circumstances under which the use of military force can be justified—and many are now concluding that, just as these circumstances could never permit the use of nuclear weapons, so they cannot permit warfare of any kind. Pacifists in some cases have also recognized the role of the restrained use of military force and coercion—for example, its minimal use in peacekeeping operations. Some extend legitimacy to limited military actions such as enforcing arms embargoes or protecting innocent victims of terrorism.

An evolving peace agenda

When Ploughshares began in the mid-1970s, disarmament and arms control were not on the action agenda of Canadian churches. Issues of militarism were, but they were seen primarily in the context of underdevelopment and human rights concerns. The link to underdevelopment was specifically articulated in the report of the Brandt Commission in the early 1970s, while the link between militarism and repression was most obviously witnessed by the churches through their involvements in South Africa and Central America.

Militarism, both as an impediment to development and as a means of repression, was the particular preoccupation of Murray Thomson and Ernie Regehr when they met in early 1976 to explore a joint study project. Thomson was at the time the executive director of CUSO and Regehr had just returned from a three-year Mennonite Central Committee (Canada) study assignment in southern Africa.

Both had witnessed first-hand the way in which military spending drained cash and military security obsessions drained energy and confidence from the development enterprise. The study project was premised on the ancient vision of transforming the material and human wealth now consumed by military preparations into resources for human development—hence 'Project Ploughshares.'[1]

In its original mandate, Project Ploughshares was described as a "working group on militarism and under-development." As we understood the issue at the time, Third World societies were being militarized as a means by which the superpowers could extend their influence over those regions of the globe in which their interests resided. In the Cold War, that amounted to everywhere. East and West sought to carve out spheres of influence and to develop political and economic relations with emerging states, drawing them into their respective spheres of influence. Military links were understood by the suppliers to be especially useful for establishing recipient dependence—cementing a sponsor-client relationship. Canadian policy and practice were understood by Ploughshares to be parasitic to this process, rather than central to it. Canadian military exports to the Third World represented Canadian participation in a process of global militarization, which was controlled by others.

The 1970s were a decade of rapid militarization in the Third World, with massive increases in military spending and military imports. In the latter 1970s there were also sharp increases in Canada's military spending, and the two trends together were making an increasing impact on churches and the non-governmental organization community in Canada.

Also during 1976, John Foster of the United Church convened a group which began meeting to look at emerging issues in Canadian defence policy. The earlier Trudeau freeze on the defence budget had been lifted and a major re-equipping process was getting under way. This new focus on Canadian military preparedness raised concerns and in some church circles—notably the United Church group CANDA (Canadian Defence Alternatives)—an interest in alternatives. The two initiatives got together as Project Ploughshares, combining both areas of concern—witnessing against the militarism that impedes development and self-determination, and exploring alternative, less militaristic, national security strategies with a particular, but not exclusive, focus on Canada. The latter was in some sense at least a consequence of the former and concerns about the former were further focussed by the first United Nations Special Session on Disarmament in 1978.

Originally planned more as a response to global militarization trends, this first Session on Disarmament was heavily influenced by another kind of militarization, that is, the Carter administration's changing security policies. President Jimmy Carter, in an effort to shore up his credentials within the American right wing, was busy backtracking on his earlier commitments to restrict arms sales and to control and reduce nuclear arms. His Presidential Directive 59 set forth an aggressive strategic agenda, including the development of nuclear war-fighting strategies, and galvanised a growing opposition. But for all his tilt to the right, Carter could head off neither the Reagan attack, nor the revival of the Cold War in the 1980s. Ronald Reagan's scary rhetoric and scarier nuclear policy decisively shifted the world's attention, as well as that of the churches and non-governmental organizations in Canada, to the nuclear threat. This had a profound impact on Project Ploughshares and its relations with the churches in two ways: first, it led to the emergence of Ploughshares-affiliated local groups and, second, it meant a growing reliance in the churches on Ploughshares for reliable information and alternative analysis of the nuclear arms race.

Forming the coalition

The development of Ploughshares local groups had begun during the lead up to the first U.N. Special Session on Disarmament in 1978. Ploughshares staff travelled across Canada conducting workshops and holding information sessions on the issues to be debated at the U.N. sessions and on related Canadian policies. In many instances, concerned groups decided to stay together and to maintain a relationship with the Ploughshares office. This process accelerated during the period of the early Reagan years, when there was an explosion of peace groups. In the larger cities, coalitions of peace and justice groups formed to protest the nuclear insanity.

By mid-1977 Ploughshares had officially become a project of the Canadian Council of Churches. It was an unusual arrangement, through which the Council became the definer and custodian of the Ploughshares mandate, but not the direct overseer of the implementation of that mandate. Instead, the Council called on churches and other institutions who shared the basic vision to come together to form a Project Ploughshares Board and take responsibility for carrying out the mandate. This meant that the Ploughshares Board could not change the group's mandate, which remained the prerogative of the Council, but was given free rein to develop appropriate programs. This resulted in a kind of hybrid ecumenical coalition which, while fully under the mandate and responsibility of the churches in the Canadian Council of Churches, operated under the guidance of a Board that included representatives of churches, non-church groups such as Oxfam, CUSO and the Voice of Women, and what were known as Ploughshares local groups, the community groups that were emerging across the country and linked to the national office.

This three-way marriage, made well this side of the pearly gates, had its strengths and weaknesses. The strengths became most obvious in the early 1980s when Canadians joined millions around the world in taking to the streets and protesting the madness of MAD (the strategic nuclear deterrence doctrine of Mutually Assured Destruction). The Ploughshares local groups gave us a strong profile in local communities and were able to multiply the impact of the research, publishing and advocacy work of the national office. Local groups also had an important hand in prompting local church communities to respond to the nuclear crisis.

The weaknesses, or tensions, in this three-way marriage were of course rooted in the divergent needs of each of the constituent groups. The development agency sponsors had joined the effort as a result of their direct stake in addressing one aspect of militarization, that is, militarism as an impediment to development. They found that their issues were largely unaffected by the rapid shift in focus to nuclear militarism. As a result, the development agencies became somewhat marginalized. While the churches and local groups were both now keenly interested in nuclear issues, each had quite different needs. The local groups needed from the national office a torrent of relevant facts and figures portrayed so compellingly and simply as to be useful in the mass mobilization and education efforts. The churches, on the other hand, looked to the national office for research and analysis on which to build institutional policy and on which to base their production of popular education materials for use in congregations.

For their part, the churches were profoundly affected by the resurgent Cold War. This was one of those rare instances, at least in some denominations, of a reversal of the usual pattern, in which the head office develops various progressive ideas and tries to sell them to a cautious constituency. In the context of the nuclear threat, conference and synod offices were inundated with calls from concerned parents who, for example, wanted to know whether the church had any materials to help them talk to their children about nuclear nightmares. Local 'international concerns' committees were being forced to respond to concerns about the nuclear threat and they in turn went to head offices to find out what the policy actually was. In many cases, the policies were in serious need of updating—a need which helped to bring the churches more directly into collaboration with Project Ploughshares.

Having originated outside official church circles, it had always been a struggle for Ploughshares to insert itself into the ecumenical family. It was in the heat of the nuclear debate that Ploughshares finally became accepted and relied on by the national churches. An important event in cementing this relationship was the churches' interest in presenting a common statement of concern to the Prime Minister. In 1982 and 1983 Canadian church leaders met with the Prime Minister of the day and presented statements drafted by Project Ploughshares specifically on the subject of nuclear weapons. Perhaps for the first time, Canadian mainline churches were challenged to articulate their faith in the context of obvious respect for their country and its institutions, a respect tempered by the knowledge of a nuclear strategy which claimed to protect the valued rights and freedoms enjoyed in Canada by threatening life on an extraordinary scale. The church leaders addressed the issue of nuclear weapons in the "knowledge that God continues to place before all people the choice between life and death." Their statement goes to the centre of the churches' approach to defence issues:

"We speak out of the knowledge that God desires for all people the abundant life of peace with justice, and are moved first to repent of our too easy acquiescence to the powers of injustice and death. The churches have too often remained silent and not understood, as the South African theologian Allan Boesak told the World Council of Churches last summer, 'that every act of inhumanity, every unjust law, every untimely death, every utterance of faith in weapons of mass destruction, every justification of violence and oppression is a sacrifice on the altar of the false gods of death; it is a denial of the Lord of life.'

"To choose life is to acknowledge that we are called to be not so much rulers as stewards of God's earth. And because we have regard for the security of the earth for not only this but also succeeding generations, we cannot accept as 'defence' any measures which threaten the planet itself.

"While we honour, and seek to preserve and strengthen, national and international institutions that serve justice, we acknowledge the transitory character of all human institutions. This knowledge leads us to place clear limits on measures that may justifiably be taken in defence of human institutions. Ultimately, human loyalty is owed only to God and when defence of human institutions undermines the abundant life of God's people and threatens His earth, then we must regard it as contrary to the will of God.

"This has particular implications for our attitude towards nuclear weapons, and we must say without reservation that nuclear weapons are ultimately unacceptable as agents of national security. *We can conceive of no circumstances under which the use of nuclear weapons could be justified and consistent with the will of God, and we must therefore conclude that nuclear weapons must also be rejected as means of threat or deterrence"* [emphasis added].

From the Defence White Paper to promoting 'common security'

The articulation of an unambiguous, principled position on nuclear weapons carried over into the churches' response to the Canadian government's Defence White Paper a few years later. Born a Cold-War cliché, the 1987 Defence White Paper came to be regarded by hawks and doves alike as an abject failure to offer any credible answers to Canadian peace and security questions. It misread the international security climate, proposed ill-conceived equipment acquisitions and either ignored or misunderstood the economic climate of the day. Its one positive contribution was to generate what is a rarity in Canada, a public debate of defence and security issues.

That debate was joined by the churches from within the broad perspective of what was called 'common security'—that is, peace and the prevention of war were understood, as militarism had been a decade earlier, in the context of political and economic justice, as well as environmental sustainability. During the latter 1980s the

churches in particular were losing their patience for a peace witness
that functioned as a protest movement. In development and human
rights policies, churches had joined the search for alternatives. Not
only were they obviously active in development projects and in
documenting human rights violations, but the churches were directly
engaged, domestically and through international institutions, in
developing and proposing alternative development policies and
formulating minimum human rights standards. Given that governments were themselves in search of new approaches to security while
the old verities of 'evil empires' and 'communist conspiracies' were
evaporating, the churches as well as community groups were anxious
to be fully involved in the debate about new directions. While the
early stages of the Defence White Paper debate took place within
old, though changing, Cold-War paradigms, the Ploughshares/church
response document was in fact a pioneering effort at applying the
common-security perspective to the much narrower question of
defence policy.

The churches' brief responded to some fundamental questions.
First, do the Canadian Armed Forces defend Canada? For the answer
to be Yes, we said that two conditions must obtain: there must be a
recognizable (or potential) threat to the territory and sovereignty of
Canada and such a threat must come from a force or enemy that is
at least theoretically amenable to military defeat. If there is no threat
that a good army could either defeat or keep at bay, the role of the
army is clearly diminished.

In Canada's case, in fact, no such threat was or is imminent.
Even when the Cold War was at its most frigid, mainstream Canadian
security analysis denied that there were direct *military* threats to
Canada. No one was or is trying to invade, to grab a piece of our
territory, or to overthrow our government or constitution by military
force.

There being no military threat specific to Canada, it follows that
the Canadian Armed Forces offer no defence. The churches noted
that this is obviously a circumstance to be celebrated, but acknowledged that, for the most part, it has added complexity rather than
simplicity to Canadian defence planning. A clear threat would have
simplified defence planning, which, no doubt, is why the white paper
first took on the job of dishing up a real defence problem, the old
Soviet threat. Hoping also to inject new zip into the Defence Depart-

ment's capital budget, the white paper set out to sell Canadians credible targets for a proposed arsenal of new weapons.

But the churches' brief seemed to beg the question: there may not now be a direct military threat to Canada, but what if one should emerge? What would the churches then say about defence policy? What if a hitherto friendly superpower decided that true friendship might require 'military assistance' (the usual euphemism for invasion)? Would it then make common-security sense to develop a military capability to repel it?

This was not an easy question for the churches to answer. Throughout the postwar period, it has actually been widely assumed that Canada is not militarily defendable. No matter how grand a military we might assemble, Canadian territory is too large, the coastline too long and the population too sparse, to mount any credible defence against a determined assailant. But the critical point for small, vulnerable powers like Canada is this: Is being militarily undefendable the same as being helpless? The defence of Canada, according to the common-security principles articulated by Project Ploughshares and the churches, cannot be accomplished through military might. Indeed, this is the case for virtually all states, even superpowers (in the sense that they have no defence against nuclear threats save counterthreats). It is the attempts to mount military defences that have helped create the currently over-armed, underfed and environmentally threatened world.

For Canada, as for all states, national defence as the protection of the integrity of national territory and governing institutions depends on a world order that respects all countries' national boundaries and their right to manage their own affairs. This led churches to conclude that the role of the military on Canadian territory is not to demonstrate a capacity to fight and win a war of national defence, but rather to monitor and police Canada's borders and territory so that violations could be detected and brought to the attention of the international community for reprobation. The international community's recognition of the legitimacy of Canadian sovereignty and territory rests in turn and substantially on the perception that we as a country are meeting the requirements for the responsible management of our affairs, internally and externally.

In extreme cases, when countries are viewed to be in chaos (Somalia) or to be run by thugs (Iraq, Grenada, Panama), they obviously become especially vulnerable to invasion (sometimes based on international consensus, sometimes based on a powerful neighbour's perception of self-interest). The point is not to shift the blame onto the victims, but the U.S. invasion of Panama, for example, met minimal international criticism largely due to the assumption that things had grown intolerable. In a similar way, Panama, Grenada and Afghanistan, for example, neglected their real defence, namely, the maintenance of a system of order and government that earned the respect and political protection of the international community. Sovereignty in the Somalia of 1992 is hardly of the same value as it is in states with stable, functioning governments (which is not to say that Somalia's dysfunction stems primarily from indigenous causes).

Canadian security thus depends substantially on Canada being a responsible member of an international community—that is, on how we manage our affairs, maintain a just domestic order, respect international law and even develop a clear, unambiguous sense of ourselves as an independent country. While these conditions do not obtain to perfection in Canada, they are present and their preservation and enhancement offer the only credible defence against invasion. Superpower invasions of smaller states invariably turn on a pretence (for example, alleged chaos or an invitation from a puppet regime), so part of Canada's (or any country's) defence is to deny a superpower a pretence and thus to ensure that the international community would find invasion to be without justification and unacceptable. That kind of political restraint is the only effective limit that can be put on a superpower's action toward its weaker neighbours or clients.

The same international community that is Canada's only defence against invasion is also the Third World's only defence. "Just, participatory, and sustainable societies," in the words of the World Council of Churches, are the best insurance against foreign invasion.

In the defence debate of the latter 1980s, the question of vulnerability to foreign intervention was an issue—not in the sense of the threat of direct military invasion, but in the sense of the gradual erosion of Canadian sovereignty, particularly in the Arctic. Canada has long had something of a complex over sovereignty. The Armed Forces are supposed to protect it, the Americans never fully recognize it and federal governments can never quite avoid the suspicion that they're prepared to squander it. Typically, sovereignty is characterized as a possession or a dependant which we are in danger of losing if we don't protect it or which will atrophy if we don't exercise it regularly. The assumption is that unless attention is paid to sovereignty in some overt way, it will erode. This, in turn, produces all that anxiety and political controversy because it is hard to agree on just how much exercise the thing needs. And not just any attention will do—real serious sovereignty protection is assumed to depend especially on a military presence and control.

Ploughshares' common-security doctrine concedes that to carry out national responsibility within one's territory requires some measure of 'control.' But we add two important qualifications: the first is that control and authority measures should be related exclusively to real law enforcement or security needs (and not to an abstract idea about the 'exercise' of sovereignty), and the second is that such control does not need to be (and, in fact, usually isn't) military.

The challenge to churches in being prescriptive about defence policy is to find the right balance. On the one hand, there must be the clear Christian acknowledgment of the reality of a fallen world in which the innocent are frequently vulnerable to abuse from the powerful or the just plain criminal. On the other hand, there must be the equally clear Christian imperative to elevate human relationships to emulate more adequately Jesus' model of non-violence. Different streams within the Christian tradition historically have emphasized different elements of this equation, but in the present circumstance in Canada one can detect some merging of these traditions. As noted earlier, mainline churches have adopted, through their evolution toward nuclear pacifism, a much more cautious, perhaps suspicious, attitude toward the use of force. The pacifist tradition, due in part to extensive involvement in situations of conflict on behalf of the victims of war, now also acknowledges that moral opposition to violence must be backed up by policies and strategies to minimize violence, if it is to be relevant. In the absence of any reliable means to eliminate the resort to violence in human affairs, the pursuit of more peace frequently means searching for lesser evils.

Toward a just world order

These dilemmas and challenges are no less a part of the post-Cold War era. In a sense, the most important Canadian defence policy question now is, "Can the Armed Forces of Canada make a contribution beyond our borders to international stability and the prevention of global war?" The question, "How do we defend ourselves?" has little urgency in the absence of a direct military threat. The pertinent question is, "How do we use our resources and geography to help prevent war and to support a just world order?"

The end of the Cold War has obviously refocussed the question of how we go about establishing a world order of stability and equity. It is not a new question for the churches—indeed it was the founding question of Project Ploughshares. By the end of 1989 and the fall of the Berlin Wall, 15 years after the founding of Ploughshares, our agenda had come full circle. Particularly with the Persian Gulf crisis of 1990 and 1991, we were back to the issue of the arms trade with a vengeance—and, for the first time, much of the rest of the world seemed to be interested as well. The critical questions of sovereignty and the justification of intervention are raised afresh. Ploughshares approaches these questions with the assumption that Canadian policy beyond its borders ought to be consistent with policies pursued within its borders. Thus, in order to build a just international order, all states can ensure that their own territory is not a threat to that order. For example, Canada can ensure that its territory is not used by, nor is in any way available to, those who would destabilize and threaten world order and equity militarily.

Prime Minister Mackenzie King was on the right track when he assured President Roosevelt that Canada would not allow the United States to be attacked through Canada. Calling it the obligation of 'a good friendly neighbour,' King declared that "enemy forces should not be able to pursue their way either by land, sea or air, to the United States across Canadian territory." In other words, Canada has a responsibility to ensure that direct military threats to the United States are neither launched from Canadian territory nor made possible by virtue of Canadian neglect.

This implies that Canada must take charge of its own territory to assure neighbours, north and south, that the other is not surreptitiously using Canadian territory as a platform from which to threaten them. Canada cannot possibly give any assurance to the satisfaction of either neighbour if it has no demonstrable capacity to carry out the necessary air and sea surveillance. So it is a contribution to international stability and the prevention of nuclear war for Canada to provide reliable peacetime patrol and surveillance of its territory between two still dangerous nuclear superpowers.

But—and this is a very big 'but'—this is exclusively a peacetime role and the size of this task should be determined by the size of the threat. This means that it is a minimal role. The point is to provide reasonable transparency in peacetime *for the purpose of preventing war*; the point is *not* to provide a strategic staging area from which to fight a war.

This domestic role really defines the basis for peacekeeping. Through peacekeeping, the international community acknowledges the importance of assisting states in maintaining internal patrol and surveillance capabilities when their own domestic circumstances make it impossible for them to do it themselves. Similarly, new models of humanitarian intervention and international enforcement measures are built on the same principle of helping states carry out national responsibilities—including meeting basic human needs and respecting minimal human rights standards. (This is so no matter what one thinks of specific interventions.)

A key element of the work of Project Ploughshares and other extraparliamentary opposition movements in the 1980s was to call for new ways of seeing the world—challenging the East-West, Cold-War, 'evil empire' lenses that framed and shaped our views of the world. In other words, these groups bore witness to 'another way.' This other way of seeing the world was most clearly articulated in the report of the Palme Commission, which early on gave currency to the language of common security.

If we think of our own community as the world and of our home as one of the many states in that community, the absurdity of the present international security regime comes into focus. In our own homes we accept certain basic security responsibilities—like locking our doors and windows. These are sensible responsibilities that members of a community must meet, not only for their own immediate benefit, but also for the benefit of the entire community (and thus also for their own long-term benefit).

But when a burglar has come through the door, either because the door was unlocked or because he forced his way in, security is no longer our individual responsibility. It is then a community responsibility. It is not required of our families that we stock arsenals of weapons and arrange for daily family shooting-practice, just to be prepared for whatever may present itself. If the worst happens, our responsibility is to appeal to the community and its police force, which we support with our taxes.

Things obviously work a little differently in the world community. There, every house on the block must be armed to the teeth to meet all possible threats. Each household stocks an arsenal, trains its inhabitants in the finer points of street fighting and makes regular trips to the local weapons dealer for new equipment (and to the bank for new credit). It is a formula for chaos and the brutalization of social and political relationships. What would happen to the social relations in our homes if we had to stock weapons to meet all comers? It would not only be the hapless burglars who would be brutalized: the main victims would be our own households. The normal arguments and quarrels, the exercise of parental prerogative and authority, the normal and healthy rebellion of teenagers—all of these social interactions and developments would be radically altered. They would become perverted and destructive as a result of the militarization of the home.

Of course, that is precisely the effect of militarization in the international community. An international-security regime that requires every country to maintain an arsenal to meet all potential threats to its security is a regime that inevitably (and sometimes, it seems, irretrievably) brutalizes societies. Heavily militarized societies, without exception, concentrate decision making in elite circles and deny popular participation in that process. Militarized societies, as surely as night follows day, engage in officially sanctioned violence against their citizens. Human rights are violated, civil rights are abrogated—and the weekly grocery money is spent to buy and maintain the weapons.

That was the chief lesson of the Cold War: the decades-long militarization of relations between and within states does not make states and communities secure; it brutalizes. It defines the old world order and when past President George Bush talked about a new world order, it was in effect a defining moment for the post-Cold War peace movement and the peace witness of the churches. When the Gulf War came crashing in on us, it exposed the fallacies of the current international military order with stunning clarity. George Bush and the U.N.-blessed coalition of anti-Iraq forces fought a convincing villain in the person and regime of Saddam Hussein, but getting him out of Kuwait was just the occasion for war, not its purpose. Many at the time took offence at the notion that the United States needed a Middle East war as part of its pursuit of a position of prevailing influence in a region long considered central to its economic and political interests. Yet when the occasion presented itself, war quickly took on the appearance of necessity. It seemed to be necessary in order to destroy Iraq's offensive military capacity and to make way for the externally designed reshaping of the region in the resulting chaos, to rid America of its lingering complex over defeat in Vietnam and to establish American military power as the final arbiter of the post-Cold War order.

Some people still insist that the attacks and mayhem of the Gulf War were the founding acts of a new international order. Somehow, it looks a lot like the old world order, a prominent characteristic of which is the inclination to regularly produce wars to end war and more wars to initiate new world orders. The Gulf crisis fit the old world order very well: it showed an undiminished faith in the proposition that war remains a useful and available means to serve the greater good. Widespread enthusiasm for a war fought to avoid future war and to bring about a new world order is the most persuasive evidence we have that we remain entrenched in the old world order— hamstrung by tired thinking and condemned to continue fighting futile wars. And, of course, it is persuasive evidence of an unfinished agenda for Project Ploughshares and the churches.

In many respects it is the same old agenda. Despite dramatic gains in the control of nuclear arms, thousands of warheads remain poised to deliver the world into nuclear oblivion. Despite a vaunted downturn in the international arms market, the world still bristles with sophisticated, lethal means of destruction and a surplus capacity to build replacements. The Gulf crisis, Yugoslavia, Somalia and all the other wars still raging, remind the churches not only of the speed with which the world's stock of weapons can transform political conflict into military combat, but also of the extent of the poverty of the world when it comes to the effective and peaceful settlement of disputes. This has led Ploughshares to propose a new initiative to focus on regional conflict and 'world order' issues.

The decision to develop a program of response to regional conflicts is not based on an inflated view of the role of churches and other non-governmental organizations in resolving conflicts that are fundamentally political and the responsibility of the state. But it is based on the assumption that there is a role. In a sense, it is analogous to the role of non-governmental organizations in economic development. While it is fundamentally the responsibility of governments to adopt the policies and create the conditions necessary for equitable economic development, it is also understood that they can't do this on their own. Governments need the help of non-governmental groups and institutions; indeed, there are some things that even some governments recognize the non-governmental organizations likely can do more effectively (for example, community development). Similarly, while the task of resolving interstate and intrastate conflicts is the responsibility of states, it ought to be clear by now that they cannot manage it entirely on their own. Not only do they need help, but there are elements of the process of resolving conflict for which the involvement of citizen groups might soon be regarded as indispensable. Unofficial diplomacy assumes that the job of building social consensus and resolving endemic conflicts is the responsibility of civil society, at least as much as it is the responsibility of government; hence it is sometimes called 'citizen diplomacy.'

For Project Ploughshares, the 1990s are surprisingly reminiscent of the mid-1970s—a period of global militarization which undermines economic development and produces intolerable human rights violations, persistent regional conflict and an uncontrolled arms trade, all precariously perched under an uncertain nuclear umbrella. (The nuclear arms agreements of early 1993 could eventually get nuclear arsenals down to pre-1976 levels.)

The agenda is familiar, but some things are radically different. One of the conditions that has changed most is ourselves. The churches today have a resource of which they only dreamt in the mid-1970s, that is, a series of effective interchurch coalitions capable of conducting sustained research, carrying out advocacy campaigns and organizing communities across the entire country. One fears that all of this and much more will be needed to face the challenges of the 1990s.

The Inter-Church Committee for Refugees

Henriette Thompson[1]

The 1970s will be remembered in Canadian church history as the decade of a novel and dynamic ecumenical experiment, a time of intense church co-operation to promote global and national justice and peace. The shape that this new ecumenism assumed was the 'coalition' in which, generally, three or more denominations united to engage in research and public action on issues as diverse as international trade and the defence of aboriginal rights. The frontline participants in these coalitions continue to be, for the most part, a blend of researchers and activists retained by the co-operating churches, denominational program staff and a sprinkling of volunteers drawn from the wider church constituencies. In late 1979 when the Inter-Church Committee for Refugees took shape—it was called the Refugee Concerns Project until May 1981—there were already a number of coalitions at work and making waves from Yellowknife to Cape Town, including GATT-Fly/the Ecumenical Coalition for Economic Justice, Project North/the Aboriginal Rights Coalition, Ten Days for World Development and the Taskforce on the Churches and Corporate Responsibility. It was only natural and even inevitable that the new refugee committee would assume the coalition form.

The beginnings: The Inter-Church Project on Population

The 1973 coup which brought General Augusto Pinochet into power in Chile and the 1974 United Nations Conference on Population in Bucharest marked critical turnings in the trail of events that finally led to the establishment of the Inter-Church Committee for Refugees in late 1979.

Formed by the Presbyterian, Lutheran, United, Roman Catholic, Anglican and Christian Reformed Churches to influence Canadian and American government policies going into the Bucharest Conference, the Inter-Church Project on Population found a new mission in the post-conference months. Bernard Daly of the Canadian Conference of Catholic Bishops, a prime mover in the Inter-Church Project on Population saga, recalls, "Back home after Bucharest, the Canadian government waited only a few months before disclosing that the population 'problem' that would be attacked as a follow-up to Bucharest was immigration. The Green Paper on Immigration was tabled in 1975.

"The Inter-Church Project on Population was ready to lead a public debate. Immigration Canada granted the Inter-Church Project on Population $50,000 in response to a detailed proposal. The 'national' Inter-Church Project on Population, upon learning that the federal government planned to have a joint committee of parliament go to every province, organized ten 'provincial' Inter-Church Projects on Population. Everywhere the committee went, the Inter-Church Project on Population was sure to go with the argument that, instead of building the palisade of a 'new and better' immigration act, Canada should plan and develop a 'new domestic economic order' that would assure jobs and security for both newcomers and those already living in Canada.

"The government committee fought off the Inter-Church Project on Population's broader arguments with the reply that they had the mandate only to look at immigration. The draft bill eventually was tabled. The Inter-Church Project on Population linked up with the Inter-Church Committee on Human Rights in Latin America to campaign for amendments. In particular, we drafted an entire section for regulating the treatment of refugees and using different criteria than those used for immigrants.

"The Inter-Church Project on Population went into its 'sunset' mode after the Immigration Act came into effect in 1978. However, that fall many of us came together again for a meeting at the Canadian Council of Churches offices in Toronto. The federal Immigration Department presented some ideas for helping refugees. We responded with ideas that led to the 'umbrella agreements' and all the other details that would become the agenda of ICCR, which emerged from that 1979 group."[2]

Working with the Inter-Church Committee on Human Rights in Latin America

In 1974, George Cram of the Anglican national office, John Foster of the United Church national office, Fran Arbour of the Latin American Working Group, Tim Draimin of the Jesuit Centre for Social Faith and Justice in Toronto and Fred Franklin of the Society of Friends in Toronto teamed together, with official blessing, in the Inter-Church Committee on Chile, later to become the Inter-Church Committee on Human Rights in Latin America. This group quickly became aware that a double-pronged program in Canada was required with regard to events in Chile and the rest of the Southern Cone, one focussing on the violation of human rights in the country of origin and the other specializing in the detailed involvements of refugee determination in Canada.

At the end of 1973, Chilean refugees took over the Canadian embassy in Santiago. Many Chileans flew directly to Canada without going through Canadian immigration procedures in Chile itself where they could be spotted by agents of the Chilean state security and listed for possible interrogation, incarceration, torture and death. These Chileans were the first significant group of in-country claimants to refugee status in Canada. This situation initiated a sharp debate between the churches and the government over the strict definition of a refugee as someone who is outside his or her country. The churches, through the Inter-Church Project on Population and the Inter-Church Committee on Human Rights in Latin America, pressured for the humane treatment of people who feared persecution for even requesting asylum. This led the government to create a special 'designated class' of refugee, one whereby a person suffering persecution and unable to leave the country safely could obtain Canadian refugee status while within their own country. The late Kathleen Ptolemy explained this mechanism in her article, "From Oppression to Promise: Journeying Together with the Refugee."[3] Problems arose, however, when the government used the designated-class mechanism to justify removing its visa exemption for people within refugee-producing countries. The churches then took the approach of stating that Canada does have the right to control its borders, but that where Canada is a 'logical and accessible' haven, that is, where it is within geographical or airline proximity (like Guatemala or Chile), a visa should not be required. Since this debate began, it has continued to dominate the Committee's work: how to balance the right of the state to control its borders with the right of refugees to protection from persecution.

Focussing on immigration policy

The new Immigration Act of 1978 ratified for the first time in law the 1951 U.N. Convention and the 1967 U.N. Protocol on Refugees. Principles of fundamental justice laid out by the churches in the mid-1970s were not seriously reflected in the Immigration Act, which seemed to be based on the premise that there would be few refugee claimants overall. These principles were: the right of a refugee claimant to appear in person and present his or her case before the people who make the decision, the right to know and to respond to information that can be used against him or her, the right to know the reasons for the decision in his or her case, and the right to be assisted in obtaining competent legal counsel.

The postwar refugee sponsorship provisions in the Immigration Act had been rescinded in 1950. This meant the imposition of immigration selection criteria on refugees. In the 1978 Immigration Act provision was made for sponsorship of refugees and the Minister of Immigration instituted a program wherein any five or more people could sponsor a refugee or refugee family, providing the sponsors could look after the refugee's material needs of shelter, food and clothing for at least one year.

In 1978, the tragic drama of the Vietnamese 'boat people' forced itself upon international consciousness. The desire to sponsor the boat people held in Hong Kong and Malaysian camps became widespread across Canada.

During this period Canadians became more aware of two needs: the need for refuge for the disabled and aged, and the need for back-up for sponsors who wished to help but were uncertain of their ability to provide financial assistance for one whole year. The result was an agreement with the Immigration Department that regional or national bodies like churches and service clubs sign Master Agreements. In this way the government hoped primarily to avoid the cumbersome bureaucracy of sponsorships.

The role of the National Inter-Faith Immigration Committee

Until the late 1970s, when the churches acted ecumenically on immigration matters, they did so in the National Inter-Faith Immigration Committee, which included Jewish participation. From the 1950s onward, this Committee, with the help of government funding, assisted in the resettlement of hundreds of refugees who came through the normal immigration offices attached to Canadian embassies. The Hungarians in 1956, the Czechs in 1968 and the Ugandans in 1973 were welcomed at this end of the 'air bridge.' An honest effort was made to have representatives of their own faith receive them locally or for others to assist them where this tie-in was not possible.

The National Inter-Faith Immigration Committee was uncomfortable with the policy approach of the Inter-Church Committee on Human Rights in Latin America and resisted the call to involve itself in advocacy. In the minds of Inter-Church Committee on Human Rights in Latin America members and many other church workers, there was urgent need in 1978 for an assertive ecumenical structure, able and willing to make overtures to Canada Employment and Immigration on questions of refugee status and on the content of Master Agreements. This need was critical by 1979. When the National Inter-Faith Immigration Committee refused to budge, the members of the Inter-Church Committee on Human Rights in Latin America resolved not to be diverted from their human rights work.

There were several factors contributing to the formation of the Inter-Church Committee for Refugees. There was strong, unequivocal interchurch support for refugees which was based in a sense of mission and of the way Canadian Christians saw their role in the world. In addition, there was a clear biblical basis for treating the refugee as neighbour. Other factors which contributed were the postwar resettlement previously mentioned, port chaplaincies as outreach efforts, the living memory of the Social Gospel movement, and Vatican and (Anglican) Lambeth encyclicals. All these factors strengthened this compassion and the desire to hear the voice of those needing refuge. Daily media coverage and aid agency publicity about refugee situations in Pakistan, Somalia and Ethiopia created a growing public awareness. Meanwhile, the World Council of Churches demonstrated concern for Iraqi and Armenian minorities and for other pockets of refugees in the mid-East and Europe. There was a growing uneasiness as well about the limitations of the United Nations High Commissioner for Refugees.

Another critical factor was Canadian Christians' experience of war and oppression. This was particularly true among Mennonite and Christian Reformed bodies, given the emigration to Canada of their people from Europe. The Rev. Arie Van Eek, the Inter-Church Committee for Refugees chairman (1980-82) and executive secretary of the Council of Christian Reformed Churches in Canada, speaks of "compassion born of their own experience in the War of 1939-45 in Holland and their post-War reception in Canada." The Dutch had known not only what it was to suffer horribly under the Nazi heel, but what risks they took in sheltering members of the Jewish community during the Nazi occupation. In the words of a Dutch person who was asked why he sheltered a Jewish family, Van Eek addresses the underlying motive for refugee work, "It was the only decent thing to do." The Mennonites too knew the reality of being a refugee. The vivid memory of hundreds of years of persecutions helped Mennonites to respond in great numbers.

The Inter-Church Committee for Refugees is born

The churches had co-operated in the National Inter-Faith Immigration Committee. They co-operated in the Inter-Church Project on Population and the Inter-Church Committee on Human Rights in Latin America. The Protestant churches were receiving World Council of Churches bulletins with refugee updates and the Roman Catholic church was on board with the work of the International Catholic Migration Commission.

On June 21 1979, the impetus to pull together a new ecumenical Refugee Concerns Project came into focus through a memo from Donald Anderson, general secretary of the Canadian Council of Churches, to "Participants in the Consultation on Refugee Sponsorship." This memo is significant because Anderson not only proposed creating an interchurch liaison office for refugee concerns, but because he alluded immediately to the 1978 Immigration Department program created primarily to meet the boat people challenge. The churches, he said, "have been concerned with finding the most adequate mechanisms... the churches now ought to propose a practical program to provide the staff back-up and facilitate the logistical support needed."

This liaison office, Anderson suggested, would operate under an agreement negotiated between the churches and the Immigration Department to take responsibility for the following tasks:

• To serve as a specific case reference bureau for ecumenical bodies and the U.N. High Commission on Refugees in relation to difficult refugee cases in need of church sponsors;

• To serve as a connecting point for local congregations and other groups which are prepared, as sponsors, to receive such difficult cases;

• To act as a support base and contact point for church groups which sponsor refugees, especially during times of difficulty (for example, facilitating sponsorship transfers and preparing a sponsor's manual);

• To monitor the world refugee situation and Canadian responses, keeping the participant churches informed and concerned.

The 'monitoring,' which in Anderson's memo is almost an after-thought, would be raised to the top of the agenda when the Refugee Concerns Project (the Inter-Church Committee for Refugees begin-ning in 1981) wrote its own mandate. It was always a concern in the Inter-Church Committee for Refugees that the issue of the local settlement of refugees in Canada, important as it was, not be allowed to take over the Committee's agenda. Members felt that energy must not be sapped from the other objectives flowing out of the concerns of the Inter-Church Project on Population and the Inter-Church Committee on Human Rights in Latin America: advocacy focussed toward root causes, durable solutions, status determination proce-dures and the setting of intake levels.

Neither Canada Employment and Immigration nor the churches responded positively to the proposal to "serve as a specific case reference bureau." In the writing of its own mandate, the Inter-Church Committee for Refugees dropped the "specific case reference bureau" down in the list of purposes and altered it to read, "To facilitate involvement of churches in difficult cases." The Committee's policy became to take on only cases where a specific government policy or practice was questioned. Even observing this limitation, co-ordinator Kathleen Ptolemy spent hundreds of hours on the phone with the Canada Employment and Immigration, provincial authorities, national church personnel and regional activists.

In September 1979, Anderson made a proposal to the Executive

Committee of the Canadian Council of Churches in which he traced briefly the Council's role in refugee work, primarily in following up cases forwarded by the World Council of Churches. He stressed the dramatic change in the reality of refugee work "dating principally from the development of the new Immigration Act." A coalition of churches "spearheaded by the Inter-Church Committee on Human Rights in Latin America entered vigorously into the review process of immigration… particularly in regard to the sections dealing with the refugee determination process in Canada for those people who arrive at a Canadian port of entry and ask for refugee status." Furthermore, he pointed out that the new Act recognized for the first time the U.N. Convention on Refugees. There was a "series of problems" at the implementation level and to correct them would require continuing church and community monitoring.

Anderson then went on to repeat his support of church sponsorship. He had already stressed this to the participants of the Refugee Concerns Project in June 1979. In the first years of the Inter-Church Committee for Refugees' work, the Committee would return again and again to the problem of bringing difficult cases to Canada—the elderly, large and single-parent families, and the physically and mentally disabled. The Committee's contribution was to advocate the streamlining of application processing.

As Anderson had evidently received a positive response to his June memo, he made the following proposals at the September meeting of the Council's Executive: to create a Canadian Council of Churches committee on refugee concerns, with a mandate to coordinate ecumenically the churches' role with refugees, and to have the staff of the Council increased in the refugee field by hiring a director of Refugee Concerns and a secretarial assistant.

In January 1980, Kathleen Ptolemy became the refugee officer of the Canadian Council of Churches. She brought into this new position her experience as a school teacher and her work through the YWCA in Canada, Sri Lanka and Zambia. She was joined by Pat Bird as secretarial assistant.

The Inter-Church Committee for Refugees' membership

In early 1980, Ptolemy moved quickly to establish relationships with Employment and Immigration, the U.N. High Commission on

Refugees, the World Council of Churches and the National Council of Churches, located in New York.

The Inter-Church Committee for Refugees (at this point still the Refugee Concerns Project) adopted the pattern established in the other interchurch coalitions of surrounding full-time staff with a committee and an executive primarily, but not exclusively, drawn from the headquarters of denominational participants. The work of the Executive was frequently assisted by Fran Arbour, the co-ordinator of the Inter-Church Committee on Human Rights in Latin America, when Latin American refugees and root causes were discussed. One glance at the matrix of networking relations that went into the founding and nurturing of the Inter-Church Committee for Refugees demonstrates the value of the wide church participation in moving the Committee's work beyond that of a bureau for settlement and social service. It is significant that Christian leaders such as Ted Scott, Donald Ray, Donald MacDonald, Nancy Pocock and Clarke Raymond were 'inside the loop' and able to give legitimation at the highest church levels to all of the coalition's advocacy endeavours.

The Inter-Church Committee for Refugees' work

By 1980 there were over 14 million refugees in the camps of a number of countries including Hong Kong, Pakistan, Mexico, Honduras, Ethiopia, Somalia, Sudan, Greece, Jordan, Lebanon, Thailand and Indonesia. These refugees required continued safe asylum in these countries, eventual repatriation in the majority of situations and third-country resettlement for many in Hong Kong, Indonesia, Thailand and Malaysia.

Scores of Canadians living abroad, the U.N. High Commission on Refugees, churches, aid agencies and ethnic organizations responded to this awesome global tragedy of refugees. Throughout Canada there was a surge of interest in congregations for resettlement and a call to their own churches to provide leadership.

Almost at once, the Inter-Church Committee for Refugees' and Kathleen Ptolemy's office were swamped by the understandable urge to 'play catch-up.' At first it proved difficult for the members of the coalition to agree on priorities. The differences were reflected in the orientation of George Cram (Anglican) and Bernard Daly (Canadian Conference of Catholic Bishops), who emphasized the problems and challenges of advocacy, and Don Groff (United Church), Arie Van

Eek (Council of Christian Reformed Churches in Canada) and Arthur Driedger (Mennonite Central Committee–Canada), who struggled to handle the Canadian settlement challenge. This inevitable tension in the early years of the Inter-Church Committee for Refugees became the focus of a working group. This group articulated the need to develop "some carefully considered goals and procedures."

The Committee's agenda, reflected in the minutes, reports and correspondence of 1981-83, illustrated the salient concerns of the co-ordinator and members of the Committee. Both advocacy and Canadian resettlement featured as the two main strands in the work. At frequent intervals the Inter-Church Committee for Refugees made a variety of overtures to Ottawa regarding refugee determination policy, Canadian intake levels, protection and aid, and exceptional individual and family cases. Every Minister for Immigration of the period, as well as their deputies and departmental assistants, became familiar with leading Inter-Church Committee for Refugees spokespersons like George Cram, Kathleen Ptolemy and Bernard Daly and with the Committee's position on issues. As well, the Standing Conference of Canadian Organizations Concerned for Refugees, with George Cram as chairman, annually brought together a number of anglophone and francophone refugee groups and agencies, interfaith bodies and community-based groups with representatives of the federal government to discuss public policy and the administration of refugee affairs within Employment and Immigration, the U.N. High Commission on Refugees and the provincial governments.

The Inter-Church Committee for Refugees also benefited from first-hand reports by people like Mennonite Central Committee (Canada) worker Annie Krasker, who gave detailed accounts of conditions of refugees in camps in Thailand. Meanwhile, requests for sponsorship from sources such as the U.N. High Commission on Refugees, Hong Kong Christian Service, the World Council of Churches, the Canadian government and individuals created great pressure on the Inter-Church Committee for Refugees to develop a clearly defined global sponsorship program. In addition, as workshops on the integration of refugees were undertaken across the country, the Committee was able to provide resources and support. In the years 1981 to 1983, Ptolemy and Executive members were called to Central America by partners in the field. They also attended meetings of the U.N. High Commission on Refugees and non-governmental organizations in Geneva, Southeast Asia, Texas and Tanzania. A 1981 conference at Stony Point, New York, was convened by the World Council of Churches, hosted by the Inter-Church Committee for Refugees and led in theological reflection by the Committee's chairman, the Rev. Robert Lindsey. Tom Clark, who became the Inter-Church Committee for Refugees co-ordinator in 1983, called it the first international conference of church agencies working with refugees. The result, he said, was deeper theological reflection on refugee movements and a greater degree of commonality in assisting refugees in different countries.

By 1982, the great pressure to arrange sponsorships had abated. The previous two years had witnessed the arrival in Canada of over 50,000 Southeast Asians with Employment and Immigration/church Master Agreements operating in full swing.

The relationship between government and non-government sponsorship makes an exhaustive subject for study itself. The Committee's interventions with Employment and Immigration with regard to settlement were primarily to ensure that the elderly and the disabled in the camps would not be passed over for the better educated and physically fit in the selection process, as would be the case in the normal routine of immigration. The success of these interventions has never been measured, but appears to have been of very limited impact. In fact, an evaluation of settlement reported by Employment and Immigration in June 1982 indicated that males outnumbered females almost three to one and 70% of them were between the ages of 15 and 35. The churches had not yet succeeded in countering arguments such as 'economic absorptive capacity' in determining refugee levels and continued to urge the government to help get the 'last and the least' out of the camps.

The early 1980s resulted in the production of several pamphlets for mass distribution in the churches. A refugee film was produced through funding by the United Church, which led to some radio interviews about Canadian refugee work. As well, Hugh McCullum's 1982 book, *The Least of These,*[4] relied heavily on input from the Inter-Church Committee for Refugees as well as from the Inter-Church Committee on Human Rights in Latin America. Clearly the receptiveness of a compassionate Christian constituency in the initial years fed the work of the Inter-Church Committee for Refugees and enabled it to look ahead.

Throughout the early 1980s Committee members discussed the root causes of refugee outflows. The Inter-Church Committee for Refugees was able to press, along with the Inter-Church Committee on Human Rights in Latin America and other church groups, for the application of human rights standards in countries of origin. This took the form of repeated intervention at the United Nations level. Similar challenges were addressed to the Canadian political and legal system, especially with respect to the 1978 Immigration Act.

In 1981 a government-appointed taskforce concluded that refugee claimants should be given a full oral hearing and that the refugee determination process needed to be streamlined. The Inter-Church Committee for Refugees intervened heavily on this issue, as it was central to the Committee's work around the refugee status question. No major change was made to the law and the government created a quasi-independent body—the Refugee Status Advisory Committee. Its role was to review written transcripts of the required examination under oath by a Senior Immigration Officer. As the number of new refugee arrivals increased, further discussion took place around the best reform process for determining refugee status. In 1984, a government advisor and a delegation of the Standing Conference of Canadian Organizations Concerned for Refugees concluded that both a full hearing and an appeal were required.

Throughout this time, the issue of protection rights caused the Inter-Church Committee for Refugees to look beyond Canada to the U.N. High Commission on Refugees. The closely observed crisis of Salvadorean and Nicaraguan refugees in Honduras forced the churches to appeal to the U.N. High Commission on Refugees in Geneva in October 1982, on the issue of protection on the ground and in the courts. The High Commission carries moral, though not legal, authority. As the U.N. body was facing a financial crisis, the Inter-Church Committee for Refugees did what it could: it pressed governments to fulfill their financial responsibilities to the High Commission and, then, appealed to other U.N. bodies like the U.N. Commission on Human Rights for action on behalf of Central American refugees.

Increasingly, the issues around the protection of refugees had become common to European and North American churches and subsequently became the focus of an international church consultation which the World Council of Churches convened and the Inter-

Church Committee for Refugees hosted in Niagara Falls, Ontario, in 1984. This meeting developed common principles for the protection of refugees and also reached agreements on basic procedures for applying those principles. These principles included a full oral hearing and an appeal, before the refugee was forced to return to another country. This consultation also recommended regional meetings to follow through in Europe and North America. Participants agreed to further international efforts to work together on refugee protection problems.

In the same year, the Canadian government requested another study and appointed as commissioner Rabbi Gunther Plaut, a highly respected advocate of human rights, to propose a new refugee determination procedure. The Inter-Church Committee for Refugees and other voluntary agencies had an opportunity to present written briefs. Meanwhile, a change of federal governments occurred. A report was finally produced in 1985.

Unexpectedly, the Inter-Church Committee for Refugees and the Canadian Council of Churches received an opportunity in the spring of 1984 to test their position that refugees had a right to full oral hearings. The occasion was the appeal to the Supreme Court of Canada by Singh *et al.* After having been denied refugee status, Singh *et al.* had successfully convinced the Court that the process did not conform to the principles of fundamental justice. Specifically, they had not been given a full oral hearing before the decision makers anywhere in the process.

The Inter-Church Committee for Refugees prevailed upon the Canadian Council of Churches to ask for intervenor status. The Supreme Court granted the Council's request. On April 4 1985, the Supreme Court allowed the appeal. The implication was that everyone physically in Canada falls under the Canadian Charter of Rights and Freedoms. They argued that the threat of loss of life or liberty if wrongly returned overseas constitutes a threat to the security of persons in Canada.

Following the Supreme Court's decision and the Plaut Report, the government looked for ways around the issues. When the Minister, Flora MacDonald, asked for speedy written replies to the Plaut Report, voluntary agencies under the Standing Conference of Canadian Organizations Concerned for Refugees responded with an unofficial boycott because they felt more time was needed for reflection and for meetings with the Minister. In September 1985, the Inter-Church Committee for Refugees presented the first brief by the churches on essential elements for a new process for refugee determination. The Committee's brief formed the basis for a number of subsequent briefs. By November the government responded that it would provide regulations for one full hearing for all claimants or, alternatively, for an appeal process, but not for both. The Standing Conference member organizations argued that justice required both a full hearing and appeal.

The government's intention to produce legislation setting limits to a full hearing without appeal resulted in a sense of betrayal for refugee advocates. This was a clear case of the government ignoring the advice that it had requested. The Inter-Church Committee for Refugees, in turn, began to work on linking External Affairs' standards for human rights with Immigration's proposals for refugee determination. The government's Immigration proposals were tabled in May 1986 and condemned by the Inter-Church Committee for Refugees in a motion at a Standing Conference meeting.

A few months later, the arrival of Tamil refugees set off a storm of national interest about the admissibility of refugees. Canadians became angry because some of the Tamils had lied about how they got to Canada and because they had arrived via Germany, which was considered to be a 'safe country.' In this situation the Inter-Church Committee for Refugees and others presented a brief for refined procedures and pointed out that justice meant protecting those who were genuine refugees and not punishing them along with abusers of Canada's system.

In early 1987 the Inter-Church Committee for Refugees and church leader delegations again pleaded genuine claimants' cases with Ottawa. When the government's Bill C-55 was introduced in May, however, it proved unacceptable. Then, when a boatload of Sikhs arrived on the east coast, negative public sentiments were further aroused. The government sensed a public mood containing racist undercurrents and it used the Sikh incident to introduce more stringent legislation in the form of Bill C-84. In the course of debate, a few amendments were made to the bill, but it still did not conform to the rights guaranteed by the Charter of Rights and Freedoms. The legislation took effect January 1 1989.

In anticipation of the passing of Bill C-84, the Inter-Church

Committee for Refugees had asked the Canadian Council of Churches to take the government to court. On January 3, the Council filed a statement of claim which called into question the constitutionality of some of the newly enacted legislation. There was an extended campaign to raise funds for the court action through the sale of sweatshirts, tapes, cards, posters, foundation grants and personal gifts. By April, $112,000 had been raised; by the end of the year it was $200,000.

The government responded to the Council's court action by filing motions that the Council was not a person who should be heard and that there was no cause for action. Committee members attended the Federal Court hearing. The decision of April 26 was favourable. The government appealed. On January 23 1990, Committee members attended the Federal Court of Appeal hearing at which the government sought to overturn a 1989 decision to allow the court action to go forward. By March, the Federal Court of Appeal allowed the Canadian Council of Churches to proceed to trial on just four concerns out of several dozen. The Council then agreed to seek leave to appeal to the Supreme Court. Just before the end of 1990, the Council received the good news that the issue of whether the Council could raise this case would be heard by the Supreme Court of Canada. In January 1992, the Supreme Court decided that the Council had no standing. The court concluded that jurisprudence should be based on practice, not theory, but it also noted that there were issues of concern in the refugee law. Disappointed but undeterred, the Council is now in the process of charging the government with violating human rights agreements through the Inter-American Commission of the Organization of American States. More directly, the Inter-Church Committee for Refugees is seeking to promote court cases about individuals whose rights have been violated.

Although the court challenge occupied much of the Committee's time in 1991 as it steered the Canadian Council of Churches through the legal effort, the Inter-Church Committee for Refugees also continued to monitor the situation in Indochina related to the protection of refugees and the faulty Hong Kong screening procedures. Also high on the agenda was the monitoring of the situation of Salvadorean refugees in Honduras who were planning to repatriate to El Salvador. This monitoring was critical, especially in the wake of the insurrection which followed the assassination of six Jesuit priests and two women in November 1989.

In the human rights arena, the Inter-Church Committee for Refugees pressed the government about its international treaty obligations with respect to proposed forced returns of certain groups in Canada, specifically Haitian, Salvadorean and Lebanese groups. The Inter-Church Committee for Refugees also identified human rights violations in Toronto with regard to the procedures followed to handle the backlog of refugee claimants. In October 1990, the Committee sent a Canadian Council of Churches delegation to Geneva to assist the U.N. Human Rights Committee in its examination of Canada under Article 40 of the Covenant. Advice from church partners has continued to aid the Inter-Church Committee for Refugees with action around refugee-related issues.

In the midst of troubling and pressing issues, there was cause for celebration. On June 2 1990, the Inter-Church Committee for Refugees held its tenth anniversary celebration in Toronto. The event included interfaith participation, supper, songs and reminiscences.

What of the future? There is evidence that particular developments will certainly influence the work of the Inter-Church Committee for Refugees. Some of these are the decline of the churches' role in society, less acceptance by the government today of the values of the churches, and less openness in Canadian society of the early 1990s.

The strands of the Committee's work at times have been more intertwined. At other times they have had a clear focus of their own. But the commitment of the churches has not wavered. As eloquently stated by the late Kathleen Ptolemy, "Whatever legislation we have in place, people will continue to become uprooted from their communities, their cultures, their climate, their language, their roots. Journeying with the refugee will continue to challenge us and test our faithfulness to the God who requires that we enable the uprooted to become subjects, and not objects, of their own history."[5]

The Interchurch Fund for International Development

Robert Fugere

Introduction

The story of the Interchurch Fund for International Development over the past 18 years has both continuing threads and several emerging patterns. During much of its earlier period, the Fund functioned fairly much on its own and tended to the funding of overseas projects on behalf of its member churches/agencies. As a fund, the Interchurch Fund for International Development has grown from $200,000 allocated to 10 projects in 1974, to $2.9 million, allocated to 116 different projects in 1991. This growth in numbers, however, reveals less of the changing nature of the Interchurch Fund for International Development than does its response to outside forces.

Throughout its history, the Interchurch Fund for International Development has responded to three major external influences: its overseas partners, the changing needs of its member churches/agencies and, finally, the changes in its government funding agency, the Canadian International Development Agency. For example, the change in southern hemisphere agencies from a popular education emphasis to income-producing activities, as well as pressure from both CIDA and the churches/agencies to create a unique mandate for the Interchurch Fund for International Development, led to the Fund's dual focus on sustainable agriculture and community health promotion. From the same forces, the Interchurch Fund for International Development more recently has become a key forum for its member churches/agencies to address important policy issues, both within the church community and with the Canadian government. We can trace the interplay of these forces over the years in three major phases: the Fund's formative phase from 1973 to 1979, its opening to Third World partners from 1979 to 1989, and its emergence as a forum from 1989 to the present. It remains to be seen, then, where the Interchurch Fund for International Development may be moving.

The formative years: 1973-79

The idea for an ecumenical fund originated with Roméo Maione, former head of the Canadian Catholic Organization for Development and Peace and in 1970 the new director general of CIDA's non-governmental organizations division. Influenced by the ecumenical movement and the growing concern for Third World development, Maione proposed several new elements in the preliminary discussions with staff of the five church development agencies, led by the Rev. Robert MacRae of the Anglican Primate's Fund and Tom Johnston of Development and Peace. The Interchurch Fund for International Development was to be a fund to "explore new avenues of co-operation between the churches and overseas projects." Right from the start, the Canadian churches provided the Interchurch Fund for International Development with a definition of development which has served it throughout its existence: "Development is a process of continuous change by which any country, any specific population, or sector of population in its natural, cultural, or social milieu and at a definite stage in history, within a framework of international rela-tions, seeks liberation, both material and spiritual, by: a) transforming its structures of production; b) establishing new social relationships; c) acquiring for itself adequate political and administrative institu-tions; d) recreating or strengthening its own culture for the purpose of achieving a better quality of life."

Although it would take some years to develop, the Interchurch Fund for International Development was also mandated "to increase the capacity of the participating Canadian churches to respond quickly and effectively to expressed development needs: 1) by working toward mutual responsibility among all participating devel-opment groups, and 2) by working toward the goal of shared decision-making and accountability" (June 1974).

Unlike its member churches (which enjoyed one-to-one project matching from CIDA), the Interchurch Fund for International Devel-opment would receive a three-to-one match for its projects, enabling CIDA to funnel more money to the churches. The Interchurch Fund for International Development was originally set up with two Board members from each of the five member agencies and four from

Development and Peace, which provided half of the church funds. In 1979, the Mennonite Central Committee (Canada) accepted associate membership and in 1981 became a full member. Right from the start, church representation to the Interchurch Fund for International Development Board usually included both a development staffer as well as a volunteer, such as the first chairman, Archbishop Ted Scott. There was even talk in 1974 of having Third World representatives on the Board of Directors, similar to the International Development Research Centre in Ottawa. Since its beginning, the Interchurch Fund for International Development Board has met three times a year, its primary task being to select projects for approval. In the early years, Bob MacRae, and then George Cram of the Anglican Church, covered the administration, until Nelson Soucy was hired in late 1977 as executive secretary. I have served as executive director since 1980.

Even in this formative period, the churches used the Interchurch Fund for International Development to present their ecumenical perspective on development to the Canadian government. In 1977 the Board was invited to present a brief to a parliamentary subcommittee, which argued strongly for maintaining Canada's international aid commitment at .07% of the gross national product. During this early period most of the Fund's attention, however, focussed on allocating the funds (which grew to $1.2 million by 1979) to a wide variety of projects.

Emerging partnerships overseas: 1979-89

During most of the 1980s the thrust of the Fund's activities was toward developing relationships with Third World groups. Regular meetings with CIDA continued to take place, but the Interchurch Fund for International Development did not take up any major policy issues. When CIDA attempted to integrate Canadian non-governmental organizations into its Country Focus program, offering much more money but making these organizations more of a delivery vehicle for CIDA's programming, the Interchurch Fund for International Development Board decided to steer clear of this path. Partly, the Fund feared being co-opted by CIDA but, more fundamentally, the Fund's lack of a solid identity was the unspoken issue. Instead, the Board decided to explore partnerships overseas in a slow, gradual fashion, primarily through a series of four consultations.

The first of the consultations took place in Aurora, Ontario, in

April 1979. Representatives from the Canadian churches, CIDA, as well as 10 project holders from overseas participated. Chaired by Tom Johnston, the consultation strongly advanced the concept of partnership and recommended that representatives from Third World agencies be included on the Board of Directors. As a result, in the following year (1980), the Federation of Organizations for Social and Educational Assistance (FASE) from Brazil, the Christian Service Committee from Malawi and the Caribbean Conference of Churches were invited to join the Interchurch Fund for International Development Board in two of its three meetings, for an experimental period of two years. These three representatives were called 'formal partners,' and the Interchurch Fund for International Development made a particular commitment to become involved in their evaluation processes, as well as to offer a preferential funding ratio of five CIDA dollars to one churches' dollar to their work. A perusal of the Board minutes from 1980 onward shows a major shift in Board discussions, moving from internal Canadian church problems to broader issues. For example, our Third World partners did not hesitate to report that subsistence, no longer development, was becoming their struggle as the debt crisis took them in its grip. For three successive meetings, the Board debated whether or how to fund projects in the homelands of South Africa.

The dual need to listen more closely to our project holders' concerns and to select a new formal partner from Latin America (as FASE's term ended) prompted George Cram to propose a consultation with our Latin American partners for February 1984. Throughout most of the Fund's history about half of its project funds have gone to Latin America. This consultation in Lima, Peru, gave an opportunity for 10 Fund representatives to interact with and listen to 25 Latin American representatives over a two-week period. After a joint exposure trip to different areas of Peru, the group met for four days to exchange common concerns. Although almost all of the groups shared an approach of popular conscientization, the differences in actual focus, from education to health to agriculture to indigenous groups, made it impossible to draw any operational guidelines or to see any way to build a follow-up network among the Fund's project holders. Experimenting with a different selection procedure, the Latin American groups elected a new Board representative from the Centre for Agrarian Education of Nicaragua, as a way of promoting Nicaragua's postrevolutionary alternative to become better known in Canada. The consultation participants called on the Interchurch Fund for International Development to become a more prophetic voice among Canadians and to offer more support to long-term integrated programs in the Third World.

The joint consultation held in Zimbabwe with Christian Care in 1987 endorsed a more specific focus, sustainable agriculture. The participants tried to open the Interchurch Fund for International Development more to the African continent. Thirty different groups from 15 countries were invited, together with eight Canadian Board representatives and Ten Days for World Development. As in Peru, we spent the first week travelling in small groups throughout Zimbabwe before assembling for four days to discuss promotion of more sustainable agricultural practices. We discovered that, although several African governments had recently approved policies for more sustainable, local food production, African churches and non-governmental organizations by and large had little experience in this area. After agreeing on a shared definition of sustainable agriculture and even some strategies for implementation, the consultation ended with a call for greater networking between the Interchurch Fund for International Development and its African project holders. As in Peru, the Fund found it difficult to respond to this call for greater presence with a limited staff of two persons.

One specific result was a small conference in May of the following year in Bolton, Ontario, in which 10 agencies from Latin America, Africa and Asia were invited to draw up a strategy for the Interchurch Fund for International Development to pursue in its support of sustainable agriculture. The expertise which one of our Board members, Lee Holland, brought from his years in Africa was invaluable. This occasion in fact resulted in the formal organization of a Latin American Consortium for Agroecology and Development. This group, led by Andres Yurjevic from the Centre for Education and Technology in Chile, moved 12 South American partners in non-governmental organizations from casual exchanges to a common commitment to train their staff, to carry out applied research in different ecological zones and to publish their results. As a result of this same small meeting, a grouping of five Philippine non-governmental organizations, also working in sustainable agriculture, emerged the following year, forming the Philippines Partners Forum.

Both of these groups were chosen to send their representatives to serve on the Interchurch Fund for International Development Board.

This series of consultations led to a basic shift in the Fund's own funding focus. This was partially promoted by an internal evaluation carried out in October 1985, recommending that the Fund narrow its focus of project funding and improve its partnership relationships. It was, however, the Review Committee, chaired by Betty Farrell, which worked for a year and a half to present "A Modest Proposal" to the Interchurch Fund for International Development Board in January 1987.

By this time the Fund's funding level had reached $2.8 million, which was spread quite widely from community development to conscientization to human rights to health projects. The Committee carried out a wide-ranging process of consultation, both with overseas partners and with Canadian church/agency members. Although they did consider focussing funding primarily on ecumenical projects, they finally decided, in the two major recommendations of the "Modest Proposal," that the Interchurch Fund for International Development should concentrate its resources on intermediary agencies working in the areas of sustainable agriculture and community-based health care and that the overall number of projects being funded should be reduced to approximately 50 over the next three-year period.

The idea behind these recommendations was that the Interchurch Fund for International Development should provide larger amounts of funds over a longer period of time to a smaller number of southern hemisphere non-governmental organizations, thus allowing the Fund to develop a more mutually beneficial partnership arrangement with a few of these organizations. Unwilling to expand the staff at this point, the Board tried to use its existing financial and personnel resources more efficiently and effectively.

One year later, in May 1988, a second, more institutional evaluation of the Interchurch Fund for International Development was conducted by Robert Thompson for CIDA. At the same time as he remarked upon the Fund's extraordinary efficiency and effectiveness with its small staff, he pinpointed a major weakness in the Fund's lack of staff time to pursue better partnership relationships with Third World agencies. By deciding to focus on fewer partnerships in the two areas of agriculture and health, the Interchurch Fund for International Development Board had taken a much more interactive

At the Constitution March, Ottawa, November 1981. *Credit:* M. Helene Laraque Photo

Some of the participants demonstrating for the Haida on
the steps of the British Columbia Legislature, Victoria,
November 1985.

Credit: Project North/Aboriginal Rights Coalition

Lubicon blockade, Lubicon Lake, October 1988.
Credit: Project North/Aboriginal Rights Coalition

Peter Hamel, Lorna Schwartzentruber, Dan Berman and Bishop Andrew
Hutchison of the Aboriginal Rights Coalition making a presentation to the
Scoping Hearings on the Great Whale Hydro Electric Project, Montreal,
May 1992.   *Credit:* Project North/Aboriginal Rights Coalition

Rev. Michael Lapsley in Harare, Zimbabwe, 10 months after the explosion
Credit: Hugh McCullum, United Church Observer

March on Parliament Hill, organized by the Inter-Church Coalition on Africa, to demand stronger sanctions against South Africa, 1989.
Credit: ICCAF

Elimo Njau, renowned Kenyan artist, at the ICCAF-sponsored "Africa: Art of the People" exhibition, Toronto, February 1993.

A delegation in support of the Lubicon Lake First Nation was hosted by the Japanese Council of Churches, supported by the Justice and Peace Committee of the Japanese Catholic Bishops, the Canadian Council of Churches, the Aboriginal Rights Coalition and the Taskforce on the Churches and Corporate Responsibility. Pictured in front of Daishowa's head office are Sam Bull of the United Church addressing the public, his son holding the banner and Lubicon Chief Bernard Ominayak in his familiar cap. Also present was the Rev. Glen Davis of the Presbyterian Church in Canada. *Credit:* TCCR

Derek Evans and Terry Gallagher sharing a ride in Pyongyang, Democratic People's Republic of Korea.

The Korean Christian Federation delegation with the CAWG Visit Planning Committee, on the steps at 11 Madison Ave., Toronto, October 1991.
Front row: Kim Nam Hyok, Pastor Kim Un Bong, Rhea Whitehead, Pastor Kang Yong Sop, Glen Davis, Daisy Francis, Choi Tje Gwon.
Back row: Kim Hyong Dok, In Kee Kim, Yu Hwan Jin, Teresa Chu, Terry Brown.

Barbara Paleczny and Vicki Obedkoff, Women and Economic Justice Committee (ECEJ), participate in a rally on Parliament Hill calling for full employment, January 1993.   *Credit:* ECEJ

ECEJ administrative committee and staff meeting, 1992: John Dillon, Diana Gibbs, Doryne Kirby, Jim Marshall (partially hidden), Rob Oliphant, Magda Horman, Ray Hodgson, David Pfrimmer, Lee Ann Purchase, Geoff Johnston (partially hidden), David Szollosy, Lorraine Michael, David Pollock (chairman), Barbara Paleczny, Dennis Howlett.   *Credit:* ECEJ

Chinese delegation at Dr. Norman Bethune's birthplace, Gravenhurst, Ontario.
Standing: Zhao Fusan, Wang Zicheng, Chen Zemin, Shen Yi-fan, Jiang Peifen,
Bishop Fu Tieshan, Kiang Wen-han. Kneeling: Bishop Tu Shihua, Han
Wenzao.

Credit: M. Terry Carter

Credit: CCP

PLURA has provided seed funding to the Pointe Adult Centre for Education (PACE), a popular education centre in a Montreal neighbourhood with 50% unemployment and functional illiteracy rates. PACE is run by and for the people of the community. *Credit:* PLURA

PLURA executive, May 1992: Mary Boyd, Susan Johnson, Mary Whyte, Faye Wakeling, Claire McIlveen. *Credit:* PLURA

Dom Helder Camara of Recife,
Brazil, speaking in Toronto, 1974.
Credit: Ten Days

Jeanne Moffat with Jaime Tadeo,
Ten Days resource speaker from
the Philippines, 1987. *Credit:* Ten Days

Ten Days resource persons on "Third World Debt" 1991: Rozette Muzigo
(Uganda), Edna Maluma (Zambia), Gertrude Kapuma (Malawi). *Credit:* Ten Days

Frances Arbour and Bishop Adolphe Proulx celebrating ICCHRLA's
10th anniversary. *Credit:* ICCHRLA

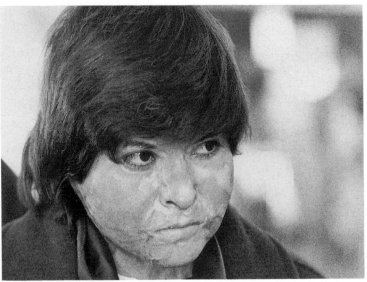

Carmen Gloria Quintana. *Credit:* Gazette, George Bird

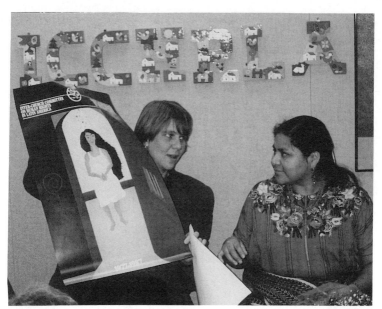
Elly Vandenberg and Rigoberta Menchu admire ICCHRLA 10th anniversary poster.
Credit: ICCHRLA

Ernie Regehr addresses the United Nations. *Credit:* Project Ploughshares

Project Ploughshares prepares annual reports and maps on armed conflicts around the world.

Credit: Project Ploughshares

Murray Thomson. *Credit:* Koozma J. Tarasoff

ICCR Board Meeting, January 1991. *Credit:* ICCR

ICFID-sponsored Consultation on Sustainable Agriculture, Zimbabwe, 1988.

Credit: ICFID

Production demonstration for farmers.

Credit: ICFID

Farmers' discuss their ICFID-sponsored projects.

Credit: ICFID

ICFID-sponsored family-based swine project in Iloilo, the Philippines.

Credit: ICFID

ICFID-sponsored farmer with the first vegetables of the new crop.

approach to development, which would require staff changes and closer co-operation with southern partners.

By choosing repeatedly to go out and engage directly in exposure trips and discussions with those southern groups working at development, the Interchurch Fund for International Development Board members reached a personal understanding of the strengths and commitments of these frontline workers and the southern groups began to trust that the Fund would really listen to them. This growing mutual trust, which went beyond staff visits, provided the basis for confidence in the Fund's own process of self-definition and identity. The special contribution of the Third World 'formal partners'— particularly that of Valentine Ziswa of Christian Care in Zimbabwe, of Makanya Bita from the Christian Council of Tanzania and of Andres Yurjevic of the Latin American Consortium for Agroecology and Development in Chile—was crucial in this transformation of the Interchurch Fund for International Development from a nondescript fund into a shared partnership tackling two major development challenges: agriculture and health. These Board partners provided not only ideas but also legitimacy for these new directions within the Board, as well as within the observant eyes of southern groups generally. Southern groups did not see this same openness in other northern non-governmental organizations. Power sharing and solidarity were working both ways.

A renewed vision: 1989-93

Since 1977, the Fund has carried out a review of its program every three years, which also serves as a remandating exercise with its member churches/agencies. Several factors came together in early 1989 to lead the Interchurch Fund for International Development to assume a stronger role as a forum for the Canadian churches on development issues. A primary influence was the turnover in church development agency staff in several of the agencies. With that came a change in the composition of the Interchurch Fund for International Development Board, with several of the longest-serving Board members being replaced and a third of its members now being women. The consciousness of women's contribution to development decisions came particularly from the Anglican and United Churches. As well, the fall of the Berlin Wall at this time dramatized the changing global context for development funding. The removal of the bipolar competition between the United States and the Soviet Union also removed a prime political incentive for Third World development assistance. Simultaneously, the return of Marcel Massé from the International Monetary Fund to become president of CIDA augured significant changes in both the policy and operations of this major Canadian development actor. A period of repeated government cutbacks to CIDA's budget was about to start. With these, Massé would turn CIDA from implementing bilateral projects to influencing southern governments' macroeconomic policy decisions. Unlike in 1981, the Interchurch Fund for International Development was now better prepared to enter into these discussions.

When the members of the Interchurch Fund for International Development Planning Committee met on a Visioning Day early in May 1989, there was for the first time a concerted, strong call for the Fund to assume a greater role in co-ordinating ecumenical policy discussions around development. Bert Lobe, the incoming Mennonite president of the Interchurch Fund for International Development, and Michel Rousseau from Development and Peace were clearest in this vision. Much as our southern partners in non-governmental organizations were deciding not to act alone any longer, so too the Canadian churches/agencies were feeling the need for more networking around policy issues. Both the changes in leadership in several churches' development staff and the growing sense that the Fund's members often shared a different, more critical vision of development than other members of the Canadian development community placed the Interchurch Fund for International Development in a natural role for more discussions at the level of policy. The key recommendations from this Visioning Day were accepted by the churches and the Interchurch Fund for International Development Board:

• That the Interchurch Fund for International Development should develop from a fund to a partnership forum;
• That partnership should be understood as a multilateral dialogue with a shared flow of analysis and the facilitation of south-south exchanges;
• That the Fund's sustainable agricultural focus should be integrated within the forum concept and that the community-based health care focus should be postponed for two years;
• That the Interchurch Fund for International Development Board should become a primary forum for policy discussions;

• That the Interchurch Fund for International Development should now be served by a three-person staff.

The first forum activity to be undertaken by the Interchurch Fund for International Development was within its church constituencies. A consultation among eight Canadian churches was called to reflect upon each of their different experiences with partnership over the past 10 years and to discuss with each other and with 12 overseas partners what improvements and new directions should emerge during the 1990s. The variety of approaches to this same term 'partnership' was quite educational for all participants. Some churches used the term synonymously with 'funding recipient,' but others described their relationship as "mutual exchange of personnel and funds," or even as "a solidarity tool to support the struggle for development." But perhaps even clearer in the discussion was a call which emerged from the southern partners for the Canadian churches and, in particular, the Interchurch Fund for International Development to address more directly the involvement of northern countries in the international economic system that affects them so grievously. All of the churches' partners called for greater involvement from the Canadian churches in their own struggles among the poor. The Interchurch Fund for International Development was mandated by this assembly to pursue improved ways of partnership and to engage the Canadian government in a discussion of the negative impacts of structural adjustment programs. In response to this clear demand, the Interchurch Fund for International Development Board decided early in 1991 to co-sponsor a study of CIDA's implementation of its 1987 policy manifesto, "Sharing Our Future."

With the International Affairs Committee of the Canadian Council of Churches (CCIA), we commissioned case studies of four countries to review CIDA's policies around structural adjustment plans, the distribution of CIDA officers in the Third World and CIDA's implementation of human rights concerns in its program activities. This study, which was quite critical of CIDA's increased tying of its bilateral assistance to the acceptance by southern countries of International Monetary Fund programs, was accepted by the Interchurch Fund for International Development Board and jointly presented to President Massé in October 1991. For the first time, this process of policy dialogue brought the Interchurch Fund for International Development into closer contact with our member churches/

agencies and with our colleague coalitions, several of which had been working on the same issues. The widespread publicity around this report, "Diminishing Our Future," led CIDA to invite the Interchurch Fund for International Development and CCIA into further policy dialogue on both structural adjustment programs and human rights. These two events—the partnership consultation and the CIDA study—quickly established the Interchurch Fund for International Development in a renewed forum function, a function which had been largely on the shelf since its early years.

The present context

The Interchurch Fund is now clearly at a point of transition. Throughout its 18 years, it has continued to increase its funding to Third World projects, in both numbers of projects and amounts of money. In 1991-92 the Interchurch Fund for International Development funded 116 projects with 40 partner groups and 55 non-partner project holders. Almost two-thirds of this project funding is committed for several years. Given the commitment several years ago to reduce the number of projects to 50 and to improve our partnership presence overseas, there is a major challenge to reorganize our operations. Our attempts to initiate more community-based health promotion, principally in Africa, are still in the initial stages and represent a primary responsibility for the second program staffer, together with a Board taskforce. In the area of sustainable agriculture, the lead is coming increasingly from co-ordinated groups of Third World partners, such as the Latin American Consortium for Agroecology and Development and the Philippine Partners Forum. As these groups themselves explore new relations, not just with their grassroots community base, but also with local universities and governments, the Interchurch Fund for International Development needs to devise better ways to keep its Board members aware of what our partners are doing.

Within Canada, the Interchurch Fund for International Development is committed to promoting the concerns of its Third World partners through a roundtable policy discussion with CIDA and key federal Finance Ministry officials. This event has been designed to allow our partners to put forward their own alternative proposals for economic policy reforms in trade, in rural development and in social services. Some of the major questions emerging have to do with staff and Board capacity to carry out this wide range of new activities.

The future

As the Interchurch Fund for International Development continues to respond to its Third World partners, to its church constituency and to the changes in CIDA, the future directions for the Board are fairly clear. Both in the north and in the south, fundamental issues around the whole development enterprise are being raised and reviewed, largely as a result of the 'New World Order.' In the removal of the ideological competition between the 'free world' and the communist bloc, the incentive for development assistance has been removed and the flow of aid from the north to the south has dried up—and even reversed! In the process, southern governments are losing their ability to deliver grand projects to improve their citizens' lives. Increasingly the whole development agenda—so much a matter of faith during the 60s and 70s—is being questioned and new values are emerging. The environment, the role of gender, the respect for indigenous cultures, greater democracy—all matter, but there are very few clear answers. As the project focus of bilateral government agencies shifts toward policy leverage and funds level off or diminish, the role in development of southern non-governmental organizations and other key actors in their civil society must grow larger. Committed since its beginning to a development approach based on community participation, the Interchurch Fund for International Development must find new ways to become present to and supportive of its partners.

Remaining responsive to and respectful of the growing competence of our southern partners to define their own development agenda has been a key trait of the Interchurch Fund for International Development. The introduction of 'formal partners' into the Board, the sponsorship of a series of overseas consultations and the acceptance by the Interchurch Fund for International Development of the challenge to address more provocatively the international system of economic injustice have demonstrated an authentic disposition to share power along with money. At the same time, the Fund's ability to be influenced by persons rather than just abstract, impersonal policies has remained. Like other coalitions, remaining small in size has gained for the Interchurch Fund for International Development a malleability to more human-scale decision making.

This shift into forum activities, however, has blurred the historical line between northern donor agencies and southern project recipients. Just as none of the Fund's member churches/agencies accept a clear division between funding to the south and northern development education, so too our southern partners are challenging the Interchurch Fund for International Development and its members to create closer links between the poor in the South and community efforts to alleviate poverty here in the north. Much needs to be explored in what is still the central focus of the Fund's work between Canadian churches and southern non-governmental organizations. More experiments need to be tried to improve our presence to each other's struggles. These efforts surely need to go beyond staff to include Board members and even volunteer groups.

At the forum level, it is not at all clear where the policy dialogue with CIDA will lead. Success will depend largely on the strength of the proposals made by our southern partners. The Interchurch Fund for International Development is committed to enhance our partners' own capacity to translate their local experiences into policy proposals. But success will also depend on the strength of church constituencies' support for these development alternatives here in Canada. Increasingly, with its limited capacity, the Interchurch Fund for International Development will have to work more closely with other coalitions, such as Ten Days for World Development and other southern area coalitions. Advocacy work, to be effective, must go beyond the coalitions to engage the churches and other concerned sectors. In the final analysis, however, both the funding function and the forum activities of the Interchurch Fund will increasingly be led by our southern partners.

The Lives of the Saints

John W. Foster

Introduction

This piece is both a reflection and a celebration. Renate Pratt well refers to the "many Board members, volunteers and staff who cared for each other, helped to nurture the organization, gave it credibility, shaped it and kept it financially afloat and in good order."[1] I was one of these for about 15 years. The colleagues were a memorable legion, the sense of joint accomplishment quite palpable.

And yet, I remember reading another volume of narratives on the church's coalitional engagement and leaving it quite disappointed, hungry one might say. For though the stories were well told, the faces and bodies and personalities of the actors were invisible. Like the authors of the early GATT-Fly research projects, they were erased in a cerebral commitment *to* collectivity and *against* ego. And yet, how do these stories take form without personality? In fact, they don't. Fortunately, the essays in this volume embody personality indeed. People, activists, researchers, investigators and advocates: people who seem to be verbs. So, in my reflection, I memorialize, celebrate, appreciate, as well as reflect. Perhaps this comes from having moved out of the immediate family into another institution with a related but different ethos. Perhaps it comes from a sense of the rapid movement of time, the occasional loss, a sense of the fragility of life. Perhaps it comes from a personal sense of all that has been gained and a desire to give something back.

Pages from an imaginary scrapbook

"The temporal equivalent of transcendence,
is it not organization?"[2]

The night that Ruth Tillman passed away, a group of folk from the Inter-Church Committee on Human Rights in Latin America happened to be together. Ruth was a staff associate of the Canadian Council of Churches during the formative period of several coalitions.

The relationship between the Canadian Council of Churches and the coalitions has seldom been as simple, warm or orderly as ecumenical theorists or bureaucrats might expect, and lately has been more clouded than ever. But, in the 1970s, Ruth was often a member of the 'Friday afternoon crisis club.' Her sense of what was right, what was worth doing, her tolerance and patience provided significant support to staff and volunteers alike. And she was not alone. Floyd Honey's erect and stubbornly righteous figure gave substance and Eoin MacKay's dry theological humour added humanity to many an encounter. I mention these things because I remember how Ruth's passing brought mourning to the little group of weary advocates. And also because Janice Acton, then editing the Inter-Church Committee on Human Rights in Latin America's newsletter, marked Ruth's life as one truly worth celebrating, one which would feed our continuing work and lives. Amid all the work, the verbiage, the difficulties, these characters shone. If they had not been there, things would have been quite different. Their yeast, flour and sugar were absolutely essential to the new bread created. I remember as well my own reaction to death, to that death. It was to dance, to affirm life and celebrate the living.

Emma Goldman linked dance and revolution; without one, the other was not worth having. There have been times when the ecumenical coalitions have worshipped work so exclusively that it was hard even to imagine freedom, release and exaltation. But deep emotional union, the celebration of commitment, the remembrance of those lost and the renaissance of hope have all come, sometimes by intention, sometimes by surprise:

•   At a magnificent ecumenical service in the great St. Paul's church in Toronto, hidden quietly near a column at the side, stood Lutheran Bishop Helmut Frenz, just out of Chile—symbol of those many seeking refuge and embodiment of those who had risked their lives to help others escape—unrecognized.

•   In the mid-70s in a quiet convent near Bogotá, Colombia, a simple mass united a fragile network of Christians fighting dictatorship from the Southern Cone to Canada. A cat wanders through the little chapel. "El gato Lopez," someone jibes later, a spy in disguise from the reactionary Cardinal a few miles away.

•   In a public funeral, held in a tiny country—El Salvador—but with global impact, Canadian clergy and lay participants witness, and by their presence there and testimony at home, mark martyrdom and strengthen the fight against its repetition.

The coalitions have often—but not always—provided a place where worship and work can be one, where the sense of fulfilment that comes from a calling answered and the opportunity to do meaningful work could be found. Coincident with the most recent great wave of feminist change in Canadian society and with a new emergence of gay and lesbian self-consciousness and self-confidence, the coalitions in some cases provided a place where women could exercise leadership and management, where gay and lesbian Christians might exercise their ministry, outside the often more confining structures and strictures of predominantly male and 'straight' religious hierarchies.

In my personal engagement with coalitions, I had the opportunity to work closely with five women coalition leaders, each with a particular and remarkable approach. The courage and self-denying persistence which Frances Arbour brought to the Inter-Church Committee on Human Rights in Latin America gave its work of denunciation a bite and a credibility which became renowned. Her compassion and interest in the situations of prisoners, mothers, refugees and victims of torture gave the Committee a reach and warmth far beyond its documentary and representational efforts. Her commitment continued that established by her predecessor, Florrie Snow Chacon.

The calm, balanced, tolerant and engaging management which Renate Pratt brought to the world of corporate responsibility was essential to the survival and impact of the Taskforce on the Churches and Corporate Responsibility. Her insight into corporate dissimulation and her eye for detail were as distinctive as Frances' investigative sense regarding human rights violations. Both had to suffer the insults and chauvinism of generals, corporate heads and politicians. Both had a way of making certain that the humanity, the fundamental claim to simple justice, shone.

With the late Kathleen Ptolemy, the road of 'accompaniment' was clear. There was a fundamental human connection which was never absent from her advocacy for and with refugees. Like Renate, she brought accomplishment to the telephone call. Whether in search of information or a commitment to action on the part of a recipient, her curiosity and her persistence were deadly. Like Frances she was committed to making the bureaucracies of the world honour their rhetoric, live up to their commitments or make new ones. And in the daily grind, when the work or the conflicts or the defeats drained the life out of colleagues, Kathleen was there to talk, joke or suggest closing the office and having a drink.

In the engagement of people, the motivation and encouragement to get involved or to continue, Jeanne Moffat brought a welcome sense of the possible to the coalitions. Through Jeanne the voices and faces of dozens of justice-seeking Canadians kept coming. When tasks threatened to get quite out of hand, assuming monumental and forbidding dimensions, Jeanne brought practical wit to bear and a sense of what could be done, born out of an experience of doing it. Remembering the subjects of the story, the actors, the learners, the voters and campaigners, Jeanne had a sense for the transparent detail, the motivating story, the transforming example.

The ideology and theology of human rights offered a supportive context in which those seeking full recognition in their own society could work with many others, in a variety of repressive situations, seeking their own liberation. That 'justice' and 'human rights' should be so motivating cannot, I believe, be separated from the personal journeys of many who worked in and with the coalitions. Some were finding ways of exercising their commitment and their talents in a new setting, having left religious orders or a more traditional denominational role. Others may have been fighting cynicism or boredom bred of repetitive inward games in shrinking institutions. Others still were finding a way to make faith real, to connect their spirits, minds and bodies in work that made a contribution to human emancipation.

* * *

> "...holding to the ground,
> while the ground keeps moving,
> I keep my balance square."[3]
> With whom better than these?

Style with substance

But there are aspects to the 'dance'—including adventure and downright fun—too often forgotten or outside the ken of theological reflection. As one reads through the narratives, like thumbing through an old moving picture book, one is overwhelmed with movement.

Project North advocates flying from Ungava to the mountain valleys of British Columbia, human rights investigators in the island battle-grounds of the Philippines, the streets of Soweto or the prisons of Chile or Argentina, the encounters with allies, victims and opponents, the bemedalled colonels of Central America, the besuited corporate giants at Bay and King, the politicians caught in the attempt to move swiftly away.

There were scenes from a Garcia Marquez novel or the histories of Eduardo Galeano—only laughter and a deep sense of human frailty could protect one—scenes of tragic reality and those perpetual, repet-itive scenes with the political or administrative functionaries of Canada or another land, where urgent cries were lost in the verbal fencing which only long training, or the distinct desire to get on to the golf course or lunch, can perfect.

Think of the church guide and the Canadian Members of Parlia-ment switching taxis and cars in Montevideo's streets and alleys, time and again until heads spun and an encounter could be secured with clandestine witnesses, free of the danger which might come from their openly meeting foreign investigators. Recall the bevy of collared clergy and upright laity in their Sunday best facing the immigration agents at the international airport as Brazilian refugees from Chile, spirited out of Panama and onto Air Canada in Jamaica by church activists abroad, are levered into safety in Canada. Imagine a cocktail lounge in a swank uptown Metro Toronto hotel, a diplomat or two, the refugee and human rights activists. The diplomat conjec-tures as to how a Canadian Forces plane could arrive in a Central American airfield to spirit some endangered witness out of the grasp of dark forces. Cynicism gives way to 'why not?' and 'can do.'

But beyond the adventure lies the unwelcome face of fear and the discovery of true courage: to sit in an airport in one of Central America's war zones and realize that one's confidential notes have disappeared, to find oneself suddenly alone facing a machine gun held by a young peasant soldier even more nervous than you, to venture into the cauldron of Ayacucho, Peru, and snatch the endan-gered from the jaws of brutal conflict.

There is a remarkable persistence in these people. The churches kept at Messrs. Trudeau, Sharp and MacEachen until Canada opened up to tens of thousands of Chileans. Bankers were petitioned, pick-eted, engaged and provoked until they began to see South Africa

through the eyes of majorities. By permitting and supporting specialized staff and volunteers to gain experience, develop expertise and
garner contacts and entrees, the churches gained through the coalitions a capacity and capability for expert and precise analysis and
advocacy which no individual denomination could sustain for long.
The depth of knowledge of the refugee system made Kathleen
Ptolemy, George Cram and others a force in Ottawa and with the
media. The analysis developed by John Dillon and colleagues over
two decades of work has earned respect for the churches in very un-
churchlike places and broadened the spectrum of debate and
economic imagination in Canada. The perceptive probing of Ernie
Regehr and Ploughshares staff has provided a spotlight on some of
Canada's most unseemly doings, when few others would take the
trouble or risk annoying the defence establishment. The commitment
and practice of 'telling the story,' the stories of injustice, the stories
of little victories, undertaken by Russ Hatton, Tony Clarke, Jeanne
Moffat or Bill Fairbairn and Gloria Shepherd has given pungency
and particularity to the work.

The sense of collectivity has always been strong in the coalitions
of my experience. I believe that this was partly an accident of time
and context, the effect of working among so many people nurtured
by the 1960s; but it was not only that. With the fresh wind which
blew through Pope John XXIII's Vatican windows came an openness
and a sense of discovery that was fresh in a way which is hard now
to conjure. Denominational executives in a variety of places made it
a point to hire across denominational lines. There was a sense of
opportunity to do things which had not before been attempted. For
some the theology of liberation was a veritable hurricane leading in
the direction of the new and the untried.

Within this context, the denominational social action and mission
advocates who came together around coalition tables made significant
leaps in working together. They were men, by and large, the majority
clergy. But there were enough Elizabeth Loweths and Bernard
Dufresnes to leaven the mixture. There was a certain sense of release,
I believe, in escaping denominational harness at least momentarily.
There was also a significant amount of new 'bonding' in action,
whether in confronting a politician, or visiting a native community
or third world prison. While coalition staff are rightly highlighted in
many of the essays, so are the indispensable representatives who

linked the work, who sought the resources, who shared the administrative duties of the coalitions. With the groundwork laid by Maxwell,
Maione, Johnson, Legge, MacRae, MacDonald, MacNeil, Proulx,
Scott, Zimmerman, MacKay and the personalities of Anthony, Davis,
Franklin, Hansen, Hatton, Clarke, Monk, Lindsey, Raymond, Smith
and Webb and many others took the reins. A considerable reciprocity
of load-sharing and mutual support emerged ...and joy.

The engagement which occurred in Ah-hah Seminars with
Dennis Howlett, the remarkable encounters and confrontations undertaken by Ten Days committees with politicians and potentates, the
prophetic interventions by a Jim Webb or a Michael Czerny in corporate annual general meetings... moments of learning, moments of
change, the joy of insight or simply of telling the truth.

Scope

In the era of the *Canadarm*, the coalitions dramatically increased
the 'reach' of the churches. Reading through the narratives is a
Baedeker of political and social theatres of activity, conflict and
achievement.

Consider the moment when Carmen Gloria Quintana addressed
the representatives of the murderous Chilean regime, in Geneva at the
United Nations Commission on Human Rights, with Canadian Bill
Fairbairn at her side: the human rights advocacy of a decade was
summed up in that moment. Think of the maimed representative of the
Bolivian opposition, whom church representatives managed to get
through the door of a reluctant Canadian bureaucrat: he became
president of his country fewer than 20 years later. The countless local
and regional representations and lobbies facilitated by a few dollars
from PLURA, the long progress from Justice Berger's table to that of
the constitution makers, the electric speed of solidarity between
Manitoba and Manila assisted by Ten Days, all contribute to the
achievement of change and of justice. The continuing research of the
Ecumenical Coalition for Economic Justice, unveiling the secret
negotiations and epic implications of the Free Trade Agreement and
the North American Free Trade Agreement, is put to the service of
women's, labour and environmental groups in Canada and beyond.
The nuclear industry, the forest industry, the mining companies and
their bankers have all found the churches at their door and in the midst
of their public deliberations. The persistent and credible investiga-

tions of Canada-Asia Working Group, the Inter-Church Committee on Human Rights in Latin America and the Inter-Church Coalition on Africa find readers in the U.N. Commission, world Human Rights Conferences, as well as being reprinted in the reports of numerous parliamentary bodies at home. The partnership with overseas groups and communities, developed by many of these groups and highlighted in Ten Days for World Development and the Interchurch Fund for International Development, now finds expression in pungent policy critique and advocacy of alternatives.

The reach is stunning, but it is not exhaustive. A new era, new forms of quiet but effective political power challenge the churches and coalitions to develop new initiatives and a more rigorous attitude toward effectiveness. A post-Cold War world offers opportunities which the wildest dreamers among Ploughshares founders might have found hard to credit, and yet is characterized by the marginalization and brutalization of the poor in ways all too consistent with those that motivated the foundation of the human rights coalitions.

Coalition personnel themselves have gone on to offer experience and expertise in many places: the headquarters of Amnesty International, the leadership of Greenpeace Canada, refugee accompaniment and advocacy in Central America, the chairmanship of the Action Canada Network, editorial responsibility with leading church and secular publications. Some have taken on leadership roles within the denominations, others in secular agencies, at least two in the offices of the Vatican. The coalitions have proved a training ground for professional expertise in social change, human rights and foreign policy successful beyond anyone's expectations.

But there is another reach embodied in these tales and it is the linkage with partners, whether in development projects, human rights and legal aid centres, native advocacy groups, antipoverty groups or camp organizations of refugees. What has fed individuals and coalitions themselves and what has made their work visible for thousands is the testimony, the visits and exchanges and, more and more, the advice, example and faith of partners. Several of the narratives detail an evolution of relationships between North and South, rich and poor. Some indicate the freedom which came because the relationship was not based on funding. Others indicate that the funding relationship could be transcended into a higher form of alliance. But this is hard to measure in its entirety. As tales of coalition experience travel from country to country, the examples of how work can be accomplished fly as rapidly and as much by intuition as the early lessons taken in by GATT-Fly and Ten Days from Paolo Freire and Gustavo Gutiérrez. This is a reach into the next century, into the next stage of global relationships and the worldwide search for justice.

Engagement

On reflection, the emphasis, particularly in the formative period, is not only optimistic, but quite outward. The emphasis is on mission, on matters largely viewed as exterior to the participating denominations or relatively far from the seats and pockets of congregations and donors. The predominance of engagement is external to Canada; even GATT-Fly—later so engaged in domestic issues—was created to address the world trading system. It could be argued that even the original engagement with native people was in a sense 'external,' its emphasis on the north and frontier areas quite other than the close-up situation of urban native peoples. Only PLURA appears to have been, from the beginning, directed at Canadian society, at internal justice in Canada.

The investigation of this orientation, the analysis of the context of the late 60s and early 70s and the self-image of those who gave birth to the coalitions is probably the stuff of theses and dissertations. Was there a sense in that time that Canadian society, its economy of resource and food exports, auto-building and branch plants, was so close to perfection that a government-funded matching grants program would provide the answers for the domestic poor which Senator Croll, Ian Adams, Wallace Smith and others had rediscovered? Was there a sense that the daily work of the denominations, the community level and downtown mission work of the churches and outreach workers would take care of poverty, and that joint work was either unnecessary or too difficult to merit the investment? Surely the limited success of the Coalition for Development following the Montreal Poverty Conference had not fed great expectations. Were the potential allies of the churches in such domestic enterprises all that interested or ready for engagement? The labour movement gave localized support and helped some limited work continue, but was its attention really on the struggle for overall justice in Canada? The antipoverty movement, struggling with limited resources and striking occasional fire, appreciated the resources offered by the churches, but no systematic or broad-reaching effort to change the structural roots of poverty developed out of the encounter. The women's movement was incipient in its new form, and the churches might not have been the first zone of attention if alliances were contemplated. The churches were as separated and confused by the national question as any other Canadian institution. Québécois might join English Canadians in common work for human rights or against economic injustice, but it was easier when directed outside Canada.

It was not that the churches were absent, entirely, from the fray of domestic politics. Although the days when a pronouncement from a leading cleric, in the style of James R. Mutchmor, could focus Canadian attention were past, the United Church of Canada worked on public issues of poverty and taxation through the 70s, as did allies in other denominations. But the promise of further extension of the welfare state by the dominant Liberal party proved ephemeral.

The battle for control of the Canadian state shifted significantly in the 70s. While the coalitions were relatively effective on resource questions (Berger) and external relations issues (Chilean refugees), other forces were rapidly outdistancing them in the Canadian policy theatre. In the mid-70s big transnational business in Canada organized itself to promote its own agenda with government and the public. Using American models, the Business Council on National Issues organized an "exclusive, by-invitation-only club" in 1976.[4] The voices and priorities of the chief executive officers of the largest Canadian private corporations were organized for maximum effect. At the same time, smaller businesses, through the Canadian Federation of Independent Business, and the ideologues of neoliberalism, through bodies like the Fraser Institute, were also intervening with government and the public in energetic and well-funded fashion.

These developments might not have been of concern had the agendas of both churches and business been otherwise, but the provocation for business' new intervention in public policy was often found in policies or innovations which the churches and at least some of the coalitions favoured: the elaboration and greater effectiveness of social programs and the reform of the tax system to provide greater redistribution and less inequality within Canada. The Taskforce on the Churches and Corporate Responsibility and a number of other coalitions came up against aspects of the 'corporate agenda.' Some church publications—notably the United Church's *Issue* "Who's in

Control?" (1977)—addressed the overall issue, but it might be remarked that the churches lagged behind the shift in political power and corporate organization which was occurring around them.

The engagement of the church social justice bodies in responding to the MacDonald Royal Commission and its competitive free trade ideology and the publication of the Canadian Catholic bishops' statement on the economy[5] signalled a shift in direction for the churches and at least some of the coalitions. The earlier work by GATT-Fly in seeking church backing for labour's struggles within Canada took a new form by engaging labour and other social forces in responding to the corporate agenda. This ultimately took shape in the Social Solidarity conversations, the Pro-Canada Network and the coalitions against Free Trade. The battle over free trade in 1987-88 and the visible role of a number of church staff and volunteers led to quiet but direct pressure by corporate leadership on denominational officials. Within denominations, divisions became more apparent between those favouring a more liberal internationalist approach and advocates of self-reliance, between those who feared or courted corporate leadership and the financial support of owners and managers and those who cared less about annoying them. At the same time, several denominations were hit with organizational crises of their own. Most of the mainline churches faced declining memberships and declining resources, and cutbacks were forced on several fronts. In the United Church of Canada, the deep and long-term conflict over the rights and participation of gays and lesbians in the roles and responsibilities of the church split the denomination and consumed much of the attention and energies of human rights and economic justice advocates across the country.

Several denominations took a further ecumenical step in the mid-80s joining coalitions in which the predominant actors were non-church bodies. The Pro-Canada (later Action Canada) Network was the most significant of these, although the Social Solidarity process offered a number of tantalizing opportunities. The level of commitment with which the churches entered these further steps was limited by some of the factors outlined above. High level leadership was often less apparent in the front lines of the fray. The durability of the Action Canada Network owed a good deal to the sustained and experienced leadership provided by coalition veterans like Tony Clarke and Dennis Howlett. The Network's survival of the 1988 election period was vindication of its value. The 1993 election posed more complex challenges to its future shape and purpose.

With the 90s, the key words of the business agenda resound through the air waves and politicians' speeches with a frequency unimagined 10 years ago: 'competitiveness,' 'globalization,' 'deficit,' 'structural adjustment.' Advocates of human rights and justice face a religion of inevitability, where a subtle economism convinces many that the fate of the nation is to be 'lean and mean' and its arbiters are world banks and corporate decision makers.

In such a climate, prophetic witness was seldom more necessary. The practice of extra-parliamentary opposition—at provincial and local as well as federal and international levels—is as vital as ever. But there are challenges to the form, challenges which need to be confronted. I perceive at least four: participation, the form of ecumenism, resources and ethos.

Participation

It is fair to assume that in the policy-oriented, information-based and participation-engaging aspects of political life which are open to those who lack the clout of major economic power, many of the forms of activity pioneered or embodied by the coalitions remain apropos. There has been at certain times—the early encounters with world trade, food and population conferences, the food campaigns, the Central American focus, the remarkable reception of refugees—an ability to engage the entire country, or even two nations, in different manners. There has also been a capacity on the part of the coalitions to mobilize the forces for justice in very difficult and controversial matters, in some alliances with labour and native peoples in struggle. But the development of a common and widely shared, locally embodied ecumenical workstyle continues to elude the churches, despite years of effort at joint prayer and joint projects. The periodic but never finalized attempts at joint fund raising for justice work may be symbolic of the limitations and appetites of denominationalism. Nevertheless, the narratives are full of examples of local ecumenical activity. The creativity which spawned one and then many coalitions on a national basis has also spawned regional coalitions to support a strike or a native struggle, and will again. What is less clear is what the governing politic of denominational leaders and legislative bodies is, and to what extent the fixations with declining personnel and revenue bases might be offset by a quickening sense of the urgency of environmental and economic challenge in society as a whole. Is it possible that a fresh generation of ecumenical experimentation, dedicated to justice, participation and sustainability, with local and regional variety and yet with clear national nurture and broad networks and focus, might emerge before the year 2000? Does the rash of national and international experimentation with electronic networking and rapid information sharing offer highways for solidarity among Christians in ways that have not yet been fully explored?

Ecumenism

The apparent decline of the Canadian Council of Churches and the continued vivacity of many coalitions lead to questions of ecumenical form at the national as well as the local level. It is hard to believe that the nurturing of a fresh generation of ecumenical endeavours can come from an emaciated and marginalized Council. It is also hard to believe that the churches can do anything but fall further out of the realm of effectiveness in public policy and social change if they continue their shrinking denominational national bureaucracies. It is also worth questioning whether 10, 12 or 20 coalitions are as effective as they might be without the ability to concentrate strength in a particular effort from time to time and particularly without adequate communications capacity, both within the Christian community and with the television-prone populace at large. During the same period in which the coalitions took form, the churches and other faith groups created Vision TV, with its limited audience but excellent commitment. The potential for engagement between the two streams of ecumenical life is considerable, but has been only slightly explored.

Resources

All this is suggestive about the use of resources. Just as the end of the Cold War was expected to bring a peace dividend to invest in new forms of security—the combat against poverty and disease, the investment in environmental sustainability—so the ecumenical vision has always had within it the idea of the release of resources for common effort. What might a significant reshuffling of assets mean? To state one example could truncate the imaginations of others, but hopefully, it could also stimulate. What might happen if the churches were persuaded to take a tithe (or more) of their reserves, however held. Let them place most of it in common, as a justice, sustainability and participation trust, and invest part of that, and part of their regular budgets, in a three-year collective effort to change the pattern of giving in Canada, a three-year joint public campaign for that trust. Let them use another portion of those funds or the income from the funds in a common campaign to address the public ethos in Canada, primarily through television (including but not only through Vision TV), but using community town halls and church services as well. Let them invest the remainder in a common organizational and communications base for ecumenical work in Canada. The research, advocacy and educational work of the coalitions would be part of that, so too would be experimentation, training and exchange among Christian communities across Canada. Mistaken? Full of holes? Indeed, but let it provoke many better ideas.

Ethos

The fourth and most essential effort may be to reshape the ethos, that is the essential content and language, of our common life. What shape does the vision, which named itself "just, participatory and sustainable" some years ago, take on for the year 2000? Does not that vision have a much greater sensitivity to gender and sexual preference now than the vision of 1970? Does not the clamour for change at home, in Canada, take on a much greater urgency in order to build sustainability into our future? Must not that vision include a way of conjecturing alternatives that was quite unknown in the girdled ideological formulas of a bipolar world?

Conclusion

The last decade has been characterized, for me and many others around the world, by a new spectre, the spectre of AIDS. Loss has been more common than our young imaginations comprehended even 10 years ago. From so many other causes, we have also lost ecumenical colleagues whose light kept darkness from our circle. In this, a very personal note, following the mention of Ruth Tillman earlier.

The liberating progress in Central America and the engagement of Canadians therein was moved forward markedly by the contribution of Father Bill Smith, Scarboro priest, lover of life and of justice.

The lives of scores, even thousands, of refugees were changed and given hope and support by Kathleen Ptolemy, who was not too busy to give my daughter a brief summer job when she was getting impatient with her work-besotted father. The quiet strength of Bishop Adolphe Proulx was particularly known to those in the struggle against poverty and for the respect of human rights. His dependable and gracious support of initiative after initiative on the part of the Inter-Church Committee on Human Rights in Latin America and other coalitions was a blessing, much missed in its absence. His generosity of spirit and wry smile were a marked loss to coalitions and overseas partners as well. These lives encourage the fuller appreciation of the living.

> *"Always, I am amazed at what we tell,*
> *how much faith we put in it.*
> *Never really knowing who is listening,*
> *how they're going to take it, where."*[6]

A Regional Perspective

Robert McKeon

Introduction

This chapter will reflect on the stories of the coalitions from the perspective of a region distant from southern Ontario. I write from my personal experience of 15 years as a volunteer and staff worker in Catholic and ecumenical social action networks in Alberta. It is important to state that this is a regional perspective.

To name a regional perspective means to stand within a specific context within Canada. National church leaders, as part of their 1973 Ten Days tour, sought to define the Alberta context: "To Canada, the Prairie region has been a Third World whose agricultural and mineral resources have been exploited at the whim and benefit of industrialized centres in the East. Rarely and inadequately consulted, Prairie citizens have had little say in the development and distribution of their own resources."[1]

While this statement refers to political and economic concerns, many from the regions, at least from the Prairies, would use similar language to describe their experience in Canadian church networks, including the ecumenical justice coalitions.

The birth of the coalitions

Ecumenical co-operation grew in the late 60s and early 70s around such issues as medicare, housing and domestic and Third World poverty. Collaboration started with informal gatherings of national church leaders and social action staff, and after a time grew to shared conferences, briefs to governments and educational events. Eventually this collaboration became institutionalized around specific justice concerns shared by the different denominations such as international trade, native rights, corporate responsibility, and human rights. A common organizational structure developed which included limited budgets and staffing, a board composed primarily of national denominational officials and a Toronto address. PLURA and later Project Ploughshares were exceptions to this pattern.

Individual coalition stories: A regional view

Most of the coalitions were organized to assist the national churches in their ongoing social action and development education programming. The materials produced by the coalitions were to be made available to national church officials and then disseminated to the grassroots in the regions through the respective denominational structures. The different coalition stories show how in most cases this was not a viable strategy and alternate approaches had to be discovered. The range of responses can be shown by examining the coalition stories and by placing the coalitions on a spectrum with respect to regional presence. On this spectrum, the Taskforce on the Churches and Corporate Responsibility would be at one pole and PLURA at the other.

The Taskforce can be described as probably the least grassroots of all the coalitions. It seeks to assist participating churches and religious orders in their investment activities; included are corporate research and shareholder action strategies. On occasion, the Task-force may venture into the regions, such as at the annual meeting of an Alberta oil company. While regional groups have appreciated the quality printed research materials, they have been distant from the Taskforce's decision making, personnel and activities.

The Inter-Church Committee on Human Rights in Latin America, the Canada-Asia Working Group, the Inter-Church Coalition on Africa, the Inter-Church Committee for Refugees—all these coalitions have a strongly centralized operation along with individual and group contacts across Canada. These coalitions work with these contacts in organizing events such as speaking tours and action campaigns. Much of the regional activity developed locally from the ground up. For example, as the Inter-Church Committee on Human Rights in Latin America gained momentum on issues of human rights in Chile and later in Central America, many regional groups were organized by Canadians who met refugees settling in local communities across Canada and developed ongoing communications and solidarity links through local Latin American networks. Over time, national networks emerged with the national coalitions playing an important role, although usually not serving as animators in the regions.

The Inter-Church Coalition on Africa has made outreach to the regions a priority since its start in 1982. Government funding through CIDA's Partnership Africa Canada has assisted the Coalition in developing and maintaining linkages with church-based solidarity groups across Canada and in organizing periodic national consultations involving regional representatives.

GATT-Fly, now known as the Ecumenical Coalition for Economic Justice, was organized by the national churches to assist the churches on issues of world trade. Part of this work involved connecting with regional networks, around actions such as the 1974 World Food Conference in Rome. The GATT-Fly story describes the shift in focus from international conferences and lobbying Canadian government officials to a strategy of research and action in empowering people's organizations and popular movements across Canada and the Third World. From this change in focus, GATT-Fly has developed extensive research and popular educational skills (i.e. Ah-hah Seminars) which have benefited regional groups. However, other than through the one-way communication of printed resources, many in the regions have experienced GATT-Fly as a distant presence whose work is marked by its Central Canadian origin. While the Coalition's mandate points to a regional collaboration, its board membership, budget allocations and staff time priorities indicate little regional presence.

Project North, now known as the Aboriginal Rights Coalition, is a coalition that has been forced to modify its whole organizational structure, operations and budgeting in order to incorporate regional native and non-native concerns. The Project North story shows how, from the beginning, coalition staff gave high priority to developing contacts with regional indigenous organizations such as the Dene Nation and to animating, supporting and strengthening a network of solidarity in the churches in the regions of Canada. Strong regional groups emerged in Victoria, Vancouver, Edmonton and Labrador/ Newfoundland. The regional groups developed primarily through the work of strong local animators together with local fund raising. The impressive record of regional groups in making submissions to bodies such as the Berger Commission and in participating in national action campaigns shows the strength of this regional solidarity network. The Project North story tells how as early as 1980 the relationship between the national coalition and the regional groups (native and non-native) had become a serious unanswered question. In 1987, Project North collapsed because the coalition had developed an institutional structure which "became mired in [national] church bureaucracy" and "did not allow for effective involvement by the network groups in decision making."[2]

When Project North suspended its operation for a year of review and restructuring, a portion of the national budget was made available to regional groups to continue their work during this period. The regional groups which had developed effective regional solidarity partnerships (e.g. Edmonton/Lubicon, Newfoundland/ Innu) continued in the absence of a national office. The new coalition which emerged under the name Aboriginal Rights Coalition had a more decentralized structure compared to what had existed previously. Regular annual general assemblies were organized, regionally chosen native and non-native representatives were included as board members together with the national denominational representatives and a significant part of the national coalition budget ($35,000) was allocated for the support of regional groups.

The Aboriginal Rights Coalition story indicates that the regional presence of the coalitions is an issue not only for regional denominational members, but also for regional indigenous organizations.

Ten Days for World Development has a somewhat similar institutional history to the Aboriginal Rights Coalition. Ten Days started in 1973 as an initiative of national church staff for a national church leaders tour across Canada to raise public awareness of Third World development issues. After this first year, Ten Days became an ongoing development education initiative. In the following years, Third World speakers, often church leaders, participated in high profile national tours. As the Ten Days story indicates, by the late 70s local Ten Days committees were organized across Canada. Some areas, such as Winnipeg, organized local committees, raised funds, hired local staff and initiated local ecumenical development education activities. The local Ten Days groups often worked in close collaboration with local Third World Learner Centres. The focus on the food issue (1977-79) provided an occasion for a whole series of regional and local hearings, meetings and workshops as part of the People's Food Commission. At that time, the Ten Days educational approach of closely integrating local and Third World dimensions of global issues was already entrenched. Such an approach demanded ongoing local and regional research, social analysis, theological reflection and action on local issues. A prairie regional network of Ten Days groups evolved in the late 70s around the planning and control of the annual speakers' tour. In 1981, these regional networks forced changes to the national coalition structure. Regional representatives demanded a voice in decisions around national programming, staffing and financial priorities. They also pressed for financial support for regional representatives to participate in regular regional and national network meetings. By the 1980s, there were over 150 local committees and a full-time staff position was created for regional network support.

Today the Ten Days network is the major national ecumenical social action network. Local and regional groups have developed their own identities, distinct from the national board and staff, distinct also from specific denominations. This regional identity issue was highlighted in the debate around the issue of developing the theme of "spirituality for justice" as a program focus. Local groups argued against national church staff who saw spirituality as a concern to be dealt with within individual denominations. Thus the regional challenge to the national coalitions was not only to relate to denominational individuals and regional groups, but also to relate to regional ecumenical groups with lives of their own.

PLURA is a unique coalition from a regional perspective. Although it was birthed by the same committee of national denominational staff as the other coalitions, from the first day it was to be decentralized with no national staff or office. It was to have a board where a majority were regionally elected members and a budget where the majority of funds were spent under the direction of regional/provincial committees. Funds were provided for regional participation in regular national assemblies which set direction for the whole organization. As with the Aboriginal Rights Coalition, PLURA recognized two distinct regional constituencies: regional denominational representatives and representatives named from local/regional low-income groups; of course, these categories need not be mutually exclusive. The national founders of PLURA hoped church funds would be supplemented by government funds in the support of local low-income social change groups. Since this hope has not been realized, PLURA has never had the resources to support an ongoing program of research, education and public advocacy on either a regional or national level in a manner similar to the Third World-oriented coalitions which have CIDA support.

Project Ploughshares is also unique with respect to the regional question. Ploughshares has a strong national office and staff located in southern Ontario. However, it also has an extensive base of individual subscribers and financial supporters all across the country, as well as a vibrant network of local Ploughshares groups. In a manner somewhat similar to the Aboriginal Rights Coalition and Ten Days, the national structure changed in order to incorporate regional representatives on the national board and to allow them to participate in national consultations.

The experiences of regional coalitions

In order to understand better a regional perspective on national coalitions, it is important to investigate the ecumenical coalitions which have emerged at the local and regional levels. Across Canada from Newfoundland to Vancouver Island, there are hundreds of ecumenical coalitions addressing local, regional, national and international issues. These coalitions are quite varied in membership, working styles and relationship to denominational church structures. Some are explicitly Christian in identity, others interfaith, while many involve Christian ecumenical participation in wider community coalitions and social movements. A full description of regional coalition work would take another book. In this section, all that is possible is to include some specific examples from Alberta.

Edmonton Church Coalition on Labour and Justice

In June 1986 in Edmonton, a strike was called by unionized workers at Peter Pocklington's Gainers meat packing plant. Edmontonians were soon presented with scenes of violent confrontation involving busloads of strike-breakers seeking physically to break through resisting picket lines of striking workers and supporters. A police riot squad intervened, mass arrests were made and a sweeping court injunction followed. Clergy and laity from several denominations gathered almost immediately. Some had already developed working relationships with organized labour through previous participation in coalitions such as Friends of Medicare and Solidarity Alberta. It quickly became apparent that there were important issues beyond this particular strike, such as Alberta labour legislation, the use of police power, the role of the courts in industrial disputes and the problems of farmers within the food industry.

During the 6 ¹/₂-month strike, the ecumenical group responded in several ways: early morning picket line prayer services, court challenges, public meetings with labour and management, a boycott, participation in mass rallies and animation within individual denominations. In the aftermath of the strike, coalition members participated in public hearings concerning changes to Alberta labour law. The ad hoc ecumenical group that gathered during the strike grew into an ongoing ecumenical coalition which became involved in subsequent strikes elsewhere. They held meetings with cabinet ministers, produced educational materials (including a video) on labour legislation in Alberta. More recently, they gathered together people from all sides of labour-management relations to explore alternative approaches to adversarial collective bargaining as presently practised. Informal links were established with similar-minded groups in neighbouring provinces, as well as with other coalitions concerned with economic justice, such as the Action Canada Network.

Social Justice Institute

For the past 13 years, a week-long ecumenical educational event, the Social Justice Institute, has been conducted in the Edmonton region. What started as a largely Catholic initiative soon became a more broadly based ecumenical organization involving several denominations. Participants came from all over Western Canada. Speakers included national church leaders and Third World, local and national resource people. The Institute has served as a forum for linking national coalitions, such as the Ecumenical Coalition for Economic Justice and the Taskforce on the Churches and Corporate Responsibility, with regional people. Probably even more important, the Institute has provided an ecumenical setting for regional people to connect with each other. For several years, the British Columbia social justice network organized a similar summer gathering.

Southern Alberta World Development Education Program (SAWDEP)/ Micah Institute

Different centres in Canada have established regional and local ecumenical and interfaith development education programs. Since the 60s, Calgary Interfaith, an ecumenical and interfaith agency, has actively supported a broad spectrum of international development education activities. In recent years, this international concern has included SAWDEP which has worked to support faith communities in southern Alberta dealing with international development and social justice issues. With funding support from CIDA and the churches, the Program has been able to hire staff and organize a wide variety of development education events. Over the years SAWDEP has been an active participant in the Ten Days network.

Alberta Youth Animation Project on South Africa (AYAPSA)

AYAPSA grew out of ongoing South African solidarity and church development education work in Alberta. In 1989, AYAPSA was organized as a project for youth by youth in order to facilitate "increased awareness of southern African issues among Alberta youth and to encourage their active participation in anti-apartheid and anti-racist work."[3] This racism focus includes an examination of racism in Canada. There are staff in Calgary and Edmonton and contact persons in several centres across the province. Programming includes a newsletter, *Cry Freedom*, provincial conferences, presentations to schools and youth groups, speaker tours and exchange visits between youth in Alberta and youth in South Africa. Funding support has come from CIDA, CUSO and several Christian denominations. AYAPSA has been able to keep in close contact and work collaboratively with the Inter-Church Coalition on Africa.

The national coalition movement: Regional voices in a national consultation

Individual coalitions have changed and adapted to varying degrees over the past 20 years. While most of the coalitions had a similar starting point (the national denominational staff serving on the Inter-Church Consultative Committee for Development and Relief), each was established independently for its own unique purpose. The coalitions were not created as part of a planned system. However, over time, there was a push to 'institutionalize' the coalitions from an ad hoc series of organizations into a more permanent and consistent structure, including a push for regular funding by the denominations and stable salaries and benefits among staff of the different coalitions. Coalition staff organized together into the Ecumenical Coalition Staff Association. Coalition board members

instituted the Coalition Advisory Committee. The funding denominations co-ordinated this broad ecumenical justice work through the
Committee on Justice and Peace of the Canadian Council of
Churches. Thus the thrust for the institutionalization of the coalitions
proceeded 'upstream' at the intercoalition and national church headquarters levels, at a distance from any ongoing regional conversation.

By the late 80s, this established coalition structure came under
increasing pressure, especially with respect to funding, because the
supporting denominations were experiencing financial shortfalls.
Coalition budgets were running a $70,000 deficit in 1990, with larger
amounts projected for future years. New coalitions had been created
over the years but, with the exception of the Inter-Church Project on
Population, coalitions once created did not close down. New issues
such as ecology, women's issues and rural poverty called for the
creation of new coalitions at a time when existing coalitions could
not be sustained at existing staffing levels.

Early in 1990, a national consultation was launched on the future
of the national coalitions. A preparatory document, "Social Ecumenism... Building Our Future Together," presented three possible alternatives: reassign the work and reduce the coalitions from 12 to 8 *or*
create 4-6 coalition clusters along thematic or geographic lines *or*
create clusters along functional lines (i.e. research, movement building, solidarity funding).[4]

A follow-up paper, "Consultation Planning Process," outlined a
national consultation process involving three primary constituencies:
sponsoring church bodies, coalition boards and staffs, and regional
church networks.[5] Each constituency was to indicate its preference
from among the three proposed models for coalition rationalizing and
down-sizing or propose alternate models. The first two constituencies
were well organized. The inclusion into the process of the regional
networks, which were not organized, provided a serious challenge.
An animator was hired, funds were allocated and eight regional
consultations were scheduled across Canada. Participants in the
regional consultations were to be named by the coalitions, individual
denominations and local ecumenical groups. The results of all the
consultations were to be presented and decisions made concerning
the future of the coalitions at an expanded Committee on Justice and
Peace meeting, at which regional representatives, one from each
regional consultation, would be present.

The summary reports from the regional consultations were compiled and a national summary report prepared.[6] This report presented a clear regional viewpoint on the work of the coalitions, including the following points:

• There was a strong affirmation of the high quality of the work of the coalitions and its importance for church social action people all across the country. Because of the importance of the coalitions to the national churches and the regional networks, denominational funding should be maintained, or even increased, rather than cut.

• A common frustration expressed was the perceived distance of most coalition activities, decision making and personnel (both staff and volunteer) from the regional social justice networks. This distance was even greater for local congregation members. The coalitions were asked to improve their overall communications with the regions, incorporate regional perspectives in coalition priority setting and include regional representatives on coalition boards. Coalition communications must expand beyond printed documents to include face to face visits and the promotion of popular education techniques. Ways must be developed to facilitate collaboration between the regions and the national coalitions in a co-operative, non-hierarchical manner.

• Regional experiences highlighted the importance of incorporating non-church partners in ecumenical social justice work, including the work of the national coalitions.

• Common regional concerns included the environment, women's issues, aboriginal rights and rural economic breakdown. These issues did not necessarily require new coalitions; rather, they should be incorporated into the work of all the existing coalitions. Regional experiences emphasized the importance of keeping the links among regional, national and international issues.

• The regional consultations were an important time for regional networking and empowerment. Many individuals were participating in such an event for the first time. Every region spoke of repeating such gatherings not just to discuss national coalition priorities, but to meet each other, share information, reflect together and discuss regional strategies and priorities. Ongoing financial support for regional networking was named a high priority. The possible decentralization of national coalition work was proposed. Regions experiencing cutbacks in church social action funding emphasized the importance of using scarce denominational funds in common ecumenical initiatives.

• There was a need to integrate more explicitly the Christian faith vision and the critical social analysis work of the coalitions. The regional experience of lukewarm church commitment to social justice highlighted the need for all in the ecumenical movement, including the coalitions, to affirm the centrality of social justice in the life of the churches.

• The absence of low-income, native and other marginalized voices was observed by many in the regional and national consultation process. Ways must be established to include these voices in ecumenical coalition work so that the churches work in solidarity *with* the poor, rather than *for* the poor.

The feedback from the three consultations (denominations, coalitions, regions) was reviewed and a proposal for coalition restructuring was prepared by a drafting committee from the Committee on Justice and Peace executive and the Coalition Advisory Committee. In response to regional concerns, the animator of the regional consultation process was included on the drafting committee. This committee prepared a proposal titled "Empowered for the Future" for the April 1991 plenary session of the Committee on Justice and Peace. This plenary session was to prepare coalition restructuring recommendations for ratification and implementation by the funding denominations. The timing of this document posed problems as the Toronto-area participants received the document, and even prepared written responses, prior to the plenary session, while most of the regional representatives did not see the document until their arrival in Toronto on the day of the session.

The "Empowered for the Future" proposal included substantial changes in the organizational working of the coalitions and overall coalition staffing cuts in response to increasing coalition deficits. Coalitions would be clustered into two groups: international (the Inter-Church Coalition on Africa, the Inter-Church Committee on Human Rights in Latin America, the Canada-Asia Working Group, the Interchurch Fund for International Development) and domestic (the Aboriginal Rights Coalition, the Inter-Church Committee for Refugees, Project Ploughshares, PLURA). The Ecumenical Coalition for Economic Justice and the Taskforce on the Churches and Corporate Responsibility would participate in both clusters. By clustering together, the coalitions would be able to share common office space, administrative and support staff. In addition to these clusters, a

"Justice and Peace Movement Building Unit" would be created by expanding the Ten Days national network into domestic issues so it could assist all the coalitions through "educational work, outreach, a common publication and regional network support."[7]

The proposal did address explicitly the demand of the regions for greater regional involvement in the life of the national coalitions and national support for regional networks. While specific recommendations for support of regional ecumenical work were not presented, the document stated: "Mechanisms should be sought which increase regional participation in what is already happening and reduce regional perceptions of isolation, without necessarily creating regional structures and the attendant expenses."[8] Hopefully, the proposed Justice and Peace Movement Building Unit would animate an ongoing regional consultation process which could result in improved communications, annual conferences or other initiatives.

Another part of the national consultation process involved a visit by three Third World partners. Their nine-day visit consisted of meetings in Ontario with national church staff and coalition personnel. Their only regional contact was with PLURA partner groups in Hamilton. The Third World visitors observed that most Canadian Christians did not know of the work of the coalitions. Their reflection on Canadian ecumenical social justice priorities had implications for the regional discussion: "We sense that the Christians in Canada find it easier to seek social transformation by responding to poverty and injustice in other parts of the world than by working for social transformation at home. Solidarity with marginalized groups in Canada helps to strengthen coalition work and to overcome middle class values."[9]

Regional reports presented at the Committee on Justice and Peace plenary were critical of the recommendations contained in "Empowered for the Future." Key issues raised included the proposed fragmentation of domestic and international issues, lack of French-language communications and resources, low priority for support of ecumenical activity at the regional level and the proposed restructuring of Ten Days. Both denominational and coalition representatives spoke critically of the separation of international and domestic issues, of the further centralization of coalition activities and of other recommendations contained in "Empowered for the Future."

Plenary recommendations included greater regional participation in all coalition boards, more affirmative action for women, aboriginals, ethnic minorities, youth, the differently abled, national financial support for regional research and meetings, and closer connection between existing regional groups and national structures.[10]

After months of intense discussions in the national and regional consultations and the Justice and Peace plenary, no consensus for changing the structure and work of the national coalitions was achieved. Little has happened subsequently with respect to changes in the coalitions and regional ecumenical social justice networks, except finding ways to cope with tightened budgets and heightened expectations arising out of the whole consultation exercise.

Issues: Competing paradigms for coalition work

The coalition stories and regional experiences show two competing paradigms for ecumenical social justice work. These competing paradigms appear within the stories of individual coalitions and within the ecumenical social justice movement as a whole.

One paradigm relates to a centralized 'top-down' operation. Staff and volunteer expertise is gathered in a national centre, research conducted and educational materials prepared and then disseminated. Financial, staffing and programming priorities are established from the centre and then communicated to the regions. There may be extensive regional networks but the relationship between the regions and the centre is hierarchical.

The coalitions were initiated primarily within this paradigm. It was assumed that the coalitions would relate to the national churches which would serve as conduits for the coalitions to communicate with the regional grassroots. This assumption was challenged in the 1990-91 coalition consultation process: "The notion that research materials, policy recommendations and educational materials trickle down from church officials and staff to the people in the pews is widely rejected."[11]

There are many reasons for this communication failure. One reason is that denominational church structures are not designed for this task. A clear example is the Roman Catholic Church which has no national structure reaching out to the regions and dealing with domestic social justice concerns. Another reason is the lack of denominational social justice staff and volunteer resources in much of the country. The recent closure of half of the English-speaking Roman Catholic social action offices in Canada due to changing church priorities and financial cutbacks is a vivid example of this.[12]

The 'distance' between the national coalitions and many in the denominations poses another obstacle. This distance has given the coalitions a niche within which an ecumenical social justice agenda has been carried out that is often more radical than the individual denominations can sustain. Thus, denominations may be unwilling to channel with any degree of enthusiasm coalition educational materials and action initiatives. A good example was the election materials prepared co-operatively by several of the coalitions during the 1988 Free Trade federal election.

Another paradigm describes a decentralized 'bottom-up' operation where staff and volunteer resources may exist at more than one location and where financial, staffing and programming decisions include regional networks as full partners. Over time, a shift toward the second paradigm has emerged in some of the coalitions. This can be seen most explicitly in the Aboriginal Rights Coalition and Ten Days stories where this shift has resulted in changed coalition structures, staffing and budgets. Several of the regional consultations spoke of the need to move closer to this second paradigm.

This clash of paradigms became quite visible as proposals to decentralize and to further centralize the national coalitions emerged side by side at the end of the 1990-91 national consultation.

Much can be learned on this question of competing paradigms by examining the experiences of other Canadian church-related national organizations, such as Citizens for Public Justice which recently centralized all its staff in Toronto and the Canadian Urban Training Project and Urban Core Support Network, both of which chose to decentralize from a Toronto centre.

Ecclesiologies and spiritualities

The growth of the national and regional ecumenical coalitions over the past 20 years has been an example of practical ecumenism. What started as shared research and social action initiatives has deepened into ongoing relationships of trust, spiritual sharing and celebration. In many local ecumenical groups, Christians of different denominations have shared their spiritual journeys, exchanged spiritual resources rooted in different traditions and prayed together. A common scripture has served as a powerful foundation for spiritual sharing lived out in countless scripture reflections in the midst of engagement in social justice struggles within communities all across Canada. Local ecumenical social action groups have provided a space where new relationships between clergy and laity, men and women and people of different ethnic backgrounds could be explored and tested. Much local and regional ecumenical work has evolved toward an egalitarian style of leadership and work that models the principles of the social justice message; this style is not often found in individual congregations and denominational structures. In local situations where particular denominations ignore or even oppose a Christian justice message, individuals experience greater spiritual solidarity in ecumenical gatherings than in their own congregations. This tension between ecumenical and denominational experiences of Christian community was illustrated in the recent discussion within the Ten Days coalition about naming 'spirituality for justice making' as a national program focus.

These are not new issues. The short-lived experiment of the social action-oriented labour churches in Canada after World War I provides a warning against ecumenical shortcuts to ongoing frustrations within individual denominations.[13] Smillie's critique of earlier generations of ecumenically minded social justice Christians within the Canadian Social Gospel movement points to the need to ground all Christian social action with deep spiritual roots.[14] Yet historical references must not blind Christians to the new ecclesial and spiritual dimensions contained in the national stories as well as in countless regional ecumenical groups across Canada. New ways of being church, ecumenically engaged while denominationally rooted, need to be explored. Spiritualities which can support and nourish these new ways of being church in a world scarred by injustice need to be identified.

Future directions: A regional perspective

Prescribing the future for the national coalitions is a difficult task. The extensive consultation process around the restructuring of the coalitions failed to provide a new direction for them. However, the feedback from the regions can provide a few suggestions:

• Within the present structure of the coalitions, increase the regional presence and participation in the decision making and programming of each coalition. The Project North/Aboriginal Rights Coalition story shows one way to do this.

• The experience of the regions in the national consultation process provided an exciting "Ah-hah" experience[15] for the whole coalition movement. A high level of enthusiasm, empowerment and ownership of ecumenical social justice work emerged in each of the regions. This type of wide-ranging networking and consultation within the ecumenical social justice movement needs to be repeated in the future. Representatives from low-income and marginalized groups in Canada as well as Third World partner groups need to be included.

• The 1991 "Empowered for the Future" document recognized the need to support and strengthen the regional networks. However, it refrained from making any specific proposals. Yet without effective regional structures, the full potential of the national coalitions cannot be realized. Ways need to be found for national funds to assist in supporting regional partners. Special priority could be given where there are gaps in the present national coalition work, such as with the issues of rural decline, the environment, and women and poverty.

Conclusion

Continuing ecumenical social action work is taking place in local and regional coalitions all across Canada. These regional voices are asking to be recognized as full partners in the work of the national coalitions. Ecumenical conversations in the regions have a similar ring to those continuing in other sectors of Canadian society. National coalitions without a rootedness in the regions are 'national' in name only. Strong regional partnerships can only strengthen and expand the work and the financial base of the national coalitions and help to build a truly national social justice movement in Canada.

A View
from the Centre

Edith Shore

The stories of the coalitions collected in this book invite our admiration for the high quality of work, the dedication of staff and the collaboration and support of their colleagues in the churches. When the coalitions began, no one knew how excellent their work would be nor that a long-term initiative was being established. All the more reason to ponder carefully any decisions that affect the future of ecumenical social justice work. Any changes that will be made must give due regard to the unlikelihood of the same work ever being duplicated within any single denominational house.

The purpose of this chapter is to offer a view from an ecumenical bureaucrat's vantage point; it is not an exalted position and it is some time since I occupied it. Since these are the reflections of one person, and ecumenical work is by definition the work of many, none of what follows is intended to be other than a possible basis for reflection within the community.

Leadership and responsible decision making

Because of the complex structure of the coalitions and the no-less-complex manner in which ecumenical work is done, leadership is always a complicated matter. There is no one person and no single church or committee that may make decisions about the coalitions. Often, decisions are achieved by a system that involves a series of agreements which come closer and closer to a final workable arrangement; this has probably been the most effective solution so far. Because each coalition has its own board and some autonomy within its own circle of funders and church representatives, many decisions are exercised within that context. This system tends to leave larger questions unasked and unanswered. Where do we place such questions as: What do we do with entirely new initiatives? Who should be included in decision making about them—one coalition at a time, or all coalitions and churches working together? For example, if the Inter-Church Committee on Human Rights in Latin America and the Ecumenical Coalition for Economic Justice propose to collaborate in a concentrated manner on North American Free Trade issues, is that business for those groups only, or should all the players in the coalition circuit take part? If a proposed new initiative, for example electoral reform in Canada, does not fall into the traditional territory of any coalition, how would we responsibly decide to include it or leave it untouched? How would the sum of coalition work and funding be changed?

It would be useful, from this writer's point of view, to establish a forum including all the parties involved which could begin to ask the questions that concern total future work. Such a forum could assign taskforces to look at overall questions of financing, accountability, program and future directions. Only by taking an active role in working on issues of programming can coalitions and churches look together for solutions to the difficult matter of beginnings and endings in a time of scarce resources. Otherwise, we may see the situation degenerate to the point where someone will be forced to make the difficult and unpopular decisions and be blamed for them. This is a classic signal of unwillingness to take responsibility, whether within families or organizations.

While a large forum would no doubt be cumbersome, it could provide a place to work on decisions for the future in a collaborative way. Leadership would no doubt continue to be shared and rotated by those involved. Decision making would not be easy or without acrimony, but an effort to resolve issues in the open has to be better than the alternatives.

Strengthening the coalition structure

The social justice coalitions of the Canadian churches exist in a profoundly institutionalized context. Not only do they have their own quite complicated network of staff, board, committees, other coalitions, denominational contacts, regional networks, funders/supporters, non-governmental organization contacts, government networks, professional and research connections, overseas connections with friends, colleagues, government and agencies, but they are invariably closely bound to the churches. Each of the churches is a larger and much less focussed entity than the coalitions, with a broader constituency and a more diffuse mandate. We would be hard pressed to diagram the whole enterprise of the coalitions with all its complexities in a way that would do justice to all that is involved.

Whereas the coalitions are, at their oldest, just becoming old enough to vote, the churches have history, some of them for millennia. While young institutions tend to have more flexibility, are usually smaller and have a firmer grip on their focus, older ones have more experience, traditions that unite their constituency and often a firmer financial base. Mixing old and new together would seem to have benefits for both sides. The coalitions gain from the stability, established constituency and money-raising capacity of the churches, and the churches are able to pursue a range and depth of social justice concerns that may require more focussed energy and risk than they would be able to gather alone. At the same time, both sides are frustrated by the other. "Why don't the churches move more quickly?" the coalitions ask. "Why are those coalitions always moving so far away from us?" wonder the churches. That's on a good day. Some days the questions from both sides are a good deal more pointed.

An outsider looking at the whole system, perhaps some peripatetic delegation from outer space, would wonder how it could ever be made to work. After some reflection, it might be clear that there are many strengths to an arrangement that makes use of many organizations and individuals in ways that complement their particular gifts without weakening the whole. Diversity is often uncomfortable but it is seldom poorer than exclusivity.

Overcoming the separation of 'insiders' and 'outsiders'

A difficulty for non-profit agencies is the concern that the centre is forever pulling away from the support base and vice versa. Whenever a staff is assembled to do a task on behalf of a wider group, they immediately begin to look at how they may shape their work in relation to that whole. They will also identify the priorities for their task. Generally the perception of the new group challenges the original parameters of the sending units to whom they are responsible. This tends to be so at all levels: congregational, regional and national. It leads to those weary reflections that our elected politicians never hear what we are saying and that the church is out of touch with what is really needed. And in one sense it is true. But it is also true that you cannot collect a staff for a national office or a coalition and expect it to function exclusively on the basis of a particular sectoral concern. Furthermore, the national groups usually locate in an urban centre and are shaped by that context. So the centre does move away from the hinterland, both intentionally and unintentionally, and the hinterland is frustrated by its inability to make the centre respond to its very legitimate interests. All of this is exacerbated in Canada by long-term regional verities: Quebec and the language issue, Western isolation, Atlantic economic issues, to name a few perennials.

Because the coalitions were set up by the national church offices to do specialized work and because they do not come under the control of any one church, the coalitions are an even more remote formation when viewed by the larger constituency. Add to that the fact that the issues under consideration are controversial and often not well understood, and it is easy to see that there are many opportunities for inside-outside tensions.

Communication from the centre becomes difficult because it is seen as coming from a distance and because the information usually requires a certain background and sophistication in order to be understood. A common perception would be that there has been no communication at all. "I didn't know about it," or "Never heard of them," probably sounds familiar. Communication from the grassroots back to the centre is always difficult. For example, a letter arrives at the offices of an interchurch coalition containing suggestions for new program directions and criticism of work to date. Unless it is signed by someone well-known and highly regarded within the coalition, the suggestions may be evaluated as being poorly informed, already done, not possible at this time, too expensive, or not central enough to the mandate of the coalition. A polite letter may go out in response, but a serious consideration of the suggestions may not ensue. It is difficult to maintain that balance between inside concerns and outside input, and it is not a flaw peculiar to the coalitions.

Becoming more responsive is not a one-time fix. It seems that we need to have considerable sensitivity, continuous support and a will to be responsive in order to do better, whether we are running a mainline church, the government of Canada or caring for a cranky baby. We can never make everybody happy no matter what we do and the spectre of all that disapproval sometimes makes it seem better just to damn the torpedoes and go full speed ahead. There are times when that may be the only appropriate solution. On the other hand, not listening may mean we miss some very good things. Being open to new ideas often leads to some better solutions than we had ourselves.

Informing our public while keeping within our budgets

Keeping the constituency informed is not a paying proposition. Paper, print and mailing have become almost out of reach. Popular magazines in Canada stay in business by continuous hard-sell subscription drives. Despite full colour production, high quality writing, professional layout and a commitment to what sells, it is a battle to get people to read more pages when most of us are already buried in paper. Newspapers are losing readership too. Consider, then, the fate of a black and white newsletter sent out by a coalition, tidily but unexcitingly laid out and full of editorial content which is often what we had particularly hoped not to know. Admittedly the commitment of those who receive social justice newsletters can overcome all barriers, but we need to keep looking at the issues of cost and effectiveness.

What if the coalitions combined some of their communication funds to produce a broadly distributed social justice newsletter or magazine that was more popularly written and laid out? Suppose the newsletter were printed as an insert to present church papers and distributed two or three times a year. Over the course of the year, major issues of all the coalitions could be highlighted. It would be a very tough discipline to scale the material down to a few pages in each issue. The effort could broaden the readership and increase the possibilities for response from grassroots members.

Even if such a scheme were wildly successful and met with congratulations on every side, it would not respond to all of the publics that coalitions have. A list of one coalition's publics would include: staff at the coalition, board, committees, other coalitions, ecumenical and denominational staff (both those working in social justice and others), funding bodies, regional and local contacts, non-governmental organizations, government people, individual contributors and friends, and out-of-country networks. When you look at all those with whom we want to communicate, it is clear that one insert is not enough, even if it has wide distribution and amazing visual appeal.

Besides the issue of how many publics to address is the question of how to explain issues. One of the aspects that is most evident in the work of the coalitions, and often difficult for church members to understand, is the shift from individual to systemic issues. A child in Peru does not go without education because her parents do not work hard enough, but because of structural adjustment programs imposed by international financial agencies. It is systemic analysis that has shaped the direction of the work. Other common sources of information do not usually talk about systems: television seldom has the time and the print media may find it does not sell well. You can read your favourite newsmagazine for a long time without noticing that the World Bank seldom brings good news to poor countries.

Perhaps those who work on communication could put their heads together, think about the total coalition budget that is used for print and mailing and determine what could be done. It is possible that some economies of scale could be achieved and some collaborative arrangements made that would save time, money and machinery while still putting the message across.

Social justice ecumenism is more than saving money

Personally, I find the ecumenical dimension one of the most vital aspects of the coalition experience. It is the ecumenical commitment of the churches which has allowed the social justice work to move as powerfully as it has in Canada. The steps that the churches have taken signify that we have decided to live in a larger context than a strictly denominational one and, to that extent, we are open to various possibilities for change, including our own transformation. Moving beyond our church walls offers us a greater ability to see the needs of the world around us.

Given the complicated and historic structural aspects of the churches, one suspects an element of pragmatism at work in the formation of the coalitions that is no surprise to anyone who has done ecumenical work. Besides the ties that bind together a particular faith community within a denomination, there is a continuum within each church along which members position themselves in relation to activities and beliefs. When church staff members in the late 60s and early 70s began to work on the tasks that led to the development of the first coalitions, they found agreement around the ecumenical table in ways that were difficult to replicate within their denominations. They were a slice across continuum lines that represented a shared vision and passion. Issues can draw kindred spirits together.

Some will remember when the threat of capital punishment arose again in the 80s. Many people and agencies raised money and awareness around this issue and, in sharing their energy, found that biblical increase of the good seed falling on good soil. Other issues, such as population, have not been able to find a home in the coalitions at all because of diverse and strongly held opinions within the churches. Indeed, the whole 'family values' agenda is full of landmines for cooperation within denominations as well as among them.

I believe that the struggle of the churches and coalitions to find ways to do their justice work effectively has led them into ecumenical advances. Furthermore, the struggle of the coalitions to keep on existing reflects the differences in constituency between the churches and the coalitions. Church members whose analysis does not coincide with that of the coalitions tug the churches in another direction. The history of this work has been necessarily full of ups and downs because it has been a continuing test of commitment to social justice, to ecumenism and to our transformation.

The coalitions have been a bargain financially for the churches and a successful way to work. They provide high calibre work, accountability, visibility in their field, a wider base of resources from which to choose, better access to government, non-governmental organizations and other agencies. The difficulty of distance from the grassroots remains, but even so, there are many advantages. Each coalition has its network of local and regional contacts and these tend to reinforce ecumenical interaction by programming in the regions. Individuals then have the opportunity to introduce new work in their congregations that may not have been highly visible before. Congregations are encouraged thereby to consider social justice issues and use the formidable resources that the coalitions can provide.

Such thoughts lead me back to the *Lund Principle* of days past which is variously phrased but says, essentially, that the churches will not do alone that which they can do together. It is a lofty goal but hard to sell when one returns to the nitty-gritty of budgets, recessions, fund raising and declining church membership. Nevertheless, in the heart of the churches and the coalitions that have served them so creatively, lies a commitment to the ecumenical task that, in Canada, has functioned more effectively in the coalition experience than anywhere else in the last 20 years. It expresses the deeply rooted theological commitment to do together in the name of Christ the work that is needed.

While the coalitions are structurally a sign of unity, they are also constantly at risk. It may be necessary for the whole community to consider theologically that the coalitions signify more than convenience or expertise. In the midst of the struggle to keep the whole wagon train of the churches together as we journey from death to life, here is a small sign that by giving something up, for instance exclusive denominational control over the social justice agenda, we have been able to participate in a unity and creativity that signifies the movement of the Spirit.

Looking to the future

If I had a dream for the coalitions, it would be that they grow in the future so that more and more of the work of the churches be done through them and through new interchurch groups. Perhaps some non-church agencies, including non-Christian agencies, would engage in the work as well when the topic brought a natural confluence of interests and goals. As well as preserving their focus and commitment to their tasks, I would hope that they would find a way to look around them at needs still unmet and share resources when necessary.

If I had a dream for the churches, it would be that they continue to educate their constituencies so that coalition work not be seen as 'other' or as threat to the 'real' work of the denomination. The churches could also work to see the spirituality that animates social justice as the rich gift that it is.

My dream for the churches and coalitions together would be for more shared planning for the big picture, asking the following questions: Who are we as a community of churches and coalitions in Canada in this decade and what are our tasks? How can we face the problem of enough money and how do we share the restraints? How can we find the flexibility necessary for beginning new pieces of work and ending them?

My nightmare is that this consideration will be put off until cost-cutting becomes so overdue that wholesale losses and changes are forced on everybody.

A biblical reflection

We live in a world that is deeply involved in change and it is in the context of these changes that the churches and coalitions work at social justice. When young David was chosen to be king over the whole of Israel, he and the subjects of his kingdom-to-be faced many deep and threatening changes. They were planning a new structural shape for the people who belonged to Yahweh. The tribes had previously held power in a way that provided them with considerable autonomy but little centralized ability to work at common tasks. Kingship was a concept foreign to Israel, particularly in the beginning, when the prophet Samuel (1 Sam 8:6f) was not happy about the idea. The earlier monarchy of Saul had been a rather rustic affair, unlike the oriental courts of surrounding nations, and did not really prepare the people for the grander court that David, and later Solomon, maintained. David moved closer to the norm of contemporary monarchies of the region and exercised great freedom to make decisions about the deployment of people and wealth within his kingdom. One of the new elements that emerged was a power shift. Being the king's favourite, for example, became more important than being the chosen leader of a tribe.

Once upon a time, the church had its grip on the jugular of power. Today, the churches feel more and more sidelined by shifts in culture and image. We no longer whisper in the king's ear, even metaphorically. Challenging the powers-that-be has not proved to be a long-term solution either. We are destined to walk a tightrope of negotiation and challenge, accommodation and resistance, in order to advance the causes of the poor who are the losers in our system.

In King David's day, he pressed his political agenda with some brilliance, relying heavily on armed conflict for the achievement of some of his most important goals. Our tools are different, but the dilemma of moving forward in the direction we feel to be God's will remains a challenge to our brilliance. For all David's success, the monarchy was apparently not a suitable vehicle for Israel; in fact, it has not been a continuing success in the history of human institutions. As it turned out, the united kingdom did not last beyond the time of David and Solomon. The separated southern and northern kingdoms maintained themselves as monarchies until the Exile and for a short time following their return to Israel, but it was not a happy experience according to the writer of Kings. He was biased, of course, as we all are, but his bias was in favour of what he felt was a bigger picture. Rather than maintaining a monarchy so that Israel could conform to the pattern of other nations, either spiritually or politically, he wanted a godly nation that focussed on its spiritual relationship with Yahweh.

We would probably find the attitude and style of the writer of Kings rather withering if he were serving on our board, but it may be important to gather ourselves to consider the whole from time to time. The future of the coalitions, particularly in a time of scarce resources, requires long-range planning and collective evaluation. The coalitions, as an amalgam of energy, vision and focus, will continue to challenge the world and the churches. The churches in Canada will, I believe, continue to participate in that challenge by upholding the work of social justice and its ecumenical character. The decisions that will make it so will not necessarily be easy, but ease has not been the guiding principle of any of the organizations involved.

"They Persevered as though They Saw the One Who Is Invisible"

Michel Beaudin[1]

Introduction

The stories of the church coalitions evoked two reactions in me. For the first time these accounts offered an integrated view of the solidarity work in which I had participated.[2] They offered me memories therefore, but above all a pride at having been closely engaged in a prophetic movement. This movement opened future pathways for churches torn between the temptation of a 'backward step' to a traditional role leading nowhere and the risk of a 'promised land,' a changed society.

The coalitions have initiated a breakthrough in the traditional conflictual relations between states, economic or otherwise. They have shown the way to a resurgent civil society and to a future where people establish among themselves relationships based on true co-operation and self-determination.

The stories told here witness to the underground work of the Spirit who sustained these "Abrahamic minorities" (Helder Camara), inspiring them, in spite of the obstacles, to give 'body' to a social experience which anticipated a world solidarity that has now become a condition for the very survival of humanity. The coalitions well deserve to have applied to them what the *Letter to the Hebrews* says of Moses, "Through faith, they left Egypt, unafraid of the king's anger; for they persevered as though they saw the One who is invisible" (Hebrews 11:27).

My other reaction was to notice a sharp contrast. On the one hand, the coalitions are strongly marked as ecclesial experiences of a lived faith. On the other hand, the spirituality and theology of these experiences remain implicit to a large degree.

Theology is not indispensable in the struggle for justice, which can stand by itself. But it is not too much to think that the scope of the questions arising at the heart of the action of the coalitions is broad enough to warrant an accounting by the coalitions themselves "for the hope that is in them" (1 Peter 3:15). The challenges call for a strong spirituality in order to 'persevere' and a reflection which identifies to what extent the social project envisioned by the coalitions is anchored in the vision of the God of Jesus Christ. This needs to happen even while unmasking the 'idols' which are secretly used by the forces of the status quo, sometimes indeed under the cover of the defence of 'Christian civilization.' Finally, in the eyes of believers, it is urgent to show how much the new way of being church developed by the coalitions—that is, a different way of situating itself in society and of 'reading' the Gospel—far from being 'delinquent,' links up again with the great biblical and patristic tradition.

Without going beyond or idealizing the experience of lived faith to which the narratives bear witness, I would like to identify the theological breakthrough introduced by the experience of the coalitions. After having underlined certain aspects of this itinerary which I find rooted in the great Tradition itself, I shall make explicit three presuppositions which undergird them and which correspond to as many theological options. Subsequent sections will display in turn the four moments of the approach by which the coalitions 'listen to' the Word of God in *history*, in the *foundational sources* of the Christian faith, in a new way of *being church* and, finally, in the new roads to *solidarity*.

Traditional roots of the coalition experience

Let me first remark on certain aspects of the history of coalitions which reveal their nearness to the founding sources of Christianity and their newness in relation to the subsequent tradition which is less critical of the status quo.

Even the idea of coalitions *for* justice reflects a renewed ecclesiology in which the churches are no longer centred on themselves but on their vocation to be at the service of the Reign of God to come in society. At once such experiences give back to the churches the ability to witness to the Gospel in significant fashion instead of 'scandalizing the Gospel' by falling back upon 'religious' preoccupations (in the modern sense of a 'separate' domain divided only along confessional lines). The coalitions make it clear once more that it is above all social exclusion which clashes with faith. They emphasize for our times the "fast which pleases God" (Isaiah 58:6) and the impossibility of dissociating the love of neighbour and the love of God according to Jesus. Besides, the narrative character of the coalitions' presentation adopts the most usual form of the biblical revelation. The Bible recounts events of everyday life in which the social stakes are determined and, thereby, the options in relation to God who makes himself/herself known in these experiences. It is also from within the historical processes of our time that the coalitions 'summon' contemporaries to create change. In turn, they 'recount' to Canadians the story and the witness of those in the Third World who, like Jesus, struggle and sometimes pay with their lives to achieve this end.

Even the form of churches' action, namely in *coalition*, is not innocent. The coalitions are aware of the need to adopt and put into practice as their principle of organization what they envisage as their objective: the re-establishment of solidarity within and between societies. Hence there is the accent on the contribution and the participation of all in an unceasing invention of forms of partnership. It is in this way that the actions in *aid* of development and in *advocacy* have ended by finding their proper perspective in a solidarity conceived as a shared responsibility in the face of a common situation. This aspect reminds us of the 'new covenant' or 'new alliance' established by God, and the commandment given to the church to be one in order to witness adequately to God's dream of a society in which God would be "all in all." By working in networks of secular and religious partners even at the international level and by reuniting 'separated' churches in a project of justice, the coalitions are pointing already in the direction of ecclesial and societal alternatives.

The accent placed in all the coalitions on *action* is also to be remembered. Anchored in the most concrete socio-economic and political reality and in continual liaison with witnesses of primary importance, the coalitions depend as well on solid analyses leading to patient and ingenious actions having in view real transformations in the structures and ethos of society. This corresponds to the priority of Jesus, not to words ("Not everyone who says to me 'Lord, Lord'…" Matthew 7:21) but rather to putting into practice the will of the Father, the establishment of a just and compassionate society. The Good

News therefore must become a 'good reality' (in Hebrew, *dabar* means 'word' and 'reality'). Without a struggle for the transformation of the world, there can be no preaching of the Gospel, since it will lack one of its constitutive dimensions.[3] The observer is also struck by the imbalance of forces between the coalitions and the weight of the powers and structures requiring change. The paradoxical logic of the Gospel only shines with a greater brilliance. After the example of the God who wishes to win over his/her peoples and only conquer evil by taking it on himself/herself from the very inside of humanity, the coalitions count on the strength of eyewitnesses who strip away evil's anonymity (for example, Project Ploughshares) and make ethical appeals to the consciences of decision makers (for example, the Taskforce on the Churches and Corporate Responsibility). The privileged place accorded to the excluded as agents of change witnesses again to the logic of salvation evidenced by David against Goliath, by the little Remnant, by the poor. It is this same logic which also enables Saint Paul to count on that which "is low and despised in the world" but which "God has chosen" (1 Corinthians 1:28).

Presuppositions and theological options

These aspects, and many others as well, do not arrive by chance. They belong to a profile, often implicit but very much in character, which I would like now to set forth at a rather formal level. Then I will return in the following sections to the stories themselves, reread this time through three perspectives which I shall develop.

A prophetic conception
of the relationship of church, society and mission

The work of the coalitions is embedded in a conception of ecclesial mission which in turn depends closely on assumptions about the relationship of church, society, and salvation. In order to put forward the 'prophetic' model to which the coalitions relate, I shall first set out two other possible ecclesiological models. These conceptions often exist side by side in the churches, but also take us back to particular historical periods of which they are more characteristic.

The 'Christendom' model

The 'Christendom' model could be illustrated by the superimposition of two figures representing respectively society and the church. Their structures penetrate one another and tend to be mixed together. It corresponds especially to a period lasting from the Edict of Milan (4th century) to the 18th or 19th century and therefore includes the age of feudalism, the crusades, and the colonializing-evangelizing of the Third World. Favouring mediation for the sake of its social integration, the church lost its capacity to challenge existing structures. In a world allegedly ordered and in harmony with God's will, the Gospel had nothing to say and the conception of justice was limited to 'good works' dealing only with the symptoms of social ills.

The perspective here is that of an integration of church and society (integrism) on the basis of a pessimistic anthropology in which humankind and the world, fundamentally separated from God and condemned, have no entry upon salvation except by conversion and adherence to Jesus Christ whose sacrificial death has redeemed us. From this flows the primary and exclusive task of the church as proclaiming the Gospel and making disciples since 'outside of the church there is no salvation.'

The 'modernity' model

'Christendom' has given way, in the reaction of the modern era, to an absolute separation of the church from the state and from public affairs. Religious faith and morality scarcely move beyond the private sphere, while the 'secular' world provides for itself other creeds and ethics, for example, the modern rules of the market. In a world perceived either as ordered or disordered (it makes little difference since only 'spiritual things' or the saving of 'souls' matters to the church), justice is limited once again to 'good works' which may still serve to draw adherents.

In this framework, the socio-historical stakes remain fundamentally foreign to faith and to the Gospel; they have no theological status. This 'accommodating' perspective seems to me characteristic not only of public institutions or the world of business, but also of a majority of the church constituency for whom nothing is less evident than the social and structural implications of faith.

The 'prophetic' model

In the third and last model, called 'prophetic,' the figure of the church is found at the heart of the figure of society. The world is recognized as being in disorder (*chaos* in the Bible) and needs to be put in order in collaboration with God. The church is distinct from society but not separate from it. The church defines itself as a group bearing 'Good News' for the world, witnessing to a hope initiated by God's intervention in a world he "so loved." This model recognizes that salvation in Jesus Christ passes by several historic routes in favour of a world which is not lost, but animated by the Spirit "who renews the face of the earth." This perspective is more society-centred than church-centred. In fact, the church-society relationships here tend to go beyond all dualisms in the direction of a third figure, that of the hoped-for Reign of God.

In such a perspective, the world is recognized for its own sake and has theological status for two reasons. It is first a place where the Word of God addresses believers through the 'signs of the times,' and also the place where the Reign of God, at once given and to be built, mysteriously comes into being in the course of time. The church is there only as an auxiliary construction, as servant of this project. It is therefore out of solidarity with society, and not as conqueror of society, that the church addresses the social structures in the name of the Gospel. The mission embraces the totality of the world's destiny which it seeks to 'animate,' and not merely its 'spiritual' aspects.

In characteristic fashion, this perspective fully recognizes social conflict and the evangelical imperative of taking sides on behalf of the excluded. This implies the necessity of a social analysis to contextualize our mission and action directed as much upon hearts as upon structures. In this way, therefore, the Gospel (and the church) and the social dynamic (and historic human freedom) are able to enter into dialogue without mutual assimilation, since God and humanity are playing out here an authentic drama.

Historically, this model touches two periods in particular: the period of the great biblical and patristic Tradition (up to the 4th century), in which the justice of social organization and the fate of the weakest concerned faith and God in the highest degree, and the period which only links up with this tradition 15 centuries later (with minor exceptions), beginning around the end of the 19th century. The recent social teaching of the churches, liberation theology and other contextual theologies of the Third World, and the young tradition of church coalitions can be classified as representatives of this model of Christian engagement.

A 'symphonic' listening to the Word of God

The following diagram illustrates and details the dynamic of the 'prophetic' model that will serve as a framework for the subsequent sections of this chapter. This approach integrates ecclesial engagement, social analysis, and theological reflection. Its explicit schematization has been developed by Carlos Mesters, a Brazilian biblical scholar who has been keeping company with the ecclesial base communities of his country for more than 25 years. The approach is based on three interrelated poles or loci for a 'symphonic' listening to the Word of God. It is this dynamic which appears to me to have also animated the journey of the coalitions and to have made of them an ecclesial experience at once fruitful and unique.

Listening to the Word of God Today

We have recently experienced a renewal of the great Christian tradition that links faith with social and human issues. The following diagram is intended to represent the implications of this renewal for the process of a faith or a theology which sees listening to the Word of God as also occurring through a discernment of the 'signs of the times' and through commitment.

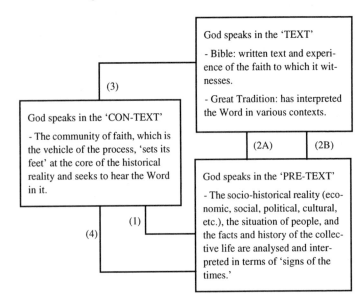

(3)

God speaks in the 'TEXT'

- Bible: written text and experience of the faith to which it witnesses.

- Great Tradition: has interpreted the Word in various contexts.

God speaks in the 'CON-TEXT'

- The community of faith, which is the vehicle of the process, 'sets its feet' at the core of the historical reality and seeks to hear the Word in it.

(2A)   (2B)

God speaks in the 'PRE-TEXT'

- The socio-historical reality (economic, social, political, cultural, etc.), the situation of people, and the facts and history of the collective life are analysed and interpreted in terms of 'signs of the times.'

(1)

(4)

Explanatory Notes

(1) The community ('con-text'), inserted in the socio-historical reality ('pre-text'), analyses the situation and its dynamics and interprets them in terms of 'signs of the times.'

(2A) Starting from this social locus and the results of the analysis, the community asks questions of the Bible and of the great Tradition, as a means of verifying the 'Word' heard in the pre-text. The historical reality therefore plays a hermeneutic role in the reading of the Bible ('text').

(2B) In their turn, the Bible and the Tradition ('text') question the socio-historical reality ('pre-text'), demonstrating its contradictions and also, sometimes, its complicity with God's purpose.

(3) This double process of questioning throws new light on the meaning and mission of the church community and brings forth calls for the 'conversion' of individuals and of the reality.

The community acts like the sound box of a guitar. The strings, on which reality plays, are the Bible. The result is a music which is God's call to us.

(4) The community ('con-text') involves itself in the transformation of the socio-historical reality ('pre-text') which fulfills the promise of salvation made by God "who so loved the world..." (John 3:16).

The process is a process of listening, not monophonically or stereophonically, but 'symphonically' to the Word of God.

I should like to add the following remarks to the explanations accompanying the diagram. First, this approach corresponds to the evolution of the people of God and to the way in which the Bible was formed. A community of faith ('con-text'), situated historically prior to the full Reign of God (in the 'pre-text,' or what comes before the 'text'), lives through events that oblige it to reinterpret and revitalize its faith. Certain events, the Exile for example, call it into question: 'Has God abandoned us?' The community seeks to read what God wants it to read in this 'sign of the times.' This listening is confronted by the written Word and by the Tradition ('text') which are then reinterpreted from the perspective of the lived experiences. Then the Word of God, forever living, begins to say 'new' things and to reveal a God-companion. This experience of faith will be in its turn recorded to become a source of reference, a part of the Bible. In this constant process of give-and-take between the socio-historical reality, the 'pre-text,' and the Written Word and Tradition, the 'text' constantly enlightens the community, or the 'con-text' (from Latin *cum* and *textum*, the group that goes with the text), causing it to rediscover its purpose or its mission in service to the coming of the Reign of God.

Second, this approach was also that of liberation theology from its birth. Resisting the process of underdevelopment, Christians became involved in popular organizations. Along with others, they analysed the reality of Latin America in terms of dependence and domination and no longer in terms of being simply behind in relation to the development of the North. This led them to set aside the received model of 'development' and to consider alternatives like breaking-away and liberation. Aware of this newness of approach, they sought to know what meaning their involvement in this direction had for their faith. That question asked of the Bible or 'text' caused the rediscovery of a God who, contrary to dead idols, frees the poor and opposes oppressors. The liberation church and liberation theologians have simply drawn the consequences of this discovery.

Third, it goes without saying that without a *practice* and a liberating *social analysis* by Christians, there never would have been any church of the poor or liberation theology. One may assume that the coalitions are also laying analogous bases for our context.

Finally, the reader will have noted the decisive role played by the taking into account of the socio-historic reality ('pre-text') in the process of faith and theology proposed in this approach. This reality is at once the privileged place for ecclesial involvement, the place for listening to the Word of God through the social analysis of the 'signs of the times,' and the place *beginning from which* (hermeneutic) Christians are called to "return to the very heart of Christianity" in order to "acquire a new awareness of its true meaning and its pressing demands."[4] I would go so far as to say that the passage through the 'pre-text' decides the authentically Christian character (incarnation) of the churches. It therefore determines their resistance to the temptation to slide in the direction of a sectarian profile (the 'con-text' enclosed with the 'text' interpreted in a fundamentalist manner and escaping from history) or of a 'Christendom' model always favourable to the status quo in the name of God.

Solidarity with the excluded as a theological paradigm

At first sight, it is justice which seems to be the keystone of the vision of the coalitions. This is related especially to the analyses prevailing at the beginning of the 70s when partners in the Third World helped us discover underdevelopment as the hidden face of the North's development, as the result of 'unjust' North-South relationships. From this emerged all the actions aimed at politically modifying unjust economic practices and the prominence of the paradigm of justice.

But an evolution will take place as the problematic evolves from development/undevelopment toward a 'mal-development,' the frontier of which will no longer pass only by the North-South line, as there emerges, alongside the market and the state, a third actor too long repressed, namely civil society. This will emerge in reaction to the violence of a market economy dislocating society by the imposition of the single rule of unbridled competition. The social reality, rendered subject to a world market without any concern for identities or for weaker partners, appears more and more as having been restructured in its very fibre according to a principle of antisolidarity, a process which is the source of endless inequalities and injustices and ultimately of the 'sacrifice' of those most vulnerable. The idea of justice is intimately linked with that of political equality and formal liberties in the Western tradition after Hobbes. It had to be enlarged to include the socio-economic conditions we now discover are decided not primarily at the level of the state or of politics but at the level of an economy which orchestrates societies and which has ended in perverting liberty and equality by cutting them off from the objective of solidarity.

It is against this background that one can explain the accelerated evolution of the church coalitions toward the formation of wider coalitions, toward a solidarity which is becoming identified with the process of at once resisting the totalitarianism of the market, reorganizing civil society and seeking a true 'development.'

My proposal is to associate this paradigm with Mesters' outline in a hypothesis that would read as follows: the analysis of the 'signs of the times' leads to an understanding of the present societal dynamic in terms of antisolidarity/solidarity. A rereading of the 'text' beginning with this key brings a rediscovery of the plan of God, or revelation, as a project of solidarity according to the very identity of the Trinitarian solidarity. The option for the excluded appears in the trajectory of revelation as the distinctive choice of a God who makes of this preference the only road possible to a solidarity of all with all. From this arises the consciousness of a kind of collision with the neoliberal project of antisolidarity and with the 'gods' at work in the 'pre-text.' This confrontation enlightens in a new way the meaning of the church, of faith and of mission: What does it mean to be a community and build 'coalitions' in a world that is coming apart? Is not faith an entry upon the 'social' commitment of God and is solidarity not its intimate fibre, salvation in action?

Solidarity with the excluded thus draws together the pathway to a future for the world ('pre-text'), the identity and the action of God ('text') as well as the meaning and mission of the church ('con-text'). It thus becomes, in our time, the focal perspective of a 'symphonic' con-vocation by the Word of God. Will the churches be able to respond to this? The coalitions for justice seem to have tried to stammer out this kind of a reply. Let us look more closely at each pole of this approach.

Listening to the Word of God in history

Contrary to the approach of the sects, the constant starting point for the coalitions is the socio-historical reality and not the biblical text or some religious doctrine. Is that a Christian way of proceeding? In fact, the Christian faith of the participants in the coalitions is always present in the approach and plays even an epistemological role in the analyses of reality. But the reference to the 'text' is not primary, precisely so as not to interfere with listening to what is and ought to be primary: the present challenging Word of God in the 'pre-text' whose work is manifested "in the process of people taking action and working together to create a new reality" (Ecumenical Coalition for Economic Justice). These convictions are rarely explicitly expressed in the writings of the coalitions; they are presupposed there and, without them, everything becomes incomprehensible.

The listening to God in the 'signs of the times' takes the characteristic form of commitment and social analysis which are intermingled. Both are controlled by a very definite choice for the excluded seen as victims. Let us make a few remarks about this.

Invariably, the history of the coalitions begins with an involvement in and an awareness of a particular situation (for example, the *coup d'état* in Chile, international commercial negotiations, demands of native people, apartheid, etc.). Associating with the victims of this situation will tend to give them voice, power, and leadership in the organization and in the struggle for their emancipation. This implies pedagogies and analyses which put the people in the picture of reality and which start from local situations that are lived (Ecumenical

Coalition for Economic Justice, PLURA, etc.). In the case of solidarity with the peoples of the Third World, priority is given to the requests of the partners. The concern is to give the latter access to the Canadian public and to the centres of decision making in the North, whether by representation or directly (the Interchurch Fund for International Development, the Taskforce on the Churches and Corporate Responsibility, etc.). Thus the traditional images which deprecated the peoples of the Third World are reversed, the challenge of difference in civilization is taken up (Canada China Programme), and the 'beneficiaries' become partners with common stakes. As Fred Franklin of the Inter-Church Committee on Human Rights in Latin America admirably expressed it: "We do know that we gained faith, insight and perspective, tools of analysis, and a much clearer understanding of our own situation and part in it."[5]

At the level of analysis, I have been struck by the capacity of the coalitions to take account simultaneously of the personal, daily, and local reality as well as of the structural stakes. Analyses and actions enter into constant dialogue (for example, the Ecumenical Coalition for Economic Justice and the praxis method), thus favouring analyses based on criticism leading to a greater effectiveness. I have everywhere noticed the importance of close and convincing social analyses (for example, Project Ploughshares with respect to 'security') and the concern to take account of the operating logic of governments and enterprises, making it possible to insert at appropriate places in these 'machines' the grain of sand (facts, demonstrations of contradictions, irrefutable criteria, etc.) which obliges them to give account of their responsibilities and to submit themselves to verifiable criteria and procedures. The analyses are continually growing larger in order to register in holistic fashion situations in terms of their real structural dynamic (for example, human rights, national security and programs of structural adjustment, immigration and neoliberal development, the growing lack of distinction between international and Canadian issues, hunger and debt, etc.). Mandates, agendas and sometimes even the names of the coalitions are thus modified according to new awareness, contact with partners, and changes of circumstances. This contextualization has also had the effect of making the coalitions work more closely together as well as with diverse secular groups.

Undeniably the coalitions are aware of the structural antisolidarity which governs present-day societies under capitalism. The establishment of coalitions can even be explained as the will to turn the logic of society upside down by means of a primary solidarity with the victims. I perceive a growing conviction that it is first and foremost in the economy rather than in politics that this process of antisolidarity is being played out, to the point that some coalitions are squarely based on this dimension (the Taskforce on the Churches and Corporate Responsibility and the Ecumenical Coalition for Economic Justice, for example). But I am not sure that the full scope of the change that has occurred has been measured. One indication is that neoliberalism is practically never named, even if the coalitions are constantly dealing with the phenomena provoked by this orientation of the market and the state. Nor have I encountered any explicit reference to the civil society as a paradigm in emergence and as a counterweight to neoliberalism, even if obviously the partnerships have no other goal. Stanley Hoffmann clearly sets out the dynamics facing each other: "the world level of the business civilization which acts as the dominant unifying force; the level of States still engaged in the traditional political game—that of Thucydides and not that of Adam Smith—and which is finding itself, for that very reason suffering from erosion; and lastly the level of peoples, that of the demand of a right to speak and of a desire to participate more and more directly asserted."[6]

In other respects, if the coalitions do concentrate with much shrewdness on the politico-economic mechanisms of injustice, I do not believe that they identify and insist sufficiently on the implicit ethics, ideology and even 'theology' which form one body with these mechanisms. Would it not be appropriate that the courageous resistance of the coalitions to the blind dynamic of the market and to politico-military interests touch more directly upon the secular 'text' which legitimates the status quo in public opinion? Are the rules of the market being contested with enough vigour insofar as they claim to take the place of common ethics? Where are we coming up with the resistance to the ideology which unilaterally gives value to the relationships of competition or antisolidarity, or again which affirms that there is no alternative to the status quo, a claim giving birth to a culture of despair?[7] Finally, even in our secularized societies, is it not appropriate to drive out the 'theology' and the hidden 'gods' of power and therefore to speak of idolatry? Sacralizations are still flourishing. Let one judge by the obstinate closure of governments to groups calling into question programs of structural adjustment or by the decision to demand the repayment of foreign debts despite the cost in the sacrifice of hundreds of thousands of children's lives, according to UNICEF. The capitalist idol holds our world firmly in its grip and is even defended vehemently by the right-wing clergy and Christian businessmen when the coalitions dare touch its politico-economic foundations in the name of the Gospel.

'Drawing the new from the old': Rereading the Word of God from the perspective of the victims, and colliding with the 'gods' of the market

The history of the coalitions does not lack for examples of fruitful reconsideration of theological and biblical tradition starting with current situations: for instance, the *just war* theology, in the light of the development of conventional wars and the destructiveness of present weapons, in the light also of the new consciousness created by pacifist groups; the biblical attitude toward the foreigner in the perspective of the phenomenon of refugees and immigrants today; the unprecedented deepening of the theology of creation and the sense of community provoked by solidarity with the native people and contact with their spirituality.

The sharp injustices of today and the scope of the social and human catastrophes arouse more and more moral and theological questions, making more urgent than ever a new, radical, and explicit questioning of the Christian 'text.' If the churches want to remain Christian they cannot return simply to the legitimacies ('text') of a system which, in creating excluded or 'useless' folk, encloses us in its own logic, refusing to recognize this Other One whom the powerful of an ancient era also excluded, crucified 'outside-the-walls.' A sign of the re-emergence of this phenomenon is the discomfort of Christians from middle- and upper-class backgrounds when pastors recall the teaching of the churches on social justice. They do not want to say that the authorities are wrong, but they are reluctant to accept their positions; and so people start to 'cough' according to the observation of theologian Gregory Baum.

In the hour of adversity and of courage, the 'confessing' churches (Dietrich Bonhoeffer) need to provide themselves with an appropriate spirituality, to take the time and the space necessary to 'see' and feel the hand of God in their work. But the coalitions must also undertake a systematic rereading of the Word starting with the stakes registered in the 'pre-text' and then confront the societal dynamic starting with the 'subversive' plan of God discovered in this new reading.

Such an approach will only bring into focus what is occurring today in social processes. The touchstone remains the position concerning the fate of the excluded. When Christians rise up beside them to 'witness' that these despised 'images of God' are more important than obedience to the absolutized law of some power, it is the God of Abraham and of Jesus Christ who rises to defend them. Then a 'battle of the gods' is launched!

There is no doubt that the coalitions are living out the essential core of this approach, but I believe that a need is being felt for a more systematic articulation of each one of its moments, in order to point out more sharply the incompatibility of the socio-economic situation with the thrust of the Gospel.

A new way of being church

The third moment of the approach consists in listening to the Word in the 'con-text,' to renew the sense of church mission in light of the confrontation between the 'pre-text' and the 'text,' or between the socio-historical drama and the plan of God. This double decentralization essential to the ecclesial identity has entailed some shifts of accent that appear clearly in the accounts of the coalitions.

The most striking is certainly the shift of the 'feet,' bringing ourselves closer to the poor, the popular groups, and all those who struggle for justice and who, in their way, *are* the church. The approach has likewise provoked a shift in the churches from internal preoccupations to social stakes. The coalitions have thus sought, by various initiatives, to pull the Christian with them in this ministry.

The churches are now more aware of the structural dimensions of their social mission. But the primary attention to the victims prohibited stopping with only approaches to the decision makers and thus pushed the coalitions to undertake, in parallel with the work of advocacy, an effort to 'empower the powerless,' taking account of the conditions for a genuine participation by the marginalized. This priority translates the conviction that it is the organizations of the people themselves—and not the churches—which are the true and primary subject of social change.

A remarkable coherence exists also among the community dimensions of the church, the 'coalition' form which the ecclesial struggle has taken against injustice, the objective of forming popular coalitions on various issues and the necessity for the coalitions to give themselves an internal functioning based on partnership principles (the role of women, of groups from the Third World, of local groups within the national leadership...) as a condition for contributing to social change (Ten Days). Community solidarity has here more than a strategic status; it has something to do not only with the road toward justice, but even with its end and therefore with the plan of a God who is himself/herself a community. Does not this perspective reverse the structural process in operation in the 'pre-text,' that of an antisolidarity which clashes with the plan of God in breaking human community?

There arises here a new paradigm in which the churches draw from their community identity (received from the Trinitarian God) the vocation to be 'co-convokers' of a new humanity. That is the astonishing mission that the coalitions are undertaking, conscious that "when there is no more prophecy in the land, the people perish" (Proverbs 29:18).

The new roads to solidarity

We arrive at the last stage of the approach diagrammed earlier, that of the return of the 'con-text' to the socio-historical reality in a renewed commitment of the coalitions which should take into account the new conjuncture and propose both prophetic vision and action in coherence with the light shed by previous stages.

Conjuncture

The present conjuncture presents new difficulties. There is first the renewed brutality of a neoliberal capitalism which marks a return to the norms of the 19th century both in the Third World and even in the North, where, with the erosion of employment and of social policies, the conditions of life decline and multiply the 'useless people' in the system. Governments cheerfully fall into step with large enterprises and with the policies of international financial institutions in an unprecedented 'adjustment' of populations to the dominant interests under the pretext of an economic rationalization henceforth locked into circular reasoning. With respect to the Third

World, the disappearance of the counterweight constituted by the Eastern block and the so-called democratization of regimes have removed all restraint to open exploitation. Depending simultaneously on public opinion that is more conservative and alert in the matter of public deficits and on a sharply neoliberal orientation, governments like Canada's manifest an increasingly harsh attitude toward the peoples of the Third World with regard to the demands of minority groups (for example, the native people).

The neoliberalism of the 80s also caused a shaking up of large social organizations and promoted a discouraging individualism. The absence of a credible alternative on the horizon encourages an apparent resignation in the face of the current disintegration. On the other hand, the setback to development has brought weariness and scepticism regarding development aid. To all this is added a weakening of the influence of the churches on society.

Vision

In terms of vision, the future of the coalitions appears to move through an accentuated vigour and coherence in their analysis of reality, their understanding of the Gospel and their conception of the church's mission. This assumes as a corollary an intense education of the grassroots members and the development of an appropriate spirituality and theology. That is a condition for the independence of the coalitions and for faithfulness in the plan to 'follow Jesus' today.

I believe that the population, despite its apparent inertia, has lost confidence in the present system and that it secretly hopes for an alternative which currently lacks a public expression. In these conditions, the coalitions must pursue their questioning of the present model of development which has been assimilated to capitalism itself. The coalitions must also pursue the search for an alternative at the structural level. This includes the work of 'harnassing' the decision-making centres of the system, if only in a pedagogical finality to draw from it more accurate analyses and to demystify the exercise of power. But does the concern to be heard and to be effective, in terms of practical measures thus obtained, oblige the coalitions to enter into the operating logic of the major interests and to content themselves with results so modestly 'reforming' that they indirectly warn the wielders of power and mask the radical nature of the changes necessary?

At the level of the search for an alternative, I fervently wish that it become the object of an approach as collective as possible at the base, indicating in its very manner the profile of this alternative. My suggestion is that it get worked out in systematic fashion according to the three poles of Mesters' diagram and that it give rise to tests of public formulation, since the expression of alternative visions appears to me an inherent condition essential to 'the art of coalitions.'

Finally, I should like to insist on the primacy of the ethical dimension. Economic liberalism has declared outdated traditional ethical values such as altruism and compassion in order to substitute for them the sole rule of the market based on their inversion, claiming that the pursuit by each person of his or her own interest will result in the end in the harmony of interests or the common good. Capitalism has substituted for ethics a supposedly self-regulating but always defective mechanism which has proved to be, in fact, a swindle. Ethics must intervene from the outset of social construction and vitalize every phase of it. The will to solidarity cannot be decreed, but without it "nothing holds together, neither village, nor city, nor the entire earth."[8] The ecclesial coalitions must no longer hide ethical values 'under a bushel' or leave to them the sole function of an interior motivation of their active members, but give them indeed a public existence.

Action

Already in several instances, I have alluded to solidarity as a paradigm consistent with the journey moving through 'pre-text' and 'text.' As for ecclesial intervention ('con-text'), the coalitions have developed a *form* and new partnerships which seem in profound agreement with this emerging paradigm. But just as justice still maintained the musty odour of the exclusion of the partners instead of representing more directly a new collective 'we,' does not the 'partnership' approach in the same way reflect only too formally the relationship (which cannot be limited to that of 'horse' and 'rider') and does it not lend itself too readily to ambiguities? For CIDA, for instance, the partnership refers only to the co-ordination of Canadian interveners in the Third World or to business agreements. Business circles further pervert its meaning in making of it a regional or local instrument of global economic competition. 'Solidarity' has the advantage of insisting both on the people themselves, their relations, and on the content of their exchanges, thereby supporting the aim of removing this relationship from structural injustice.

Following this track of solidarity, the work of the coalitions could be radicalized in several convergent directions which I simply list:

• Develop a grassroots network to reweave the church cloth straight out of social solidarity and to give weight to the coalitions.

• Work diligently on the blockages of faith among the grassroots members of the churches with respect to social justice; promote familiarity with social analysis and in particular with the false sacralizations of the metaphysical, anthropological, and ethical presuppositions of an economic and political modernity which has succeeded in convincing the faithful of the possible coexistence of faith and injustice (Romans 1:18).

• Support the self-organization of the excluded here and elsewhere and mutual presence in their struggles; this structural transformation could serve as a criterion for any initiative.

• Support and participate in social coalitions going beyond the ecumenical or ecclesial framework, while at the same time safeguarding an institutional independence.

• Despite the national character of coalitions, work on local issues; at the other end, support the formation of international coalitions with the aim of creating an entity on the world level capable of calling to account the world economic and political actors.

• Propose to various social movements the integration of international solidarity into their programs rather than reserving this for specialized and isolated groups (this presupposes the breaking-down of the partitions in national and international issues).

• Propose to the groups coming together a process and pedagogies of continuing education touching at once upon analysis, organization, inspiring vision and the search for alternatives, such that solidarity being lived out in the course of struggles, as experience of the alternative, sustains a journey which promises to be long.

• Publicize the experiences of solidarity here and with the peoples of the Third World so that they serve as landmarks for the decision makers and the institutions.

• Elaborate and circulate the criteria (ethical, organizational or others) which mediate the major perspectives growing out of the confrontational journey of 'pre-text,' 'text,' and 'con-text,' so that they could become popular instruments of intervention.

• Develop a greater capacity and financial independence for the coalitions so that the work can gather scope and depend less on a restricted number of sources. Can they, for example, be financed also by the groups with which they collaborate? Politically and financially, should not the coalitions become ever more immersed in the social movement, and that as the result of deliberate church policy?

Conclusion: Spirit and solidarity

One expression has continually impressed me in reading the accounts of the coalitions: 'advocacy.' It summarizes well the long march of these coalitions if one gives it its full theological scope. In John 16:5-11, the Holy Spirit is presented as the force through whom God raises Jesus from the dead, against his accusers, justifying the one who had sided with the excluded to the point of death. The Spirit is also presented as the Paraclete, the Advocate who, in all subsequent history, will appeal the verdict and undertake a vast revision of the trial of Jesus condemned unjustly as are always the 'least' in societies founded on the arbitrary use of power (John 14:16, 26).

The coalitions, even in their work of advocacy, are not the advocates of the excluded. It is rather the Spirit who assumes this role. But for the new trial, the Spirit calls Christians and every person of good will to the stand so that they may witness in favour of Jesus who, if we may paraphrase the evangelist Matthew, assures us: "Every time you will have defended the least of these (followers) of mine, you will have defended me..." (Matthew 25). This witness, in a secularized world like ours, cannot be credible by words alone. Is it not rather the *practice of solidarity* with the excluded which alone, in the absolute sense, declares and truly witnesses that their cause is just as was that of God in Jesus? This practice alone truly proclaims the Good News of the Good Reality, salvation for everyone. It is on this Trinitarian height, the height of the drama of salvation, that the commitment of the coalitions is situated. Long life to these builders of peace!

An Ecumenical Model
for Participation
in Civil Society

Rebecca S. Larson

For a long time the Canadian ecumenical community has had a particular preoccupation with the public participation of the churches in civil society. The coalitions' history documented this preoccupation as one with fundamentally ecumenical characteristics which mark the work of the coalitions as unique. The following observations attempt to position the work of the coalitions within the contemporary discussion of civil society and to suggest that it is precisely the ecumenical characteristics which make the interchurch coalitions a significant and effective voice in Canadian public discourse, as well as an important resource for the international ecumenical family.

Most discussions of civil society take as their starting point the breakdown of old ideologies and with them simplistic and *a priori* systematized answers and analyses of global questions. This breakdown is most dramatically seen on a macro scale in the dissolution of the former socialist states; however, there are many other less obvious points at which the limitations of ideologized and systematized answers to social problems are evident.

The current discourse of civil society moves away from the use of absolute or forced-choice categorizations of analysis such as we/they, rich/poor, good/bad, powerful/powerless, north/south, east/west, reform/revolution. Rather, the lexicon of civil society is filled with words such as: compromise, multiplicity, diversity, partiality, mediation, multidirection, contradiction, co-operation, relativity. These words point to the complexity of relationships between individuals and societies and to the symbolic systems which give them meaning. They suggest the need for more nuanced—though no less effective—strategies of response, which relate more appropriately to the internally contradictory nature of contemporary socio-political systems from the family, to the neighbourhood, to the state and international settings.

There is a great deal of debate within international ecumenical social justice circles as to whether the new look of civil society is not just the latest form of co-optation to ongoing systems of oppression. At the June 1993 session of the United Nations Commission on Sustainable Development—that part of the U.N. system responsible for implementing the decisions of the *Earth Summit*—five government delegations seated non-governmental organization representatives as official members of their delegations. Canada was one of them. Is this cause for celebration or concern? Or, as one staffer at the World Council of Churches put it: "If we spend our time being a mediating institution and brokering policy decisions with those we have never been willing to trust, who will fight the struggle?" It is, perhaps, a question that Nelson Mandela has had to wrestle with over the past months and years.

Although precise definitions seem to be lacking at this time, it is possible to identify certain characteristics of civil society which characterize the resurgence of the term on the contemporary social action agenda:[1]

• Civil society refers to a politically active and informed 'third sector' of society which is distinct from either government or market-based business sectors.

• One distinguishing feature of this third sector is that it is made up of institutions and groups which operate out of an intentional and identifiable value base and whose purpose is that of the social good.

• The credibility of these groups is determined not by representation or membership, but by the moral authority derived from their purpose together with the competence of their public participation.

• Such groups have the capacity to bring together coalitions of people from otherwise unrelated sectors.

• Such groups and institutions are generally multivalent in their capacity for movement within and across social boundaries and sectors. For instance, it is often possible within such groups to move from local to national to international fora, or across economic, gender or professional lines.

• Civil society holds in tension at one time multiple and conflicting systems of symbolic meaning relating to individuals, families, communities, ethnic groups, nation states, gender, religious groups, etc.

• Civil society requires mediating institutions which, although private, take for themselves a public mandate. This mandate includes constituting a public institutional infrastructure which creates opportunity for social public discourse and the building of diverse coalitions. The work of mediation is the key factor within civil society.

• Civil society is a pragmatic arena of public participation which creates coalitions around concrete and specific issues. It is the issues which are the catalysts for convening sometimes improbable allies for common action.

• Within civil society issues of public policy are not important as matters of ideological principle, but are addressed as the logical 'next step' in responding to specific cases of human need.

• Civil society knows only partial and sometimes even contradictory victories. Diversity and multiplicity are the norm, not the stumbling block.

• The primary role of civil society is to negotiate a public social agenda.

For people in Canada who know the work of the interchurch coalitions, these points sound surprisingly familiar. What is not so familiar is an understanding of this work as an inherently ecumenical activity.

The whole inhabited earth

The work of the coalitions as a model for participation in civil society calls for an inclusive understanding of what it means to be ecumenical.

The Greek word *oikoumene* suggests a certain meaning of 'the whole inhabited earth.' For over 40 years, this term has provided a conceptual framework for ecumenism. It is a concept to which the unity of the church is integral, but it is more than that. Words such as *koinonia* and *household* point to that aspect of right relationships within the whole inhabited earth that is central to the meaning of ecumenicity. Konrad Raiser, general secretary of the World Council of Churches, argues that the *oikoumene*: "is not a matter of structures, but of dynamic, real relationships... What we are speaking of are the actual and at the same time endangered connections and relationships between churches, between cultures, between people and human societies in their infinite variety, and between the world of humankind and creation as a whole."[2]

Within Canada, the ecumenical work of churches is framed by these concepts and the years of work which brought them about. The coalitions carry this heritage and their work reveals distinct characteristics which mark their participation in civil society as ecumenical.

Working together co-operatively

It is no small achievement that the coalitions work together as partners within coalitions and with one another. This foundational ecumenical principle is derived from what is called the *Lund Statement* which challenges the churches to "act together in all matters except those in which deep differences of conviction compel them to act separately."[3]

There is debate within the church community in Canada as to whether the coalitions are interchurch or ecumenical ventures. Certainly, for people outside the churches, the coalitions are perceived as ecumenical in that they demonstrate in a most visible way the reality of churches working together. Within the coalitions too, there is a commitment to act together and a principled willingness to go to great lengths to make common action possible for all. Bonnie Greene, former member of the national Ten Days committee, described the ecumenical commitment of the coalitions in Canada to work together in this way: "We bite our tongues constantly so as not to come into conflict, but we believe that what we do together is so critical we will not abandon each other."[4] This statement echoes the mutual commitment made by churches at the time of the 1948 formation of the World Council of Churches: "We intend to stay together!"[5]

Acting together in all matters

The ecumenical task of the coalitions, however, involves much more than working co-operatively. It also involves recognizing that the churches as one sector of society have a contribution that is best made if they get their act together as churches rather than, either in reality or in perception, offering conflicting and counterproductive interventions into public policy debates. This is a matter not only of internal mutual accountability but of public responsibility.

At one point in pre-coalition history, it was a decision of political strategy that public participation is better served when churches speak with one voice to Canadian society. It was the creation of the National Committee on the Church and Industrial Society in 1965 which

provided the opportunity for churches to come together on an inter-
church basis from which they would relate as one to various sectors
of industrial society. It was this felt need to relate ecumenically first,
and then to the various sectors of Canadian society, which prompted
the national church social action officers, meeting at the 1965 convention of the Religion-Labour Council, to forge the unique "ecumenical
approach to social issues and the social action approach to
ecumenicity"[6] of which the National Committee on the Church and
Industrial Society is the pre-coalition model.

The twofold dimensions of this relationship still hold across time.
First, the "ecumenical approach to social issues" provides an effective
and credible opportunity for the churches, as one sector within
society, to engage commonly in work with other sectors concerning
social issues. Secondly, the "social action approach to ecumenicity"
raises particular issues within specific social, historical and political
contexts around which effective ecumenical theological reflection
can take place.

Holding together the abidingly different

A third aspect of the ecumenical task of the coalitions is located
in the nature of ecumenism, the very purpose of which is to hold
together in creative tension that which is different. For churches and
people of faith, it is the Holy Spirit which "creates fellowship between
the abidingly different, and precisely thus enables us to experience
new life, life in its fullness."[7]

Building coalitions, therefore, is an intrinsically ecumenical task.
The challenge is to find ways for this holding together of the "abidingly different" to form and inform the methodology and relationships
of the coalitions. "Our experience has confirmed that coalitions are
one of the most hopeful means for social transformation," writes
Dennis Howlett.[8] Building coalitions is ecumenical work precisely
for the two reasons that Dennis elaborates in those wonderful images
of the 'arithmetic' and the 'chemistry' of the art of coalition politics:
groups have more power and effectiveness by working together, and
groups educate and change one another through working together.[9]

It is also ecumenically responsible to find ways for the work to
reflect the goal both in symbol and in substance. If the goal of the
ecumenical movement is understood as including the renewal of

broken human community, then one important task of the coalitions is to create, seek out, discover, nurture and invite into relationship a myriad of groups and individuals for the sake of the *oikoumene*.

One thing this means is to bring together those with whom one has common cause. This is one of the strengths of the coalitions and examples abound. Although it began as "one of the most daring, creative and controversial experiments in ecumenical history," the relationship between the churches and the aboriginal peoples of Canada through Project North and the Aboriginal Rights Coalition developed into a "solid bond of trust."[10] PLURA committed itself to a partnership of church and low-income groups and took organizational decisions to decentralize and to promote participation in decision making to reflect that commitment. Ten Days for World Development built a national network of over 200 groups capable of remarkably focussed political action. The Canada-Asia Working Group participated with CIDA and a broad cross-section of non-government organizations in the Philippines and Canada to broker the Philippines Canada Human Resources Development program. Farmers, sugar workers and textile workers connecting with the Ecumenical Coalition for Economic Justice, human rights groups relating to the Inter-Church Committee on Human Rights in Latin America, forum-based partnerships in the Interchurch Fund for International Development: the documents reveal the history of the coalitions to be blessed with a variety of creative relationships and productive partnerships.

Coalition building, however, also means bringing together those with whom the motivations of building common cause are more tenuous. Here, the challenges are to articulate and establish broader bases of common cause which are grounded in the common humanity and common future shared by all on a fragile planet. This too is ecumenical, for living together in the church as well as in the 'whole inhabited earth' means that widely opposing perspectives and mutually exclusive approaches must be brought into relationship. Although these relationships are not always easy, precisely because the issues are difficult and the interchurch coalitions bring strongly reasoned and principled arguments to bear, an astounding array of relationships have been built over the years which include governments, crown corporations, banks, and energy boards as well as some difficult years with the Confederation of Church and Business People.

Oikoumene-grounded analysis

Building coalitions also means raising hard questions about the mutual responsibility and accountability of all people within a common *oikoumene*. Over and over, coalition analyses of issues are grounded in a comprehensive perspective of the whole of the human family and broader social and political systems. This comprehensive approach to issues analysis is fundamentally ecumenical and constitutes one of the significant and unique contributions of the interchurch coalitions to Canadian public policy debates. Not only are abidingly different relationships held in tension, but the inseparable connections of seemingly isolated issues are revealed and become the basis for the visioning of alternative possibilities, policies and strategies.

One good example of how this works within the interchurch coalitions is the formation of the Ten Days' Policy Integration Committee, particularly as it functioned around issues related to Central America from 1983-85 to create a broad base of analysis to advise Ten Days on the action component of their program.[11]

There are a host of other examples of coalition analysis being grounded in a clear articulation of the linkage of issues. This has led to the Inter-Church Committee on Human Rights in Latin America adopting an unusually broad definition of human rights and linking human rights in Latin America with Canadian policies of refugee accessibility and political settlements of internal military conflicts.[12] The Inter-Church Project on Population insisted that immigration is related to economic sustainability.[13] The Taskforce on the Churches and Corporate Responsibility recognized the incongruity of taking seriously Canadian business investment policies without dealing with Canadian foreign policy issues. The Aboriginal Rights Coalition incorporates environmental issues into the task of social justice for aboriginal peoples of Canada.

This comprehensive approach to issues led to the formation of the Debt Study Network which in 1989 produced a major study paper for the Canadian churches' use in addressing governments and banks. This was part of a major advocacy effort on debt.[14] This comprehensive approach found the Taskforce on the Churches and Corporate Responsibility and Project North together with the Nisga'a in New York in 1981 protesting the dumping of molybdenum mine tailings into Alice Arm, British Columbia; the Canada-Asia Working Group, the Inter-Church Committee on Human Rights in Latin America and the Inter-Church Coalition on Africa together developing briefings for the United Nations Commission on Human Rights; the Taskforce on the Churches and Corporate Responsibility and the Canada-Asia Working Group co-operating on challenging the decision of Petro-Canada to continue to drill for oil in Myanmar (Burma);[15] Ten Days, the Ecumenical Coalition for Economic Justice and the Taskforce on the Churches and Corporate Responsibility appearing before the Standing Committee on External Affairs and International Trade in February 1990; and the Inter-Church Committee on Human Rights in Latin America and Project Ploughshares together questioning governments on their failure to link human rights with strategies for disarmament or campaigns to stop arms sales.[16]

Pastoral care as an ecumenical responsibility

The issue-specific nature of the coalitions is also important, however, because it makes possible that ecumenical work which relates to pastoral care. Pastoral protection of those loved by God is part of the ecumenical vocation (John 17:11, 21). Addressing public policy is the churches' expression of pastoral care in the political arena. Therefore, it is important that the work of the coalitions around particular issues be, to use the word of Renate Pratt, "incremental":[17] behind every policy paper and every government submission lie stories of human life and human need, the policy aspects of which unfold in relation to historical events and human experiences. The extensive policy work of the Ecumenical Coalition for Economic Justice, Ten Days for World Development and the Taskforce on the Churches and Corporate Responsibility on economic and debt issues are human stories writ large in political terms. A military takeover in Chile leads to two decades of policy work in Canada for the Inter-Church Committee on Human Rights in Latin America; the increasing poverty of a Lubicon Cree community in Little Buffalo, Alberta, takes a church-related delegation to Japan to address issues of a Canadian subsidiary logging company.

The "sociological impossibility" of ecumenism

One of the reasons this pastoral task is possible is because of the multivalent social complexity of the constituencies and groups to which the interchurch coalitions relate. An assembly of the World

Council of Churches was described by Margaret Mead as a "sociological impossibility."[18] No comparable gathering, she claimed, could bring together so diverse a cross-section of humanity.

The ecumenical movement and the groups to which it relates open to the Canadian coalitions peoples and partners around the world in almost every sector of society, and through its commitment to justice issues over the years, it has developed trust relationships with hundreds of other groups and networks. One of the reasons that the work of the coalitions is effective is, for example, that the Taskforce on the Churches and Corporate Responsibility can refute Alcan Canada on South Africa investment issues on the basis of a personal conversation held in the garden of an archbishop in Durban.[19] As Cynthia McLean concisely puts it in referring to Canada China Programme's work on China which is rooted in relationships established a century ago: "If we weren't Christians we would probably have little to do with each other."[20]

Moral authority and ecumenical theology

The diversity of these ecumenical relationships, coupled with the pastoral task of grounding public policy work in the daily experience of people allows the coalitions to exercise the ecumenical responsibility of making public witness to the realities of these experiences. The word 'witness' is, of course, a technical theological term. It is interesting to note that the words 'witness' and 'martyr' are different levels of meaning given to the translation of the same Greek word used in the New Testament. Both the witness and the martyr bear testimony to what they have seen and believed; the differentiation is that the martyr bears testimony also by death.

Ernie Regehr effectively describes this ecumenical work of witnessing practised by the coalitions in some detail.[21] It is an important strategy for the work of all the coalitions. For instance, in 1989, Ten Days was able to arrange for Jaime Wright from Brazil to appear as a witness to the Standing Committee on External Affairs and International Trade sessions on the international debt crisis. In March 1987, the Inter-Church Committee on Human Rights in Latin America coordinated the testimony of Carmen Gloria Quintana before the 43rd session of the U.N. Commission on Human Rights in Geneva.[22]

One of the reasons that the role of witness is effective in the work of social justice is that it introduces moral authority into policy debates. The coalitions undertake the monitoring function of their witness work by way of their technical competence on issue analysis. Moreover, through the coalitions, the churches as values-based moral communities—these values and morals being ecumenically vested interests—are engaged with other vested interests—business or military for example—in the political sphere.[23] This role implies that in order for the coalitions to be effective, their work must also be informed, accompanied and grounded theologically. The ability to speak in spiritual terms about political issues constitutes one of the public responsibilities of churches in civil society.

Coalitions are challenging themselves and being challenged by the churches, by their partners and by their own work on this point. For example, in 1988, when determining their vision statement and new structure, the Aboriginal Rights Coalition made theological reflection and spiritual development related to the struggle for aboriginal justice a prime objective. Peter Hamel writes: "We have a major role in bringing the spiritual dimension to the issues. Our challenge is to talk in spiritual terms about the meaning of self-determination, aboriginal rights, economic development and resource exploitation. We are being challenged to deepen our own Christian spirituality, to relate aboriginal spirituality to our own Christian faith. If we are unable to do this, it will be impossible to create a new covenant with the aboriginal peoples of Canada."[24]

In the much different situation of Project Ploughshares, it was agreed that it would be strategically counterproductive for Project Ploughshares to factor the churches' just war theological histories and debates into the program and policy work. It is significant that their work together has in fact had the effect of moving the churches forward, individually and together, in their theological understandings of the moral decisions related to war.

Symbolic systems and social analysis

The coalitions carry another ecumenical responsibility within civil society to enhance understanding and communication among the various groups and institutions with which they work, given their differing systems of symbolic meaning. The coalitions are linked in a particular way to an enormously rich repository of symbolic meaning related to the biblical, cultural, theological and liturgical history of Christianity. This wealth of story, symbol and ritual, together with an informed experience of the creative power of symbolic clusters of meaning for individuals and communities, equips the coalitions to address the conflicts of symbolic systems which are central to social struggles. This enables them to be particularly responsive to the multiple and diverse symbolic and cultural ways in which people give expression to meaning in their lives and their struggles for survival and liberation, and aware of the many factors which inhibit shared understanding.

The written histories of the coalitions hint at the awareness of the need to address issues of symbolic meaning and language as part of their social analysis. Surprisingly, few examples are given of the use of symbolic meaning as a resource for addressing issues. Likewise, there is little evidence of policy or program decisions which take up this ecumenical task of the coalitions in a serious way.

Ecumenical mediating institutions

The last important role of the coalitions as ecumenical participants in civil society relates to their unique situation as 'institutionally based' coalitions able to create the conditions for mediating between various other sectors, groups and institutions.[25]

The task of mediation is an important dimension of the ecumenical vocation of the coalitions. The role of mediation in the life of the church has a rich biblical and theological history: the Bible presents Moses, the prophets and particularly Jesus in the role of mediator—one who restores to right relationship what has been broken or separated.

The fact that the oldest of the coalitions have now been active for 20 years suggests that a certain degree of institutionalization has taken place in what was originally to have been a flexible and issue-specific organizational model. 'Permanent coalitions' present, for some, a contradiction in terms. Those who are critical of the coalitions on this point in fact miss the point, for it is precisely the relationship of the coalitions to long-term and publicly identifiable values-based institutions which makes much of the coalition mediation work viable. These are the institutions which can call on people of all sectors and persuasions for public dialogue, discussion and confrontation. These are the institutions which can provide a vital public forum for attempting the restoration of broken social relationships.

Certainly, churches lend a certain level of credibility to the work of the coalitions by virtue of their public role as moral communities, as has been discussed above. But, in addition, the institutional base of churches provides the umbrella of public conceptual space—as well as the infrastructure—which create the conditions for the coalitions to carry on work as ecumenical mediators in civil society.

Gary Kenny describes the inspiration to the Inter-Church Coalition on Africa board of the deft capacity of the churches in Africa "to act as mediators and reconcilers among conflicting groups within the anti-apartheid movement and between anti-apartheid groups and the government."[26] The Inter-Church Committee on Human Rights in Latin America took up this role in relation to the Central America peace process as it related to a host of governments and groups holding different and conflicting positions. The Canada-Asia Working Group functions in this way in relation to enhancing communication and understanding between North and South Korea. Local ecumenical groups practise mediation in a host of courageous and creative ways, attempting to restore right relationships between people, groups and institutions in Canada and throughout the world.

Looking ahead

What is the particular contribution of the Canadian interchurch coalitions to civil society at this point in history? Quite simply, to be ecumenical. This ecumenical vocation suggests a particular orientation in both identity and methodology: to work co-operatively together; to be the vehicle for churches to act as one on social issues; to hold together the 'abidingly different'; to ground analysis within an understanding and articulation of the *oikoumene*; to approach public policy as an aspect of the pastoral ecumenical task; to embrace the sociological impossibility of diverse relationships; to be a moral community formed and informed by theological reflection; to provide institutional opportunity for public discourse; and to bring a sensitivity to conflicting symbolic systems into the analysis of socio-political events.

As their histories reflect, this is not a new vocation for the coalitions. This same history, however, challenges the coalitions in their work for the future. These challenges can be stated as questions related to the role and responsibilities of the Canadian interchurch coalitions as part of the ecumenical movement at this time in history:

- To what extent do the coalitions understand theirs to be an ecumenical task within civil society? What implications does this have for the content and methodology of their work?
- What responsibilities do the coalitions have toward the churches and their ecumenical work in Canada? What does this mean for relationships between the coalitions and the Canadian Council of Churches?
- A recent World Council of Churches meeting on Koinonia and Justice, Peace and the Integrity of Creation tackled "one of the most persistent and damaging divisions within the ecumenical movement today, that between the search for the visible unity of the church and the church's call to prophetic witness and service."[27] What responsibilities do the coalitions have to other ecumenical work being done in Canada? How does the healing of broken relationships within human community relate to the healing of broken relationships within and between churches, many of which have significant justice elements?
- What are the theological responsibilities of the coalitions as participants in civil society?
- What is the capacity of the coalitions to take up symbolic systems of meaning as a particular category of socio-political analysis?
- What are the contributions the Canadian coalitions have to bring to the international discussion of civil society?

I have heard it said internationally that the Canadian interchurch coalitions are 'the envy of the ecumenical movement.' This is more than envy for the financial contributions of CIDA, the churches and individuals; it is also more than respect for the fine and creative work that is done. Rather this statement acknowledges the participation of the coalitions within civil society as ecumenical work in the most profound sense and invites the contribution of this experience as a gift to the wider ecumenical community.

Policy Impact
and Political Empowerment

David Langille[1]

Students of politics take great risks when they try to make definitive statements about the impact of social movements or organizations. Those who label the women's movement the strongest or most
effective instigator of change in Canadian politics must hesitate when
they witness the increasing levels of violence toward women and
their growing economic insecurity. Similarly, the degradation of our
environment continues even though the environmental movement
attracts generous media publicity and political rhetoric.

It is therefore appropriate to ask whether the ecumenical coalitions have been politically effective—given that Canada is now a
meaner, less equitable and more unjust society than it was before the
first coalitions were established in the early 70s.[2] The short answer
to the question is that, while the coalitions have made a progressive
contribution to Canadian political life, they have encountered considerable opposition, both direct and indirect. This opposition has been
led by very powerful business interests which have helped orchestrate
a conservative offensive to roll back the welfare state and restore
corporate profits.

However, our evaluation of political effectiveness or political
impact will very much depend on our overall conception of politics
and society and, in this case, of the role of the church as a social
institution. For instance, if one holds an organic conception of
society, whereby those at the top of the hierarchy have an obligation
to protect those below, then one is more inclined to favour a system
of elite accommodation. Under such a system, the church leadership
negotiates with the leaders of other social and political institutions
on behalf of its parishioners. If, on the other hand, one favours the
notion of individual and collective empowerment, it becomes more
important to increase people's capacities and capabilities to assert
more control over their lives—and thereby create a more democratic,

humane and just order. We have to examine, therefore, to what extent
the ecumenical coalitions lobby governments on behalf of their particular constituencies or participate in the broader movements for democratic social change.

In practice, some coalitions follow one model and some the other,
or combinations thereof, depending on their mandate from the
churches, the policy community within which they operate,[3] and their
history, i.e. how they were organized and who was in control (national
churches, staff, or grassroots activists). The Taskforce on the
Churches and Corporate Responsibility, the Inter-Church Coalition
on Africa, and the Canada-Asia Working Group offer but a few
examples of the lobbying approach. The Ecumenical Coalition for
Economic Justice initially attempted to change public policy via
lobbying, but now seeks to exert more pressure as part of a wider
coalition of popular sector groups.[4] Project Ploughshares continues
to function in both realms, doing research and lobbying on behalf of
the member churches while also maintaining its own network of local
peace groups. Ten Days for World Development offers yet another
model, developing a grassroots network within the church community
which it can then employ in lobbying efforts.[5]

To reiterate, then, how we evaluate the ecumenical coalitions
will depend on our political interests, power base and point of view.
The following criteria are designed to evaluate the complexities of
social movement and coalition politics:

- Have they been able to change public policy?
- Have they set other objectives for themselves and achieved them?
- Have they helped to educate and to change public opinion?
- Have they built a stronger movement for a longer term struggle
  for social change?
- Have they changed the political system, its structures or proc-
  esses, preferably in a democratic direction?

Changes in public policy

Despite their best efforts to enhance peace and social justice, the
churches and their interchurch coalitions have not been setting the
agenda for Canadian politics. They have been forced into a very
defensive, reactive posture, due in part to the growing secularization
of Canadian society but, more significantly, to the very successful

political offensive of the corporate community that helped turn Canadian politics to the right.

The changing context for political action

The economic and political context within which the interchurch coalitions operate has changed a great deal since the first coalition was established in 1973. If one evaluates their political effectiveness in light of these changes, one is struck by three significant trends: the growing structural and political power of business; the relative weakness of labour and the other social movements that constitute the 'popular sector'; and the consequent weakening of the welfare state and the social safety net that it offered.

The strengthening of free-market forces around the world has been due to a mixture of increased capital mobility, the internationalization of production, the erosion of protectionist trade barriers, and technological change.[6] Business leaders in many of the capitalist countries became better organized and mounted a very effective political campaign to restore their image, which had reached a low ebb by the late 60s and early 70s. The most significant step in this direction was the formation in 1976 of the Business Council on National Issues, composed of 150 chief executive officers representing major multinational corporations that currently control over $925 billion in assets and employ nearly two million Canadians.[7] These executives now constitute the senior voice of business in Canada, the most powerful interest group in the country, and one of the strongest bastions of patriarchy.[8] The Business Council offers them the opportunity "to contribute personally to the development of public policies and the setting of national priorities."[9] They concentrate on trying to set the overall framework for public policy and their record of success is phenomenal.

In the early 80s, the Business Council on National Issues helped to alter the direction of government intervention in the economy—the new focus on opposing inflation meant opposing 'inflated' wage expectations, the growth of public spending, and the regulation of the free market. When the Canadian Conference of Catholic Bishops responded with their *Ethical Reflections on the Economy*, Tom d'Aquino, the president of the Business Council, advised the bishops to stick to religion since they knew so little about economics.[10] Since then, the Business Council on National Issues has played a major role in bringing about the Free Trade Agreement with the United States and having it expanded to Mexico. It also deserves a great deal of the credit for the Goods and Services Tax, for the reform of competition legislation to encourage greater corporate concentration, and for the slow but steady erosion of our social security system.

Labour and the other social movements which have been forced onto the defensive by the growing influence of business have relied on two strategies. They have coalesced to protect their interests—the Action Canada Network being one example—and they have invested much of their hopes in the New Democratic Party, leading to the election of NDP governments in three provinces. These governments have disappointed the social movements, not only because of the NDP's capitulation to neoliberal notions of fiscal restraint, but because of the political constraint they have shown—their unwillingness to fundamentally change the processes of government so as to help empower individual citizens and social movements and enhance their capacity to control their lives.[11]

Consequently, the interchurch coalitions cannot take credit for many changes in government policy. In the 70s, the Inter-Church Committee on Human Rights in Latin America and the Inter-Church Committee for Refugees played a critical role in improving Canada's acceptance and treatment of refugees.[12] Similarly, the Inter-Church Coalition on Africa and the Taskforce on the Churches and Corporate Responsibility were instrumental in curbing Canadian investment in South Africa and thereby helping to dismantle the apartheid system. However, the coalitions have not managed to stop the Free Trade Agreement or megaproject development in the North, to entrench the aboriginal right to self-government, achieve fair tax reforms, or remove the root causes of poverty. Nor can Project Ploughshares take much credit for ending the Cold War or substantially reducing military spending in this country. Fortunately, there are other criteria by which we can give the coalitions a more positive evaluation.

Meeting other objectives

Although changing public policy would seem to be the most obvious measure of political effectiveness, social movements sometimes adopt other, less direct objectives. For instance, many within the women's movement have concluded that we must first change individual values, attitudes and behaviours before we can achieve meaningful political change. Such common objectives as education or movement building are discussed below. However, social movement organizations sometimes pursue more questionable objectives, particularly if they have suffered goal displacement, become distracted from their original mission or consumed by problems of organizational maintenance or empire building. The interchurch coalitions must examine whether their objectives and actions remain appropriate to their mandate or the political priorities of their sponsors. To cite an example, some observers question whether the Taskforce on the Churches and Corporate Responsibility should be trying to alter the conduct of individual corporations at a time when corporate leaders are systematically removing the regulations that constrain corporate behaviour. Would it not be fairer and more effective to campaign for a strict set of rules governing all corporations, so they could compete on a level playing field? At the same time, the Taskforce could educate Canadians about corporate activity and posit a clear alternative to the agenda of competitiveness and greed.

There are other voices within the churches that do not see it as their role to intervene in specific issues of public policy. For example, there are pacifists (many of them Mennonite) who prefer to bear witness, believing in the integrity of a particular action or position, regardless of whether it influences anyone in the short run. They choose to stand by their principles without necessarily intervening in the immediate policy debates. Such action (or inaction) can play a critical role in the beginning of a cause or issue by helping to raise public consciousness, and such steadfast commitment can also help to keep an issue alive when other activists lose energy and the media lose interest. The record of Project Ploughshares and the role of Ernie Regehr deserve credit in this regard.

Furthermore, the coalitions can play a prophetic role by leading the churches in a progressive direction. This is always a risky role to play, and all the more so in a time of social conservatism and fiscal restraint. But many of the ecumenical pioneers had hoped that the coalitions would help to build and strengthen the participating churches by developing expertise in social justice issues that would inspire both the leadership and their parishioners to action.

Education, consciousness raising and changing public opinion

Given how much of the coalitions' efforts are premised on a democratic process leading to changes in public policy, it is critical to measure their impact on public opinion and, if possible, to assess whether they have had any influence over election results. This is not so difficult as it might appear.[13] There are national surveys which track how the public's support for issues such as aboriginal rights, foreign aid, or military spending changes over time. These surveys can help us gauge the effectiveness of those national campaigns in which the coalitions and the churches play a leading role. Focus groups can help clarify whether people have heard of particular campaigns or coalitions, what attitudes have been formed, and how communications can be improved in the future. While it would be foolish to give such techniques priority over other forms of analysis, the coalitions might benefit from more rigorous evaluation of their communication and education efforts.

The interchurch coalitions have often played a critical role in the early stages of developing a political issue or campaign—attracting media attention, raising public awareness and putting issues on the political agenda. The coalitions are also noteworthy for contributing resources to the less popular causes and for sustaining support when attention faded and the issue went out of fashion. One of their most effective contributions has been the publication of popular printed materials, such as the book by Karmel Taylor McCullum and Hugh McCullum, *This Land Is Not For Sale*,[14] which greatly aided Project North in its support for the Dene; the Taskforce on the Churches and Corporate Responsibility brochure, "Banking on Apartheid," and its 'No Loans to South Africa/Chile' stickers which helped to expose the behaviour of our chartered banks; and the long string of books and popular education materials produced by the Ecumenical Coalition for Economic Justice, including 750,000 copies of its cartoon booklet on tax reform. The Ecumenical Coalition for Economic Justice also deserves recognition for developing the effective popular education tool, the Ah-hah Seminar, that helps participants develop confidence in their own abilities to analyse situations and devise appropriate strategies.[15] In several cases, the coalitions have played a valuable role in leveraging resources out of government. Countries such as Canada, Sweden and the Netherlands were for many years distinctive for the support they gave to their non-governmental organizations engaged in international development, peace, women's and environmental issues, etc., and the inspiration often came from the churches or church-based organizations.[16]

Elitism versus democracy

Concern has grown over the degree to which some of the coalitions cater to the small elite of established decision makers in the churches, government and corporate community, rather than to a wider base of church members or community activists. By what means can those persons across Canada who identify with the objectives of the various coalitions contribute to their work and help control their direction? How can these coalitions effectively reach and involve a wider constituency when the churchgoing population is declining? Once we identify the various factors which contribute to the relative elitism of the coalitions, we can begin to answer these questions.

First, most of the coalitions were not given the mandate to communicate with or involve a large audience. The one coalition given a clear mandate to do so, Ten Days for World Development, certainly has demonstrated its effectiveness at developing a grassroots network. If it were to assume much of the educational and communications responsibilities of the other coalitions, the latter could then be free to concentrate on research, the monitoring of public policy, consultations with government and the provision of other services to their constituency. Such a division of labour might also help to resolve the debate over appropriate tactics and strategies—the coalitions would conduct research and collaborate with government as necessary, but they would be well-equipped to mount highly effective publicity campaigns and apply political pressure when required. This would not preclude coalitions from maintaining their own network of community activists, where they were able to do so.[17]

Secondly, the ecumenical movement has been far more effective at promoting the values of peace and social justice than it has been at promoting democratic empowerment. Has it been handicapped in this regard by the relatively undemocratic character of some of the member churches which may still find it troubling to encourage a more egalitarian political order? Even some of the most progressive theology may prove a handicap. One of the major influences on the interchurch coalitions has been the theology of liberation and the appeal to extend "a preferential option for the poor." This theology helped to define the Catholic left in Quebec which shows many parallels with the ecumenical coalitions. Gregory Baum observes that the theology of liberation made an enormous contribution to "the field of popular education and the promotion of a culture of solidarity."[18] While there is no doubting its many positive connotations,[19] the discourse of solidarity and sacrifice derives from and reinforces a more elitist world-view than does the discourse of democracy. Baum goes on to note that "the Catholic left is a minority movement in the Church. The great majority of Catholics who attend Sunday mass in their respective parishes are only vaguely aware of the progressive documents published by their bishops and have never heard of the left-wing Catholic organizations... However, activists of all tendencies, progressive or not, are almost by definition minorities; their influence and example do not depend on their numbers."[20]

The various coalitions need to examine on a regular basis with whom they are in solidarity and to what end[21] and whether popular participation is being sacrificed for a more vanguardist politics, whereby a small cadre of activists sharpen their analysis but grow distant from their base.[22]

There is no doubt, however, that the principal factor accounting for the limited outreach of the coalitions is the mandate they received from the sponsoring churches who envisaged that the coalitions would merely feed information into existing church networks and that the churches themselves would be responsible for disseminating the research and mobilizing their members to action. This limited mandate assumed that the churches were capable of following through—in fact, their networks were often very weak or overloaded. The coalitions are now beginning to appreciate the weaknesses inherent in their design, as they find themselves without a strong base of support during a time when the churches are reconsidering the very existence of the coalitions.

Movement building

Given their limited mandate and resources, the coalitions have been grappling for over 20 years with how best to effect political change. Although they often succeeded in mobilizing church leaders to take a progressive stand on a particular issue, the federal government appears increasingly unmoved by such appeals. Naturally enough, some coalitions, such as Ten Days for World Development, the Ecumenical Coalition for Economic Justice and Project Plough-shares, have widened their net and appealed directly to the church membership and beyond to the secular community or non-religious public. However, many coalitions still seem to be confused about who is their constituency, clientele, audience or target group. They know they risk losing the support of ordinary church members if they cater exclusively to the national church offices. On the other hand, if they spend all of their time with marginalized minorities, whether in Canada or overseas, it will be difficult to mobilize support for political change. It would certainly be counterproductive to involve only a narrow range of activists and become no more than a small sect at odds with the church community and without strong ties to a base outside the churches.

Meanwhile, the past 20 years have witnessed the development of an impressive infrastructure of social movement institutions in Canada. Despite all of the cutbacks in the welfare state (or perhaps because of them), the organizations, networks and coalitions of the 'popular sector' have managed to survive the recent era of reaction. Some of the coalitions have made important contributions to this longer term process of community building—fostering a sense of social solidarity, forging alliances amongst the popular sector, and building a coalition for a more progressive politics.[23] The Ecumenical Coalition for Economic Justice and PLURA appear most committed to coalition work. It has been the Economic Justice coalition's experience that the leadership for social change is more apt to come from people's organizations, such as labour or women's groups, than from governments which are allied with the rich and powerful.[24] In fact, popular sector leaders can seldom make significant social changes unless they first democratize the process of government. Yet, as Mary Boyd notes, many of our interchurch coalitions are still reluctant to forge the sort of coalitions with labour and other popular sector organizations that might bolster their political power.[25]

In any case, coalition politics tends to be a relatively elitist enterprise somewhat divorced from the 'rank and file' membership or parishioners. This problem is very difficult to avoid if the coalition occurs between national organizations, as is the case with the inter-church groups. It is also a serious problem for the Action Canada Network.[26]

The attempt to involve regional coalitions or local networks in the national decision-making process is an imperfect compromise since local bodies tend to be dominated by activists rather than be representative of the average church member or citizen. This can develop into a problem if the membership feels no sense of identification with or control over the coalitions and, consequently, becomes reluctant to support them financially or politically.

Although the ecumenical coalitions have cooperated with one another around issues such as food, energy and the debt crisis, there are grounds for far more systematic collaboration—just as the corporate sector is learning the advantages of clustering together to achieve synergies. For example, the best means of broadening and deepening support for the coalitions and the cause of social justice would be to renew and enlarge the supply of activists. The churches and the coalitions might collaborate in sponsoring leadership training schools, camps and workshops, and educational tours—especially for youth who have not hitherto been involved in church programs.[27]

The ecumenical coalitions may not have attracted many people to become active churchgoers, but they have helped maintain the faith of many of the poor and oppressed, and of many progressive young people who were becoming disillusioned with mainstream religion. Perhaps one of their greatest accomplishments has been to maintain such faith during these dark ages which are so often marked by fundamentalism, intolerance and a cynical despair. The coalitions are full of modern-day missionaries who have maintained or resurrected the best of the Judaeo-Christian tradition—and inspired many by their actions—working hard to change the values and attitudes, actions and behaviours of Canadians rather than trying to convert 'pagans' overseas.

Systemic change, democratization and empowerment

Our notions of political effectiveness also have to take account of different time frames—short-term versus long-term. Over the short term we can change government policies or programs, or deliver services that will improve the immediate conditions in which people find themselves. While it is absolutely critical that this important work be done, we need to be working toward a longer term vision of societal change and development. In earlier eras, religious leaders contributed to the eradication of slavery and serfdom, the introduction of democracy, the emancipation of women and the abolition of capital punishment. In this present climate of economic recession and political reaction, it is still not too ambitious to consider the elimination of warfare and interpersonal violence, nor too grandiose to imagine the democratic control of our economic enterprises and the agencies of global government, such as the International Monetary Fund, the World Bank and the United Nations. It may help the coalitions sort out some of their strategic dilemmas if they set tangible policy objectives that transcend all denominational or national boundaries.

Canada's interchurch coalitions are laying the foundations for systemic change by their educational campaigns, their coalition-building efforts and their attempts to encourage popular participation and empowerment. Obviously the record of the coalitions in this regard is very uneven. Only a few have tried to alter the balance of forces in Canadian politics so as to empower the poor and the marginalized.

Yet a very significant step in the work of the interchurch coalitions has been their linking of global and domestic issues. It is increasingly apparent that environment or trade issues, or the supply of food or energy questions, cannot be resolved at one level or the other. The coalitions have helped people to appreciate their interdependence and develop a sense of common interest and solidarity. Still greater results might be expected if those coalitions engaged in development and solidarity work with Africa, Asia, China and Latin America were to function as a more cohesive unit, so as to promote more co-operation on issues both in Canada and internationally.

Nonetheless, the coalitions have managed to raise the consciousness of Canadians on the implications of free trade, the nuclear arms race and the global debt crisis. And even if they have managed only to moderate the corporate agenda and help lessen its impact on Canadians, their contribution has been worthwhile. The coalitions have also played a critical role by making the resources of the churches—from finances to photocopiers—available to various movements working for social justice. And finally, they have served as an intellectual refuge wherein church people and others could develop a vision of progressive possibilities.

Confrontation versus consensus

It is important at this point that we put to rest a long-standing debate over appropriate strategies or tactics for the coalitions, i.e. the relative merits of a consensual or confrontational approach. Schwartz and Paul have drawn a distinction between social movements that operate on a *conflict model*—those which confront organized opposition in trying to change the social structure, fundamental policies or the balance of power among groups—and those that operate on a *consensus model*—with broad institutional support and little or no opposition. Their research shows clearly that conflict movements, such as the labour movement, the women's movement and even the Woman's Christian Temperance Union, have more success in mobilizing people than do consensus movements such as Mothers Against Drunk Driving.[28] The consensus movements may be able to gain minor amendments so as to fine-tune public policy, but they are seldom responsible for more substantive changes in policy.[29]

Therefore, research, logic and experience all dictate that one's political approach should vary according to the objectives sought, the issue being dealt with and the degree of openness or responsiveness experienced. Alienated youth may favour confrontation (largely on account of their own relative powerlessness), but most of us prefer a more harmonious approach, adopting confrontation only as a last resort. The coalitions are fortunate, therefore, if a low-key process of consultation generates a consensus and their objectives are achieved. However, if not, it may well be appropriate for them to confront the government or corporation with whom they are dealing and to exert more pressure.

Conclusion

Although the interchurch coalitions have contributed to peace and social justice and helped to encourage a more progressive politics here in Canada, they have certainly not been able to prevent the drift to the right and the erosion of much of our social safety net and national institutions. As has been shown, many of these changes can be attributed to developments in the world economy, facilitated by the political efforts of the business community as its seeks greater security in the face of increased competition. Therefore, what at first glance appear to be two contradictory social trends—the growing power of transnational capital and the growth of a popular sector committed to a more democratic and egalitarian society—are in fact very much related to one another. Just as former President Reagan contributed to the growth of the peace movement in the early 80s, the political offensive of the New Right has sparked a defensive movement on the part of its victims. The churches and their social justice coalitions have played a critical role in this movement to maintain the quality of life in Canada and protect us from the competitiveness and social decay common in the free enterprise culture to the south.

However, it is important to ask how the ecumenical coalitions could have been *more effective* in shaping Canadian politics. The coalitions depend on their base in the churches, yet the status and strength of the churches has eroded. Could the coalitions have made more effective use of the diminishing resources that were available for social justice work? While the conventional techniques of cost-benefit analysis may be inappropriate to judge whether the churches are getting good value for their money or assess how the coalitions might become more efficient, more effort could be made to obtain independent evaluations of their effectiveness. Of the 12 coalitions, only PLURA, Ten Days, ICCAF and the Aboriginal Rights Coalition have commissioned such studies.[30] In any case, one of the more remarkable features of the ecumenical coalitions is their low level of funding—the combined annual budgets of all 12 coalitions is $2.5 to $3 million annually.[31] It is intriguing to speculate how much more could be accomplished if their budgets were substantially increased.

Ideally, the coalitions could raise more of their own funds and be less dependent on the churches. The greatest obstacle appears to be the tax regime. It is ironic, given how the corporate agenda seems so inimical to the values and priorities espoused by the Christian churches, that corporations can obtain an easy tax deduction for their lobbying activities, while many popular sector or public service groups have to curtail their political activity for fear of jeopardizing their charitable status.[32] If the coalitions were able to do their own direct fund raising, they could appeal to the wider public, a large portion of which shares the same values, even if a declining number attend church on a regular basis. These appeals can also educate a wider constituency about the issues and recruit more political support.

The churches have generally opposed such direct fund raising in order that the coalitions remain within their purview rather than function independently. This fear could be mitigated if the churches collaborated and organized a 'united appeal' for social justice. Such collaboration would also save money, given the high cost of modern fund-raising techniques. It makes little sense for the coalitions to mount separate campaigns and compete with one another in the quest for funds. A joint campaign would not preclude the coalitions from tapping into their own natural constituency, as Project Ploughshares does with its direct mail campaigns. Nor would it prevent them from contracting with governments to provide services to their constituency, as does the Inter-Church Coalition on Africa which accepted funds from the Canadian International Development Agency for its Educational Project on South Africa.[33] However, as the coalitions become more financially independent, they will have to take care to maintain close ties with the churches if they still wish to call upon their political clout.

A strategic vision for the 90s and beyond

As Joe Mihevc has noted, "the coalitions were formed in the 1970s when there was a positive climate of opinion, strong leadership and a progressive ecumenical vision"[34]—conditions reminiscent of the 1920s and 30s when many Christians became advocates of the Social Gospel. However, it is no use complaining that a vision of the future path no longer exists—the same values inspire us today as before, even if they seem harder to attain. Rather than succumb to the latest corporate agenda, one can easily imagine the components of a democratic agenda and strive for its attainment. Although the rich and the powerful deny there is any alternative, they are merely asserting their own interests in response to the possibilities offered by new technologies and new trade opportunities.[35] We must encourage experiments and alternatives—whether in Cuba, China, Singapore, Sweden, or right here in Canada. Those in search of a practical alternative vision can find plenty of inspiration in Marcia Nozick's work on building sustainable communities.[36] It must be recalled that visions or agendas seldom arrive as fully fleshed-out manifestos but are patched together over time through a process of trial and error.

Those who make peace and social justice their priorities still have some critical strategic choices to confront. It would be unwise to place too much faith in the NDP at a time when social democracy appears to be in crisis in all of the industrialized countries, finding itself unable to escape the constraints imposed by international capitalism which has effectively escaped the bounds of Keynesian economic policy. On the other hand, many social activists and social scientists are overly impressed with the political potential of social movements and coalitions. If they reject not just electoral politics but all forms of 'statism' and concentrate instead on strengthening 'civil society,'[37] they risk reinforcing the right-wing attack on government intervention and undermining the provision of public services to those most in need, particularly those in the less industrialized countries. Our experience of the decade of greed indicates that wealth does not trickle down to the poor, competitiveness curtails co-operation, insecurity inhibits risk taking, deregulation contributes to corporate concentration, and increased reliance on the free market leaves people more dependent on social welfare and less in control of their lives.[38]

The churches, in particular, face some difficult choices, given the weakness and vulnerability of so many in our society. As their membership shrinks and their resources diminish, they could turn inward, reacting to these challenges with policies of exclusion, catering only to their chosen few.[39] Or they could open up and become ever more inclusive, practising their religion in the larger community, showing not only a preferential option for the poor but a stronger commitment to the democratic empowerment of all citizens. During these hard times, the churches and the ecumenical coalitions can help sustain us, help us maintain our humanity and our ethical standards, instil good values in our children and educate us about how we can apply these values in contemporary society so as to resist the corporate ideology of greed and selfishness. They still have enormous resources to contribute to Canada's social movements—not only via the networking activities of the various coalitions, but also at the local level, where each church can become a more active community centre helping to publicize and participate in the work of the various ecumenical coalitions.

Missiology

Roger Hutchinson

Introduction

The Canada China Programme described itself as an anomalous coalition on the assumption that its focus on partnership and mission sets it slightly apart from other coalitions which emphasize social justice advocacy. However, when attention is focussed on the fact that all of the coalitions can be seen as agents of their sponsoring churches' mission, the Canada China Programme no longer appears to be particularly anomalous. Whether or not a particular coalition stresses listening to and interpreting the concerns of partner churches or advocacy on behalf of human rights, social justice or environmental protection depends on who the partners are and what witnessing against evil requires in a particular context.

The continuing role of each coalition as an agent of the mission of its sponsoring denominations cannot, however, simply be taken for granted. In the past, organizations such as Oxfam and Crossroads International initially depended heavily on church funds but they became increasingly independent. They are sometimes viewed as the churches' partners but, in relation to the budgets and priorities of each denomination and the identities of the organizations themselves, they are not the churches' agents of mission. As budgets tighten and pressure grows on a shrinking number of denominational staff members who serve on coalition administrative committees, each denomination will have to clarify its own priorities and its own understanding of what its mission is and how it can best be pursued.

My main aim in this chapter is to bring to the level of conscious articulation the view that the coalitions are agents of the churches' mission. It is interesting to notice, of course, that the other side of this proposition is that, through their contributions of denominational funds used to support the coalitions, church members are agents of mission and not simply financial contributors to someone else's good works. My secondary aim is to introduce a framework which might be useful for continuing discussions about mission and partnership, interchurch and ecumenical activities, and denominational priorities.

David Bosch's major study of mission[1] provides a good starting point. His characterizations of biblical models of mission and the emphases he detects in the emerging ecumenical missionary paradigm provide a suggestive framework for thinking about coalition activities as integral parts of the mission of their sponsoring denominations. Three of the biblical understandings of mission which are of particular interest are: Luke's emphasis on solidarity with the poor, Matthew's stress on making disciples and keeping the commandments, and the Pauline emphasis on membership in the covenant community. Themes that are central to both the emerging ecumenical model of mission and the coalition stories are: partnership, contextualization and witnessing.

The framework I will use in this chapter involves looking first at mission as solidarity with the poor and partnership, next at mission as keeping the commandments and contextualization, and finally, at mission as membership in the covenant community and witnessing.

Mission as solidarity with the poor and partnership

According to the frequently cited passage in Luke (4:18-19), when Jesus returned to Nazareth where he had been brought up, he went into the synagogue on the sabbath day, as was his custom, and read the following verses from the book of the prophet Isaiah: "The Spirit of the Lord is upon me, because he has anointed me to bring good news to the poor. He has sent me to proclaim release to the captives and recovery of sight to the blind, to let the oppressed go free, to proclaim the year of the Lord's favour" (Isaiah 61:1-2, 58:6).

This passage, combined with Jesus' claim that "Today this scripture has been fulfilled in your hearing," stands at the centre of Luke's interpretation of the basic purpose and meaning of mission.[2] What Bosch finds particularly interesting in Luke's account of Jesus' appearance in the synagogue at Nazareth is that the line "to let the oppressed go free" has been taken from Isaiah 58 and added to the passage from Isaiah 61. The oppressed referred to in this passage are "the poor Jews who, in order to pay the taxes levied by the Persian king, had to mortgage their vineyards and homes and even sell their children into slavery to rich fellow-Jews who grasped the opportunity to capitalize on the predicament of the poor."[3]

Among the other causes of poverty, Luke pays special attention to "those who have become destitute because of their ever-growing debts... For them, as well as for the other oppressed groups listed here, the 'year of the Lord's favour' is being announced."[4] His emphasis on relief from debts represented good news for the poor and a message for the rich. He expected the rich to be converted to a way of life more in keeping with the social teachings of Jesus. One model for this was the tax collector, Zacchaeus. He both repaid those from whom he had collected too much and gave half of his wealth to the poor. The rich young ruler, on the other hand, was not prepared to meet Jesus' criterion for conversion and went sadly away.

There is a clear connection between the churches' recent emphasis on partnership and their commitment to be in solidarity with the poor. The various interchurch coalitions were created to increase the effectiveness of the churches' solidarity activities.

The coalition model itself is an innovative exercise in partnership. During the 70s the Canadian churches—Protestant and Roman Catholic, mainstream and minority—devised a way to work together in concrete ways that did not require full agreement in areas of doctrine, worship and political ideology. This dimension of partnership is for the most part presupposed in the coalition stories.

Partnership presupposed equality. In Western missionary circles, the idea of the autonomy and equality of the 'younger' churches became popular during the last decade of the 19th century, but did not immediately transform the practice of either the older or the younger churches. The commitment to equality was kept alive, however, and at the Jerusalem and Tambaram conferences of the International Missionary Council in 1928 and 1938, the younger churches were referred to as equals. The phrase 'Partnership in Obedience' was coined at the 1947 meeting of the Council held in Whitby, Ontario. Although it took a long time for practice to catch up with theory, there was an unmistakable movement away from characterizing churches as autonomous or dependent, older or younger, and toward an understanding that the church-for-others was in the process of becoming the church-with-others.[5] Coalition activities represent concrete expressions of this commitment to be partners with, or in solidarity with, other churches and groups working for peace and justice.

The notion of partnership is either explicitly mentioned or clearly implied in each of the coalition stories. In the chapter on the Aboriginal Rights Coalition, for example, Peter Hamel refers to sponsoring churches, aboriginal organizations and regional support groups as three integral partners. For GATT-Fly, the early emphasis on partnership as solidarity with sugar workers was gradually extended to include partnerships with workers, farmers, peasants, women and other 'popular movements.' There are numerous references in other chapters to the relationships among the coalitions, their sponsoring churches and their partner churches overseas.

Collaboration with other development, environmental and peace groups has been standard practice for most of the churches, as is the habit of referring to churches in other countries, with shared denominational identities or compatible agendas, as partners. Where the coalitions differ from one another regarding their understanding of partnership is over the extent to which they carry out the policies of their sponsoring churches and the extent to which they seek church and other sources of funding to carry out their own agendas. Such organizational and ecclesiological issues raise important questions about accountability and participation.

Denominations will no doubt continue to allocate some of their resources to independent partners as an effective way to pursue particular goals. Such decisions should, however, be made on the basis of renewed understandings of mission and not as the result of residual commitments made during an earlier phase of an organization's development. Denominations must be able to reassess their priorities and commitments, or the present generation of church members will lose their sense of being agents of mission rather than financial donors without a say in how their money is being spent and how their church carries out its mission.

Participation is perhaps an even more important question than accountability. Although in my own church, the United Church, many members feel alienated from the processes used to determine church policies, the fact remains that structures are in place to allow ordinary church members to participate in discussions about the ethical and theological implications of public policies and to take an active part in the development of church policies. Although membership is declining in many of the formerly mainline denominations, they continue to play important roles as intermediate structures linking otherwise isolated individuals and the large institutions which dominate the public realm.

When attention is focussed concretely on denominational budgets and priorities, the distinction between partners and agents of mission might be useful. This should not, however, lead us to forget that God's mission and the churches' mission cannot simply be equated. Identifying the real followers of Jesus in particular contexts involves more than asking about church membership and denominational affiliation. Sometimes, as Luke, Matthew and Paul all realized, the signs of the Gospel are more clearly evident outside the churches than within. For Matthew, the crucial question was who was actually keeping the commandments. Luke, on the other hand, looked for signs of the Spirit.

Luke's Gospel and the book of Acts were written for followers of Jesus who were at a distance both in time and space from the events which had such an impact on those who knew Jesus. Whereas the first generation of followers expected the immediate return of Jesus, Luke and his readers knew that life must go on. His aim was to retell the story of Jesus and the Christian movement for followers who must find inspiration and guidance in the absence of their Lord.

Luke established continuity between Jesus and his later followers by stressing the presence of the Spirit. Just as God was present to humans through Jesus, Jesus continued to be present to his followers through the Spirit. "The gift of the Spirit is the gift of becoming involved in mission, for mission is the direct consequence of the outpouring of the Spirit. Luke's pneumatology excludes the possibility of a missionary command; it implies, rather, a promise that the disciples will get involved in mission."[6]

In addition to initiating mission, the Spirit guides and empowers mission. "This manifests itself particularly in the boldness of the witnesses once they have been endowed with the Spirit."[7] According to Bosch, "For Luke, the concept of the Spirit sealed the kinship between God's universal will to save, the liberating ministry of Jesus, and the worldwide mission of the church."[8]

Not all spirits, however, are the Holy Spirit or the Spirit of Jesus

Christ. Being spirit-filled and confident that God is present is in itself an ambiguous phenomenon as the tragic events in Waco, Texas, remind us. In addition to looking for signs of the Spirit, Christian discipleship requires discernment and the ability to test the spirits. For Luke, the forgiveness of sins and solidarity with the poor were signs of the presence of the Spirit of God. Matthew also presupposed forgiveness of sins as a sign of God's grace and stressed justice for the poor, but he talked more about discipleship and keeping Jesus' commandments than he did about the Spirit.

Mission as keeping the commandments and contextualization

The 'Great Commission' in Matthew 28:19 which provides a mandate to make disciples of all nations, baptizing them in the name of the Father, the Son and the Holy Spirit, and teaching them all that Jesus had taught is usually associated with an evangelical rather than an ecumenical understanding of mission.[9] Social justice Christians find more obvious roots for their concerns in the story in Matthew 25 which identifies the real followers of Jesus with those who feed the hungry, give a drink to the thirsty, welcome the stranger and so forth. Bosch argues convincingly, however, that the Great Commission, the culmination of a theme which runs throughout Matthew's Gospel, provides a view of mission which is as relevant for seeking justice in the world as it is for saving sinners from the world.[10]

Matthew's Gospel was written during the early 80s of the first century to address the identity crisis of a small Jewish Christian community which had fled the Jewish war and was living in a predominantly Gentile area, probably in Syria. It was a time of growing hostility between Pharisaic Judaism and Jewish Christianity, but the complete break which came in A.D. 85 had not yet occurred. The community wanted to maintain continuity with its Jewish roots, but it was clearly in the process of becoming something other than a renewal movement within Judaism. The situation was aggravated by tensions between legalists who equated faithfulness with obedience to the law and enthusiasts who looked to the Spirit for guidance and miracles. Contradictory passages in Matthew's Gospel reveal the author's reluctance to side completely with one side or the other. He wanted both sides to move toward a new understanding of who they were as followers of Jesus and how Jesus continued to be present in their midst.

Whereas Luke found continuity with Jesus through the Spirit, Matthew stressed the continuing presence of Jesus through disciples who do what Jesus taught and who try to keep his commandments. Matthew's account of the final appearance of the risen Jesus to his disciples is very sober and low key. The 11 disciples went to the mountain in Galilee and were commissioned by the same Jesus who had walked the dusty roads of Palestine with them. "He is risen from the dead, yes, but his glory is wrapped in a mystery. No ascension into heaven or outpouring of the Holy Spirit is reported or even anticipated... Nothing spectacular! Nothing for the enthusiasts!"[11]

The continuing presence of Jesus is "intimately linked to his followers' engagement in mission. It is as they make disciples, baptize them, and teach them, that Jesus remains with those followers."[12] This is a reversible proposition for Matthew. On the one hand, disciples of Jesus do what he taught and follow his commandments. On the other hand, those who do what Jesus taught are his real followers. "There is, for Matthew, a certain tension between church and discipleship; at the same time they may never be divorced from each other... Ideally, every church member should be a true disciple, but this is obviously not the case in the Christian communities Matthew knows."[13]

Insofar as the missionary paradigms of Luke and Matthew both stress doing justice in the world, they provide suggestive models for coalition activities in the present. Their differing understandings of how Jesus continues to be present to his followers points both to diversity within Christian communities and to the recurrent tension between Spirit-filled innovators and more sober efforts to discern which activities most adequately embody the commandment to love our neighbours. A shift in attention from the general commitment to being on the side of the poor to asking in concrete cases what effective discipleship requires in particular situations brings us to the question of contextualization.

The term 'contextualization' was coined in the early 70s by Asian theologians preparing for the 1972 meeting of the Theological Education Fund. Background for the concept had been laid by Shoki Coe, a Taiwanese theologian, in a 1966 address entitled *Text and Context in Theological Education*.[14] He pointed to the need for a more interactional understanding of the relationship between traditional Christian teachings (text) and Asian societies (context). Coe and his colleagues came to see that 'indigenization,' the term used at that time to describe efforts to make theological education and mission better suited to their Asian situations, was too static in a double sense. The term indigenization implied that the problem was how Christian beliefs brought in from the West could be adapted to traditional Asian societies. This was a past-oriented approach which treated both the imported message and the existing social order in too static a fashion. A more future-oriented, dynamic approach was captured by the terms 'contextuality' and 'contextualization.'

There is no serious debate within coalition circles, or on the part of their sponsoring churches, over the need to recognize the relationship between our theologies and factors in our contexts such as gender, geography and social location. White, male, European and North American theologians no longer assume that their theology is universal and objective while the theologies of Asians, Africans, Latin Americans, indigenous peoples, American Blacks and women are partisan and subjective.[15]

There is, however, an ironic tendency for some post-church Christians to assume that Christians speaking on behalf of, and being accountable to, particular denominations are being partisan and therefore less ecumenical than Christians without a denominational home. Future discussions of mission, coalition activities and denominational priorities will be difficult unless all participants become more self-consciously contextual and more sensitive to different understandings of what membership in the covenant community means, that is, more sensitive to the third biblical model of mission.

Membership in the covenant community and witnessing

Until his conversion on the road to Damascus, Paul had persecuted followers of Jesus for their 'unconventional' beliefs and 'subversive' activities. As a result of his dramatic experience, Paul was convinced that he had been commissioned directly by Jesus to proclaim the astounding news that, in Christ, God had reconciled the world to himself and had entrusted Jesus' followers to be the messengers of this reconciliation.

In looking to Paul for a missionary paradigm which might have continuing relevance for us, it is important not to underestimate the difficulty of bridging the gap between his context and ours. Bosch suggests that we can both remember our differences in context and look to Paul for insights into the apostolic mission of the church if we "allow him to 'fertilize' our imagination and… to prolong, in a creative way, the logic of Paul's theology and mission amid historical circumstances that are in many respects very different from his."[16]

Paul was a church planter, but the church was not, for him, the ultimate aim of mission. His commission was "to proclaim that God has effected reconciliation with himself and also among people."[17] Bosch points out, "The life and work of the Christian community are intimately bound up with God's cosmic-historical plan for the redemption of the world. In Christ, God has reconciled not only the church but the world to himself (2 Corinthians 5:19)."[18]

Although Paul departed from his Jewish roots by stressing the role of Jesus, the concern which motivated him was in continuity with the Jewish message "of the one God who lays exclusive claim to people's loyalty."[19] His passion to proclaim this message to the whole world was fired by the pervasiveness of idolatry.

Idols are fabrications of the perverted human mind (see Romans 1:23, 25), and yet, in spite of the fact that they are human creations, they take control of people who are "led astray to idols" (1 Corinthians 12:2) and are "enslaved to beings that by nature are not gods," slaves of "weak and beggarly elemental spirits" (Galatians 4:8-9). Their being in bondage to idols is therefore due not to ignorance, as the Stoics would argue, but to wilfulness. In fact, 'idolatry' is not limited to worship of idols but includes a broader sense of allegiance to anything that is false.[20]

Paul's concern about proper allegiance to God extended to his views about the transformation of society. He attempted to avoid the one-sidedness of apocalyptic sects on the one hand, which considered the world irredeemable, and enthusiasts on the other hand, who could ignore the world since in Christ the final victory over evil had already been won. "Precisely because of God's sure victory in the end Paul emphasizes not ethical passivity but active participation in God's redemptive will in the here and now." The Christian life is not limited "to interior piety and cultic acts, as though salvation is restricted to the church, rather, believers, as a corporate body, are charged to practise bodily obedience (see Romans 12:1) and serve Christ in their daily lives." For Paul, the basic human problem is not ignorance but the wrong orientation of the will. His basic concern is not that we do not know what is good but that we lack the will and motivation to do what we know we ought to do.[21]

Paul's emphasis on the motivating power of Jesus does not, however, require an imperialistic, intolerant attitude toward persons who do not believe in him. The starting point and foundation for his message is the 'solution' he experienced rather than the 'plight' of unbelievers. "Only in light of the experience of the unconditional love of God could he recognize the terrible abyss of darkness into which he would have fallen without Christ." Statements in 1 Thessalonians 1 such as "For we know, brothers and sisters beloved by God, that he has chosen you" (v. 4) and "Jesus who rescues us from the wrath that is coming" (v. 10) are "a confession of being saved by God's act in Jesus, not a pronouncement about others who do not believe." To focus on the state of persons who have not experienced the love of God through Christ would be to begin with plight. "Rather, he knows, on the basis of the 'solution' he has found—better, which has found him—that the gospel he has to preach is one of unconditional love and unmerited grace. His missionary gospel is therefore a positive one."[22] The churches he planted were not closed and exclusive. They were covenant communities in which love was experienced and in which members lived an exemplary existence which worked like a magnet to draw outsiders toward the church.[23]

Paul's critique of idolatry has affinities with the attacks of the coalitions and the churches on the bondage of rich people, including rich Christians, to false gods of economic growth, wasteful patterns of consumption and military power. His emphasis on the experience of reconciling, sustaining love as the primary motivation for mission is consistent with the view of the coalitions and their sponsoring churches that the experience of injustice and brutality is a primary motivation for effective action against such evils.

Paul's reluctance to pronounce judgment on those who are not believers does not mean that he was unwilling to share the good news that through Christ the whole world was restored to right relations with God. The issue for Paul, as for Bartolomé de las Casas and the many Christians who do not feel compelled to try to convince their Buddhist, Jewish and secular humanist neighbours that they should become Christians, is how the Christian story should be shared, not whether it is ever appropriate to confess one's faith. As Las Casas insisted, the "one right way" to share the Christian story is through humility, graciousness, and perseverance as witnesses against evil.[24]

Perhaps a more open discussion of how the Christian story is being shared in different ways could lead to renewed confidence that sharing the story remains an important and legitimate part of the witness of organizations which are both the churches' partners and their agents of mission.

The image of witnessing is used most directly and powerfully by Ernie Regehr in his chapter on Project Ploughshares.[25] He makes it clear that, in witnessing *against* evil, the churches are also witnessing *to* the truth. The role of the churches as witnesses can be illustrated with an anecdote from the days of the Mackenzie Valley pipeline debate. At a meeting between church leaders and representatives from the business community, one of the business people said rather angrily that church leaders should stick to their main task of filling the pews. One of the church leaders, Clarke McDonald of the United Church, replied that filling the pews was not the churches' main job. The central responsibility of the churches was, he said, to witness to the truth. Clarke McDonald's claim about witnessing *to* the truth and Ernie Regehr's emphasis on witnessing *against* evil point to a central feature of the mission of each coalition. Underlying different choices of partners and the work in different contexts is an unchanging aim to witness to the truth and against evil. The need to discern what this entails at particular times in particular places is illustrated throughout the coalition stories. The presence of this commitment provides the non-negotiable core of absolute values which allows the churches and coalitions to adopt a pluralistic stance regarding different understandings of mission and different assessments of what is going on in different contexts.

Conclusion

My main aim in this chapter has been to encourage discussion of the ways in which the coalitions can be viewed as agents of mission. My secondary aim was to introduce a framework which might be useful for discussions of mission, partnership, coalition activities and denominational priorities. An important requirement of a framework for discussion is that the framework itself should not predetermine the outcome of debates over the nature of mission and the priorities of the churches. Some readers will no doubt observe that I have met that requirement by appearing to have taken both sides on the question of what it means to be an agent of mission.

On the one hand, I pointed out that in all three biblical models of mission there is an ambiguous relationship between the mission of God and the visible church. To discern the presence of Jesus in our world, one looks for signs of the Spirit in acts of solidarity with the poor and evidence that the commandments are being kept by witnessing to the truth and against evil. Sometimes these signs and this evidence are found in the churches, but for increasing numbers of people—even those with a Christian upbringing—the churches are neither spirit-filled nor faithful.

On the other hand, I have claimed that being partners with the churches is not necessarily the same as being partners in mission. In making this claim, I have had at least three different things in mind. First, I have been pointing to the obvious fact that denominations are accountable to their constituencies for the allocation of their resources and entitled to determine their own priorities. Concerns about the survival and priorities of one's own denomination does not necessarily indicate a weakening commitment to ecumenism.

Second, I have been circling around a more provocative point. Ecumenical agencies, such as the interchurch coalitions, the Canadian Council of Churches and the World Council of Churches, depend upon strong and self-assertive sponsoring denominations. Just as love between persons requires mutuality rather than self-sacrifice, long-term co-operation among Christian organizations requires self-affirmation rather than self-denial.

Finally, I have prepared the ground for asking what it means to be an agent of mission as well as a church-funded partner. The claim that coalitions are agents of the mission of their sponsoring denominations presupposes a continuing intention to remain grounded in the Christian "grand narrative"[26] and a willingness to share that story in appropriate ways. Understanding how this intention is being honoured in different ways will require occasions when stories can be told and conflicting claims about mission, coalition activities and denominational priorities can be assessed. I hope the framework used in this chapter which relates biblical models of mission to themes central to the coalition stories will be useful for such discussions.

The Wisdom
of Doing Justice

Nancy L. Cocks

> *"See, I am sending you out like sheep*
> *into the midst of wolves;*
> *so be wise as serpents and innocent as doves."*
> (Matthew 10:16)

Reflecting on the accounts of more than 20 years of Christian social justice coalition work reminded me of these words of Jesus. I recalled the time I spent as a Presbyterian representative on the Taskforce on the Churches and Corporate Responsibility between 1982 and 1985. In those days, the Taskforce Board met regularly in the Sunday School rooms at Deer Park United Church in Toronto. There we sat amid the telltale signs of children, their wild and woolly art dripping from the walls, as we poured over detailed accounts on nuclear waste disposal or possible military applications of Canadian exports to South Africa. There, perched on stacking chairs at paint-flecked tables, we planned the next management meeting with the board of a large corporation or heard the reports of those freshly returned from raising concerns at some company's annual general meeting. There, in the domain of the children, the churches' advocacy against acid rain and apartheid took shape. So it was that the lens of the wisdom tradition began to focus my study of the coalition histories. I was amused by the profound paradox—in the simplest of settings, some of the most complex and challenging issues of our time were studied. A far cry from the polished board rooms and plush corridors of corporate power! The paradox of God's wisdom will always confound the world's power-brokers: "I thank you, Father, Lord of heaven and earth, because you have hidden these things from the wise and the intelligent and have revealed them to infants" (Matthew 11:25).

My participation in the work of the coalitions has been as a church volunteer and it is from the perspective of someone active in local congregational ministry that I have been invited to write this essay. Trained in theology and in pastoral practice, I am interested in exploring the implications of coalition analysis and advocacy for the daily vocation of doing justice, a vocation which all Christians share. The work of those coalitions, primarily focussed on Canadian issues and institutions, has provided the main field for my analysis. Using the Canadian landscape as common ground seemed the most simple and logical way to identify both common methodological features and distinctive developments among coalitions whose inter- ests and history vary so greatly. I will therefore concentrate my remarks on the work of the Taskforce on the Churches and Corporate Responsibility, the Ecumenical Coalition for Economic Justice, the Inter-Church Committee for Refugees, PLURA, Project Plough- shares, the Aboriginal Rights Coalition, and Ten Days for World Development. Some of the observations offered may also fit with the work of the other five coalitions whose mandates span the globe, but time and space would not do justice to an analysis of their work.

This chapter will seek to highlight different influences and emphases within the justice work of the coalitions in relation to the dominant themes of wisdom literature. It has become almost a commonplace, however, to refer to the work of the social justice coalitions as the 'prophetic' voice of Canadian churches. Why bother, then, to examine ancient wisdom as yet another biblical category to frame this justice work? Perhaps most importantly this task is under- taken because the term 'prophetic' by itself conveys very little clear or consistent meaning apart from the biblical collection of prophetic literature. Leon Epzstein, writing on social justice in the ancient Near East, comments that "it seems very difficult, if not impossible, to extract a uniform prophetic doctrine," noting that it is necessary for interpreters to take account of the individuality of the great prophets.[1] Given that each biblical prophet expressed a profoundly personal sense of divine call and offered visionary pronouncements to audi- ences situated somewhere across several centuries of the history of Israel, it is not easy to condense the passion and proclamation of these rather elusive figures into a single word, prophetic. To speak of the work of the coalitions as 'prophetic' is not to convey much specific information or even a common perspective.

Coming from a church which values highly the biblical founda-

tions for ministry, I wonder whether a more nuanced appreciation of
biblical views on justice making might not help to guide ecumenical
coalition work through times when the circumstances of the churches
are changing. By examining the major themes of wisdom literature,
which also emerge in prophetic writing, I intend to explore a biblical
framework which offers some clearly defined concerns and stylistic
features to see how the components of ancient wisdom illuminate the
work of the coalitions. In a time when consensus around the public
role of religion and religious values is quite fragile, I hope to lift up
the implications of the wisdom tradition for the future of Christian
social witness which may engage our context with both the passion
of the prophets and the patience of Job!

In the coalition accounts of their roots and their vision, 'prophecy'
is often linked to 'justice,' as if these two terms in some sense determine each other's meaning. Yet the word 'justice' also defies simple
definition. Karen Lebacqz, for example, surveys six theories of justice
including both philosophical and theological points of view. Her concluding questions are pertinent: "Does justice require maximizing
utility, benefiting the least advantaged, accepting the consequences of
choice, honouring human dignity, treating equally, or liberating the
poor and oppressed?... Are the requirements of justice derived by
deduction, by reason complementing revelations, by faith compromising with history, or by biblical and Marxist analysis?"[2]

There is not a single biblical or theological definition of justice
or justice making. Scriptural references to justice span the canon,
suggesting that interest in just and right relations was not only a
prophetic concern, but one woven throughout the testimony of God's
people. The wisdom tradition in Israel is very much a part of the
prophets' heritage, a tradition which informed their imagery and their
concern, a tradition they in turn influenced by their forceful insight
into specific crises in the history of the nation and the people. Biblical
scholars interested in the interrelationship of traditions within
Hebrew scripture note that justice is a consistent theme in wisdom
literature, a theme shared with the prophets through both the
substance of their concern (fair treatment for the poor, for example)
and the style of argument (use of the 'woe' pronouncements in Amos,
Proverbs and Luke, for example).[3] Given that the legacy of wisdom
is found in the writing of prophets, psalmists and evangelists, a simple

identification of God's justice as prophetic proves inadequate as a grounding for contemporary justice ministry in the church.

Wisdom literature in its many forms is full of concern for covenantal and cosmic justice. Bruce Birch, in his study *Let Justice Roll*, proposes that wisdom developed a 'creation theology' which understood God as "the source of order and value in creation" and as the source of the wisdom needed to discern that order. He further notes that wisdom did not simply affirm divine ordering, but linked belief in God's creative power to issues of God's justice.[4] Although wisdom writing is most popularly associated with the aphoristic style of the Book of Proverbs, wisdom strands in biblical literature are both more plentiful and more complex in their vision of God's redeeming purposes in creation than a single book suggests. In a study of wisdom in Old Testament traditions, Donn Morgan argues for an appreciation of the reciprocal relations between wisdom and prophetic traditions. Rejecting the assumption that wisdom was simply a 'late' tradition in Israel, he believes that prophets were reinterpreting contemporary wisdom teaching, using the forms, vocabulary and theology found in wisdom literature.[5] Like the prophets whose proclamation occurred across several centuries, wisdom literature reflects a lengthy period of development and expresses a variety of views on Israel's institutions, reflecting different sociological roots within Israel.[6]

The complex social context in which the prophets wrote points to a further complexity in applying prophetic words to contemporary Canadian Christian work for social justice. The 'word of the Lord' spoken by the prophets might well have addressed monarchs of Israel or even neighbouring kings, the priests of the Hebrew cultus, or the people themselves, with a word of warning, a pronouncement of judgment, or a vision of hope. The canvas of the prophetic horizon is coloured by a spectrum of concerns, all in some way related to Israel's covenant relationship with God. Yet it is not a simple step from breaches of that covenant within a theocentric monarchy to the problems of a liberal democratic state in which we live and our churches undertake their mission.

In ancient Israel, rulers, priests, prophets and people recognized mutual obligations to Yahweh, God of their ancestors. However, we find ourselves in a social setting in which religious voices are greeted with increasing nonchalance and even suspicion. The issues of church and nation which face Canadian churches are framed in a very different context, one in which the role of the ancient prophet does not readily fit. In a time when some churches regard themselves as voluntary associations, or at least some church members regard participation as a matter of personal choice and preference, and when churches guard themselves from interference by the state in matters of belief and polity, one must ask about the nature of authority 'prophetic' statements can claim in contemporary church and society. A prophetic voice is appropriately addressed to the churches where there remains some sense of common commitment to the ministry of Jesus, even though we may interpret the implications of that ministry differently. In a society where a plurality of religious and ethical commitments exist, Christian proclamation must reframe its witness to the need for justice in order to interpret that need to diverse audiences and interests. The wisdom tradition offers many strategies to make its appeal for just ways of living.

Working by wisdom's ways

Two major features generally characterize all forms of wisdom literature: a) an emphasis on knowledge, especially knowledge of God, and b) the "explicitly experiential basis" of wisdom teaching, which draws examples from nature and from the world of daily human experience and relationships. In his treatment of wisdom in Israel, Gerhard von Rad sees a combination of what might sometimes be termed faithful and secular knowledge in wisdom literature which offers a theological foundation for connecting knowledge of God with knowledge of the world.[7] Donn Morgan presses this view further to question whether what he terms "the contemporary epistemological dichotomies, such as reason–revelation," are operative in biblical texts. He suggests that the expanding interest in wisdom in recent times is "at least partially related" to a movement away from revelation-centred theology in the latter decades of this century.[8] He goes on to illustrate this theme in his treatment of Amos, commenting that the authority of Amos' arguments "rests as much on experiential observation as on the revealed word of Yahweh."[9] Wisdom therefore offers timely insight into two key aspects of coalition work which shape the basis of authority claimed for their social analysis but which also meet with objections from time to time.

Knowledge of the world in the language of faith

Whether focussed primarily on research or on advocacy, the work of Canadian coalitions has depended on knowledge that is both detailed in its accuracy and broadly based in both national and international networks. The analysis of complex issues such as global economics or international human rights is rehearsed in the essays from the coalitions with obvious facility in the 'dialect' of each area of public policy. Such competence in their subject areas, accrued persistently and diligently over the years, appropriately sets the work of the coalitions in the domain of wisdom which respects the capacity of human knowledge.

Still, for 'revelation-centred' churches, my own included, which value a word from God, coalition expertise in tracking the currents of politics, human rights and economics is sometimes found wanting because its analysis is conveyed in a vocabulary that avoids the typical language of faith. One notes the lack of explicitly theological language in this collection of essays to frame either the mandates or the vision of most coalition work. Justice is sought and defined in the language of our social context. Now the need and desire to address analysis to the world—its policy makers, its corporate planners, as well as its advocates who share similar concerns with Church coalitions—makes this vocabulary a useful tool to carve out Christian witness to unjust systems and to propose workable alternatives in terms understood by the surrounding culture. However, church members not yet convinced that faith provides an alternative vision of justice which challenges prevailing social structures often remain unconvinced in the face of detailed social analysis. What does wisdom say to the tension between what might be termed the language of politics and the language of faith?

First, the wisdom of wisdom literature is that knowledge of God and knowledge of the world are intimately related, based on a dialectic of experience and understanding which arises in the world God created. As von Rad puts it, in the wisdom tradition "thinking entered into a new form of responsibility" in which faith in Yahweh had to express itself in new ways, forced out from "the security of patriarchal-sacral orders" into "its own 'worldly' domain."[10] To fail to engage the world with our capacity for reflective thought would be faithless. Hence the vocabulary of the streets and stock markets ought not to be regarded as inappropriate to express Christian concern. Yet wisdom literature also sets observations about daily life and divine truth side by side. The easy flow from one aspect of truth to another, as shown often in the Book of Proverbs, exemplifies the possibility and even the ingenuity of braiding the domestic and the cosmic dimensions of faithfulness.[11]

The task of interpreting theologically the insight and information offered by coalition work is an ongoing responsibility for supporting churches, one which calls for more direct dialogue between coalition researchers and theological interpreters in order to encourage cross-fertilization between analysis of the world and confession of faith. Both church and coalition communicators need to consider carefully how best to draw upon the language of faith, which is often the language of the heart, to portray concerns for justice in ways that call both church members and church structures to conversion. This is not a plea to obscure the poignancy of the issues addressed by coalition work with pious sentiment. It is, however, to raise a concern that we remember the importance of shared language in community for communication and commitment.

A kind of dualism seems to exist between the language of social analysis and the language of confession, a dualism which threatens the integration of social justice at the core of the church's understanding of its identity and its mission in this age. If justice speaks one language and faith another, have we not set up 'two solitudes,' a situation which we know too well from the history of this land can lead to misunderstanding and fragmentation? When the community of the church is addressed with complex justice issues, the language of boardroom, immigration panel and editorial needs to be set alongside cogent words of faithful conviction, illustrating the connection between faith and life. The ability to present more clearly the theological framework that supports analysis and advocacy would strengthen the claim of coalition work as central to the church's mission in the face of opposition like that described in the Taskforce on the Churches and Corporate Responsibility story.[12]

The theological importance of wisdom's ways of knowing is worth highlighting. Linking of knowledge from life in the world with knowledge from faithful encounter with God grows from the conviction that God, who is the source of creation, is also source of all truth. The framework of wisdom thinking overcomes the sacred/ secular dichotomy which pervades much Western thinking and which persists in the privatization of faith. Coalition work testifies against this dichotomy as well, implicitly at least, by taking the concerns of compassionate faith into the public arena and by bringing the broken-ness of society before church altars and assemblies. Yet one wonders if this reciprocity of knowing represents a true theological consensus among supporting churches, or whether the limited theological language of coalition life itself speaks of a limit to the shared under-standing upon which coalition work is undertaken by Canadian churches. It will be the task of the latter part of this essay to examine further the theological implications suggested by coalition concerns and ways of working. Expressing more directly the theological assumptions imbedded in coalition work may help to identify points of tension as well as fruitful insights which are significant for the future work of doing justice.

Experience gives authority to knowledge

The second central methodological feature of biblical wisdom stems from the source of its inspiration in the voices of experience collected and tested over the ages. Distinguished from the call and pronouncement of the prophets which emerged from an individual's profound experience of God's word, the life experience collected in wisdom literature finds its appeal through its broad applicability. As Bruce Birch puts its, "the authority of wisdom is based on the cumu-lative experience of observing what brings life and what does not. Wisdom believes that we have the capacity to choose life and live wisely, and that these choices cannot be avoided."[13] Donn Morgan finds in prophets like Amos and Hosea stylistic applications of this feature of wisdom, both in the kinds of illustrations drawn from nature and daily work and in the prophets' appeals to common sense to support conclusions.[14] Wisdom ethics are marked by examples of general validity which point to God's order of just and right relations as the sensible way to live.[15] While wisdom shows little interest in political formation among the people of God, it presents goodness as "always something public, never something merely internal... always a social phenomenon."[16]

Daily experience of living out this public vision enacts what von Rad terms a dialectic in which God's presence both limits human planning and yet carries human beings beyond the goals they had envisaged. "Experience... teaches that you can never be certain. You must always remain open for completely new experience. You will never become really wise, for in the last resort, this life of yours is determined not by rules but by God."[17]

Wisdom, then, combines respect for knowledge and for the unknowable. The unknowable dimensions in human experience make justice a constant concern for the community of God's people. In the dialogues of the Book of Job and the pensive soliloquies of Ecclesiastes, wisdom ponders the theological significance of human experience, especially the experience of suffering and encounters with the limits of life. Suffering often illumines the experience of injustice when human choices create competing interests and conflict. Attention to justice in sorting through human choices points to the limits of knowledge encountered in both the intended and unintended consequences of what we do and what we know.

The work of the coalitions has honoured the authority of human experience in a variety of ways. When one reads the early accounts of the Aboriginal Rights Coalition and PLURA, for example, one cannot but be struck by the tremendous personal energy and vision which shepherded a growing conviction about the significance and the possibility of common Christian action on matters of urgent social concern through those demanding early years of shaping coalitions. Many individuals built on their experience in the churches, and beyond, to focus attention on concerns long ignored on the Canadian social landscape. Yet a much larger chorus of witnesses has also been given voice in and through the coalitions, testifying to experiences of poverty, environmental risk, tyranny or racism in Canada and beyond. Whether it is the story of a refugee caught in the depersonalized system of bureaucratic rules or fresh word received from global partners whose homelands are wrecked by violence, whether it is a request from a First Nations organization for solidarity or from a local self-help group seeking PLURA funding, the voices of daily experience have shaped coalitions' understanding of the limits to life which people impose upon each other and upon the natural systems which sustain us. Experience has named injustice and pointed the way to a more just ordering of relations and resources in the world.

By honouring the testimony of marginalized groups and by pointing out the suffering caused by the systems of our society, the coalitions have identified the limits to the knowledge upon which Canada has framed its common life. It is no wonder that the authority of this testimony is often called into question, inside the churches as well as beyond, for these voices disturb the confidence and comfort we as citizens take from the institutions we have created. In their role as truth tellers, coalitions point again and again to the cracks in cherished theory, whether they speak of a theory to eliminate nuclear waste or a strategy to reinvigorate trade and economic relations. Yet how can ordinary life experience be addressed to such sophisticated schemes as the Free Trade Agreement or proposals to bury radioactive material in the Canadian shield, schemes which have not yet been fully implemented? Here, coalitions have demonstrated their own sophisticated ability to address careful analysis to complicated social and scientific theory and to advocate for appropriate public partici-pation in decision making, especially by those who experience in their daily lives the consequences of policies under scrutiny. Coalition wisdom has been forged by combining expert knowledge with the realities of injustice experienced by so many people each day.

The authority granted the voices of experience is a source of controversy for social justice coalitions. Just as an epistemology which seeks truth solely through revelation resists the truth discerned through exploration of the world, so the voices of victims, the margin-alized and the average concerned citizen are greeted with suspicion by the presumed experts, the designers of social policy and those who find that existing economic systems function, more or less, to serve their interests. The need to challenge 'prevailing wisdom' (which might be understood simply as knowledge and experience which have won current acceptance) remains a dynamic in both prophetic and wisdom literature. Von Rad finds in the book of Job, for example, a wisdom argument against "a rigid theological position masquerading as experience."[18] Experience of the world and of God serves to liberate what is known from control and lack of authenticity. Wisdom's dialectic presses toward openness. The analysis of the coalitions has also pressed for openness, in both church and society, openness in participation and in perspective, by insisting that justice can only be achieved in dialogue and action which take account of the knowledge and experience of all those affected by policy and practice.

This study of the work of the social justice coalitions from a wisdom perspective will now shift to explore other core dimensions of the biblical wisdom tradition in relation to methods and concerns demonstrated in the coalition histories. Through this, I hope to show

some of the theological choices which coalitions have put into practice both in defining and working for justice.

Theology of creation—a unifying vision

In an age of mounting concern for the integrity of God's creation,
it has often been noted as an anomaly that none of the justice coalitions has a mandate exclusively focussed on environmental research
and advocacy. However, several coalitions have been able to dovetail
concern for the earth in its fullness with their working strategies and
mandates. This is a wise strategy, to be sure, one which illustrates
the unifying force of the wisdom tradition to connect social and
natural dimensions of the created order.

The work of the Taskforce on the Churches and Corporate
Responsibility is an important example of a unifying vision behind
very specific strategies related to corporate policy. The Taskforce's
work has interpreted justice to include responsibility for destructive
consequences to the earth caused by corporate practices. Through its
research and advocacy on acid rain, nuclear waste disposal, lead
emissions and forest management, the Taskforce makes the case for
eco-justice in corporate circles. At the same time, its work stands as
a testimony to the fundamental interconnectedness of life, an important aspect of a theology of creation inherent in the Taskforce's
research and advocacy. Project Ploughshares, with its concern for
defence policy, raises the same appreciation of creation in its outcry
against nuclear proliferation and the devastation nuclear disaster
would bring to the earth. As a statement quoted in that essay declares:
"To choose life is to acknowledge that we are called to be not so
much rulers as stewards of God's earth. And because we have regard
for the security of the earth for not only this but also succeeding
generations, we cannot accept as 'defence' any measures which
threaten the planet itself."[19]

Defence is redefined from a strategic category related primarily
to military planning and resources to a category that embraces the
survival of all life. Theology is not only inherent within the work of
this coalition, but explicitly stated as the vision under which the
intricate study of defence policy has been undertaken.

The essay on the Aboriginal Rights Coalition notes that work
with aboriginal peoples in struggles for human justice expanded the
coalition's appreciation of the interconnectedness of creation. "The

aboriginal peoples have taught us that social justice is inextricably linked to environmental justice. Justice in the social order cannot be achieved in isolation from a recovery of the integrity of creation."[20] This insight from First Nations' wisdom is a reminder that the wisdom tradition in biblical literature also finds its ancient parallels beyond the canon of scripture, suggesting to some scholars that this stream of Scripture is part of a broader international wisdom tradition, much of which has been ignored or devalued in the development of Western philosophical and theological traditions.[21] That Canadian churches learn about the wisdom of creation from indigenous cultures is an appropriate recovery of spiritual concern not foreign to our own ancient spiritual sources.

Experience of suffering as a source of knowledge

The authority granted the voices of daily experience in coalition work has already been noted along with the role of suffering in pointing to injustice. Wisdom literature has probed the mystery of human suffering and the struggles of those who suffer to know the presence of God in times of adversity. Situations of human suffering, especially those caused by oppression in recent times, have been particularly influential in shaping the work of several coalitions. The determination of the Inter-Church Committee for Refugees, for example, has been fed by those churches whose members themselves experienced life as refugees or who faced the rise of oppressive regimes and recall the impetus of faith to shelter those who were at risk.[22] The passion and commitment which accompany the Inter-Church Committee for Refugees' ability to interpret the plight of each new wave of refugees in the face of public uncertainty and government resistance express faithful conviction that trusts in God's power to reverse the tide of injustice against the apparent victories of intransigence.

However, it is not always co-sufferers who have connected through the concerns of coalitions. PLURA, for example, has made a deliberate strategy to bring poor people from self-help groups together with church representatives on to the PLURA boards. The account of how this partnership has developed over the years shows it is not easy to build understanding and maintain trust between partners in different economic circumstances, even when concerns for justice are held in common. PLURA's undertakings have worked to demonstrate that the economically disadvantaged are not objects of Christian charity but subjects of their own choices and actions. The decision-making model in PLURA's provincial organizations is an important expression of working more justly together and a reminder that justice is lived in the balance of decision making within church and coalition structures as well as in larger social arenas.

In yet a third method of working with people who have suffered injustice, Ten Days for World Development learned early in its educational efforts that visitors from the Third World are the most effective interpreters of their own reality. Ten Days' visitor program has enabled the human face of complex global situations to meet Canadians face to face. These authentic witnesses to the social cost of international monetary policy, for example, have enriched immeasurably the education and advocacy accomplished through the Ten Days' network.[23] Personal connection with those who live in situations of injustice, locally and elsewhere in the world, has remained one of the wisest strategies of coalition work throughout the years. Proposed policy alternatives can be explored with those who will feel their effects most directly. Advocates have learned first-hand, often with remarkable speed and effectiveness, the daily gains and losses in the struggle for justice all over the world.[24] In all our strategies to work for justice, there is no substitute for the voices of those who must stand in the face of injustice.

Individual and corporate dimensions of justice and right relations

The proverbial form of wisdom found in the Bible has often given the impression that wisdom's chief concern was the behaviour of the upright individual. Studies on wisdom in the prophets make clear the implications of righteousness for the people of God in their collective identity and activity.[25] It is interesting to observe how coalition work for justice has tried in various ways to develop both collective and personal strategies for doing justice.

Ten Days for World Development portrays this combination most clearly in its program on international debt. Responsive to individual interest to follow up study with action, its program material on debt was expanded to provide people in local communities with action guides to address bank managers and politicians on this issue. Ten Days also notes the value of intercoalition study on the same theme, instigated by the Ecumenical Coalition for Economic Justice.[26] Furthermore, its own effort and analysis were recognized by the Standing Committee on External Affairs and International Trade.[27] On this one issue, the flexibility and responsiveness of a coalition's structure has demonstrated its ability to facilitate individual and corporate action. The Taskforce on the Churches and Corporate Responsibility's concern for responsible action by shareholders has also been beneficial to individual as well as corporate investors once the publicity on the coalition's work increased interest in ethical investment in and beyond the Churches.[28]

This twofold emphasis in justice work is also present in other coalitions which attend to community groups and local networks as part of their strategy. The Ploughshares essay notes that demand for information on nuclear disarmament from church and community groups focussed resources on the education of children as well as the articulation of alternative policy for the Canadian government.[29] The the Ecumenical Coalition for Economic Justice's project on popular education, which embodies their change of strategy to "empower the powerless" rather than "convert the powerful," is another method that recognizes the role of the ordinary person in justice making. "If we are working for a society that is democratic and supports the participation of all in making decisions that affect them, then it is important to employ participatory educational approaches and develop action strategies that will allow for participation by many, rather than lobbying by a few leaders."[30]

The pattern of enabling individuals and small groups to share in the strategies of Church institutions also involves a pattern of connecting local, national and international partners in work of common intent and sometimes common action. Several of the coalition essays point to the strains of this working style, given the geographic size and the demographic diversity of Canada. Through their painful lessons and their satisfying achievements, from the Aboriginal Rights Coalition and PLURA to Ten Days and Ploughshares, the churches in Canada have much to learn from the national coalitions with local connections. The future of coalition and church work may in large part depend on how wisely networks for justice and for spiritual life are established and tended.

Sustaining spirituality for justice making

Earlier, the ability of wisdom literature to connect knowledge of God and knowledge of the world was presented as an important dimension of coalition work, albeit one that is most often implicitly understood. However, in the account of the Aboriginal Rights Coalition, this relationship is clearly expressed in the excerpt from a submission to the Berger inquiry, speaking of the stewardship of the earth and the 'social sin' at issue in the development of the Mackenzie Valley: "The Gospel proclaims that God's sovereignty includes all realms of life. Nothing that is human can be outside the Church's mission... We are calling for a conversion within our social and economic structures whereby policy making and decision making will begin to reflect and make practical the values of justice."[31] Yet the essay concludes by noting the lack of opportunities within the coalition for "deep theological reflection and spiritual development related to the struggle for aboriginal justice." The challenge for the future is "to talk in spiritual terms about the meaning of self-determination, aboriginal rights, economic development and resource exploitation."[32] The Ten Days essay also reports that, as local action strategies began to provoke strong reaction, a need for reflection on the "spirituality for justice-making" was expressed from local committees.[33] Knowledge of God is an important restorative when one knows and faces the effects of injustice.

The need to connect with the presence of the living God in the midst of doing justice, day in and day out, is powerful for all those involved, whether researcher or advocate or fund raiser, whether one suffers the consequences of injustice personally or debates the merits of policy alternatives with cabinet ministers. Yet the coalitions began with an impetus for action rather than meditation to engage the serious and complicated issues of an unjust world. In the coalition world of public engagement, the work of prayer and reflection—the word 'work' having been chosen deliberately—is often left for private or personal discipline. This, I think, is ultimately unwise and allows the forces of the world's systems and the dynamics of organizational life and institutional survival—for even coalitions have a form of institutionalized life after 20 years—to take a heavy toll on justice makers. The call for a spirituality for justice making is, in wisdom's view, a cry to tap the strength of the mystery of God in order to be able to make a stand for justice when the foolish and the unjust threaten. It reminds me of that voice of wisdom: "Come to me, all you that are weary and are carrying heavy burdens, and I will give you rest. Take my yoke upon you, and learn from me; for I am gentle and humble in heart, and you will find rest for your souls. For my yoke is easy, and my burden is light" (Matthew 11:28-30).

The paradox of wisdom—
our capacity to act and the limits of action

Spirituality, however, is not the only way in which those who work for justice appropriately acknowledge the mystery of God's power. One of the features of the wisdom tradition is its recognition of the limits to human knowing and enterprise. Wisdom writing is characterized by the paradox between knowing what to do and knowing when to wait upon the unfathomable mystery of God's time. There is little sense of an inherent limit to justice making glimpsed in the coalition essays. From time to time, conviction about the goal of total social transformation rings through. While a vision of the transforming goals of justice work is vital to people of faith, there is wisdom to the theological confession that transformation is ultimately the work of God, beyond even the most faithful advocacy and daring civil disobedience.

If commitment to faithful action for justice rather than social transformation is identified as the theological grounding for coalition work, then I think the churches' social justice movement can remain more flexible and responsive to the changing circumstances in which Canadian Christians find themselves. Although many of these essays rehearse histories of growth and change, I miss any serious plumbing of the depths in the shifting seas of Canadian church life to ask if there is a more effective and more faithful way to do justice as Christians facing the turn of the millennium. The Aboriginal Rights Coalition essay adds a sober reflection in its account of the collapse of one structure and the emergence of a new strategy. It ought not to be surprising that more than a decade of working in one pattern may lead to a moment—whether of crisis or of opportunity—which calls for a new pattern. Here is a lesson in the limits within our capacity to organize and an example of the wisdom in knowing when to restructure in order to respond more effectively to a changed and changing situation. Wisdom asks justice makers and churches alike to remember the limits to human action and to be faithful in the moment, as the familiar words of Ecclesiastes suggest: "For everything there is a season, and a time for every matter under heaven: ...a time to seek, and a time to lose; a time to keep, and a time to throw away; a time to tear, and a time to sew; a time to keep silence, and a time to speak" (3:1, 6-7).

Concluding reflection: Wisdom's network

If a single symbol or model of coalition work emerged for me in my reflection on these essays, it was the network. From the bold commitment to the Action Canada Network on the part of the Ecumenical Coalition for Economic Justice to the persistent commitment of PLURA to a decentralized, volunteer organization, again and again I saw the fruits and frustrations of existence as a network in these accounts. Both flexible and yet fragile, sometimes overlapping yet often struggling against isolation, networks of information, letter writing, education, action and fund raising span the land, west to east, north to south, connecting individuals and institutions, small groups and large organizations, both within churches and insistently outside their walls. The coalitions have spun and connected existing threads of commitment to justice making that literally reach around the globe.

But what a different image to consider compared to the church as body of Christ or household of God! Church as network implies quite different ecclesiological connections and patterns of authority than church as body, household—or even kingdom—would suggest. A network creates an expansive sense, yet its connections can grow weaker if the flow of energy and information is interrupted or is not met with reciprocal commitment. The organic nature of a body suggests tighter connections and some sense of mutual identity and co-operation, with more clearly defined functions for the parts and perhaps some valuing of one part over another—despite what Saint Paul had to say in 1 Corinthians! So with a household or a kingdom, questions of authority and ownership colour relationships in a way that the model of network does not suggest.

There is wisdom in the formation of responsive networks that connect and inform Christians and others committed to the work of justice, wisdom that in some sense has always stood in judgment of institutions. (Both prophetic and wisdom writers invested little loyalty in the organized priestly cult, we can recall.) Yet networks take energy and attention on all sides to maintain their effectiveness. What would it mean, therefore, for churches to take seriously the concerns and needs and gifts of people and groups dispersed in every region? To ask this question is really to ask about the nature of authority and community in far-flung churches. When does a church 'own' a decision or an action for justice—when a church council debates and votes on a policy, when church leaders proclaim policy in public statements, or when local groups and active individuals throughout the churches join the discussion to share the fruits of their labour and the knowledge of their situation? The wisdom tradition upholds the vision that God's community lives out just and right relations day by day in the exchange between individuals as well as in the faithfulness of leaders and their communities. The future of justice making in a time when the social profile of the churches has diminished depends on the connections we make between individual lifestyles and ecclesial commitments which do justice in the whole of creation.

Several coalitions look to the future as a time to increase co-operation with those outside the churches who share our concerns for doing justice. Yet there is still much more to be done to link people within the churches, in local and regional groups, formed denominationally and ecumenically. Could the heartbeat of Christian justice ever be measured elsewhere than in centralized groups—in the pulsing day-to-day connections of networks which quite literally cover the country? The polities of the churches which support social justice coalitions seem to defy serious reckoning with this expansive sense of church as network. Existing models of ecclesial authority concentrate decision making in centralized conferences, councils and courts. Be that as it may, it seems important to press the theological insight into the nature of being church which has emerged over 20 years of Christian coalition work for justice. So much has been accomplished by networks of committed Christian people who meet in small groups connected as often by the design of the Holy Spirit as by the intentional planning of churches or coalitions. Yet through this network, God's justice flows into hidden crevices as well as into well-known streams. We need in this moment to consider wisely how to tend and strengthen justice connections so that justice can flourish at a time when institutional energy is low.

For me, the possibilities of strengthening our network of just and faithful action are portrayed in the wisdom parables of Jesus. Parables portray the sometimes illusive connection between everyday experience and living in the reign of God, but in ways that are difficult to express in words. They offer only a glimpse of the paradox which Jesus embodied—that knowledge of God, creator of all things, and knowledge of this creaturely world are intimately connected. Two brief parables suggest to me why 'network' is an appropriate model of God's people at work in the world: "The kingdom of heaven is like a mustard seed... it is the smallest of all the seeds, but when it has grown it is the greatest of shrubs and becomes a tree, so that the birds of the air come and make nests in its branches... The kingdom of heaven is like yeast that a woman took and mixed in with three measures of flour until all of it was leavened" (Matthew 13:31-33).

Here we see the paradox of God's wisdom portrayed in a tiny seed that becomes a great and hospitable tree, sheltering vulnerable creatures. Justice grows by the grace of God, defying the odds of humble beginnings and what seem like meagre resources. The parable of the bakerwoman punching a tiny bit of leaven into an incredible mound of flour speaks of patience. Our efforts for justice, which some days face insurmountable odds, are kneaded by the hands of God to yield surprising results.

These parables are not pictures of the power of the church in its institutional expressions. They witness to faith in the power of God to work in expansive ways, through sometimes imperceptible change, to create astounding conclusions. The wisdom of knowing the limits to even our most faithful attempts to make justice rests on the trust we place in God's power to defeat principalities and powers, to multiply a few loaves to feed the multitude, and to raise up new life out of the clutches of death.

The coalitions for justice supported by Canadian churches have lived out these paradoxical images of Christian faith in their justice making. Often the faith implicit in coalition work has been left unspoken, even unnamed. Yet to continue to stand in the face of the forces of injustice, there is wisdom in naming the source of our confidence so that weariness or discouragement will not overwhelm us. There is wisdom in knowing who stands with us so that our witness for justice may continue undaunted, amid the wise serpents and the innocent doves. God's wisdom is the source for our justice making, to give discernment for the times and strength to persevere.

Relinquishing Control

Lorraine Michael

Introduction

Only three of the national interchurch committees involved in the struggle for social justice include the term 'coalition' in their name. Furthermore, two of these, the Aboriginal Rights Coalition, formerly Project North, and the Ecumenical Coalition for Economic Justice, formerly GATT-Fly, took on these new names after 15 or so years of existence; ICCAF has considered itself a coalition since 1982. The interchurch groups that are now so familiarly known as 'ecumenical coalitions for social justice' have grown gradually into understanding who they are as coalitions and what are the implications of their work.

In forming the ecumenical bodies, the participating churches were being prophetic as they responded to the needs of the moment both in Canadian society and globally. They were reading the signs of the day not knowing the implications of what they were proclaiming. The extent of the prophetic nature of their vision comes out in many ways in the 12 stories that form Part One of this book. Continually the words 'solidarity,' 'partnership' and 'mutual respect' are used matter of fact. And rightly so since these words are at the heart of what being in coalition is all about. Some of the terms being used come out of today's reality and the experience that has been lived by the coalitions. It is clear from the stories told by coalition members that those who were originally behind the movement for ecumenical social justice work did not fully know where the road they were exploring would lead.

It is now obvious that there were visionaries in the churches who were giving leadership in a whole new understanding of bearing Christian witness. In Ernie Regehr's reflection on the experience of Project Ploughshares, he points out three parts to the witness bearing: the active bearing of witness against evil which requires systematically identifying injustice, the bearing of witness to "another way," and the standing watch over what is happening on all levels in our society, thereby robbing evil of its anonymity. The churches have learned through their coalition experience that there is another dimension to witnessing. The bigger the circle of witnesses, the greater the chance of stopping the evil. That was obviously one of the insights that brought the churches together in working for social justice.

As the churches began to live being in solidarity and partnership with one another, they began to experience how very challenging it is to do solidarity work. For the ecumenical coalitions there are two dimensions to the nature of the solidarity to which they have committed themselves. One is the solidarity that the churches confess to one another; the other is the solidarity that they strive for with the groups in whose name they have become involved. In either case the churches opened themselves to a massive challenge when they decided to work together in the cause of social justice.

All of the coalition stories indicate in one way or another that they learned very early in their work what it would mean to witness together in solidarity with those who were suffering the injustices that concerned the churches. It did not take long for the coalitions to realize that effective witnessing would mean being in coalition not just with one another but with groups outside of the church constituency such as development agencies, unions, and antipoverty organizations working on similar concerns. More importantly, the coalitions realized that they could not work on issues of social justice without listening closely to the people who were most affected by an issue. In many cases the very formation of a coalition came about because someone in the churches heard the call from the oppressed to get involved, whether it was to seek justice for the aboriginal peoples, for peoples of the Third World, or for the poor of Canada.

In whose name

The coalitions learned very quickly the theological principle of solidarity with the poor and oppressed. The realization that the Christian message calls Christians to take an option for the poor and the oppressed came out of the liberation theology of the church in the Third World in the late 60s and early 70s. This radical concept meant that, in doing its theologizing, the church was challenged to take as its starting point the experience of those who suffered most in society—the poor and the marginalized.

The writers of some of the coalition stories appear to take this principle for granted without acknowledging that this theology is not yet understood, let alone taken for granted, throughout the Canadian Church. However, it was an understanding of this theological point that dictated the work of the coalitions. No matter how it is described in the various stories, it was the lack of understanding and acceptance, in certain quarters, of the principle of solidarity with the poor that created some of the struggles that the coalitions experienced in trying to do their work.

The ecumenical coalitions have been marking out a whole new way of operating. While being bodies of the churches, at the same time they have tried to be true first to those with whom they have stood in solidarity rather than to church bureaucracies. This direction is something which has not been consistent in the way in which the churches have operated historically. Whether it was PLURA or the Interchurch Fund for International Development recognizing each in its own context that it is the experience of those living in poverty which must inform decision making about funding, or the Canada China Programme opening itself to be led by the voice of the Christians in China, or Ten Days for World Development changing its structure to allow direct involvement of the local and regional groups in policy and decision making, the coalitions were urged to listen closely to those who were most involved in the situations of injustice about which the coalitions were concerned.

In some cases, the call to the churches to become involved in social justice work came directly from church partners in the south. Such was the case with the post-independence crisis in Africa which prompted the All Africa Conference of Churches to appeal to churches in the north to support them in responding to the social, political and economic crises that they were facing. It was the challenge thrown out by the Latin American churches as they tried to stand in solidarity with the poor in their countries. In responding to their partners in the Third World, the Canadian churches were learning to work in a new way among themselves as well as with others.

One of the things that the coalitions learned was that they had to listen to their partners. While they did not just follow them uncritically, the coalition leaders realized that they alone did not possess all the answers. As church coalitions they had to remain faithful to the experience of the churches in the Third World who were trying to hear the voice of the poor and the oppressed in their context. This way of operating was certainly different from the mentality that had sent the churches out as missionaries in earlier times to the very parts of the world that were now calling out for solidarity from them.

As the coalitions listened to those who were suffering injustices, they had to become involved in speaking out against the system, whether it was the system at work in Africa, Latin America or Canada. The churches soon learned that the system, which was used to having the church be a docile member, was going to object to the churches' involvement in issues of social justice. The churches also learned that being led by the poor and marginalized implies a loss of the control and power that they had come to enjoy.

Several of the stories talk about the role of the coalitions in their earlier years in lobbying government and business as a key way to obtain the social and economic justice for which they were struggling. However, they seemed to learn a common lesson that changed the approach of the coalitions over the years. A choice was made sooner or later to identify more closely with 'the people' in the struggle for change. Gary Kenny puts it well when he describes the Inter-Church Coalition on Africa's determination "not to become too comfortable in its movements within government circles and... to relate to government on a strategic rather than an ongoing basis."[1] Dennis Howlett is even more pointed in talking about GATT-Fly/the Ecumenical Coalition for Economic Justice: "GATT-Fly's frustrations with lobbying government on both the sugar and food issues led us to conclude that the kinds of fundamental social change which we sought were not likely to be supported by the powerful who benefited from the present unjust system. Rather than trying to convert the powerful, we began to focus on empowering the powerless."[2]

Consequences of opting for the poor

The effectiveness of this approach is shown in the reaction of business people to the work of the ecumenical coalitions. Some of the stories refer to these forces, which exist also within the churches, that work against the struggle for social justice. The formation of the Confederation of Church and Business People was one of the clearest signs that not all church members, including the ordained, accepted the theological principle of promoting social change from the perspective of the poor and oppressed. The level at which the

Confederation operated was evidence that the power structures of the church were being challenged by the new directions of the struggle for social justice. Businessmen who were used to positions of power in their churches wanted to stop the critical voice of the churches from speaking out.

The two coalition stories that speak specifically about the Confederation are the Taskforce on the Churches and Corporate Responsibility and the Aboriginal Rights Coalition, two of the coalitions overtly challenging corporate power. Obviously the corporate people who were part of the institutional churches understood the power issue. Why else would they take the stance of opposition that they did? It is difficult to feel empathy for the business executives who spoke out against the work of the coalitions. It is even harder to understand the "former moderators, bishops and clergy" who supported these businessmen, unless the struggle is understood as one of power. The self-identification of these people as "the real church," as opposed to the poor and the oppressed, clearly illustrates the nature of the struggle. They did not believe that the groups with whom the coalitions stood in solidarity should be listened to. They certainly did not want the churches calling for a moral condemnation of the corporations of which they were a part.

Some of the coalition stories imply that the Confederation of Church and Business People was a solitary moment in history that happened and was overcome. Just because the official church institutions challenged the forces of the Confederation at the time they first became active does not mean that such opposition does not still prevail among church people. The coalition stories could have pursued more thoroughly the power struggle that has gone on between the ecumenical coalitions and their partners on the one hand and those who have been historically used to holding power in the churches as well as in the broader society on the other. They could have reflected as well on how the churches can deal pastorally with individuals who are caught in the moral dilemma of considering themselves Christian while at the same time being part of the systems that the churches condemn as oppressive of the poor and marginalized.

At the bottom of the issue is the whole relationship between church and society referred to at the end of the story of the Inter-Church Committee on Human Rights in Latin America. There is an inherent contradiction in the fact that church institutions which enjoyed a place of favour in society turned around and began to criticize the system of which they had been a part. Obviously it is not what is expected by church members who support the social and economic system as it exists. None of the stories deals adequately with this issue.

There are several allusions in the coalition stories to the fact that the openness to the experience of the oppressed has sometimes placed the coalitions in situations of alienation within the structures of the very churches which make up the coalitions. Mary Boyd states this dilemma clearly in the PLURA story: "our churches... are made up, by and large, of relatively affluent people who have interests other than spending time locating the injustices within our society." She goes on to say that it is up to coalitions like PLURA to ask the question, "Who are the poor in Canadian society?"[3]

The implied breakdown between what the churches officially teach and what the church membership understands has created tensions that are only hinted at in the stories. As has been pointed out, while the coalitions pursue being in solidarity with the poor and oppressed, they are in the position of being prophets within the churches—a position that for the most part places them on the periphery, always having to prove themselves.

There are not many signs that the majority of the people who sit in the pews of the churches are imbued by the spirituality of active involvement in struggling for social justice. However, it is these people who form the recognized church community and who sit on church committees that determine policy. The moment has come for the official church to reflect on whether or not it wants to follow the way that has been forged by the ecumenical coalitions for social justice or be led solely by the voice of the faithful who in many cases do not reflect aboriginals, the poor, the oppressed, either in our midst or in other countries. Because the churches' involvement in the ecumenical work has not resulted in a mass movement for social justice, there is the danger that the success of this work will not be recognized in discussions of restructuring that have been going on in some of the churches. As Peter Hamel puts it in his reflection on the Aboriginal Rights Coalition, "We are also being challenged to address the internal reality within the institutional church... Despite the valiant efforts of a few across the country, [we] remain a community on the fringe."[4]

Several of the coalitions indicate that the late 80s and early 90s were a time when the churches began to look at the work of the coalitions with new eyes. The experience of the Ecumenical Coalition for Economic Justice shows where working in solidarity with other groups in the struggle for justice can lead. The struggle that is described as having occurred during the remandating process is a clear example of the difficulties encountered by the churches when coalitions identify themselves unequivocally with broader struggles for justice. According to the Ecumenical Coalition for Economic Justice story, some in the churches did not see the Coalition "spending enough time providing services to the church constituency" and were critical of "the large amount of time and energy that it put into working with 'non-church' groups."[5] While the remandating process did not stop the Coalition from doing the work it had always done in "empowering the powerless," there did seem to be a moment in the process where the churches made their presence felt.

None of the coalition stories actually uses the words 'power struggle.' However, it seems clear that there has been an ongoing struggle for power within the life of the coalitions. Peter Hamel is probably the most forthright on this subject as he relates the shock to both the church bureaucracies and to the groups which made up the Project North network when he describes the dissent and divisiveness that existed in all aspects of the coalition. Hamel notes the divisions between the official churches on one side and the solidarity groups on the other when he claims that "the Project's structure did not allow for effective involvement by the network groups in decision making. They had no formal access."[6] The change of the name and of the structure of Project North in 1988 indicates that this coalition joined several others in learning what solidarity work is about—the Aboriginal Rights Coalition is "a coalition of churches working in partnership and alliance with both aboriginal organizations and regional network groups."[7]

In solidarity with one another

The coalition stories deal very peripherally with the difficulties that have been encountered as Christian churches of different traditions chose to work together in the struggle for social justice. None of the coalition writers deals in great depth with the issue of the obvious theological and disciplinary differences that exist among the coalition partners. In some cases there is a passing reference to the fact that not all the churches hold the same position on an issue.

Ernie Regehr writes about the change in positions on pacifism and war that were obvious during the Gulf War when it was easier to get the participating churches to agree on a common position than at other times in the history of Project Ploughshares. He credits this phenomenon to the fact that the churches over the years have learned from listening to and working with one another. He does not, however, go into much detail about the struggles that obviously occurred. The Canada China Programme story also makes reference to the differences between the Protestant and Catholic churches that were overcome at certain points. The tensions are alluded to in some cases without much reflection on what the differences have meant for the work of the coalitions.

The most tantalizing such comment is the one by Bill Fairbairn at the end of the Inter-Church Committee on Human Rights in Latin America story. He refers to the economic realities and political pressures in Canada that "*continue* to test the commitment of Canadian churches to issues of justice and ecumenical co-operation."[8] Unfortunately, there is very little in the story that talks about how the commitment to ecumenical co-operation was tested over the years.

Undoubtedly, working through the differences that existed among the churches was a reality and a source of growth. One has to imagine in reading the stories that there were times also when the differences held back the work of the coalitions.

Staying true to the vision

The difficulty in working in solidarity with the poor and oppressed in the context of the institutional churches does not seem to have deterred the coalitions from their vision. The commitment to the option for the poor and the oppressed does seem to be a principle to which the coalitions have been strongly committed from the beginning as is attested by the experience of the Aboriginal Rights Coalition. The formation of the initial Inter-Church Project on Northern Development was a response to the urging of the aboriginal leaders for the churches to "do more than pass resolutions and issue statements on the continuing pattern of paternalistic, colonial development in northern Canada that was destroying aboriginal life and culture."[9]

The current challenge to the churches is to involve themselves on all levels in reflection on what it means to work for social justice. The coalitions, through their stories, are asking for this reflection. The coalitions have committed themselves to a path from which it would be very difficult to stray without raising some serious questions among those in the church who believe that the struggle for social justice is an essential part of the Gospel. Questions will also arise among the social partners whom the coalitions have developed over the years. Involving themselves with the victims of oppression, the coalitions have raised the hopes of these people that the churches are on their side, rather than on the side of the oppressors in our society. The churches continue to be called upon to deal with the challenge of speaking out in the cause of social justice even when there are individuals who maintain the status quo breathing down their necks while sitting on church committees, taskforces and commissions.

The churches will have to reflect on the resource that the coalitions are both to the churches who form them as well as to the non-church groups which have come to depend on them. The research that is done by the ecumenical coalitions serves not just the churches but the broader society that is involved in the struggle for social justice. To take away that resource at this time of reactionary political decision making would be to undermine seriously the strength of the struggle for justice both in Canada and in the Third World. The churches ought to examine carefully any decision which might suggest that it is not necessary to work together for social justice at a time when the need to work in coalition for social change is at its height.

There is no doubt that it is frightening to continue to walk with the poor and oppressed when there are people in the church congregations who promote the status quo and disagree with the social change that is being demanded. Susan George's warning must be taken to heart more than ever before—"Sides must be taken in this conflict."[10] To take the side of the poor and the oppressed means giving up the power of control and taking on the power of the witness who stands watch over evil.

Seeds of Hope
in the New World
(Dis)order

Lee Cormie

Introduction

Perhaps too rapidly for our imaginations to grasp yet, especially for those of us who enjoyed some of its fruits, the foundations of the old order established in the years following World War II have been radically undermined. A growing number of voices across this country—unemployed fisher folk in the Maritimes, street people in Toronto, landless farmers in the West—and many more throughout the Third World are speaking of the deepening suffering of millions of people, of the devastation of the biological foundations of life on earth, and of the deaths of thousands of species. The prospects for progress in addressing these problems, though, are bleak. As Gregory Baum has soberly confirmed, unlike the 70s and even the early 80s when social justice struggles in Canada were characterized by a sense of optimism, the 90s are a time of mourning and of wandering in the wilderness.[1]

In this context, issues of hope and faith are urgent and central, religiously and politically. Strangely, however, the mainstream churches have provided little support or leadership in clarifying these matters and in charting responses to them. In particular, the ecumenical interchurch coalitions have been at the forefront of the churches' commitment to the victims in wrestling with the challenges of our history over the last 25 years. Yet, with little discussion in the churches, there are even clear signs in recent years of declining official church support for social justice activities. It is as if church leaders and officials are looking in another direction, as if the church's business were elsewhere, on other matters more important than following the Spirit in this world.

In this journey over unfamiliar, hazardous and dimly lit terrain, I have turned to the stories of the coalitions with a sense of urgency, at times even desperation, searching for some signposts of the path of the Spirit of truth and justice, peace and the integrity of creation. To this nascent but urgent dialogue, I offer five meditations—admittedly partial, incomplete and provisional—as probes to test our shared understanding of the recent history of struggle and faith, and its implications for our hopes for the future and for the life of the church in Canada.

A word of thanksgiving

Against the background of the domestic and global social order created at the end of World War II and of subsequent historical struggles to broaden access to the halls of culture-defining and policy-making power, the coalitions have incarnated a Christian commitment to helping those who have been historically marginalized from the centres of power. The poor and working people in the so-called Third World and in Canada, indigenous peoples, women, all those longing for peace and for ecological balance, in fact the great majorities of this world have been given a voice to speak for themselves and to shape the decisions on which hinge their fate and, ultimately, the fate of all life on earth. For me, the first and most important word concerning the history of the interchurch coalitions is one of thanksgiving for these signs of grace in history.

The coalitions have witnessed in Canada to a worldwide "explosion of compassion and solidarity" unique in Christian history.[2] They have helped to inspire a transformed faith and a renewed church. Along with many other popular groups, networks, and organizations, they have helped to give birth to new networks of solidarity with oppressed groups across Canada and throughout the world. Through their research and publications they have added immeasurably to our knowledge of major issues confronting the world, and helped to clarify the options before us. In many cases they have helped to change government and corporate policies.[3] Even when they have failed, they have educated, challenged and inspired many Canadians, thereby helping to nurture the seeds of greater witness and deeper change in the future. Above all, in these days of neoconservative darkness and mourning, this insight and inspiration should be joyously celebrated.

Troubling questions

Yet, over the years, certain troubling questions have emerged among thoughtful coalition staff, board members and supporters. My concern is not with individual staff or board members, nor with the policies of particular coalitions. Rather, this second probe is concerned with the overall structuring of the agendas of the coalitions in the broader context of social change, their overall significance for the church, and the churches' significance in these struggles for re-ordering the world. In general, it seems fair to say that the coalitions were not mandated or structured to reflect in an ongoing, disciplined way on the lessons of their history of involvement in struggles for social change or on the implications for their own work or for the church as a whole.

There is no space here to analyse the political and ecclesial context of the 70s and early 80s, or the ways in which it left its mark on the coalitions. It is important, though, to recall the optimism of a period when possibilities for reform in the near future and faith in history, as progress reflecting the cumulative gains made in individual struggles, seemed more plausible. In this context, a focus on influencing government as the key terrain of social struggle and agent of change was natural. Since reform seemed possible, avoiding the high plane of ideological debate concerning the social system as a whole, and alternatives to it, also seemed more realistic and promising. In the churches too, awash with enthusiasm for ecumenical collaboration and a widely diffused sense of the importance of social justice in the ministry of the church and with early support from key church leaders, it was also easy to avoid theological debate which might raise contentious issues. Support was available, change seemed possible in those days, and there were many concrete demands requiring attention.

In a radically changed and changing social context, however, many questions have arisen concerning the agendas, structures, and strategies of every progressive group in Canada and around the world.[4] As we approach the end of the end of the millennium, they are increasingly urgent.

Pragmatic Approach

The first query concerns the generally pragmatic and activist orientation of the coalitions. Certainly it facilitated avoidance of abstract, time-consuming and divisive ideological debates. But it also seems generally to have inhibited serious, sustained reflection on the lessons of the experience of the coalitions.

This tendency is not hard to understand. The continuing pressures on understaffed coalitions to act in the present in response to growing suffering and an endless list of urgent needs undoubtedly functioned continuously to marginalize such reflection and to compel the coalitions and their supporters to rely on prevailing common-sense versions of the lessons of the past and especially on the insight and leadership of key coalition staff and board members. But to the extent to which this is true, this tendency is problematic in four ways.

1) It has inhibited coalition members and supporters from taking their own experience seriously, from trying to learn in self-conscious and disciplined ways from their own history about the character of their work. In terms of the work itself, this has left the door open to unrealistic, often impossible expectations concerning what should be accomplished, a continuing lack of attention to a framework for identifying priorities within individual coalitions and within the churches concerning the coalitions as a whole, frustration, exhaustion and burnout of some staff members and key supporters.[5]

2) This pragmatic approach has also inhibited the cross-fertilization of insights, inspiration, and challenges flowing from the whole range of sensibilities, commitments, and struggles reflected in the broad range of coalition activities. Of course, some cross-fertilization has gone on; the defunct project Connexions existed specifically to serve this process. But this process has been largely informal, and very uneven, in terms of its impact on individual coalition staff and board members, their active supporters, and those addressed in the broader church.

3) It has also inhibited the development of broader, more historically grounded perspectives on the problems and challenges in the present, confronting each coalition, each denomination, and the Christian community as a whole. In an incredibly complex and rapidly changing world, these tendencies are self-defeating.

We have all learned how easy it is to miss the forest for the trees in such matters. In the last 30 years activists have learned the hard way that it is often possible to make progress in saving a particular tree or two from imminent destruction while the forest as a whole is being irreversibly destroyed. This bitter lesson is clear in a number of struggles: some progress on some issues as defined by movement leaders for some members of particular constituencies (people of colour, women, the poor, lesbians and gays, peace or environmental issues) has been possible, but in the context of defeat and even regression on a broader front.

The great majority of people committed to these struggles share John Williams' observation that "on almost every front, the social justice situation in Canada worsened during the 70s and especially the 80s."[6] But there is little evidence that this observation and its implications have been seriously addressed. Without efforts to sort out these matters, it is impossible to make reasoned calculations in anything more than an informal manner concerning the character of human experience in a shifting social, economic, cultural and political context, the challenges to faith and hope arising from these radical changes, and the implications of this shifting social ground for the overall mission of the church, and for the coalitions in particular.[7]

4) Without a broad discussion of the lessons of the coalitions, it is impossible for most supporters to appreciate the rationale for particular strategic decisions made by policy makers in individual coalitions and in the churches.[8] Sometimes we must rely on intuitive, 'seat of the pants' navigating in hazardous waters, or on the intuition of our leaders, for lack of time and space to do anything else. But such trust in the intuition of leaders inevitably has its limits. Without a broader framework, it is impossible for them to sort out these matters and to maximize learning from experience. Without broader discussions of such matters, it is impossible genuinely to empower a broader cross-section of people in making and owning the decisions of these groups, in attempting to transform society in the churches or the world or, most importantly, in learning from the consequences of these decisions.

'New' social issues

A second question which emerged early in the life of the coalitions concerned the church's response to 'new' issues. Without a broader framework for discussing the changing context and shifting priorities, it has been difficult to discern whether and how to respond to emerging social issues that became so important in the 80s and early 90s, including for example discrimination and violence against women, racism, environmental degradation, the farm crisis, devastation of Maritime fisheries, oppression of gays and lesbians, violence against children, violence against Palestinians in Israel and the widespread conflict in the Middle East as a whole. In a shifting political climate, failure to respond to these new movements and the issues they were raising risked both alienating potential supporters and causing a more pervasive fragmentation benefiting those in power with their own, radically different agenda.

Theology aside

The third question concerns the lack of attention to theology within the coalitions. The coalitions emerged in the spirit of the ecumenical theological renewal of the 60s and early 70s pushing the churches to take society and history more seriously. Subsequently, this impetus was reinforced by the liberation theologies emerging in Latin America and elsewhere in the Third World and, to a lesser extent, by North American feminist and Black theologies. In general, though, while there were exceptions[9] and there are signs that this is changing,[10] the coalitions have been marked by a neglect of theology.

Indeed, this was not accidental. As Ernie Regehr reports about the founding of Project Ploughshares, "we deal with some problems by ignoring them—which in effect was the Ploughshares' strategy regarding theology."[11] Elsewhere, Joe Mihevc reports the widely shared view that the "original genius of the creation of the interchurch coalitions was to overlook traditional divisive theological issues (over church authority, the sacraments, etc.) to allow for work in areas of common social concern."[12] It is probably true that theology, understood in this way as fixed doctrinal and ethical positions, would only have been divisive.[13]

But it is also true that theology is the discourse of the life of the churches. There is evidence that this neglect has been costly in terms of the work of individual coalitions themselves.[14] Continued lack of attention among the coalitions and their supporters to developments and debates in theology has risked a self-imposed marginalization from the ongoing debates within the church and among church leaders over the nature of Christian faith in a conflictual and radically changing world, over the changing character of mission, and over shifting pastoral priorities.[15]

Neglecting theological discourse, which for Christians articulates the deepest meaning and hope of our lives most powerfully, also left marginalized the deep spiritual needs that overburdened coalition staff and supporters have felt, especially in the face of increasingly powerful opposition and declining resources. It also left marginalized questions concerning the formation and nurture of communities and of future leaders.

Unfulfilled assumptions

The fourth question concerns the understanding—or taken-for-granted assumptions—concerning the process of social change underlying the founding and management of the coalitions.

Many coalitions were organized to do 'research' on particular issues and to promote some kind of action, typically mobilizing church leadership in support of briefs to government and support for certain shifts in government policies. Some, notably Ten Days and, to some extent, Project Ploughshares with its grassroots groups and GATT-Fly/the Ecumenical Coalition for Economic Justice with its Ah-hah Seminars for popular groups, have taken the fruits of their research directly to the people.[16] In general, though, the operative assumption has been that individual denominational offices and structures would be responsible for disseminating this information and educating their own members on the matters addressed by the coalitions.

Certainly a great deal of education has taken place. However, as many coalition staff privately admit, this operating assumption built into the structuring of the agendas of the coalitions has simply not reflected the reality in most cases. On the contrary, there is much anecdotal information that, by and large, the denominational structures and priorities have not fulfilled this function. In fact, very often they have functioned as obstacles. This apparent contradiction has weighed heavily on coalition staff and supporters, seemingly giving the lie to official church sponsorship of these efforts and further inhibiting coalition efforts already severely constrained by impossibly great demands and grossly inadequate resources.[17]

More fundamentally, this situation reflects a failure to grapple with profound analytic questions concerning the nature of social order, visionary questions concerning alternative structural principles, and strategic questions concerning how social change occurs.

Reflection

Of course, there is no one 'right' analysis explaining all of these matters, and there is need for widespread discussion and debate. However, simply ignoring such questions, or leaving them at the level of impressions and incompletely articulated intuitions, is like shooting in the dark. It ignores the massive, well-funded campaign by neoconservative forces to manufacture analyses reflecting their biases and interests and to sell them to the public. However strong the research and analyses of particular issues generated by the coalitions, it abandons by default public discussion of larger issues concerning the economy as a whole and, after the end of the Cold War, the emerging 'new world order.'

The failure to grapple with these questions has also impoverished discussions of alternatives to the reigning global (dis)order.[18] Of course, it is possible to imagine alternative policies on a number of specific issues, and the coalitions have been strong in promoting alternative policies on many issues. However, throughout the 80s and into the 90s, pressure for such alternatives has been increasingly sidestepped by neoconservatives who have shifted the debate to another level, concerning the supposed 'logic' of the global marketplace and its inevitable 'requirements.' Those hoping for alternatives can only avoid addressing questions at this level at the cost of surrendering our imaginations to the constraints of a single global rationality.

In view of these characteristics of coalition structuring and functioning, then, many in coalition circles have long wondered whether, in effect, a 'subconscious' accord was struck in the establishment of the coalitions. On the one hand, coalition supporters would receive substantial support for their efforts with the official backing of the churches, so long as they did not raise fundamental theological issues or press for fundamental reforms in the churches. On the other hand, the denominations would contribute to some change and reap the benefits of moral leadership in these struggles, but without committing any denomination to the particular stand of any coalition and without having to address more seriously denominational responsibilities for internal conversion and renewal in terms of the imperatives to solidarity and of insights flowing from these experiences of hope and struggle.

Rewriting Genesis

The 70s were a 'golden age' for ecumenical social action programs.[19] However, the world has changed greatly since then and the story of the coalitions has been profoundly complicated by these changes. My third probe concerns these changes. In general, it seems fair to say that in every domain, however the causes are analysed, the world is witnessing changes on a scale never before seen in history, transforming literally the nature of creation—and the Creator?—itself.

Travel, massive immigration and refugee flows are changing the faces of those around us and the makeup of our workplaces, schools, neighbourhoods, and churches. This international flow is contributing to an unprecedented worldwide mixing of cultures and religions, transforming the content and horizon of each and challenging every notion of purity and authenticity. New forms of human subjectivity and sociability ('community'?) are literally being created.[20]

Daily, it seems, we witness new miracles of technology, endlessly pushing back the frontiers of human knowledge and capacity to transform and manage life. Perhaps none is more remarkable than the rapidly developing capacity of genetic engineers to create new forms of life. Previously, since the dawn of creation, such power, now being harnessed in the pursuit of private profit, was only in God's hands...

But we are learning to recognize another side to this human capacity to transform the world—the capacity of the developers and managers of industrial technology to poison the air and water and land, to sicken and kill many forms of life, even whole species and the ecosystems of whole regions, and to undermine the very foundations of life as we have known it on earth. These developments are challenging every notion of nature and human nature, of sin and grace, of human freedom and responsibility. It is hard for most of us to imagine, since so few of us have any experience of wielding such power, but there are some human hands on policy-making levers which will determine the fate of life on earth. Previously too, since the dawn of creation, such definitive power was solely in God's hands...[21]

Among other things swirling around the globe is capital, its managers ceaselessly transferring it from place to place at the touch of a computer keyboard, in search of the quickest and highest profits. In this process, the power of unions has been drastically undermined, workers everywhere are forced to compete with one another, wages and working conditions of the vast majority are deteriorating, and governments are forced into ever more vicious competition necessitating cutbacks in social programs and in their right to 'interfere' in the workings of the market.

In the wake of these developments and as the world becomes more 'interdependent,' established ways of achieving a sense of place are becoming decentred, resulting in growing centrifugal pressures toward the establishment of smaller and smaller ethnically- or culturally- or religiously-based nations each competing with all the others for investment, jobs, and markets. The concept of 'nation' is becoming increasingly fictional in view of the growing power of transnational corporations and international institutions like the World Bank and the International Monetary Fund which are governed by elites.[22] Everywhere, the process of social development becomes more volatile and uneven, affecting different groups and regions in different, contradictory ways, widening gaps in quality of life, life expectancy and power between groups of people, even as, in limited ways, *some* progress is possible for *some* constituencies on *some* issues in *some* contexts.

These developments are everywhere calling into question traditional categories, frameworks, and methods for thinking about and managing our lives, individually and corporately. As Richard Barnet has recently pointed out, they "have dealt a mortal blow to the nineteenth-century ideologies that have defined our world: communism, socialism, social democracy, and free-market capitalism... none of which provides an intellectual framework for the survival of the planet."[23] The institutions promoting the development of knowledge and of knowledge elites (experts and authorities) are in crisis too, evident in the widespread crisis in education and generalized crisis of authority at the heart of every tradition of knowledge and wisdom, including religion and all the sciences. Indeed, some commentators have gone so far as to refer to the "death of development," of the categories, frameworks, institutions, structures, and priorities which have been the cornerstones of social order throughout the post-World War II period.[24]

Inevitably, this questioning raises the most fundamental issues of hope and faith too. These are simultaneously political and religious questions. What solidarities, which 'others,' define *me/us*? What do *I/we/others/humanity* dare to hope for on this earth? What hope can we communicate to our children and to their children? Against such great odds, how do we ground these hopes? How do we join together to make our voices heard in the great debates over the future of the world? How do we nurture spiritualities, cultures of resistance and hope in ourselves and our children? How do we witness concretely to the Spirit of Life, day in and day out, throughout all the stages of our lives?

In the midst of such questioning, it can hardly be surprising that the mainstream Christian churches, whose theologies, institutional forms, and pastoral programs over the last 50 years have been worked out in some kind of accord with the social order created at the end of World War II, are in crisis too, reflecting as many disagreements, tensions and conflicts within denominations as among them, or that newer forms of Christianity are breaking out and gaining ground in many directions as people search for meaning and direction. Certainly the same process of questioning and search for renewed forms of the tradition are evident within other religions too.

Of course, the matter is far more complicated than classically liberal versions of abandoning 'tradition' in favour of modern 'scientific' insights and answers would have it. For all the sciences themselves have been thoroughly implicated in the problems facing us. Thus there is no going forward without mining the past for deeper insight into the character of the system and the roots of the problems we now face, for clues about perhaps still lively alternatives previously rejected, and for inspiration.

As risky as this process is, this challenge should not surprise Christians. For throughout the Bible, it is evident that there can be no escape from history by naive appeals to the tradition. Rather, members of each generation must reread their tradition(s) and, from among its many diverse and sometimes conflicting strands, identify anew, in terms of their own experiences and insights, its deepest currents inspiring them in addressing the challenges of their own context and the challenges to renew themselves, their communities and institutions. After all, Jesus was a Jew, drawing on some strands of the Jewish tradition in responding to the pervasive social crisis of

Palestine under Roman imperial rule and calling for a profound renewal of his own tradition.[25]

Re-creating the world: The New Right agenda

In the midst of this earth-shaking process of global change, we have also heard the eruptions of a growing range of new voices and points of view in addressing every issue. This new pluralism of voices and perspectives is real in many regards and must be respected in the ongoing renewal of each community and tradition. Yet, in a very real sense, it is also limited. My fourth probe concerns this limitation. It is becoming increasingly clear that the supporters of the so-called New Right, or the neoconservatives (also referred to in Latin America as 'neoliberals'), have amassed perhaps the greatest concentration of power that the world has ever witnessed. And they have a radical project for re-ordering the whole world.

In the wake of the Cold War, this concentration is clear in terms of the military power of U.S. policy makers, above all evident in the Gulf War. But the concentration of economic power, though not vested in a single government and therefore harder to detect, is of perhaps even greater import for the future of the world.

The reign of neoconservative economics is the singularly author-itative discourse for discussing every important issue in the media, in virtually every national capital and in the major international institutions like the World Bank, the International Monetary Fund and the GATT. The triumph of this global orthodoxy would make any stereotypically authoritarian leader green with envy. In this 'new world order' there is only one language for discussing the world's problems and its basic terms and orientation have been fixed by a few: there is only one path to salvation, for all people, no matter what their own traditions, values and historical starting points—east or west, north or south, rich or poor.[26]

While it did not invent the new global age, this economic ortho-doxy signifies a particular approach to the changes sweeping the world, a radical project for redefining and re-ordering not only the 'economy,' but the whole social order. This is a genuinely radical project—not in the usual sense of the word—involving the transfor-mation of the foundations, structures, cultures and politics of the domestic and global social order established after World War II. In its ideologically explicit form, this project has never been as popular in Canada as it was in the 80s in the United States among supporters of Reagan and Bush or in England among Thatcher's supporters.[27] It is clear, though, that the Mulroney-Reagan Free Trade Agreement is part of this project. As John Warnock has pointed out, closer economic integration with the United States has been seen by its promoters as "the means of moving the Canadian people in the direction of the New Right agenda."[28] Looking back over the effects of the first three years of the Free Trade Agreement with the U.S., Bruce Campbell has noted its effectiveness as a "multipurpose device for securing and advancing the conservative-style restructuring of Canada."[29] The Mulroney-Bush-Salinas North American Free Trade Agreement simply represents the further deepening and entrenching of this agenda.[30]

Like every form of fundamentalism, this orthodoxy has depended on short-circuiting basic questions and marginalizing those who ask them.[31] Among the faithful, its triumph generated, especially at the beginning of the 90s, a kind of ecstasy concerning the appearance of a 'thousand points of light' at the 'end of history,' a new era of global harmony, prosperity and peace for all. But the ecstasy was short-lived as consensus among the powerful behind this orthodoxy began to fragment on the shoals of competing interests. The circle of true believers began to shrink, leaving some new space for other voices to be heard clamouring for different kinds of changes. In the U.S., President Bush's defeat in the 1992 elections signalled this growing scepticism there, if not a clear turn to an alternative agenda reflected in the ambivalences and contradictions in the Clinton administration's early policies and Clinton's widely fluctuating popularity. In Canada, though, while there is widespread and growing public opposition, this faith lives on in the agenda of the Reform and Conservative Parties and, shockingly to many, apparently even in the agendas of the 'born-again' provincial NDP governments.[32]

Not surprisingly, there are many signs of generalized crisis in politics, as established political institutions seem incapable of protecting their constituents from the ravages of these changes and more and more crucial decisions are being made elsewhere, in 'private' think tanks, corporate headquarters and lobbying groups, and in specialized institutions like the International Monetary Fund, the World Bank, and the G-7 meetings, far from public input and accountability.[33]

In this global context, many in the so-called Third World are speaking of the 80s as the 'lost decade,' even as the 'worst period' in their history.[34] While not so advanced yet, the feeling grows here too that Canada is "on the edge of disintegration,"[35] and with it increasing underemployment and unemployment, deepening poverty, the destruction of communities, alienation, racism, pathology, and violence on the streets and in the homes, "as if we were all taking part in some kind of assisted national suicide."[36]

The need for radical changes

The ecumenical interchurch coalitions, and the churches more generally, need to be seen today in this light—more accurately, darkness. My fifth probe concerns the response of the churches to these shifts. It seems clear that, as important as the work of each coalition is, individually and together they do not represent an adequate response to the magnitude of the questions and challenges currently before Canadians and the churches. Indeed, born in a different world, the coalitions were never intended to address tasks of the magnitude required by the global changes under way and the unprecedented concentration of power in the hands of a few. No other agency or organ of the church has taken up these challenges to faith.

In particular, given the wide-ranging character of the neoconservative agenda and its implications for every aspect of Canadian life, it is surprising and disappointing that Canadian church agencies and official teachings have done so little to promote widespread public debate and informed choices concerning it.[37] Indeed, so far it is social scientists more than theologians and church leaders who have been calling attention to the religious dimensions of these issues. For example, political scientist Terrence Downey has pointed out that "underlying the [free trade] deal were assumptions which constituted a fundamental challenge to the traditional Canadian vision of the good society."[38] Political economist Manfred Bienfeld has soberly concluded: "If we as a nation simply accept the challenge of becoming competitive within the parameters determined by today's unregulated economy, we will either fail, or we will succeed through actions that will destroy most of that which is worth preserving, including our environment, our welfare system, our social stability and even our compassion and humanity."[39]

Indeed, while so far few in the churches have recognized the matter in these terms, growing numbers of commentators are calling attention to the significance of faith—more accurately, idolatry—in the neoconservative agenda of global capitalist reconstruction.[40] For example, political scientist James Laxer refers to this agenda in terms of the "false god that has done vast destruction in many parts of the world."[41]

Clearly, these insights call into question conventional definitions of the allegedly separate spheres of the 'economy,' 'culture,' 'religion,' and 'politics,' and the larger framework in which these spheres have been defined, institutionalized, and managed. In particular, they pose historic challenges to church leaders to rethink the very definition of faith, the church's mission in the world, pastoral priorities in this renewed mission, and the appropriate forms of institutionalization for carrying out this mission.

Of course, over the last 25 years, there have been many bold experiments in new ways of following the Spirit in this new era, reflected especially in the various liberation theologies in the Third World. While they cannot simply be imported into other contexts, these quests in renewed ways of living the faith have inspired many Canadians and been richly flavoured with initiatives flowing from feminist, Black, gay and lesbian theologies, and indigenous spiritualities. Many seeds of renewed faith and witness have been sown within the coalitions and the wider circles of their supporters.

The signs of growing concern for theological and spiritual reflection, as integral to the agendas of the coalitions, are encouraging. Still, there has so far been little sustained discussion of these challenges, of how the church might respond, of a specifically Canadian theology self-consciously rooted in and responding to our own context.[42] There has been little encouragement for experiments in alternative ways of concretizing the mission of the church in this context.

More generally, the relative silence on these matters in official church circles in Canada suggests the view that the struggles over (re)ordering and managing society and the world are not 'religious' matters. Ironically, then, while an agenda with profound religious dimensions is being implemented with life and death implications for all—concerning the fate of whole classes and racial/ethnic groups, whole regions and nations, whole species and the foundations of biological life as we know it on earth—the church appears to be standing on the sidelines. Church leaders and officials seem to be looking in another direction, as if the churches' business were else-where, on other matters more important than following the Spirit in this world. This failure suggests deep contradictions, confusion and paralysis within the churches. It contributes to loss of credibility at a time when questions concerning the meaning of existence and of hope for the future have never been more historically urgent.

Of course, there are happy exceptions, especially the recently published pastoral statement by the Social Affairs Commission of the Canadian Conference of Catholic Bishops, *Widespread Unemployment: A Call to Mobilize the Social Forces of Our Nation.*[43] Perhaps this signals an important shift in the churches, one drawing deeply on the hard-earned legacy of Christian involvement in social justice struggles over the last 25 years and on the rereadings of the Bible and of other often marginalized dimensions of the Christian tradition nurtured in these movements. Perhaps it signals a revitalized courage to address deeper questions and to confront fundamental choices.

But there are many reasons for grave concern. For there is a widespread sense among social justice activists that the mainstream churches are not only not increasing their efforts on these matters, but are turning away from them and indeed cutting back on their commitments. There is evidence of this trend in the United Church,[44] and in the Catholic Church too, as Patrick Jamieson has confirmed: "even with a brand-new bishops' message on unemployment to rally their thinning ranks, these are shaky days for Catholic social justice workers in English-speaking Canada."[45]

Generally these cutbacks have not been advanced in a principled way, as an overt expression of a neoconservative agenda. Rather, ironically in view of the legacy of questioning the dominant logic and its priorities, decisions to freeze and cut back personnel and funds are being made on apparently simple fiscal grounds—declining income—and they are being made administratively, with little discussion within the churches or consideration of other options.[46] It seems that the neoconservative logic has in effect triumphed within the churches, as if theology had nothing to contribute to the discernment of issues and options, as if the church operated according to exactly the same logic as the world of business, as if even in the Spirit there were no other ways of viewing issues or possibilities for responding to them. The result is that many concerned Christians feel compelled to conclude that a kind of idolatry is operating within the church. For the fruit of following this spirit of economic and administrative efficiency is the continued suffering of a growing number of victims and of the earth itself.

Conclusion

In conclusion, I wish to celebrate the immense richness of the coalitions, expressions in Canada of the worldwide "explosion of compassion and solidarity" marking the last 25 years. Surely they are concrete expressions of God's grace in our history.

In a radically changed and changing context, there are many reasons for concluding that a significant restructuring of the coalitions is in order, concerning the visions, agendas, structures and strategies of individual coalitions, the relationships among them and to broader movements for progressive social change, the relationship of each to the denominations, and their collective significance for the church as a whole.

However, simply cutting back on coalition budgets and staff in the face of growing suffering should be unthinkable for all aspiring to be disciples of Jesus. Indeed, proceeding on the basis of the reigning administrative and fiscal criteria promises only to turn the back of the official church on the deeper questions of our history, and on the vast majority of its victims. It is to turn away from the most basic questions concerning how to witness to the Spirit of the prophets and Jesus in our history. Addressing such historic questions only in small circles of church officials simply reinforces global patterns of concentration of power, knowledge and expertise in the hands of a few and the marginalization of the great majorities.

The path of the Spirit of truth and justice is riskier and more challenging. It starts on the margins, among the historically oppressed and powerless and those in solidarity with them. It involves a willingness to question conventional wisdom in the world and in the church, to re-examine patiently the foundations of our thinking and acting, and to confront many challenges to conversion. The risks are great, but, as evident in expanding communities and networks around the world, this path is more promising too, leading to deepening and expanding solidarity among and with all the oppressed, and, in the midst of great suffering, real joy in the Spirit.

Much has been learned in these struggles over the last 25 years.

As I re-examine the history of the coalitions, in the context of other groups and movements, I see an emergent clarity around eight key issues, concerning:

• The option for the poor and oppressed, expressed in terms of support those who have historically been marginalized—the poor, women, people of colour, gays and lesbians, and those speaking on behalf of the earth and on behalf of peace—to speak for themselves and to have a voice in the centres of decision-making power;

• The interconnectedness of the basic issues raised by all of these movements, and the need to address them together;

• The irreducible centrality of the struggles over 'economic' order in all the struggles for equality, justice, peace, and the integrity of creation;

• The global character of all of these struggles;

• The importance of linking local, national and international responses, with a priority on nurturing solidarity and effective action from the bottom up;

• The irreducible significance of matters of hope and faith in these struggles and thus, for Christians, the importance of ongoing theological reflection in discerning the deeper meaning of these struggles and in identifying the resources available to us in our tradition for articulating anew who we are and where we are going in this world;

• The crucial significance of these issues for the soul of the church and its mission in the world, and the magnitude of the challenges to conversion we still face;

• The importance of collaboration between church activists and organizations and those in the broader social movements in the shared struggles for the future.

All on earth and in the heavens above is at stake in the quest for a different kind of faith besides that in the spirit of (ir)rationality currently dominating the centres of power in the world, promoting not order but disorder—chaos—which is killing millions of peoples and countless species, and threatening the very foundations of life as we know it. In the rich history of the ecumenical interchurch coalitions in Canada, there are many insights concerning these and other signposts along the path of the Spirit in this disordered world. There is much to be thankful for and to celebrate joyfully.

Endnotes

PART I

Introduction

1   Memo from the Ad Hoc Committee, April 1982.
2   Virginia FABELLA and Sergio TORRES (eds), *Doing Theology in a Divided World: Papers from the 6th International EATWOT Conference* (Maryknoll, NY: Orbis Books, 1983).

The Aboriginal Rights Coalition

1   Charles HENDRY, *Beyond Traplines* (Toronto: Ryerson Press, 1969).
2   ACC General Synod, *Journal of Proceedings* (1969), p. 36.
3   Tony CLARKE, "The Cry of Justice," in *Project North Journal*, 11:4 (1987), p. 2.
4   Hugh MCCULLUM and Karmel T. MCCULLUM, *This Land Is Not For Sale: Canada's Original People and Their Land, A Saga of Neglect, Exploitation and Conflict* (Toronto: Anglican Book Centre, 1975).
5   Clifton Monk, personal communication.
6   PROJECT NORTH, "A Call for a Moratorium: Some Moral and Ethical Considerations Relating to the Mackenzie Valley Pipeline." Submission to the Mackenzie Valley Pipeline Inquiry in Ottawa (1976), pp. 1-2.
7   H. MCCULLUM, "No Last Frontier," in *Risk*, 13:1 (1977), pp. 1-44.
8   K. T. MCCULLUM, "The Dene" in "Land Rights for Indigenous People," *PCR Information Report and Background Paper No. 16* (1983), pp. 47-52.
9   PROJECT NORTH, "A Call for a Moratorium," pp. 7-9.
10   R. WILLOUGHBY, "Business Replies: 'Using the Church to Promote a One-sided Economic View'," in *United Church Observer* (August 1978), p. 20.
11   Staff report to Project North for the period May 17–June 18 1977, p. 10.
12   CLARKE, "The Cry of Justice," p. 3.
13   T. CLARKE, "The Future of Project North," internal discussion paper (1979), p. 2.
14   C. MONK, "Spirited Actions of Conviction," in *Project North Journal,* 11:4 (1987), p. 6.
15   *A New Covenant: Towards the Constitutional Recognition and Protection of Aboriginal Self-Government in Canada. A pastoral statement by the Leaders of the Christian Churches on Aboriginal Rights and the Canadian Constitution* (Toronto, February 1987).
16   Anwar BARKAT, Letter to the Rt. Hon. Pierre Trudeau re: Concerns of the Lubicon Lake Indian Band, Northern Alberta (November 1983), p. 1.

17 ARC, "A New Ecumenical Coalition for Aboriginal Justice in Canada" (remandating document, January 1989).

18 M. ANGUS, "...And the Last Shall Be First" (Toronto: NC Press, 1991), pp. 71-76.

19 Paul Bresee, personal communication.

20 Minesque (Rod Robinson) address to WCC 6th Assembly, Vancouver, July 1983.

The Taskforce on the Churches and Corporate Responsibility

1 TCCR membership has grown since 1975 when it comprised the Anglican, Lutheran, Presbyterian and United Churches, the Baptist Federation of Canada, the CCCB, and four religious orders. By 1992 the original church membership remained the same, except for the withdrawal of the Baptists, while the number of religious orders had increased to 15. CUSO and the National Board of the YWCA hold consultative membership. TCCR has been financed by the participating denominations and orders. It publishes an annual report with an audited statement. It has never received grants from either government or business.

2 Space constraints limit us to selected case studies. Although this will not do justice to the scope of TCCR activities, it should typify the incremental nature of TCCR work as it has evolved over the years.

3 The Royal Bank, the CIBC, the Toronto Dominion Bank, the Bank of Nova Scotia and the Bank of Montreal. There were minor loan involvements of smaller banks as well and correspondence was also conducted with them.

4 SPECIAL JOINT COMMITTEE ON CANADA'S INTERNATIONAL RELATIONS, "Independence and Internationalism" (June 1986), p. 103, and SCEAIT, "For Whose Benefit?" (May 1987).

5 Quoted in TCCR *Annual Report 1989-1990*, p. 26, "The World Bank and Human Rights," in *The Bank's World* (February 1988).

6 The term 'North/South' in the context of international development is increasingly describes relationships between the industrialized 'North' and the non-industrialized 'South.' 'Partner churches' denotes the long-term nature and mutuality of relations between Canadian churches and churches in other countries.

7 The document was prepared by TCCR in co-operation with GATT-Fly (now ECEJ) and the Inter-Church, Inter-Coalition Debt Network.

8 "The International Debt Crisis" (1989), p. 26.

9 "Alas poor bankers," in *The Globe and Mail*, January 11 1992.

10 International action includes TCCR collaboration with Lingkod Tao-Kalikassan, a Filipino environmental organization, on the harmful discharge by Marcopper Mining of tailings into Calancan Bay on the island of Marinduque.

11 *The Fisherman* (Newsletter of the United Food and Allied Workers Union), February 1983, cited in TCCR *Annual Report 1982-83*, p. 67.

12 TCCR works on issues in Brazil (violations of aboriginal rights, environmental abuse due to the construction of the Balbina Dam with World Bank funds) and issues related to Electronorte and operations in the Amazon region by Brascan.

13 See also David HALLMAN, "Assessing Corporate Responsibility in the Forest: A Model from Canadian Churches," Annual Meeting of the Canadian Institute of Forestry, September 1991, Toronto.

14   The Brundtland Report (1987) initiated and strongly advocated the concept of 'sustainable development.'

15   TCCR, "Corporate Environmental and Social Responsibility: Recommendations to the United Nations Conference on Environment and Development–Third Preparatory Committee Meeting," July 1991, p. 2, point 4.

16   See also Moira HUTCHINSON, "Shareholder Action: Recent Canadian Experience," presented at the Strategies for Responsible Share Ownership Conference, University of Toronto, December 1990.

17   M. HUTCHINSON, "Shareholder Action," p. 67.

18   *The Globe and Mail,* January 20 1983.

The Ecumenical Coalition for Economic Justice

1   John DILLON, "Limitations of the Trade Issue" (Toronto: GATT-Fly, 1973).

2   S. AMIN, *Accumulation on a World Scale: A Critique of the Theory of Underdevelopment* (NY: Monthly Review Press, 1974); A. G. FRANK, *Capitalism and Underdevelopment in Latin America* (NY: Monthly Review Press, 1969); A. G. FRANK, *Latin America: Underdevelopment or Revolution* (NY: Monthly Review Press, 1969); W. RODNEY, *How Europe Underdeveloped Africa* (Dar es Salaam: Tanzania Publishing House, 1972);C. THOMAS, *Dependence and Transformation: The Economics of the Transition to Socialism* (NY: Monthly Review Press, 1974).

3   GATT-FLY, *Ah-hah! A New Approach to Popular Education* (Toronto: Between the Lines, 1983).

4   Paulo FREIRE, *Pedagogy of the Oppressed* (NY: Seabury Press, 1968).

5   Cranford PRATT and Roger HUTCHINSON (eds), *Christian Faith and Economic Justice: Toward a Canadian Perspective* (Burlington: Trinity Press, 1988); Dale HILDEBRAND, "The Inter-church Coalition GATT-Fly, Theological Praxis and the Option for the Poor: Towards a Canadian Contextual Theology." Master's thesis, University of St. Michael's College, Toronto School of Theology, Toronto, 1987.

6   GATT-FLY, *Power to Choose: Canada's Energy Options* (Toronto: Between the Lines, 1981).

7   GATT-FLY, *Debt Bondage or Self-Reliance: A Popular Perspective on the Global Debt Crisis* (Toronto: GATT-Fly, 1985); GATT-FLY, *Free Trade or Self-Reliance: Report of the Ecumenical Conference on Free Trade, Self-Reliance and Economic Justice* (Toronto: GATT-Fly, 1987); GATT-FLY, *Recolonization or Liberation: The Bonds of Structural Adjustment and Struggles for Emancipation* (Toronto: GATT-Fly, 1990); Brian RUTTAN, "GATT-Fly and the Basis of Economic Development," in *Toronto Journal of Theology* (Fall 1989).

8   B. RUTTAN, "The Inter-church Project GATT-Fly 1972-1980: A Reconstruction." Ph.D. dissertation, University of St. Michael's College, Toronto School of Theology, Toronto, 1986.

9   Gustavo GUTIÉRREZ, *A Theology of Liberation* (Maryknoll: Orbis Books, 1971); B. RUTTAN, "GATT-Fly and the Churches: Changing Public Policy," in Christopher LIND and Terry BROWN (eds), *Justice as Mission: An Agenda for the Church* (Burlington: Trinity Press, 1985).

10   Dennis HOWLETT, "The Arithmetic, Chemistry and Art of Coalition Politics," in *Action Canada Network Dossier,* 37 (July 1992), pp. 7-9; D. HOWLETT, "Social

Movement Coalitions: New Possibilities for Social Change," in *Canadian Dimension,* 23:8 (November-December, 1989).

The Canada China Programme

1   The language of the 'Three-Selfs' originated with 19th century Western missionary theorists whose aim was to establish autonomous self-governing, self-supporting and self-propagating churches in China. Reality, however, never matched the ideal, as Western agencies held title to most of the schools, hospitals and churches, basically regarding the 'younger churches' as extensions of themselves.

PLURA

1   Roméo Maione in an interview with Mary Boyd, September 1990, Ottawa.
2   He was no doubt referring to the Latin expression, *mea culpa,* 'through my fault.'
3   The Rev. R. D. MacRae in conversation with Mary Boyd, April 1992.
4   Tom Johnston in conversation with Mary Boyd, April 1992. See also the Minutes, Ad Hoc ICCCDR, October 1971, p. 3.
5   Addenda to the Minutes, Ad Hoc ICCCDR, December 1971, p. 1.
6   The Rev. Donald G. Ray, deputy secretary of the Inter-Church Committee on Poverty, Letter to Heads of Churches, October 23 1972.
7   Minutes, Board Meeting, CCODP, November 1972, Montreal.
8   Minutes, Ad Hoc ICCCDR, October 1971.

Ten Days for World Development

1   See the story of the antipoverty group PLURA for more information on this conference and its impact.

The Inter-Church Committee on Human Rights in Latin America

1   In March 1991, the Aylwin government made public a report on some of the worst human rights abuses committed during the Pinochet dictatorship. The report is a 2,000-page six-volume compilation of testimonies. It confirms a total of 2,279 political assassinations, including 957 enforced disappearances, which occurred between September 1973 and March 1990.
2   The Canadian government recognized the new regime after only 18 days.
3   Prior to the coup, Chile had provided refuge for many Latin Americans: those who had fled the torture and state terror of Brazil, those who had seen the democratic government in Uruguay fall to military rule, those who had escaped the long repression of the Stroessner regime in Paraguay and those who had suffered a military takeover in Bolivia were among the thousands of refugees living in Chile.
4   The seven-person delegation was led by Dr. Floyd Honey, general secretary of the CCC, and the Rev. Everett McNeil, general secretary of the CCCB.
5   "Chile issue," mimeographed (1974), ICCHRLA archives.
6   The Inter-Church Committee on Chile was comprised of representatives from the ACC, the Religious Society of Friends, the CCC, the Lutheran Church of America (Canada Section), the Presbyterian Church in Canada, the CCCB, the Scarboro Foreign Mission Society, the Toronto Passionist Community and the UCC.

7   Between October 1973 and March 1974, the Inter-Church Committee on Chile sent four ecumenical delegations to Ottawa to raise concerns around Chile directly with Canada's Minister of External Affairs (three meetings with Mitchell Sharp and one with Alan MacEachen).

8   Over 1,300 prisoner petitions for exile were approved by Pinochet by early 1977. This practice continued until at least 1980.

9   "Open Letter to North American Christians," reproduced in part in Inter-Church Committee on Chile, "One Gigantic Prison: The Report of a Fact-Finding Mission to Chile, Argentina and Uruguay," November 1976.

10   ICCHRLA, "Submission to the Standing Committee on External Affairs and National Defence on Canada's Relations with Latin America and the Caribbean," Toronto, July 1981, p. 4.

11   In 1977, an ultra-right death squad threatened to kill all 47 Jesuit priests living in El Salvador unless they left the country. Two of these were subsequently assassinated, including Father Rutilio Grande.

12   This phenomenon was not entirely new. At its January 1974 meeting, the executive committee of the CCC moved that the CCC "prepare a document recording its actions and reasons for same, to be distributed to groups who question our actions for Chilean refugees, in the hope of counteracting false information and unreasonable opposition to immigration from 'socialistic' countries."

13   B. AMIEL, "Color those clerics red," in *The Toronto Sun,* January 29 1984.

14   ICCHRLA, "Mandate of the Inter-Church Committee on Human Rights in Latin America 1988-1991," Toronto, September 1988, p. 2.

15   INTER-CHURCH COMMITTEE ON CHILE, "Canada-Chile Bulletin," December 1976, pp. 2-3.

16   Fred FRANKLIN, "Reflection on the ICCHRLA: Experience and Grace," in ICCHRLA *Newsletter,* 4 (1987), p. 4.

17   ICCHRLA, "Submission to the Canadian Ambassador to the 36th Session of the United Nations Commission on Human Rights," in ICCHRLA *Newsletter* (April 1980), p. 5.

18   Frances ARBOUR, "Canada: The Inter-Church Committee on Human Rights in Latin America," in FABELLA and TORRES, *Doing Theology in a Divided World.*

19   FRANKLIN, "Reflection on the ICCHRLA," p. 4.

Project Ploughshares

1   Micah 4:3: "...and they beat their swords into ploughshares... nation shall not lift up sword against nation, neither shall they learn war any more..."

The Inter-Church Committee for Refugees

1   The author wishes to thank and acknowledge the input to this chapter made by Robert Lindsey, Tom Clark, Arie Van Eek, Ellen Turley and George Cram.

2   Personal interview with Bernard Daly.

3   Kathleen PTOLEMY, "From Oppression to Promise: Journeying Together with the Refugee," in Bonnie GREENE (ed), *Canadian Churches and Foreign Policy* (Toronto: James Lorimer & Co., 1990).

4   H. MCCULLUM, *The Least of These* (Toronto: United Church Observer, 1982).

5   PTOLEMY, "From Oppression to Promise."

PART II

The Lives of the Saints

1   Renate PRATT, *TCCR*, p. 64.
2   Pier Paolo PASOLINI, "Trans-humanize and Organize," in *Poetry*. Selected and translated by Antonino MAZZA (Toronto: Exile Editions, 1991), p. 118.
3   'Trina' in William FINN and James LAPINE, *Falsettoland. Vocal Score* (Secaucus, NJ: Warner Bros. Publications, 1991).
4   Linda MCQUAIG, *The Quick and the Dead: Brian Mulroney, Big Business and the Seduction of Canada* (Toronto: Viking Press, 1991), p. 96.
5   Donald MACDONALD, *Royal Commission on the Economic Union and Development Prospects for Canada* (Ottawa, 1984); CCCB, Social Affairs Division, *Ethical Reflections on the Economy* (Ottawa, 1982).
6   Bronwen WALLACE, *Keep That Candle Burning Bright and Other Poems* (Toronto: Coach House Press, 1991), p. 21.

A Regional Perspective

1   TEN DAYS, "Development Demands Justice, The Alberta Context," March 1973.
2   Peter HAMEL, *ARC*, pp. 31-32.
3   AYAPSA brochure, Winter 1992.
4   "Social Ecumenism... Building Our Future Together," in *Future Directions of Ecumenical Justice Work*, Document 1 (July 1990), p. 9.
5   "Consultation Planning Process," in *Future Directions*, Document 2 (1990).
6   Elaine BRUER (ed), "Report of the Regional Consultations," in *Future Directions* (February 1991).
7   "Empowered for the Future," in *Report and Recommendations of the Drafting Committee*, Results of the Consultation Planning Process, April 1991, p. 10.
8   "Empowered for the Future," p. 14.
9   Dina GUERRA, Mary MXADANA and Carlos OCAMPO, "An Input to the Consultation Process on Ecumenical Social Justice Work in Canada," April 1991, Toronto.
10 "Record of Proceedings," *CJP Plenary Meeting*, April 1991, Toronto, pp. 16, 17.
11 SOUTHERN ONTARIO REGIONAL CONSULTATION, "Notes on the Restructuring of the Ecumenical Social Justice Coalitions," February 1991.
12 See Patrick JAMIESON, "Social Justice Ministry Worries about Its Future," in *Catholic New Times* (May 02 1993), pp. 10-11; P. JAMIESON, "Social Justice Ministry Worries about Its Future: II–The West and the North," in *CNT* (May 16 1993), pp. 14-15; P. JAMIESON and Janet SOMMERVILLE, "Social Justice Ministry Looks for Its Future: III–Maritime Canada," in *CNT* (May 30 1993), pp. 16-17; J. SOMMERVILLE, "Who's Minding the Faith and Justice Store: IV–The National Office," in *CNT* (June 13 1993), pp. 12-13.
13 Richard ALLEN, *The Social Passion* (Toronto: University of Toronto Press, 1971), pp. 159-74.
14 Benjamin SMILLIE, "The Social Gospel in Canada: A Theological Critique" in R. ALLEN (ed), *The Social Gospel in Canada* (Ottawa: National Museum of Canada, 1971), pp. 317-42.
15 GATT-Fly, *Ah-hah! A New Approach to Popular Education*.

"They Persevered as though They Saw the One Who Is Invisible"

1   This paper was translated by Dr. Charles JOHNSTON, Professor Emeritus of St. Andrew's College, Saskatoon.

2   In the Quebec francophone milieu, it is mainly with secular social groups that CCODP effected coalitions. This is because of the almost total absence of non-Catholic churches, especially outside Montreal.

3   SYNOD of Bishops, *Justice in the World* (Rome: 1971), note 7.

4   SYNOD of Bishops, *Justice in the World*, note 38.

5   FRANKLIN, "Reflection on the ICCHRLA," p. 4.

6   S. HOFFMANN, "Le monde nouveau et ses problèmes," in *Commentaires* (Spring 1991).

7   Franz J. HINKELAMMERT, "Theology of Empire," in *Amanecer*, 2 (March-April 1988), pp. 22-28.

8   A. SOLJENITSYNE, *La maison de Matriona* (Paris: Julliard, 1974), pp. 78-79.

An Ecumenical Model for Participation in Civil Society

1   I am grateful to Rubem César FERNANDES of the Instituto de Estudos da Religião in Rio de Janeiro for his analysis of civil society which has informed this summary (*Back and Forward to 'Civil Society,'* an unpublished discussion paper written for the WCC) and to Leo J. PENTA of Villanova University.

2   Konrad RAISER, *Ecumenism in Transition* (Geneva: WCC, 1991), p. 86.

3   See documents of the WCC Conference on *Faith and Order* (Lund, 1952).

4   Taken from personal recorded interview with Bonnie Greene.

5   See documents of the First Assembly of the WCC (Amsterdam, 1948).

6   R. HUTCHINSON, *Ecumenical Social Action in Canada: Selected Documents,* unpublished (University of Toronto: Dept. of Religious Studies, 1983), p. 3.

7   RAISER, *Ecumenism in Transition*, p. 78.

8   Dennis HOWLETT, *ECEJ*, p. 114.

9   HOWLETT, "The Arithmetic, Chemistry and Art of Coalition Politics."

10   HAMEL, *ARC*, pp. 16, 26.

11   Jeanne MOFFAT, *Ten Days*, p. 163.

12   Bill FAIRBAIRN, *ICCHRLA*, pp. 174, 176, 180.

13   Henriette THOMPSON, *ICCR*, p. 204.

14   R. PRATT, *TCCR*, p. 71.

15   Terry BROWN, *CAWG*, p. 93.

16   FAIRBAIRN, *ICCHRLA*, p. 181.

17   R. PRATT, *TCCR*, p. 68.

18   Quoted by David GILL (ed), *Gathered for Life*. Official Report of the 6th Assembly (Geneva: WCC, 1983), p. 5.

19   R. PRATT, *TCCR*, p. 81.

20   Cynthia MCLEAN, *CCP*, p. 133.

21   Ernie REGEHR, *PP*, pp. 185-87.

22   FAIRBAIRN, *ICCHRLA*, p. 182.

23   See Larry L. RASMUSSEN, *Moral Fragments and Moral Community, A Proposal for Church in Society* (Minneapolis: Fortress Press, 1993), for a helpful discussion of the role of the church as moral community in society.

24 HAMEL, *ARC*, p. 36.

25 I acknowledge the unpublished paper by Leo J. PENTA "Theses on Power, Social Change and the Churches" in which he outlines the role of values-based institutions in civil society.

26 Gary KENNY, *ICCAF*, p. 51.

27 WCC Consultation on Koinonia and Justice, Peace and the Integrity of Creation, *Costly Unity*. Final document of the meeting of representatives of the Justice, Peace and the Integrity of Creation process and the Commission on Faith and Order (Rønde, Denmark, 1993).

Policy Impact and Political Empowerment

1 Thanks to Joe Gunn, Jenny Cafiso, Dennis Howlett, Martha McGuire and Joe Mihevc for their helpful comments.

2 L. MCQUAIG, *The Wealthy Banker's Wife: The Assault on Equality in Canada* (Toronto: Penguin, 1993); Daniel DRACHE (ed), *Getting on Track* (Montreal/Kingston: McGill-Queen's University Press, 1992); and David ROSS and Richard SHILLINGTON, *The Canadian Fact Book on Poverty* (Ottawa: Canadian Council for Social Development, 1989).

3 Each coalition operates within a distinctive policy community comprised of relevant government departments and responsible interest groups, that is those willing and able to seek an easy accommodation with government, refraining from outrageous demands or confrontational behaviour that would threaten the established order. For a sympathetic reading of the concept, see William D. COLEMAN and Grace SKOGSTAD (eds), *Policy Communities and Public Policy: A Structural Approach* (Mississauga: Copp Clark Pitman, 1990).

4 See HOWLETT, *ECEJ*, p. 100.

5 Thanks to Jenny Cafiso for this insight.

6 See Daniel DRACHE and Meric GERTLER (eds), *The New Era of Global Competition: State Policy and Market Power* (Montreal/Kingston: McGill-Queen's University Press, 1991); and M. Patricia MARCHAK, *The Integrated Circus: The New Right and the Restructuring of Global Markets* (Montreal/Kingston: McGill-Queen's University Press, 1991).

7 See David LANGILLE, "The Business Council on National Issues and the Canadian State," in *Studies in Political Economy,* 24 (Autumn 1987), pp. 41-85; MCQUAIG, *The Quick and the Dead*; Lawrence MARTIN, *Pledge of Allegiance: The Americanization of Canada* (Toronto: McClelland & Stewart, 1993).

8 In recent years, BCNI's membership has expanded to include 2 women.

9 BCNI, *Information Brochure* (Ottawa, 1989).

10 CCCB, *Ethical Reflections on the Economy*; Thomas D'AQUINO, "The Bishops' Reflection on the Economic Crisis: A Business Response," Address to the Empire Club of Canada (Toronto, January 1983).

11 See Gregory ALBO, David LANGILLE and Leo PANITCH (eds), *A Different Kind of State: Popular Power and Democratic Administration* (Toronto: Oxford University Press, 1993).

12 See Joan SIMALCHIK, *Part of the Awakening: Canadian Churches and Chilean Refugees, 1970-79* (Master's thesis, University of Toronto, 1993). Credit also

goes to Ten Days for its influence on Canadian policy toward Central America, described in Rebecca LARSON, *Ten Days for World Development: A Case Study in Development Education* (Ph.D. dissertation, University of Calgary, 1988).

13   For instance, Howlett notes how the campaign against free trade influenced public opinion and election results (HOWLETT, *ECEJ*, p. 110). See also MCCULLUM and MCCULLUM, *This Land Is Not For Sale*.

14   MCCULLUM and MCCULLUM, *This Land Is Not For Sale*.

15   HOWLETT, *ECEJ*, pp. 103-105.

16   See Leslie A. PAL, *Interests of State: The Politics of Language, Multiculturalism, and Feminism in Canada* (Kingston/Montreal: McGill-Queen's University Press, 1993). Pal shows how the idea of 'citizen participation' made popular in the late 60s led to the direct government funding of interest ('advocacy') organizations.

17   On the other hand, if there is only one central organization to channel the churches' message, that organization becomes a 'gatekeeper' of information. Ten Days could become a political battleground as groups champion their cause. Alternatively, it might lose any focus if it sought to campaign on all issues at once.

18   Gregory BAUM, "The Catholic Left in Quebec," in Colin LEYS and Marguerite MENDELL (eds), *Culture and Social Change: Social Movements in Quebec and Ontario* (Montreal: Black Rose, 1992), p. 150.

19   Credit must be given to the Social Affairs Commission of the Canadian CCCB and the very special contribution that Bishop Remi De Roo and Tony Clarke have made toward a more egalitarian politics in Canada. See George MORTIMORE, "Remi De Roo," in *Canadian Forum*, LXIX:789 (May 1990), pp. 8-12.

20   BAUM, "The Catholic Left in Quebec," pp. 150-51.

21   The Common Frontiers Project offers one such example of a new approach to solidarity. According to Howlett, ECEJ is involved alongside social movements from the United States and Mexico in a new form of solidarity "in that we are not just supporting them in their struggle, but supporting each other in a common struggle which affects us all" (HOWLETT, *ECEJ*, p. 115).

22   The same caution applies to the notion of 'prophetic praxis' as practised by small groups within the churches rather than by the church at large. Although Boyd agrees that PLURA is a "prophetic organization" capable of spiritual growth, contemplation, analysis and vision, she also demonstrates a strong commitment to grassroots organizing (Mary BOYD, *PLURA*, p. 150). Despite Boyd's strong commitment to grassroots organizing, it may not survive long without a strong leader.

23   See Howlett's chapter on the important role that ECEJ has played in coalition building (HOWLETT, *ECEJ*, pp. 114-15). Many popular sector groups endorsed the consensus document produced by the WORKING COMMITTEE ON SOCIAL SOLIDARITY, *A Time to Stand Together: A Time for Social Solidarity* (Ottawa: Canadian Union of Public Employees, 1987) when it was published, but it has since proved difficult to broaden and deepen their national network.

24   HOWLETT, *ECEJ*, p. 103.

25   BOYD, *PLURA*, p. 150.

26   See Peter BLEYER, "Coalitions of Social Movements as Agencies for Social Change: The Action Canada Network," in William K. CARROLL (ed), *Organizing Dissent: Contemporary Social Movements in Theory and Practice* (Toronto: Garamond, 1992), pp. 102-17; HOWLETT, "The Arithmetic, Chemistry and Art of

Coalition Politics"; HOWLETT, "Social Movement Coalitions"; Randy ROBINSON, "Democracy from Below—Action Canada: The Story of a Movement," in *Canadian Forum,* LXXI:818 (April 1993), pp. 8-14.

27   It is noteworthy that the Fraser Institute, perhaps Canada's most vocal neoconservative advocate, sponsors student conferences and a student newspaper.

28   Michael SCHWARTZ and Shuva PAUL, "Resource Mobilization versus the Mobilization of People: Why Consensus Movements Cannot Be Instruments of Social Change," in Aldon D. MORRIS and Carol McClurg MUELLER (eds), *Frontiers in Social Movement Theory* (New Haven/London: Yale University Press, 1992), pp. 205-23. They found that "most successful conflict movements also experience, at some time or another, major failure as well," in which case the key to survival "is the creation of new programs and strategies that encompass the lessons learned from past defeats" (p. 217).

29   The coalitions which receive the most media attention seem to be those with a clearly identifiable opposition or those which manage to stir up opposition!

30   BOYD, *PLURA,* p. 142, HAMEL, *ARC,* pp. 33, 34 and communications with Dennis Howlett.

31   This excludes the financial aid which ICFID channels into overseas development projects. Joe MIHEVC, "The Christian Left in Ontario: Reflections on the Current Juncture of the Interchurch Coalitions," in LEYS and MENDELL, *Culture and Social Change,* p. 156.

32   See A. Paul PROSS and Iain S. STEWART, "Lobbying, the Voluntary Sector and the Public Purse," in Susan D. PHILLIPS (ed), *How Ottawa Spends 1993-94: A More Democratic Canada...?* (Ottawa: Carleton University Press, 1993), pp. 109-42.

33   KENNY, *ICCAF,* p. 53.

34   MIHEVC, "The Christian Left in Ontario," p. 167.

35   See John Kenneth GALBRAITH, *The Culture of Contentment* (Boston/New York: Houghton Mifflin, 1992).

36   Marcia NOZICK, *No Place Like Home: Building Sustainable Communities* (Ottawa: Canadian Council for Social Development, 1992). See also Herman E. DALY and John B. COBB, Jr., *For the Common Good: Redirecting the Economy Toward Community, the Environment and a Sustainable Future* (Boston: Beacon Press, 1989).

37   They can certainly play a critical role in social transformation, which may eventually lead to political change. See HOWLETT, *ECEJ,* p. 114; Carl BOGGS, *Social Movements and Political Power: Emerging Forms of Radicalism in the West* (Philadelphia: Temple University Press, 1986); Warren MAGNUSSON, "Critical Social Movements: De-centering the State," in Alain GAGNON and James BICKERTON (eds), *Canadian Politics: An Introduction to the Discipline* (Peterborough: Broadview Press, 1990), pp. 525-41.

38   GALBRAITH, *The Culture of Contentment*; Kevin PHILLIPS, *The Politics of Rich and Poor* (NY: Random House, 1990).

39   MIHEVC notes ("The Christian Left in Ontario," p. 166), "There is a hesitancy... to form alliances and new structures with non-church groups based on the assumption that in periods of scarce resources, churches should draw inward."

Missiology

1 David J. BOSCH, *Transforming Mission: Paradigm Shifts in Theology of Mission* (Maryknoll, NY: Orbis Books, 1992).

2 BOSCH, *Transforming Mission,* p. 100.

3 BOSCH, *Transforming Mission,* p. 101.

4 BOSCH, *Transforming Mission,* p. 101.

5 BOSCH, *Transforming Mission,* p. 379. For a sobering discussion of the problem of neocolonialism in Third World churches, see T. BROWN, "Neocolonialism in the Third World Church," in LIND and BROWN, *Justice as Mission,* pp. 7-16.

6 BOSCH, *Transforming Mission,* p. 114.

7 BOSCH, *Transforming Mission,* p. 114.

8 BOSCH, *Transforming Mission,* p. 115.

9 See Donald A. MCGAVRAN, "What Is Mission?" in A. F. GLASSER and D. A. MCGAVRAN (eds), *Contemporary Theologies of Mission* (Grand Rapids, MI: Baker Book House, 1983), pp. 15-29.

10 See R. HUTCHINSON, "The Dene and Project North: Partners in Mission," in William WESTFALL, Louis ROUSSEAU, Fernand HARVEY and John SIMPSON (eds), *Religion/Culture: Comparative Canadian Studies,* Canadian Issues 7 (Ottawa: Association for Canadian Studies, 1985), pp. 391-410.

11 BOSCH, *Transforming Mission,* p. 77.

12 BOSCH, *Transforming Mission,* p. 77.

13 BOSCH, *Transforming Mission,* p. 82.

14 Shoki COE, "Contextualization as the Way Toward Reform," in Douglas J. ELWOOD (ed), *Asian Christian Theology: Emerging Themes* (Philadelphia: Westminster Press, 1980), pp. 48-55. See the chapter "Mission as Contextualization," in BOSCH, *Transforming Mission,* pp. 420-32.

15 For a fuller discussion of contextualization as applied to the coalitions and the Canadian churches, see R. HUTCHINSON, "Contextualization: No Passing Fad," in Theresa CHU and Christopher LIND (eds), *A New Beginning: An International Dialogue with the Chinese Church* (Toronto: CCC, 1983), pp. 68-74; R. HUTCHINSON, *Prophets, Pastors and Public Choices: Canadian Churches and the Mackenzie Valley Pipeline Debate* (Waterloo: Wilfrid Laurier University Press, 1992).

16 BOSCH, *Transforming Mission,* p. 170.

17 BOSCH, *Transforming Mission,* p. 178.

18 BOSCH, *Transforming Mission,* p. 178.

19 BOSCH, *Transforming Mission,* p. 134.

20 BOSCH, *Transforming Mission,* p. 134.

21 BOSCH, *Transforming Mission,* p. 176.

22 BOSCH, *Transforming Mission,* p. 178.

23 BOSCH, *Transforming Mission,* p. 137.

24 Helen Rand PARISH (ed), *Bartolomé de las Casas: The Only Way.* Trans. by Francis Patrick SULLIVAN, (Mahwah, NJ: Paulist Press, 1992), p. 71: The way to preach Christ's law should be based upon the way of "Christ Himself, Son of God, Wisdom of the Father." This "form of preaching a living faith wins the mind with reasons, wins the will gently, by attraction, by graciousness."

25 REGEHR, *PP,* pp. 185-86.

26   For a discussion of the way grand narratives articulate historical experience in
     terms of ultimate convictions about truth, salvation, justice and peace, see J. M.
     BERNSTEIN, "Grand Narratives," in David WOOD (ed), *On Paul Ricoeur: Narra-
     tive and Interpretation* (London/New York: Routledge, 1991), pp. 102-23.

The Wisdom of Doing Justice

1   Leon EPZSTEIN, *Social Justice in the Ancient Near East and the People of the
     Bible* (London: SCM, 1986), p. 93.
2   Karen LEBACQZ, *Six Theories of Justice: Perspectives from Philosophical and
     Theological Ethics* (Minneapolis: Augsburg, 1986), pp. 118-19. See also Bruce C.
     BIRCH, *Let Justice Roll: The Old Testament, Ethics and Christian Life* (Louis-
     ville: Westminster/John Knox Press, 1991) for a study of various emphases in the
     understanding of justice in Hebrew scripture.
3   See, for example, Donn MORGAN, *Wisdom in the Old Testament Traditions*
     (Atlanta: John Knox Press, 1981); R. B. Y. SCOTT, *The Way of Wisdom in the Old
     Testament* (New York/London: Collier Macmillan, 1971); Gerhard VON RAD,
     Wisdom in Israel (London: SCM Press, 1972).
4   BIRCH, *Let Justice Roll,* pp. 326-27.
5   MORGAN, *Wisdom in the Old Testament Traditions,* p. 65.
6   MORGAN (*Wisdom in the Old Testament Traditions,* pp. 66, 67, 76) discusses the
     idea that clan wisdom influenced Amos and Micah, providing rural examples for
     illustrations and contributing a note of hostility toward leaders in Jerusalem.
7   See VON RAD, *Wisdom in Israel,* "Knowledge and the Fear of God," pp. 53-73.
8   MORGAN, *Wisdom in the Old Testament Traditions,* pp. 14, 15, 29.
9   MORGAN (*Wisdom in the Old Testament Traditions,* p. 70) compares the rhetorical
     style in Amos 3:3-8 to Proverbs 29:13 and the style of comparative questions in
     Amos 6:2 and 9:7 to the use of questions in Proverbs, for example in 14:22 and
     23:29-30. See SCOTT, *The Way of Wisdom in the Old Testament,* pp. 126-27.
10   VON RAD, *Wisdom in Israel,* p. 95; see pp. 62ff.
11   See, for example, Proverbs 15 and 16 which move from observations on the dis-
     cipline of speech to God's commitment to justice for the widow, then on to the
     concerns of the righteous kings to verses which echo Psalm 19 and its image of
     God's wisdom as the sweetness of the honeycomb.
12   R. PRATT, *TCCR,* pp. 64-65. The CCBP is the most clearly described and organ-
     ized lobby against the economic analysis provided by the coalitions. The TCCR
     story notes that this early criticism dissipated, yet various issues still raise critical
     reaction in supporting churches. For example, educational material on the pro-
     posed Free Trade Agreement circulated to congregations in 1988 just prior to the
     federal election was judged in some churches to be too partisan for distribution.
     Clearly expressed convictions about faith in action could rebut this argument by
     more clearly interpreting such vital issues in terms of discipleship or witness.
13   BIRCH, *Let Justice Roll,* p. 330.
14   MORGAN (*Wisdom in the Old Testament Traditions,* pp. 69-70) cites examples in
     Amos 3:3-6, 8; 5:25; 6:12; pp. 72ff examine examples in Hosea 5:12; 6:4; 7:11
     and 10:7, among others.
15   One is here reminded of the comment offered in the ICCR story to explain com-

mitment to refugee work: "It was the only decent thing to do" (THOMPSON, *ICCR*, p. 208). Recapturing this sense of compassion as an obvious way to put faith to work is a wise dimension of doing justice.

16 VON RAD, *Wisdom in Israel,* pp. 82, 78.
17 VON Rad, *Wisdom in Israel,* p. 106.
18 VON Rad, *Wisdom in Israel,* pp. 70-71.
19 REGEHR, *PP*, p. 193.
20 HAMEL, *ARC*, p. 30.
21 See, for example, SCOTT, *The Way of Wisdom in the Old Testament*, for his chapter on "The International Context" of wisdom, pp. 23-47.
22 THOMPSON, *ICCR*, pp. 206-208.
23 MOFFAT, *Ten Days*, p. 157.
24 Consider the example of solidarity work in MOFFAT, *Ten Days*, pp. 151-53.
25 MORGAN, *Wisdom in the Old Testament Traditions,* pp. 90-93.
26 MOFFAT, *Ten Days*, p. 164.
27 MOFFAT, *Ten Days*, p. 165.
28 R. PRATT, *TCCR*, pp. 79-80.
29 REGEHR, *PP*, p. 192.
30 HOWLETT, *ECEJ*, p. 105.
31 HAMEL, *ARC*, pp. 21-22.
32 HAMEL, *ARC*, p. 36.
33 MOFFAT, *Ten Days*, p. 162.

Relinquishing Control

1   KENNY, *ICCAF*, p. 54.
2   HOWLETT, *ECEJ*, p. 107.
3   BOYD, *PLURA*, p. 150.
4   HAMEL, *ARC*, p. 36.
5   HOWLETT, *ECEJ*, p. 112.
6   HAMEL, *ARC*, p. 31-32.
7   HAMEL, *ARC*, p. 33.
8   FAIRBAIRN, *ICCHRLA*, p. 184.
9   HAMEL, *ARC*, p. 16.
10 MOFFAT, *Ten Days*, p. 158.

Seeds of Hope in the New World (Dis)order

1   G. BAUM, "Good-bye to the Ecumenist," in *The Ecumenist*, 29:2 (1991), p. 2.
2   BAUM, comments made at a Toronto conference (April 1991) sponsored by *Compass*, cited in *Compass* (November-December 1991), p. 10.
3   For example, Peter MCFARLANE, in *Canadians and Central America* (Toronto: Between the Lines, 1989), refers to the shifts in the churches in attitudes toward Central America between the 60s and 80s, and to the important role that organizations like ICCHRLA played in the development of expertise on the region, in pressuring government on behalf of refugees and with respect to its policies in the region. See also GREENE, *Canadian Churches and Foreign Policy.* Concerning the role of ECEJ in articulating an alternative to the neoconservative agenda,

centering on community self-reliance and promoting the formation and development of new kinds of political coalitions, see John WARNOCK, *Free Trade and the New Right Agenda* (Vancouver: New Star Books, 1988), pp. 293-95, 299-300.

4   Concerning progressive social movements in general, see BOGGS, *Social Movements and Political Power*; George KATSIAFICAS, *The Imagination of the New Left: A Global Analysis of 1968* (Boston: South End Press, 1987). Concerning movements in Canada, see Joan Newman KUYEK, *Fighting for Hope: Organizing to Realize Our Dreams* (Montreal: Black Rose Books, 1990); LEYS and MENDELL, *Culture and Social Change.* Concerning movements in Latin America, see Arturo ESCOBAR and Sonia ALVAREZ (eds), *The Making of Social Movements in Latin America* (Boulder, CO: Westview Press, 1992).

5   With the exception of the PLURA account, these coalition stories reveal little focussed attention on the forms in which the coalitions have been institutionalized, the organization and management of work and staff relations, staff-board relations, etc. These 'micro' questions are central to the concern for social change. For example, issues of employment equity, pay equity and promotion are crucial and issues of interregional communication and regional input into often centralized decision making are especially important. There is certainly much anecdotal evidence of a widely shared sense in the regions that their perspectives, concerns and suggestions are often ignored in the development of coalition agendas.

6   John WILLIAMS, "What Has Church Social Justice Work Achieved Since 1970?" in *Compass* (November-December, 1991), p. 8. Some coalition stories point to a similar conclusion. For example, the CAWG story notes that "it has become much more difficult to influence Canadian foreign policy in the areas of human rights, development and foreign aid" (BROWN, *CAWG*, p. 94). The PLURA story refers to the success of the neoconservative agenda in chipping away at the meagre gains won in earlier social justice struggles (BOYD, *PLURA*, p. 149).

7   Joshua COHEN and Joel ROGERS point out (*Rules of the Game: American Politics and the Central America Movement* [Boston: South End Press, 1986], pp. 46, 48), "without a strategic perspective, it is very difficult to make sense even of the short run, to devise coherent but flexible tactics, or to develop realistic measures of success." Thus organizations without such a perspective "are typically more susceptible to disruption by shifts in tactics, or the manipulation of terms and information, by policy producers."

8   In her account, Thompson refers to the support of influential denominational leaders who were " 'inside the loop' and able to give legitimacy at the highest church levels to all of the coalition's advocacy endeavours" (THOMPSON, *ICCR*, p. 211). It seems clear that all the coalitions benefited from this kind of support, which undoubtedly contributed significantly to their denominational support and to their capacity to mobilize pressure on government policies. However, this situation was inherently precarious, subject to significant shifts with the replacement of even one or two of these key leaders with others less supportive, indifferent or even hostile. Such shifts have in fact contributed to the reduced level of official church support for coalitions in recent years.

9   Moffat refers specifically to an emerging awareness in the mid-80s within local committees which "pushed the issue of a 'spirituality for justice-making' to the top of Ten Days' agenda" (MOFFAT, *Ten Days*, p. 162). McLean reports that study

of the theological implications of what was happening in China was part of the original mandate of CCP (McLEAN, *CCP*, p. 119).

10 Concerning signs of a renewed interest in theological reflection, see BOYD, *PLURA*, p. 150 and HAMEL, *ARC*, pp. 35-36. ICCHRLA staff and board members have affirmed the need for a new emphasis on theological reflection: see "ICCHRLA Spring Retreat, 1993," in *Alerta: Canadian Churches Reporting on Human Rights in Latin America* (March-April 1993), p. 3.

11 REGEHR, *PP*, p. 186.

12 MIHEVC, "The Christian Left in Ontario," p. 166.

13 R. Hutchinson elevates this practical wisdom reflecting the particular historical context of Canada in the late 60s and 70s into a principle of method for Christian social ethics. See R.HUTCHINSON, "Study and Action in Politically Diverse Churches," in C. PRATT and R. HUTCHINSON, *Christian Faith and Economic Justice: Toward a Canadian Perspective*, pp. 178-91. Perhaps a case can be made that the neglect of theology was fruitful then in promoting ecumenical collaboration among mainstream churches in social justice ministry. In my judgment, however, the cost of avoiding basic questions concerning the nature of faith and the mission of the church in a radically changing world has long since outweighed whatever benefits were gained through this strategy (see Lee CORMIE, "On the Option for the Poor and Oppressed in Doing Social Ethics," in *Toronto Journal of Theology*, 7:1 (Spring 1991), pp. 19-34). Ironically, the Third World expressions of Christian renewal which have so inspired many Canadians focus explicitly and intensively on specifically theological issues, as in Latin American liberation theology.

14 For example, Hamel refers to the costs to ARC of the lack of theological reflection: "Despite the valiant efforts of a few across the country, [we] remain a community on the fringe... partly because we have not facilitated opportunities to deepen theological reflection and spiritual development" (HAMEL, *ARC*, p. 36).

15 Certainly theological issues have been central to some of the debates concerning coalitions and their agendas. For example, a different view of the church and its mission is undoubtedly involved in the pressure from some church quarters concerning the priorities of working with 'church' versus 'non-church' groups (HOWLETT, *ECEJ*, p. 112).

16 See too the Moment Project of the Jesuit Centre for Social Faith and Justice, its periodical, *The Moment*, and the wonderful organizing handbook *Naming the Moment: A Manual for Community Groups* (Toronto: The Jesuit Centre for Social Faith and Justice, 1989). Also, see the rich description of the grassroots organizing approach in Social Action Commission, DIOCESE OF CHARLOTTETOWN, *From the Grass Roots: A Critical Consciousness Approach to Social Justice in Prince Edward Island* (Charlottetown: Social Action Commission, 1987).

17 Clearly, the notion of educating the Christians in the pews is not always considered so important by church leaders and coalition founders. Brown notes, CAWG "can be considered a broad-based grassroots or people's organization only insofar as Canadian national church bodies can be considered broad-based grassroots or people's organizations... [Its] resources are intended to be fed into the Canadian networks of the churches and organizations which are its members. Sometimes, however, these networks are not strong" (BROWN, *CAWG*, p. 91). Boyd reports that " 'members did not feel supported by the churches.' " They felt that the

churches didn't really want this type of education and that they preferred to do their 'churchy things' rather than look at the causes of poverty (BOYD, *PLURA*, p. 143). See also Lorraine Michael's painful conclusion: "I can no longer believe the lie that has been fed to me since 1965, that this church—and when I speak of church here it is the formal [Roman Catholic] institution that I mean—truly wants change" (L. MICHAEL, "How I Lost Faith in the Church," in *The Toronto Star* [March 09 1991, J8]). Given her deeply committed involvement in social justice ministry—she helped initiate a parish social action team in Toronto in the late 70s and served for 10 years as co-director of the Office of Social Action, Archdiocese of St. John's, Newfoundland—this is a searing indictment.

18   A GATT-Fly initiative articulates an alternative development agenda and reflects the importance of this agenda and the limitations of efforts to date. The GATT-Fly publication, *Community Self-Reliance: A Canadian Vision of Economic Justice* (Toronto: GATT-Fly, 1987) proposed self-reliance as an alternative development agenda, but was quickly and seriously criticized even among those sharing the hope of an alternative. To their credit, GATT-Fly organizers took the initiative in promoting public discussion of this alternative and publishing the sometimes very critical response. See GATT-Fly, *Free Trade or Self-Reliance: Report of the Ecumenical Conference on Free Trade, Self-Reliance and Economic Justice* (Toronto: GATT-Fly, 1987), especially the criticism by Cy Gonick who pointed to the unimaginably radical, rigid, profoundly unrealistic and scary character of this alternative (pp. 36-37). I agree with Gonick that this fundamentally apolitical proposal lacks a strategic sense; it fails to incorporate concern for the political process of articulating and organizing on a broad grassroots level. Surely, the content of the vision of an alternative will change as more people become involved in agitating for change and as the definitions of the issues and estimates of the possibilities for change evolve. So far, there is little evidence that the debate has advanced much beyond this point, especially in church circles. Political scientist Cranford Pratt, an important voice in coalition and CCC circles, has also criticized this version of self-reliant development (see C. PRATT and R. HUTCHINSON, *Christian Faith and Economic Justice*, pp. 148ff). I agree with much of his criticism, but also wish to note that this vision is not the only one compatible with the option for the poor or with the kind of critical analysis advanced by GATT-Fly, as Pratt seems to imply. A good overview of the concerns and positions informing the debates: Fred HALLIDAY, "Self-reliance in the 1980s," in *Monthly Review,* 39:9 (1988), pp. 47-55.

19   R. HUTCHINSON, "Ecumenical Witness in Canada: Social Action Coalitions," in *International Review of Mission,* 71 (July 1982), p. 347. Hutchinson refers to the first half of the 70s in these terms; I extend it to the whole decade.

20   It is now possible to play a television video game with a friend on the other side of the world via phone connections. How are these new possibilities changing the nature of friendship? And what do we parents say when our children ask if they can 'play' with a friend?

21   Consider the revelatory power of the Bible in this respect. Biblical peoples imagined that their sins condemned the whole of creation, as in the story of the fall in Genesis. In our more secular world we think in terms of 'natural' causes and effects. In other respects though, this story of the fall has never in history been so true as it is at the end of the 20th century: through the sins of (some) humans all

of creation (on earth) is suffering and in need of redemption.

22   Political scientist James Laxer insists that, in the absence of any other remotely democratic international forums, the nation-state is still crucial. See J. LAXER, *False God: How the Globalization Myth Has Impoverished Canada* (Toronto: Lester Publishing Limited, 1993), p. 35.

23   Richard BARNET, "Inquiries into the Human Prospect" (review of Paul KENNEDY, *Preparing for the Twenty-First Century* [NY: Random House, 1993]), in *World Policy Journal*, 10:1 (1993), p. 91. See also LAXER, *False God*, p. 28.

24   See the contributors in Wolfgang SACHS (ed), *The Development Dictionary: A Guide to Knowledge as Power* (London: Zed Books, 1992).

25   This perspective on the internal biblical dynamic of renewing faith in each new historical context is developed in CORMIE, "Revolutions in Reading the Bible," in Peggy DAY, David JOBLING and Gerard SHEPPARD (eds), *The Bible and the Politics of Exegesis* (NY: Pilgrim Press, 1991), pp. 173-93.

26   In Canada, Murray Dobbin notes, the "convenient notion that there is no alternative to BCNI's formula for the future has permeated all public discourse about economics, public policy and our future." See M. DOBBIN, "Thomas d'Aquino: The De Facto PM," in *Canadian Forum*, LXXI:814 (November 1992), p. 7. Concerning BCNI, see also LANGILLE, "The Business Council on National Issues and the Canadian State"; Mel WATKINS, *Madness and Ruin: Politics and the Economy in the Neoconservative Age* (Toronto: Between the Lines, 1992), pp. 159-64: "The Deficit Scam: From the Folks Who Brought You Free Trade."

27   This neoconservative new right was never so popular in the U.S. as media made it appear. See Thomas FERGUSON and Joel ROGERS, *Right Turn: The Decline of the Democrats and the Future of American Politics* (NY: Hill and Wang, 1986).

28   WARNOCK, *Free Trade and the New Right Agenda*, p. 314.

29   Bruce CAMPBELL, *Canada Under Siege: Three Years into the Free Trade Era* (Ottawa: Canadian Centre for Policy Alternatives, 1992), p. 7.

30   There is widespread evidence that NAFTA is viewed with great suspicion by popular groups in Mexico and the U.S. See, for example, contributions in John CAVANAGH, John GERSHMAN, Karen BAKER and Gretchen HELMKE (eds), *Trading Freedom: How Free Trade Affects Our Lives, Work, and Environment* (Toronto: Between the Lines, 1992).

31   LAXER, *False God*, p. 65.

32   See Thomas WALKOM, "No More Party of the Underdog," in *The Toronto Star* (May 22 1993, D1); Carla LIPSIG-MUMMÉ, "Reaction to Neo-conservative Rae: New Directions for the Left," in *The Toronto Star* (August 18 1993, A17).

33   Concerning the growing concentration of power and the corresponding political crisis and its effects in Canada, see L. MCQUAIG, *Behind Closed Doors: How the Rich Won Control of Canada's Tax System... and Ended Up Richer* (Toronto: Penguin Books, 1988); MCQUAIG, *The Quick and the Dead*. Concerning the U.S., see William GREIDER, *Who Will Tell the People: The Betrayal of American Democracy* (NY: Simon & Schuster, 1992).

34   Concerning Latin America, see A. ESCOBAR, "Culture, Economics, and Politics in Latin American Social Movements Theory and Research," in ESCOBAR and ALVAREZ, *The Making of Social Movements in Latin America*: "Latin America is going through its worst crisis in history" (p. 64). Concerning Africa, see Godfrey

M'MWERERIA, *The Root Causes of Debt Crisis in Africa: An Agenda for Continental Collective Self-Reliance* (Nairobi, Kenya: Southern Network for Development, Africa Region, nd).

35   LAXER, *False God*, p. 3.

36   T. WALKOM, "Silent Night, Holy Night, All's Not Calm, All Is Blight," in *The Toronto Star* (December 23 1992, A25).

37   See Terrence Downey's lament that despite years of prophetic teaching "the bishops have provided little by way of coherent leadership for the Church and for the broader society" concerning the free trade agenda. T. DOWNEY, "The Bishops and the Mulroney Revolution," in *Grail,* 6:1 (March 1990), p. 31.

38   DOWNEY, "The Bishops and the Mulroney Revolution," p. 34.

39   Manfred BIENFELD, "Financial Deregulation: Disarming the Nation State," in *Studies in Political Economy,* 37 (Spring 1992), p. 56.

40   Indeed, supporters of this agenda are the first to point to the importance of faith in it. The chairman of the Royal Commission, Donald MacDonald, insisted that "at some point Canadians will have to take a 'leap of faith.' While there are risks in acting, there are greater risks in not acting" (Rod MCQUEEN, *Leap of Faith:* An Abridged Version of the Report of the Royal Commission on the Economic Union and Development Prospects for Canada [Toronto: Cowan & Co., with assistance from Woods Gordon, Clarkson Gordon, 1985], facing the page of contents).

41   LAXER, *False God*, p. 2.

42   On the importance of making theology contextual, indeed of its inevitably contextual character, see Douglas John HALL, *Thinking the Faith: Christian Theology in a North American Context* (Minneapolis: Fortress Press, 1991).

43   CCCB, Social Affairs Division, *Widespread Unemployment: A Call to Mobilize the Social Forces of Our Nation* (Ottawa: CCCB, 1993).

44   MIHEVC refers to these cutbacks in the United Church ("The Christian Left in Ontario," p. 163).

45   A recent series of articles documents cutbacks in diocesan social justice offices and in the staffing of the Social Affairs Commission of the CCCB. See JAMIESON, "Social Justice Ministry Worries about Its Future"; JAMIESON, "Social Justice Ministry Worries about Its Future: Part II–The West and the North"; JAMIESON and SOMMERVILLE, "Social Justice Ministry Looks for Its Future: Part III–Maritime Canada"; SOMMERVILLE, "Who's Minding the Faith and Justice Store: Part IV–The National Office."

46   Of course, fiscal matters are important. And in this connection, it is important to note a significant gap in the coalition stories. It concerns financing. Some of the accounts—ICFID, Ten Days, ICCAF, PLURA—refer to government funding. None, however, provides accounts of the sources and amounts of funding, how funding decisions are made and by whom, and shifts over time. These matters are crucial for understanding the past history of the coalitions and the debates over their future.

Acronyms

ACC	Anglican Church of Canada
ACN	Action Canada Network
ARC	Aboriginal Rights Coalition
BCNI	Business Council on National Issues
CAWG	Canada Asia Working Group
CCBP	Confederation of Church and Business People
CCC	Canadian Council of Churches
CCCB	Canadian Conference of Catholic Bishops
CCIC	Canadian Council for International Cooperation
CCODP	Canadian Catholic Organization for Development and Peace
CCP	Canada China Programme
CIBC	Canadian Imperial Bank of Commerce
CIDA	Canadian International Development Agency
CJP	Committee on Justice and Peace
CTRP	Canadian Theological Reflection Project
EATWOT	Ecumenical Association of Third World Theologians
ECEJ	Ecumenical Coalition on Economic Justice
GATT	General Agreement on Tariffs and Trade
ICCAF	Inter-Church Coalition on Africa
ICCCDR	Inter-Church Consultative Committee for Development and Relief
ICCHRLA	Inter-Church Coalition on Human Rights in Latin America
ICFID	Interchurch Fund for International Development
ICCR	Inter-Church Committee for Refugees
ICPOP	Inter-Church Project on Population
NDP	New Democratic Party
MP	Member of Parliament
NAFTA	North American Free Trade Agreement
NGO	Non-Governmental Organization
PC	Progressive Conservative Party

PLURA	Presbyterian, Lutheran, United, Roman Catholic and Anglican
PP	Project Ploughshares
SCEAIT	Standing Committee on External Affairs and International Trade
TCCR	Taskforce on the Churches and Corporate Responsibility
Ten Days	Inter-Church Committee for World Development Education
UCC	United Church of Canada
WCC	World Council of Churches